I O N

# Skill Set

## STRATEGIES FOR READING AND WRITING IN THE CANADIAN CLASSROOM

## Lucia Engkent

OXFORD

UNIVERSITY PRESS

# OXFORD

UNIVERSITY PRESS

Oxford University Press is a department of the University of Oxford.
It furthers the University's objective of excellence in research, scholarship,
and education by publishing worldwide. Oxford is a registered trade mark of
Oxford University Press in the UK and in certain other countries.

Published in Canada by
Oxford University Press
8 Sampson Mews, Suite 204,
Don Mills, Ontario  M3C 0H5 Canada

www.oupcanada.com

**Library and Archives Canada Cataloguing in Publication**
Engkent, Lucia Pietrusiak, 1955–, author
Skill set : strategies for reading and writing in the Canadian
classroom / Lucia Engkent. – Third edition.

Includes index.
ISBN 978-0-19-902013-3 (pbk.)

1. English language–Rhetoric–Textbooks.   2. College readers.   I. Title.

PE1408.E486 2015                428                C2014-907347-X

Cover image: lightpoet/Shutterstock.com

Oxford University Press is committed to our environment.
This book is printed on Forest Stewardship Council® certified paper
and comes from responsible sources.

Printed and bound in Canada

1  2  3  4 — 19  18  17  16

# CONTENTS

# Introduction

## Introduction for the Instructor

This text is intended for students who need to hone their English writing and reading skills in order to meet future academic demands. It was developed in a non-credit college course for students who had not achieved the required reading and writing skills for the credit English course. The students in this course were of different backgrounds and mixed abilities: some were native speakers of English who were reluctant readers, some were newly arrived international students who had university degrees from their native countries, some were mature students looking for a change in career, and some were immigrants who had spent many years in the Canadian school system and spoke English fluently. These students were taking regular college courses in their own discipline at the same time that they were studying English. In addition, some of the material was tested in English as a Second Language (ESL) academic preparation classes.

Although some institutions have separate streams for ESL students and native speakers, at this level the two groups have enough in common that they can be taught together. Even some of the grammatical errors are similar. Instructors see incorrect verb forms, article and preposition errors, difficulty with complex sentence structures, and misuse of vocabulary. Reluctant readers struggle with the more complex vocabulary and structures of academic English.

*Skill Set* is very much a product of the classroom. It focuses on the problems generally seen in the writing of students in the developmental English course. The exercises address problems these students have, such as distinguishing general and specific points in order to write supporting statements in paragraphs. Some of the sample paragraphs and essays were generated from student writing assignments. In addition, many of the sentences used for error correction in Unit 7 were taken from student writing samples.

### Native Speakers and ESL Students

This book has been designed to meet the needs of both native speakers and ESL students. It is therefore important to start with a few definitions because of the confusion with such terms as *first language*, *second language*, and *mother tongue*.

Native speakers of English speak English as their first language—their strongest and dominant language. Native speakers use English fluently and idiomatically. They speak without a noticeable foreign accent. In Canada, second-generation immigrants (those born or raised in Canada) generally become native speakers even if they speak another language at home. Once they start using English at school, their English gets much stronger than their mother tongue, and English gradually becomes their dominant language. The Canadian census defines mother tongue as "language first spoken and still understood."

ESL students are those whose dominant language is not English. *First language* and *second language* do not refer to the order the languages are acquired—the terms refer to the relative strength of the language. ESL students are more comfortable in another language. Some speak several languages, and English may be the language they learned third or fourth, but they are referred to as English as a second language students because English is not their first language. ESL students may have studied English for many years in their native country. Their fluency depends on the type of instruction they received and whether they actually used the language instead of just doing language exercises, such as filling in blanks in sentences.

Note that these definitions focus on the spoken language. Writing is an entirely different matter. Written English should be considered a separate language. Native speakers of English who do not read much could be called "WESL students" because for them written English is a second language, an unfamiliar one. This explains why students in developmental English classes make similar errors whether they are native speakers or ESL students. Native speakers often write by ear and thus drop verb endings that are not pronounced clearly. For example, they may write "he use to" and "I'm sposta." Both ESL and WESL students have weak vocabularies and struggle with complex sentence structures and the conventions of academic English.

## Organization of the Text

This book is designed to let instructors move around from section to section as needed. It is organized so that smaller units (vocabulary and sentences) are discussed before larger units (paragraphs and essays), but that does not mean units have to be tackled in that order. The material is organized by skill areas, such as constructing complex sentences and writing topic sentences, so you can focus on the weaknesses your students have.

It is important to remember that students do not come to a course like this as a blank slate. They have been introduced to the writing process and essay structure. They do not have to master sentence structure before they move on to paragraphs, and they may even chafe at working on paragraph structure when they want to write essays.

You may wish to move on to the unit on paragraphs (Unit 4) after a brief introduction to writing (Unit 1) and then work on vocabulary (Unit 2) and grammar (Units 3 and 7) in bits as students practise writing paragraphs and then essays. You can draw from Unit 6, Rhetorical Skills, as you assign different types of writing tasks.

The reading units in Part 2 offer you a range of choice. Each article and short story is a self-contained unit and thus can be studied on its own, in any order. The non-fiction units have two articles on the same theme—you can do both or just one. The variety of topics allows you to pick selections according to the curriculum, your students' needs, and your own tastes. Moreover, the readings have been chosen so that there is not a wide range in length or difficulty, which means that they can be treated equally. Thus, for example, you can assign different readings for summary assignments or group presentations, and the work load would be fairly divided. You can also change the readings you present each semester to keep the course fresh.

## Paragraphs and Essays

Students are given an opportunity to work on independent paragraphs before they move to the essay. This allows them to practise their skills in shorter writing assignments. The focus is on the basic academic skills of making points and supporting them.

Some educators argue against teaching the five-paragraph essay, since it is so formulaic and not "real world" writing. However, it is a useful pedagogical structure that teaches the skills students need for all kinds of writing—the ability to organize thoughts, present ideas, and support them. Whether they have to write a cover letter for a job application or a business report, they still have to introduce a topic, divide their arguments into well-structured body paragraphs, and write a conclusion—just as they do in an essay. Students who struggle with writing benefit from having a well-defined structure to follow.

## Readings

Reading and writing go hand in hand. It is not enough to add some readings to a writing text as an afterthought. Students with weak writing skills often have weak reading skills, and this must be addressed. Good reading comprehension is paramount—no instructor would deny that as skills are ranked, understanding the main idea of a newspaper article is surely more important than being able to fix a comma splice. Furthermore, to become good writers, students need to read more in order to learn the written language—its structures and vocabulary.

It is essential to test students' reading ability with comprehension questions, paraphrasing, and summarizing. Otherwise, it is easy to miss students' reading problems.

The readings in this text serve several functions. First, they give students an opportunity to improve their reading skills and their vocabulary. Second, students are asked to look at sentence, paragraph, and essay structures in the readings so that they can carry over what they learned about grammar and writing into their reading. They can see different writing styles at work. Third, the readings provide the students with interesting subjects to discuss and write about.

The non-fiction readings are presented in seven thematic units (Units 9–15). Each unit includes two articles and a five-paragraph essay on the theme. A wide range of writing topics is given in the Discussion and Assignment topics for each article and in the Additional Topics at the end of the unit. Each unit includes both journalistic and academic writing styles.

The book also contains four fiction readings—three short stories and one excerpt from a novel. It is important to include fiction in students' reading diet because students sometimes have difficulty understanding the difference between fiction and non-fiction. Moreover, reading fiction develops language skills, captures and exercises the imagination, and even improves social skills.

Besides the typical comprehension questions, discussion topics, and assignment suggestions, the readings are accompanied by language study and notes on structure and technique. These elements are intended to make students more conscious of the language as they read. They can then apply what they learned about vocabulary and sentence structure to actual words and sentences in the reading.

## Vocabulary Study

In developmental English courses, building vocabulary is crucial. Spoken English uses a fairly small range of words, so reluctant readers have limited exposure to less common words and need more guidance to learn the patterns that can help them make connections between words. For that reason, this text has work on collocations, parts of speech, and common roots and affixes.

Each of the readings is accompanied by a variety of vocabulary exercises. Students can use the context to find the meaning of the less common, more difficult words in a matching exercise. The Word Families charts allow students to figure out the derivatives of some more common words, including words from the Academic Word List. The lists also draw students' attention to idioms, common expressions, and collocations. The exercises are designed to make students more conscious of the words and expressions they come across; they are not simply supplied with the definition and asked to read on.

Interesting and problematic words and expressions (such as *toonie* and *afford*) are explained in the context of the reading, but because these explanations are useful beyond their use in the specific reading, such words and expressions are listed in the index.

## Grammar

Grammar can be a contentious issue. Instructors all agree that grammar instruction is necessary, but there is so much to learn and practise that the areas to focus on must be carefully chosen. Most ESL students have been given formal grammar instruction, whereas native speakers have not. However, native speakers have a better sense of the structure of English even if they have trouble with basic labels, such as *noun* and *verb*.

Grammar exercises have little carry-over to actual writing ability; some students excel at the exercises but make errors on the same grammar points in their writing. Error correction and the construction of complex sentences are two areas that are more like real writing work. Unit 7 focuses on error correction, explaining the process and highlighting common errors. Most of the sentences used for error correction are taken from actual student writing.

Grammar labels can be another problem: students are unfamiliar with the words, and terminology can vary. Therefore, the terms are kept simple and are defined the first time they are used; the index points to these definitions.

## Discussion and Assignment Topics

Assignments are left open-ended so that you can tailor them to your class needs. For example, if your class is still working on paragraph structure when you do a particular reading, your assignments will focus on paragraphs. If you are working on reports or research essays, you can choose a topic for students to explore in such an assignment. You may want to specify length and format. The discussion topics can be used as writing topics.

## The Third Edition

Instructors who have used earlier versions of *Skill Set* will find the third edition quite different. Besides its new readings and rewritten explanations, the book has been reorganized, and some sections have been moved. For instance, the explanation of the use of *you* in academic writing can now be found under Correcting Pronoun Errors in Unit 7.

## Teacher's Resource

The online Teacher's Resource offers supplemental material such as sample course outlines and lesson plans, answers to exercises, and sample quizzes. It also offers guidance for beginning instructors.

## Introduction for Students: Developing Study Skills

*Skill Set* is a book that will help you improve your reading and writing skills, but it cannot do so unless you do your part. It is important to develop good study habits in order to be successful in college or university.

Passing your English course is not your end goal—improving your reading and writing skills is. The stronger your literacy skills, the more success you will have both in your education and in your future career, so it is important to attend class, participate, do the work required, and strive to improve.

### Using the Textbook

A textbook is a valuable resource for any course. Once you have bought your book, your first step is to familiarize yourself with the contents and organization. Look over the table of contents and the index. Check out what the appendices have to offer. Scan the textbook by reading subtitles to identify the different sections. Be sure to bring your textbook to class.

How the instructor uses the textbook depends on the individual instructor. Two teachers may have the same book but present very different courses. Whatever the approach, instructors generally ask you to do homework from the text. Be sure to do the assigned reading. It is a waste of your time and tuition money to come to class unprepared.

Textbooks generally offer more than can be covered in a course, but you can use the rest of the book as a resource and for reading practice. For example, you can read the section on Punctuation and Capitalization if punctuation is a particular weakness you have. Moreover, instead of just covering the assigned reading selections, you can read the other articles and short stories when you have some free time. You will be improving your reading skills and your background knowledge.

Unit 8 gives details on how to read the textbook and how to prepare assigned readings.

The index is a valuable resource for locating topics and for finding definitions of grammatical and literary terms. For example, if you forget what a transitive verb is, you can find the term listed in the index with the page reference for the explanation of the meaning. The index will also help you to locate the usage explanation for words and expressions, such as *used to* and *clothing*, from the notes for the reading selections.

## Time Management

One of the biggest changes students face when they make the leap from high school to post-secondary school is the need for time management skills. In high school, your time is often managed for you. Much of your work is done in class, and your assignments may be divided into smaller chunks. In college and university, however, you may have several weeks to complete an assignment, but how and when you do it is your responsibility. For every hour spent in class, you are expected to do two or three hours working on your own.

It is important to use some sort of calendar to organize your semester. Schools often provide specially printed handbooks or agendas that include important dates in the school year, such as holidays and exam week. Alternatively, you could use an electronic format, whether it be on your laptop or on your phone. Enter test and assignment due dates as you get them. Make daily and weekly "to do" lists, and use them.

Start assignments as soon as you get them while the instructions are fresh in your mind. Work on them in manageable chunks. Finish early so that you can review everything before you hand it in. Getting an assignment done early clears the way for other work. It also helps you to avoid last-minute problems such as a malfunctioning computer. (Remember to back up all your work on other sites, such as your school electronic folders, or other media, such as flash drives.)

Review and study your material as the course goes on. Last-minute cramming is never as productive as keeping up with the flow.

Your schedule should allow for some flexibility and downtime. Take breaks, get some fresh air and exercise, and try to get enough sleep. Your mind will function much better if your body is healthy.

## Multi-tasking

Today's technology encourages multi-tasking. Students have multiple windows open on their computer screen. They send text messages while they walk, talk, and study. However, the human brain has not evolved to handle more than one task at a time. It can switch rapidly between tasks, but it cannot do two at once. Studies show that you lose time and efficiency when you try to multi-task. You will work more efficiently if you commit to the task at hand and avoid distractions. While background music can be beneficial, anything that draws your attention away from your work is a problem.

## Active versus Passive Learning

People learn things much better when they are active rather than passive learners. Active learning requires doing something—taking notes, summarizing material, asking questions, making comments, and talking about the topic. Passive learning is just reading or listening. Even telling your roommates or family about what you studied in class will help you to remember it.

Classroom discussion is an important part of active learning. Good students are attentive and engaged. They answer the instructor's questions and ask questions when they need more information. Instructors do not want to lecture for an hour—they would rather hear their students' opinions. Unfortunately, many students today are reluctant to speak up in class. Those who do, however, are rewarded with better learning.

## Taking Notes

College and university instructors expect you to take notes in class. This does not mean simply copying down what the instructor writes on the board or shows on a screen. You need to process the information that is being presented to you and write down the main ideas. Pay attention to what the instructor stresses as important.

Capturing electronic records is not the same as taking notes. An audio recording of a lecture is more difficult and time-consuming to review than good handwritten notes. Taking pictures with your smartphone is also no substitute. Even typing notes on a laptop may not help you to remember as well as handwritten notes. Muscle memory and the hand-to-brain connection play an important part in processing and remembering information.

A good strategy is to flesh out the notes soon after class while the information is still fresh in your mind. For example, you can write down the meanings of the new vocabulary items you jotted down during class.

Making reading notes is also useful. You can summarize a chapter in a few notes after you have read it to aid your comprehension and memory. Moreover, notes are useful when you study for tests and exams.

Keeping a separate vocabulary notebook allows you to create a useful learning tool, much like your own dictionary. Write down new words and expressions. Add grammatical information, such as the part of speech. Write down the phrase or sentence that the word appeared in. Jot down the meaning and related words.

## Following Instructions

While some people think that following instructions is only for mindless automatons, it is vital in the workplace where failure to do so can result in lost workhours and added expense or even lead to life-threatening situations. In school, following instructions is the key to getting good grades. One of the common complaints of all instructors in any institution is that students often do not do what they have been asked to do.

Read written instructions carefully, more than once. For example, you can read them when you first get an assignment, while you are working on the task, and again as a final check before you hand the work in. Highlight important instructions you do not want to overlook. Listen to oral instructions carefully, taking notes. Instructors repeat directions because they are so important and because students often do not pay enough attention to them.

## Developing Language Skills

Students who are learning English as a second language (ESL) should recognize that it takes years to develop the language skills required to function in an English-speaking academic environment. If their goal is a diploma or a degree from a Canadian institution, they must work at their language skills all the time—not just for the duration of English class. They need lots of exposure to both written and spoken English, so they should read, watch educational television, and surf the Internet in English.

Students whose native language is English have mastered the spoken language, but if they do not read much, they may still be considered language learners for written English. They also need to build their vocabulary and learn about the structures of academic English.

## Learning from Mistakes

Making a mistake creates an opportunity to learn. Indeed, learning would not take place without mistakes. Of course, errors also mean lower marks, so you should try to avoid making them. However, for those mistakes you do make, be sure to learn from them and avoid them in the future.

Writing instructors spend a lot of time marking essays. They write corrections and comments. Students who take the time to go over their marked essays can see where they have problems and how they can improve for the next assignment. Unit 7 guides you in the process of correcting and editing and highlights common problem areas.

## Practice

In his 2008 book *Outliers*, Malcolm Gladwell explains what leads to success and shows that talent and skill are not enough. He argues that it takes 10,000 hours of practice to become a world-class expert at something. Wayne Gretzky undoubtedly had a lot of natural talent, but he would not have become "The Great One" without the hours he spent practising his hockey skills every winter on his backyard rink.

While you do not have to put in 10,000 hours to become an expert essay writer, you must recognize that you cannot hope to become a competent writer without lots of practice. Take advantage of any practice opportunity you are offered. Some instructors mark practice essays and allow you to rewrite them.

Some students find journal-writing a low-pressure way to practise expressing ideas in writing. A journal is a notebook that you write in on a regular basis. You can record your thoughts about almost anything—a movie you saw, a class you attended, what you think about a political issue, or your observations of your class-mates. Keep in mind, though, who might read your writing. If you are keeping a journal as part of your class work, your audience is your instructor. If the journal is just for you, you do not have to be as careful about what you say.

Furthermore, writing in a journal and reading a chapter in a novel are good ways to wind down at the end of the day. Studies show that watching television and staring at a computer screen immediately before bedtime can interfere with sleep rhythms.

Reading comprehension and speed also improve with practice. At the end of Unit 8 are some tips for building reading skills.

## Seeking Help

Colleges and universities offer many services to help students succeed. They may offer a study skills course, for example. The library may have tutors and seminars. Conversation groups may be arranged for ESL students. Remember that you have paid for these services in your tuition fees, so take advantage of them.

It is important to ask questions in class when you do not understand something. Do not be shy about it—chances are that other students are wondering the same thing. Moreover, the instructor would prefer that such general questions be asked during the class instead of several students asking the same question immediately after class.

If you have concerns about the course or your progress in it, be sure to talk to your instructor before taking a drastic measure such as dropping the course. Sometimes students give up prematurely, thinking they have no chance of passing the course when in fact they are making good progress.

---

**Abbreviations and Conventions Used in the Text**

| | |
|---|---|
| n: | noun |
| v: | verb |
| adj: | adjective |
| adv: | adverb |
| tr: | transitive (verb) |
| U: | uncountable (noun) |
| C: | countable (noun) |

In Part 2, Reading Selections, numbers in square brackets refer to the number of the paragraph where a vocabulary item can be found.

## Acknowledgments

This material was class-tested at Seneca College in Toronto and at Renison College at the University of Waterloo. Many thanks to my students, whose work provided the base for many of the examples and exercises. In particular, Sharon Nuan-Yu Liu gave me detailed feedback on the readings from a student's perspective. I would also like to acknowledge the suggestions and support of my colleagues, especially Sharon Vignaux, Adriana Neil, and Dara Lane.

Thanks as well to the editors and staff of Oxford University Press Canada for their hard work and dedication to this project, especially Carolyn Pisani and Jason Tomassini.

And as always, a big thank you to my family—my husband, Garry, and my children, David, Susan, and Emily. They contributed their literary criticism, editing, and writing skills to the cause.

Lucia Engkent

## About the Author

Lucia Engkent has more than 30 years' experience teaching English and writing instructional materials, (including six textbooks.) She has taught at Seneca College, the University of Waterloo, York University, and the University of Alberta. Her academic background includes the study of 10 languages, a master's degree in applied linguistics from the University of Ottawa, and a master's degree in library science from the University of Toronto.

# PART 1

# Skill Development

# Writing Skills

Writing is a skill that you develop through practice. Unlike learning to speak a native language, it does not come naturally or without effort. Moreover, as a school subject, it is not one you can master by memorizing facts from a textbook. In a writing course, it is important to come to class and do the work so that you can take advantage of every opportunity to learn and practise.

Reading and writing go hand in hand. You cannot become a better writer without reading, because the written language is different from the spoken language. Through reading, you expand your vocabulary and learn the conventions of writing. In addition, avid readers find writing easier because they have more vocabulary and background knowledge to draw on.

Whatever the type of writing, whatever the purpose and audience, writing is a form of communication, so the qualities of good writing remain the same: Documents must be legible, clear, concise, and correct. The writing must engage and inform the reader. The style of language should be appropriate to the situation.

This unit introduces these basic principles of good writing—ones that you will apply throughout your writing course and throughout your life.

## Distinguishing Spoken and Written Language

One of the first steps to becoming a good writer is recognizing the difference between spoken and written language. Even though the written system is fundamentally based on spoken language, the differences can be quite marked. Writing is not just speech written down.

The essential difference between spoken and written English is that the spoken language is simpler in both vocabulary and sentence structure. This is just a generalization, however, since there are different spoken and written forms. A casual conversation differs from a formal speech, while a text message is written language but is more similar to spoken conversation.

In spoken English, you use tone of voice, gestures, and context to get your meaning across. You can get away with calling something a "thingamajig," for example, if you can point to the item in question. You can get immediate feedback if your communication is unsuccessful—ranging from the bewildered look on the listener's face to direct questions such as "What do you mean?"

In written English, you have no such back-up system. Your meaning must be clear from the outset. You must anticipate what your readers need to know. You have to use precise vocabulary. Consequently, written English calls upon the huge vocabulary of English more than the conversational language does. For example, someone demonstrating how to transfer photos from a camera to a computer might use a vague term like "this wire thing here," but the instruction manual might refer to "a USB cable."

You speak mainly in simple sentences, but in writing you use longer, more complex sentences. You can layer meaning with clauses. Your attention span is greater when you read than when you listen, and you can go back and check meaning, so you can handle complexity better in written form. Academic English, the language of essay writing, is even more sophisticated. For your English course, you need to be able to produce this level of language, which is also used in both business and technical writing.

## Addressing Audience and Purpose

Your first job as a writer is to consider why you are writing (your purpose) and who your readers are (your audience). You may write to inform, persuade, or entertain your readers. The purpose of a technical manual is to give information. A novel or short story entertains and perhaps along the way informs and enlightens its readers. Academic essays are essentially arguments in a presentation of organized and supported points.

What you write has to be tailored to your audience, so you need to know who will be reading your document. Imagine telling someone how to use a new smartphone app—instructions to your grandparents would be very different from instructions to your classmate. Recipe directions for an experienced cook would be different from those for a novice. If you write an essay about traditions in your native country, you need to say enough to make your essay clear to readers who have never visited that country or who are not familiar with the traditions.

The information you give and the words you use will vary depending on your audience and purpose, as in this example:

| | |
|---|---|
| That patient is suffering from separation anxiety disorder, but I think it is developing into full-fledged agoraphobia. I'd like to try cognitive behavioural therapy. | Audience: another psychologist Purpose: to give information for a treatment program |
| It's okay, sweetie. Don't cry. Your mama will be back soon. | Audience: small child Purpose: to reassure and calm the child |

Knowing what your audience knows and needs to know is not easy. It can be especially difficult if your audience is diverse, but keep in mind that you cannot follow your document around to explain it, so it is better to give too much information than too little. Lack of information is one of the most common problems in student essays.

## Writing for School

Academic writing—the writing you do for a college or university course—has a specific audience and purpose. In an English composition class, your primary audience is your instructor, and your purpose is to show the instructor what you have learned, how you can connect ideas, and how well you express those ideas. And, of course, your purpose is also to get a good grade on your assignment.

The writing you do in school is artificial in the sense that it is not communicating new information to your reader. You are writing for a teacher or professor who may be an expert on the subject. Your essay on sibling rivalry is not going to tell your psychology professor much that he or she does not know; however, it will tell the professor how well you have learned the required material, researched the topic, and expressed your ideas. Sometimes you may be tempted to leave out information that you know the professor has, but it may be required for the logical links in your argument.

Writing courses vary in their requirements, and different instructors vary in where they put the emphasis. For example, some instructors invite creative, personal essays while others may want you to produce tightly structured impersonal writing. You may feel frustrated if your English instructor prefers a style very different from the one your previous instructor did, but remember that it is the same situation in the work world: each supervisor wants a job done in a specific way, and this may require you to adjust how you do the job for a different manager.

The section Understanding Writing Evaluation at the end of this unit lists some common criteria for writing assignments.

## Achieving Clarity

The success of any communication depends on how clear it is to the audience. Clarity is the most important criterion. When you speak, you have immediate feedback for your words because you can interact with your audience and ensure that everyone understands what you are saying. However, as a writer you cannot follow your document around to every reader to make sure that it is understood. Your job is to make your writing clear from the outset. Writing that is not clear does not succeed as communication and is, therefore, essentially worthless.

To achieve clarity, you must choose your words carefully. You cannot just point to something if you forget the name of it. You cannot get away with imprecise words like *stuff* and *whatever*. The vocabulary of the written language is much larger than that of everyday spoken language, and these words are needed to ensure precision and clarity. You can get by with fewer words in your everyday speech, but for good writing you need an arsenal of words, words that you can use correctly and words your audience will understand. Clear, simple language is always preferable to overly ornate, complicated language.

Clarity depends on more than vocabulary choice. Writers must use proper grammar and sentence structure to make sure their ideas are clear. Paragraphs must have coherence—that is, sentences must follow logically (see pages 121–22 for more on coherence). Transition signals, such as *for example* and *in addition*, help readers to see the relationship between ideas. General points need to be supported with specific examples to make them easier to understand. Following conventional writing patterns also helps readers to follow what you are saying.

Here are some examples of student writing that lacked clarity:

Men do not carry purses because purses are too big for men to carry without a handbag. Therefore, men have to put their purses in their clothes bag.

This example of student writing is unclear because of vocabulary problems. The question was "Why don't men use purses?" The student mixed up the words *purse* and *wallet* and did not know the word *pocket*.

Cars come in many forms as perceived by a viewer. In the past century, cars have contributed to many criteria of human development. To view cars as an advantage is a benchmark, but to view them as a disadvantage is a learning curve. Owning a luxury car can be an advantage and disadvantage.

The essay prompt was "Explain the advantages or the disadvantages of owning a luxury car." This student's essay introduction shows that writing can follow basic grammar rules and be technically "correct" yet not be clear.

Hover is a problem on both parents and children because it is related to each other.

This example shows why students are asked to answer "in their own words." The writer picked up the word *hover* from the reading but did not know how to use the word correctly.

It is difficult for writers to evaluate the clarity of their own writing. They may not know they are using words incorrectly. They may be relying on references that may not be clear to their audience. One way to improve clarity is to let a document sit for a while and come back to it with fresh eyes. Getting a second opinion is also vital. That is why published works go through several readers and editors.

### How to make sure your writing is clear

- Use standard spelling and grammar.
- Do not use words you are unsure of without checking the meaning and usage.
- Support your statements with examples and explanation.
- Be specific; clearly identify what you are talking about.
- Do not overload sentences with too many phrases and clauses.
- Stay on topic; do not wander and include irrelevant information.
- Make sure your timeline is clear so that the sequence of events is not confusing.
- Use transition signals such as *moreover* and *consequently* to help the reader to see the relationship between ideas.
- Attentively reread what you have written—after a bit of time has passed, if possible.
- Get a second opinion.

## Strengthening Content

Writing is judged by what it has to say as well as how it is said. In English class, your essays are evaluated on the strength of your argument—the logic of your conclusions, the support for your points, and the relevance of your examples. Instructors may disagree with your point of view, but as long as the argument is sound and well expressed, they will not penalize you.

Writers build on what other writers say. The more you read, the easier you will find it to come up with ideas for your essays. For example, as you read newspaper stories about gang violence and the editorials and comments of people discussing the issue, you will get a better understanding of the complexity of the problem. When you write an essay suggesting ways to tackle the problem, your ideas will be founded on this strong understanding.

### Answering the Question

Your content is only good if it is on topic. Your ability to answer the topic question is, after all, a main part of what is being tested in academic writing assignments. If you order a steak dinner in a restaurant and are given chicken instead, it does not matter how good the chicken dinner is. Similarly, it does not matter how well written an essay is if it does not deliver what was asked for.

Writing assignments start with reading. Your topic may be related to an article you read in class. You may be given a short passage that leads to an essay prompt. At the very least, you are given a question or direction that you have to understand in order to write the essay. For example, the question "What are the factors that determine student success?" hinges on the word *factor*. To answer the question, you could write about factors such as motivation, study habits, and home background but not about attending class, previewing material, or taking notes, which are activities, not factors. Throughout the book, you will have a chance to consider writing prompts and what is required to answer them.

It is important that you understand exactly what the instructor is asking you to do. Be sure to ask your instructor if you do not understand the assignment. Stay focused on your topic question as you write so that you do not wander off-topic.

### Critical Thinking

Content is built through critical thinking. You develop critical thinking skills as you read others' opinions, especially opinions you do not agree with. While reading, you can weigh the strength of the arguments, follow the logic in the reasoning, and evaluate the validity of the examples. Then you will be able to apply these skills to your own writing.

An essay is a test of the way you think. Your writing should be logical and clear. For example, you cannot argue that roadways should be expanded to relieve traffic congestion and then go on to say that there should also be less construction on the roads. You should be able to distinguish general and specific statements. You should be able to recognize statements that say the same thing even if the wording is quite different. Be sure not to make contradictory statements. Show the flow of ideas with transition signals (pages 119–20) to help the reader follow your argument.

## Organizing Ideas

Writing is more structured and organized than speech. Readers can more easily follow ideas when they are presented in a recognizable structure and logical order. Writers make organization decisions from the sentence level through to the structure of the whole essay.

While everyday speech is mostly in simple sentences, complex sentences allow the writer to layer meaning. For instance, subordinate clauses contain information that is less important to the main idea of the sentence. (See Unit 3 for an explanation of sentence structure and different kinds of clauses.)

Most modern writing has very short paragraphs, often only a couple of sentences. Academic writing, however, still uses more structured, longer paragraphs. General points are followed up by explanation or by examples to make the points clear. (See Unit 4 for an explanation of paragraph structure.) Even with shorter paragraphs, it is important to understand how to connect ideas and provide logical links with and between paragraphs.

Most college and university writing courses focus on the essay, using the five-paragraph essay as a base. Even though five-paragraph essays are not generally found in the "real world," the organizational patterns that students learn through essay writing are applicable to other kinds of writing. The standard essay structure of introduction, body, and conclusion is also used in business reports and technical writing. Moreover, learning and following the basic structure is one of the easiest ways you can show improvement in writing skills, thus raising your marks on writing assignments.

## Writing Concisely

Unless you are writing a novel, conciseness is valued in writing. No one likes to read more than they have to unless they are reading for pleasure. Business and technical communication must be short and to the point. The Internet favours brevity, as shown in a comment used by online posters: "tl;dr" (too long; didn't read).

Wordiness frustrates readers; it not only causes readers to lose interest but also confuses them. Everyone has had the experience of listening to or reading the words of someone who repeats ideas, wanders off-topic, and drags out a report or story with unnecessary details.

Students faced with a required length for an essay assignment may pad their writing because they do not know what to say. This is always a mistake. Writing instructors know when you are padding and will find fault with such an essay.

These examples illustrate how writing can be made more economical:

| Wordy | Concise |
|---|---|
| at this point in time | now |
| woman whose husband has died | widow |
| There are many students who had to repeat the course. | Many students had to repeat the course. |
| Failure helps students learn. For example, a student does a homework assignment. He makes some mistakes. His teacher points out the mistakes and gives the student some advice. The student takes the advice. He corrects his work. He does not make the same mistake the next time he writes an assignment. | Failure helps students learn. For example, students can use feedback from assignments to improve their writing. |

Learning to communicate concisely takes practice but it is worth the trouble. Concise communication is invaluable everywhere, especially in the workplace. Conciseness is addressed throughout this text. Specific exercises include 7.22 (page 225) and 8.4 (page 248).

**How to make your writing concise**

- Choose precise vocabulary instead of long descriptive phrases.
- Use pronouns and short phrases to refer back to what you are talking about.
- Eliminate unnecessary repetition of ideas.
- Organize your points logically.
- Use complex sentences instead of many short sentences.
- Eliminate unnecessary points, such as those that are off-topic.

## Striving for Correctness

Written work should be correct—that is, free of errors in vocabulary, grammar, spelling, and punctuation. Some mistakes are serious in that they impede comprehension. Some are minor; readers can understand what is meant, but they may get annoyed, and their impression of the writer's ability and credibility will be negatively affected.

Perfection, however, is impossible to attain, and even professional writers make slips in language use. Editors and proofreaders work hard to keep publications mistake-free, but errors seem an inevitable part of the final product.

Moreover, language correctness is not a black and white issue. Languages constantly change and evolve. New words come into use, pronunciation changes over time, and grammar "rules" can shift as acceptability of usage evolves. As a result, even language experts (such as writers, lexicographers, and linguists) have spirited disagreements over what is "correct." For instance, the word *irregardless* makes most educated English speakers cringe, with many insisting it is not a proper word at all. However, it is gradually moving into acceptability and being included in dictionaries.

Even though achieving correctness may seem an unattainable goal, it is important to strive for Standard English. Writers can easily correct many errors themselves: for example, spelling errors may be caught by using spellcheckers and dictionaries. But such methods are not sufficient by themselves. You must take time to check your writing and make the necessary corrections and improvements. (See Unit 7 for more on editing and correcting errors.)

It is also important not to take the quest for correctness too far. Some students stick to basic words and simple sentence structures in order to avoid making mistakes. This practice can hinder their ability to express sophisticated ideas. To develop your writing skills, you may need to experiment with language you are not entirely comfortable with and learn from your mistakes.

## Writing Personally or Impersonally

A personal voice in writing is important and indeed unavoidable, but many documents in business and technical writing must be less personal and more objective. Because of your years of practice with compositions in English class, you may be able to handle personal writing more easily. You are probably used to personal assignments like "What I did on my summer vacation" but may have more difficulty with topics like "Why vacations are necessary for a healthy workforce." Therefore, as a college student you should practise writing impersonally so that you can be prepared for the work world, where you might, for example, have to produce a business report that represents the company viewpoint instead of your own.

Impersonal writing is generally in the third person (*he, she, they*) instead of the first person (*I*). It is also more objective. For example, instead of arguing in an essay that an increase in tuition fees is wrong because you cannot afford it, you would write that the government should pay more than its current share because public spending on post-secondary education is an investment in society.

Students writing essays often struggle with making their writing more formal and less personal. The most common problem is that they have trouble avoiding the use of the personal pronouns *you* and *I*. Pronoun usage is explained in Unit 3, pages 69–71, and pronoun errors are addressed in Unit 7, pages 201–07.

When student writers overuse *I* in their essays, they often come up with such phrases as "In my opinion, I personally think that . . ." Unless you say otherwise, your writing is your opinion. If you say, "SUVs are a waste of money," that is clearly your point of view, and you don't need to say, "I think SUVs are a waste of money." If you say, "Many people think smoking is a personal, free choice," you are distancing yourself from that idea; the reader expects the next sentence to express a "but" idea that shows your viewpoint: for example, "However, teenagers start to smoke without a true, rational decision, and they get hooked quickly and cannot stop."

Another problem is that "I think" can weaken your writing. From a grammatical point of view, a sentence such as "I think that the college should lower its parking rates" has the emphasis on the main clause "I think." You can use "I think" and "in my opinion" in your essay when you need to emphasize that this is your point of view, but use such expressions sparingly—only when you really need the emphasis.

You need to develop a sense of when personal writing is appropriate. Instructors will indicate whether an essay should be personal or impersonal by the assignment question. For example, "Would you want to be married?" is a personal question, but "Discuss the benefits of marriage" indicates that a less personal response would be appropriate.

Even in an impersonal essay, you are giving your opinion and speaking from your experience. You can give personal examples, but be sure that they are appropriate and expressed impersonally so that they can apply generally and not to a specific person. For instance, in an essay arguing for a decrease in tuition fees, you could illustrate how poor students live:

| | |
|---|---|
| As a student, I am so poor that I live on macaroni and cheese. My friend lives on his version of "tomato soup," which is boiled water flavoured with ketchup from packets collected from fast food restaurants. | uses first person: *I, my friend* |
| Students can't even afford food. They are forced to go to food banks or live on macaroni and cheese or boiled water flavoured with ketchup. | makes the same points but generalizes to "students" |

Remember that personal writing is not wrong, but it may be inappropriate for certain purposes. You need to be able to write both personally and impersonally, but usually you need more practice in the latter. Notice also that it is a matter of degree; you can make something more or less personal. Many of the articles in Part 2 start with a personal reference but move on to general statements. Moreover, it is possible to take impersonal writing too far. Governments and businesses use this style when they want to obscure who actually performed an action.

You will read examples of both personal and impersonal writing in this book, in both sample paragraphs and essays and the reading selections. Study the sample essays beginning on page 154 for an example of two treatments of the same topic. Practice in making writing impersonal can be found in Unit 7 (pages 203–05).

### How to make writing less personal and more objective

- Use the third person (*he, she, they*).
- Use the passive voice when you want to emphasize the action rather than the person who did it (see pages 54–56 for an explanation of the passive voice).
- Make general statements that apply to many people.

## Using Appropriate Style

Every language has different styles and varieties. In spoken language, dialects and accents vary considerably. For example, in everyday conversation Australians use a kind of English very different from the one Canadians use—they might even have trouble understanding each other because of differences in expressions and pronunciation. However, since written English is more standardized than spoken English, essays written by Australian students would not differ greatly from those written by Canadians.

The style of language we use depends on our audience and purpose. We speak casually to our family and friends in everyday conversation, but we would use a more formal speaking style as a witness in a trial. Even though it is written language, online messaging is in a more conversational style.

It is important that our language is appropriate to the situation, just as we dress appropriately for an occasion. For instance, a job candidate would not wear old jeans and a grubby T-shirt to a job interview even if that is typical attire for the job itself.

The term *academic writing* refers to the style expected in essays and reports in college and university. While compositions in high school and ESL classes may be informal and personal, you need to graduate to the more formal and impersonal academic style because it is similar to the one used in business and technical writing.

It is also possible to write too formally. However, this is not a common problem among college and undergraduate students. It is more often seen in the writing of professionals and academics who use jargon and complex expressions, often obscuring what they mean, as when the military refers to civilians dying in war as "collateral damage."

North American society has moved toward greater informality. Casual work dress has replaced business suits in many occupations. People rarely use a title and surname, preferring to address business associates by their first name. Written communication has also seen a lessening in formality. For instance, instead of using *one* to refer to people in general, the less formal pronoun *you* is commonly used today.

Here is an example of conversational style:

Well, the thing is, the guys did a real good job on that project. They busted their butts getting all the info together. And they figured out all the stuff that could come up. Like, let's say, the power went out, they'd have this back-up plan all set to go. And they made this list of people to call, you know, if you had some sorta problem.

This sample of conversational English contains 67 words. It contains conversational expressions (such as *Well* and *let's say*) and slang (*busted their butts*). *Sorta* is not Standard English and would only be used to imitate speech.

Note how the same activity can be described in academic style:

| | |
|---|---|
| The team did a commendable job on that project. They all worked diligently to assemble the required information. They planned for contingencies such as power blackouts and prepared an emergency contact list. | This sample of academic English contains 32 words, less than half of words used in the conversational sample. The words are longer. |

The writing styles used in this textbook vary. The explanations are addressed to the reader directly, so *you* is used. The sample paragraphs and essays are in a slightly more formal style—in the academic style usually required for your English assignments. Many of the readings in the text are in a less formal, journalistic style. You can learn from reading all kinds of styles. Your instructor will give you direction as to which type of writing style you are expected to use for assignments.

| Conversational English | Academic English |
|---|---|
| regional (different dialects, accents) | standardized |
| mostly spoken but also written to friends (letters, email, chat messages) and in dialogue in novels and short stories | mostly written but also in formal speeches |
| immediate feedback so speaker knows what listener needs to understand | writer must anticipate what reader knows and what questions reader will have |
| meaning from gestures, tone of voice | meaning from punctuation, use of space |
| use of visuals from situation, scene | some use of visuals from pictures, graphics |
| personal (use of *I* and *you*) | less personal, more detached and objective; more use of passive voice to depersonalize |
| *you* for people in general | focus on third person (*he, she, they*) |
| imprecise words (*stuff, thing*) | precise vocabulary for clarity |
| very limited vocabulary (~2000 words) (basic English has only 800 words) | huge vocabulary in use (~20,000 words) |
| conversational markers (*let's see, well now, you know*) | use of transition markers to show relationship of ideas (*moreover, however*) |

| Conversational English | Academic English |
|---|---|
| short, simple sentences | longer, more complicated sentences |
| use of slang, colloquialisms | little idiomatic language |
| contractions to show speech forms (*don't, gonna, would've*) | contractions not used |
| sentences starting with coordinate conjunctions (*and, or, but, yet, so*) | use of conjunctive adverbs (*however, nevertheless, furthermore*) |
| conversations can meander, digress; ideas may not be fully explained or completed | in long, structured paragraphs; with logical sequence; ideas supported and explained; with introductions and conclusions |
| repetition, interruptions | more development, less repetition |
| shorthand among friends, relatives referring to common experiences | reference to other works of literature, film, history, current events |

**Activity**

Generally, a piece of writing stays in one style of language. Academic pieces that use hip hop slang would be disconcerting to readers, and a newspaper column in an overly formal tone would sound unfriendly and cold. The following article breaks this rule to create a humorous effect. The author switches from formal language to conversational English throughout the piece.

Read the article, and then work together in groups to answer the questions that follow it.

### A Global Warming Deal to Do Nothing Still Possible

*by Linwood Barclay*

1    If, as it appears, the Kyoto Protocol to reduce global warming is going straight into the toilet, it's time to consider drafting a new deal that all of the world's nations can get behind.

2    Let's face it. The United States isn't signing on to Kyoto. Australia's not on board. Russia isn't going to ratify the agreement. And our soon-to-be Prime Minister is kind of waffling about it, too. So it's finished. It's done. It's over. The deal to cut greenhouse-gas emissions has gone up in smoke. But that doesn't mean an agreement regarding global warming is impossible. It just needs to be worded a bit differently.

3    Chances are, world leaders like US President George W. Bush and Russian President Vladimir Putin and even our own Paul Martin would be more likely to consider an agreement with the following provisions:

4    "Be it resolved that, given that the worst effects of global warming—continents disappearing under oceans, skin frying the moment you step outside,

that kind of thing—aren't likely to happen for another hundred years or so, there's no sense getting your shorts in a knot about it today. Why not take in a ball game instead, so long as it's not outside."

5       "We are united in the belief that it's not our own children, and maybe not even our children's children, who will be devastated by global warming. In all likelihood, it will be our children's children's children. And ask yourself this, 'What have they done for you lately?' Have you seen so much as a thank-you card from any of them?"

6       "It is acknowledged, without prejudice, that while massive Hummer-style SUVs may contribute to the problem of global warming, they're also part of the solution. Those suckers sit high enough that when the oceans start rising, you'll be drier longer than that guy in the Neon."

7       "The people of the nations of the world are in agreement that, well, you've got to die from something, right? You could spend billions trying to curb emissions, then cross the street and get hit by a bus."

8       "We must accept, unreservedly, that it is within the realm of possibility that maybe we're just plain wrong about how dangerous these greenhouse gases really are. Isn't it possible the scientists, with their oversized glasses and little slide rules and pocket protectors, are not only the people we beat up in grade school but a bunch of naysayers who've got it all wrong? Consider this: Who could have imagined that not just one but both Matrix movie sequels would suck? If something like that can happen, anything's possible."

9       "As responsible nations we are committed to the financial well-being of our citizens. Strict environmental protection rules stifle economic growth. We believe strongly in the principle of being able to make as much money as we can and acquiring really neat things, right up until the moment that we collapse onto the sidewalk, hacking and wheezing and gagging."

10      "You have to admit, sometimes, when the sun is setting, and the rays hit the smog clouds just the right way, it can be quite beautiful."

11      "It is hereby affirmed that we, the leaders of the world, must get re-elected every few years, and that's not going to happen without substantial campaign donations from the leaders of the business community, and given that it is the aforementioned business community that has to pay the costs of greater environmental controls, well, do we have to connect the dots for you here or what?"

12      "Just for fun, let's go to David Suzuki's place and let the air out of the tires of his hybrid car."

13      Now there. Isn't that something our world leaders, visionaries every one, could sign on to?

---

[5 December 2003]


1.  What are the features of conversational English that this article contains? (Use the chart on page 13 as a reference.) Consider the verb forms, the beginnings of sentences, and the use of questions. Are these features suitable for use in an essay?

2. Find examples of conversational expressions (such as "let's see") that would be inappropriate in an essay.
3. Find three idioms in the article. (See page 37 if you need an explanation of *idiom*.)
4. Find examples of slang. (See page 38 if you need an explanation of *slang*.)
5. Find examples of "legalese"—overly formal language that a lawyer (or politician) would be likely to use.
6. What one word could be used instead of "children's children" and "children's children's children" [5]?
7. What are some words you would use to describe "scientists, with their oversized glasses and little slide rules and pocket protectors" [8]?
8. How does the author create humour in the article? What do you find particularly funny?
9. How do you know that the author is not serious about his opposition to environmental initiatives, that he is in fact kidding?

---

**How to write in academic style**

- Do not use *I* or *you* (see pages 203–06 in Unit 7).
- Do not use conversational expressions (such as *let's see* or *right?*).
- Do not use slang (see page 38).
- Avoid asking your reader questions.
- Do not start sentences with coordinate conjunctions (*and, or, but, so*) (see page 77).
- Use transition signals (see pages 119–20 in Unit 4).
- Write fully developed paragraphs (Unit 4), not one- or two-sentence paragraphs.
- Avoid vague words like *thing* and *stuff*; use precise vocabulary instead.
- Use complex sentences with adjective and adverb clauses to layer meaning (see Unit 3).

---

## Understanding the Writing Process

Essentially, there are three stages to the writing process: planning, writing, and editing. These stages can be broken down into smaller steps. For instance, planning includes choosing a topic, brainstorming, and outlining. Several drafts may be written in the second stage. Editing includes making both major revisions and minor corrections.

Writers do not always progress from one stage to the next in an organized fashion. Working on a computer allows writers to go back and forth in their writing, changing their plans and editing as they write, until they are satisfied with the final product. However, they do still start with planning and end with proofing and correcting.

Student writers sometimes spend too little time on the first and third stages of the writing process. They may skimp on the planning stage, not thinking enough about what they want to say and how they want to say it. They also tend to neglect the editing stage: they may look for obvious mistakes they have made, but they are reluctant to toss out or rework full sentences, especially sentences they have sweated over. However, all three stages are necessary.

Students sometimes do not have the luxury of time for their assignments. When they have to write an essay in class, they have to get words on paper fast, but even then they can follow the basic process even if they have only a few minutes to plan and a few minutes to edit and correct.

## Planning

Choosing a topic is generally the first step in the planning process. How much choice you have depends on your instructor and the nature of the assignment. Although students sometimes grumble about the choice of topics and say that they want to choose their own, students given complete freedom to choose a subject often flounder because of too much choice. They are better off with the instructor's topic choices because these topics are tailored to the level of the students and related to the readings and discussions in the course.

You often have to narrow your subject down from the question asked. Most subjects cover a broad range of ideas. For example, an essay topic might be "Discuss one of the problems that second-generation immigrants face." Not only do you have the choice of problem you wish to explain, but you may choose to narrow this further by writing about one specific ethnic group that you are familiar with. Often, you are given a choice whether to disagree or agree with a statement or to write about advantages or disadvantages of something.

If you cannot decide among a selection of topics, do some brainstorming on two or more of them. If you jot down some ideas in point form, you will be able to see which issue you have more to say on. Pick the subject you are most comfortable with.

Sometimes students are asked to show the process in the work they submit. They may be asked to include the brainstorming, essay outline, and/or drafts with the final product. Often, instructors evaluate the outline and give feedback that the students can use to write their essay.

You can read more about brainstorming and outlining in Unit 5.

## Writing

The planning stage makes writing the draft easier. It helps to prevent writer's block—when a writer stares blankly at the screen or paper and does not know what to say.

It is also easier to write if you just go for it without worrying about perfection. Remember that you can correct spelling and grammatical errors in the editing stage. Essentially, you want to get your ideas down in a clear, coherent order with a logical flow from one idea to the next.

Remember to support your ideas with explanations and examples. Academic writing is all about making points and supporting them. You can see how this is done in Units 4, 5, and 6.

## Editing

Editing involves making both major changes and minor corrections to your draft. You may want to revise what you have said, changing parts of the essay around and taking out sections. Do not hesitate to delete what does not work in your essay—even if you feel you worked hard to get those sentences written. One important difference between professional writers and student writers is that professionals keep revising their wording until they are satisfied with it.

Remember that you have to proofread carefully. It is better if you do this after the essay sits for a day so that you can view it with fresh eyes. This is impossible to do with an in-class writing assignment, but you can still reread your work before you hand it in. It is important not to leave take-home writing assignments until the last minute so that you can take advantage of the time to revisit your work.

Unit 7 explains the basic principles of editing and correcting and gives you an opportunity to practise with common errors.

## Understanding Writing Evaluation

Students may question or even challenge the marks they receive for a writing assignment. Unlike mathematics and science where right answers usually cannot be debated, writing is evaluated in a more subjective fashion. However, writing instructors usually explain what they are looking for and often use a detailed marking scheme.

Because instructors have likely read thousands of student papers, they can size up an assignment very quickly and know where it ranks from excellent to unsatisfactory. Students, on the other hand, may think they deserve a good mark based on the time and effort they put into the assignment. However, their view of their work is quite narrow. For instance, some students rarely see how their work compares with other students' writing.

Here are some questions that writing instructors generally consider when evaluating an assignment:

Did the student follow the instructions for the assignment?

Does the essay answer the topic question?
Does the assignment follow the required structure and format?
Is the work in the required writing style?
Are citations and referencing correct?

How strong is the content?

Does the student use his or her own ideas and not just repeat ideas from the reading?
Do the statements follow logically?

Are arguments organized and supported?
Does the writer stay on topic?

How well are the ideas expressed?

Is the writing clear? Is it easy to understand what the writer is saying?
Is the writing concise, or is it padded with repetition and wordiness?
Does the writing flow from one sentence to the next? Is it easy to read?

Is the language used correctly?

Are the basic sentence structure and grammar sound?
Are words and expressions used correctly?
Are there very few mistakes in spelling, punctuation, and capitalization?

Does the work show improvement in writing skills?

Has the student worked on error correction for mistakes he or she consistently makes?
Does the work show that the student has learned the principles taught in the course?

These are the basic criteria used to evaluate writing assignments. Sometimes they are listed on a marking rubric, and your assignment is graded on each scale separately. For example, you may get a mark for content and another for essay structure. Sometimes instructors give a holistic mark, a grade that encompasses all the criteria. For example, an A paper is considered excellent—the essay is properly structured with a clear thesis, the ideas expressed are on topic, and there are few errors in language use. B means very good, C is satisfactory, D may be a bare pass, and F is given if the basic criteria are not met. Instructors usually explain these criteria at the beginning of a course and may show sample papers.

**How to become a better writer**

1. Read more—in order to learn the written language, to develop vocabulary, and to acquire background knowledge.
2. Think critically—be curious about the world around you, listen to others' ideas, and develop your own opinions.
3. Practise—writing is a skill that you develop the more you use it.
4. Check your work—be critical of what you write, look for mistakes, and check whatever you are unsure of.
5. Learn from your mistakes—use corrections and comments on your work to help you improve.

# Vocabulary Skills

Words are the building blocks of language. Grammar tells you how the words fit together in sentences, but without the words there is no meaning and no communication. The most important thing you can do to improve your reading and writing skills is to increase your vocabulary so that you can more easily comprehend what you read and express your own ideas clearly and concisely.

Reading increases vocabulary knowledge because you are exposed to more words when you read than when you listen to English. Standard Written English uses—and needs—a lot more words than spoken English does. You can get by in conversational English with only 2000 or 3000 words, but to read and write at the post-secondary level, you may need to know 20,000—which is still only a small number of the estimated 700,000 words in the English lexicon. (This is a rough estimate based on dictionary entries. Getting the exact number of English words is an impossible task; much depends on what is counted as a word. Moreover, new words get added to the lexicon every year.)

Reading is vital to vocabulary learning because that is where you see the words in action—used in sentences. Through repeated exposure to the words in context, you develop a sense of what they mean and how they are used. Vocabulary learning is incremental—you continuously build on your knowledge.

Vocabulary knowledge is not just how many words you know but how well you know them. A crucial distinction is between **passive vocabulary** (words you understand, also called **receptive vocabulary**) and **active vocabulary** (words you use, also called **productive vocabulary**). Everyone has more words in their passive vocabulary. As you get to know the words better from seeing them used, you start to use them yourself, and the words move from passive to active vocabulary.

Word knowledge encompasses several different aspects in addition to understanding the meaning of the word in its encountered context:

- other possible meanings of the word
- its part of speech (noun, verb, adjective, or adverb)
- its pronunciation
- its spelling
- what words tend to appear along with the word
- what grammatical structure is required to use the word in a sentence

- whether a word is positive or negative and how strong that connotation is
- whether the word is limited to a specific group (British vs. American English, for instance)
- how common the word is
- how that word is distinguished from its synonyms and other related words

These different aspects of vocabulary are explained in this unit. You will learn how words are formed and how they work. This will increase your word consciousness and help you to increase your vocabulary.

Because word knowledge is complicated, an analogy may help you to understand. In some ways, words are like people.

- They are born (or *coined*, as we say about words).
- They grow and change over time.
- They have different origins and ethnic backgrounds.
- They have families and relatives.
- They are quirky and often do not make sense.
- They like to hang out with friends (collocation).
- They can be found in specific locations (in a sentence).
- They may behave differently in different contexts.
- You have to meet them several times to remember them and get to know them.
- You might not recognize them in different contexts.

## Learning Pronunciation

A fundamental part of knowing a word is knowing how to pronounce it, even if that is not a priority in a reading and writing course. Electronic and online dictionaries often have audio files that can guide you; they are easier to use than the pronunciation guides found in print dictionaries. Remember that words often have more than one correct pronunciation. For instance, British pronunciation can be quite different from the way North Americans say the words.

Make sure you know how different letter combinations are pronounced. Greek letter combinations can be especially confusing. Because Greek uses a different alphabet, some English letter combinations represent Greek letters: *ph* (from *phi*, φ) sounds like "f"; *ch* (from *chi*, χ) sounds like "k"; and *ps* (from *psi*, ψ) sounds like "s"—as in the words *philosophy*, *chaos*, and *psychology*.

Word stress is an important part of pronunciation, especially since unstressed vowels reduce to the "schwa" sound (an "uh" sound) in English. Words sound very different if the syllable stress is changed. As an example, compare the pronunciation of *table* and *vegetable*.

Examples of different stress in noun/verb pairs:

The company can <u>produce</u> different versions of the same product. [verb]
They buy their <u>produce</u> in the market. [noun]

The <u>convict</u> was quickly caught. [noun]
They couldn't <u>convict</u> him because of the lack of evidence. [verb]

Because the English language is not written the way it sounds, it is difficult to figure out how to pronounce a word just from the spelling and to figure out how to spell a word when you hear it pronounced. Moreover, because the written language uses a much larger vocabulary than spoken English, avid readers may know the meaning of many words, but they may not know how to pronounce them.

When you learn new words in your English course, pay attention to how your instructor pronounces the word. Ask for a repetition if you did not hear the word properly, and ask questions if you find anything confusing.

## Learning Spelling

Spelling is an important part of word knowledge, but it is particularly difficult in English. Essentially, English spelling is not phonetic—it does not mirror the pronunciation.

As English evolved over time, its pronunciation shifted away from its spelling, with changes such as these:

- Silent letters used to be pronounced. This includes the *k* and *gh* in *knight* and the *e* at the end of words like *name*.
- Vowel sounds are not pronounced as the letters indicate, because unstressed vowels are reduced in English. (This is why *than* and *then* sound the same in a sentence, for example.)
- English spelling was standardized with the printing press, but printers used different dialects as a base, and the pronunciation of English underwent major shifts afterwards.
- Words entered English from other languages and introduced non-English letter combinations, such as the *ph* from the Greek letter *phi* (φ), which is pronounced as an *f* sound.

### Tips for learning spelling

- As you learn new words, pay attention to the spelling. Look for spelling patterns.
- Use spelling rules (like the "*i* before *e*" rhyme) even though there are often exceptions.
- Use mnemonic devices—tricks to help you remember. (For instance, the first letters in the phrase "I go home tonight" gives you the *–ight* spelling combination.)
- Learn common letter combinations. For instance, *–ough* is never *–uogh* or *–ouhg*.
- Write and/or type the word out several times because muscle memory plays an important part in spelling—sometimes your fingers "know" how to spell a word.
- Make a list of words you tend to misspell. Memorize them.

Note that there can be more than one way to correctly spell a word. For instance, British spelling is sometimes different from American spelling. Canadian spelling is somewhere in the middle, sometimes following British conventions (like *colour*) and sometimes following American (like *organize*). In these cases, it is important to be consistent. For example, if you use the *–our* spelling in *colour* then you should also use it in *neighbour* and *favour* and not switch between variations.

When we talk about spelling, we are mainly concerned with avoiding and correcting spelling mistakes. See Unit 7, pages 195–198, for more on spelling mistakes.

## Recognizing Parts of Speech

Words belong to different classes: nouns, verbs, adjectives, and adverbs are the main parts of speech we consider when we talk about vocabulary learning. These are called **content words**, and the list of content words is infinite because we keep making new words. The other parts of speech (prepositions, conjunctions, articles, etc.) are considered **function words**. This is a closed set of words—it is much harder to invent a new preposition and have it accepted in the language than it is to invent a new noun. You can learn all the function words but not all the content words, so vocabulary learning centres on nouns, verbs, adjectives, and adverbs.

### Nouns

Nouns tell the listener or reader who or what is being talked about. In a sentence, nouns can be **subjects** (doing the action) or **objects** (receiving the action). How they work in a sentence is explained in Unit 3.

Nouns are essentially the names of persons, places, things, animals, and ideas. **Concrete nouns** refer to things you can touch (*stone, chair, eggs*), while **abstract nouns** name emotions and qualities (*love, truth, success*). **Proper nouns** are specific names and are capitalized (*Tom, Vancouver, the Bible, Saskatchewan, Mr. Smith*). **Collective nouns** refer to a group of people and things; collective nouns are singular (*staff, team,* and *herd*). **Compound nouns** are two words that are used together as a unit (*girlfriend, bookcase, boom box, lunch break, slip-knot, mini-bar*). The unit may be written as two separate words, hyphenated words, or one word.

**Countable nouns** have two forms of the word—**singular** (one) or **plural** (more than one). For most nouns, an *–s* is added to the singular to make the plural form (*book/books, holiday/holidays*). Nouns that end in an *–s* sound (using one of these: *–s, –sh, –ch,* or *–x*) are spelled with an *–es* plural ending (*box/boxes, bus/buses, wish/wishes*). Nouns that end in *–y* preceded by a consonant have an *–ies* plural ending (*story/stories, spy/spies*). **Uncountable nouns** (such as *information, furniture, advice*) are not made plural.

Many nouns have irregular plurals. Some involve a change of letter (*knife/knives*) or an added letter (*potato/potatoes*). Some do not have a different plural form (e.g., *deer, moose*), while others are plural with no singular forms (*scissors, jeans*). A few words from Latin and Greek have plural forms that follow the form of their original language (*criterion/criteria, phenomenon/phenomena, analysis/analyses*). Some common words have plurals that students often write incorrectly (*man/men, woman/ women, child/children*).

If you are not sure of the plural form of a noun, look up the singular form in the dictionary. Any irregular plurals or plurals that have spelling changes (like *y* to *i*) will be listed in the main entry for the noun; otherwise, the plural is a regular –*s* ending.

| **Common noun endings** | **Examples** |
|---|---|
| –age | breakage, marriage, mileage |
| –ance, –ence | alliance, difference, silence |
| –er, –or | actor, escalator, inventor, teacher |
| –dom | freedom, kingdom, wisdom |
| –hood | knighthood, neighbourhood |
| –ism | feminism, heroism, plagiarism, realism |
| –ist | artist, cyclist, finalist, racist, typist |
| -ity | capability, fatality, morality |
| -ment | document, enjoyment, entertainment |
| -ness | goodness, happiness, sadness |
| -ship | friendship, kinship |
| -sion, -tion | celebration, fusion, nation, permission |

## Verbs

Verbs are words that describe **actions** (*jump, swim, break*) or **states** (*be, seem, signify*). They are crucial to a sentence. This section introduces verbs as vocabulary items. Verb tenses, forms, and uses are explained in Unit 3 as part of sentence structure. Common errors made with verb forms and tenses are discussed in Unit 7, page 215.

When we talk about a verb or look it up in a dictionary, we use the **base form**, the simplest form of verb, the one without any endings (for example, *wait, listen, feel*). With a *to* in front of this base form, we have the **infinitive** form, also considered a fundamental form (for example, *to sleep, to answer*). We often give the infinitive when we talk about verbs because that clearly identifies the word as a verb.

English has fewer verb endings than other European languages do. An –*s* ending is used to denote the third-person singular in the simple present tense (*he walks, she laughs, it makes*). For regular verbs, an –*ed* ending makes the simple past form (*he walked*). It also makes the past participle, which is used with *have* for present tenses (*he has walked*). An –*ing* ending is used to make the form used in continuous tenses (*he is walking, she is reading*).

In English, the most common verbs are irregular in their formation. Instead of just adding an –*ed* ending to the base form to make the simple past form and the past participle, you may have verb forms with vowel changes. If you look up an irregular verb in the dictionary, the entry is the base form of the verb, and the simple past and the past participle are listed. If the dictionary does not give the past form and the past participle, you can assume that the verb is regular (that both past forms are made by adding an –*ed* ending to the base form).

| Principal parts of the verb | | | |
|---|---|---|---|
| | **Base form** | **Simple past** | **Past participle** |
| Regular verbs: | talk | talked | talked |
| | exist | existed | existed |
| | | | |
| Irregular verbs: | sing | sang | sung |
| | take | took | taken |
| | run | ran | run |
| | think | thought | thought |
| | swim | swam | swum |
| | make | made | made |
| | go | went | gone |

For almost every verb, knowing these three principal forms will allow you to make all the tenses and structures you need. For instance, the base form is the same as the simple present tense, and you use that form to add the −s ending for the third person (*he sings*) and to make the −*ing* form (*singing*). Of course, as with all endings, some spelling rules may apply—such as dropping the silent *e* before adding the ending (*making, dating*).

The two most common verbs have even more irregular forms:

> **to be:** being, am, is, are, was, were, been
> **to have:** having, has, had

One tricky part about verbs is that some verb forms can act as other parts of speech. The −*ing* form can also work as a noun (called a **gerund**) or as an adjective (called a **participle**).

For example:

| | |
|---|---|
| She <u>is sleeping</u> right now. | verb—present continuous tense |
| <u>Sleeping</u> is the best way to spend Sunday morning. | gerund, acting as the subject |
| The <u>sleeping</u> children looked angelic. | present participle, acting as an adjective describing the children |

The past participle can also function as an adjective.

| | |
|---|---|
| The <u>elected</u> officials were sworn in on Friday. | past participle, acting as an adjective describing the officials |

The difference between the two participles is that the present participle is **active** (doing the action), while the past participle is **passive** (receiving the action). See pages 54–56 in Unit 3 for more on the passive.

| | |
|---|---|
| The woman <u>wearing</u> the crown is the queen. | active participle |
| That crown is <u>worn</u> on state occasions. | passive participle |
| He found the explanation <u>confusing</u>. | active participle |
| He was <u>confused</u> by the explanation. | passive participle |

Sometimes a verb is derived from another part of speech (as *personalize* is derived from the adjective *personal*). You can identify verbs by certain beginnings (prefixes) and endings (suffixes).

| Word endings and beginnings that can identify verbs | | |
|---|---|---|
| **Prefixes** | **Suffixes** | **Examples** |
| be- | | bejewel, belittle, bewitch |
| en- | | enable, endanger, enjoy, enlarge |
| in-, im- | | inflame, impassion, imprison |
| | –en | blacken, lighten, soften, toughen |
| | –ate | activate, discriminate, motivate |
| | –fy, –ify | identify, modify, notify, signify |
| | –ize, –ise | exercise, idealize, maximize, realize |

Note that British spelling tends to use *–ise* (*organise*, *penalise*) whereas North American spelling favours *–ize* (*organize*, *penalize*).

## Adjectives

Essentially, adjectives describe nouns. They usually appear before the noun in English, as in these examples:

> brown dress, tall man, close escape, unparalleled beauty, questionable actions

They also appear after the verb *to be* and other verbs that describe the state of something:

> Working in this classroom is <u>difficult</u>. The air feels <u>stuffy</u>. The noise is <u>annoying</u>.

In many European languages, adjectives have endings to agree with the verb they modify, but English has no plural adjective forms. The only endings used on English adjectives are *–er* for comparative forms and *–est* for superlative forms.

Moreover, these endings are only used on short adjectives (one or two syllable words). (*More* and *most* are used in front of longer adjectives.)

> short, shorter, shortest
> pretty, prettier, prettiest
> long, longer, longest
>
> expensive, more expensive, most expensive

The use of these adjectives is explained in Adding Modifiers (Unit 3, pages 71–73).

| Common adjective endings | | |
|---|---|---|
| **Suffix** | **Meaning** | **Examples** |
| –able, –ible | able to, suitable for | acceptable, capable, flexible |
| –en | made of | golden, wooden |
| –ful | full of | beautiful, grateful, powerful |
| –ic, –ical | relating to | classical, comic, musical, public |
| –ive | tending to | descriptive, sensitive |
| –less | without | careless, worthless |
| –ous, –ose | quality, state | mountainous, poisonous, verbose |
| –y | having, being like | funny, sunny, hairy |

## Adverbs

Adverbs explain how, when, or where something is done. There are two main kinds of adverbs. Some are function words (*now*, *there*, *yesterday*), and there is a finite list of them. As function words, they are not a part of vocabulary learning. The other kind of adverbs are content words; they are derived from adjectives.

Most adverbs are formed from an adjective by the addition of an –*ly* ending (*carefully*, *quickly*, *realistically*, *slowly*). If the adjective ends in –*able*, the adverb form is made by changing the final *e* to *y* (*reliable/reliably*).

Note that there are a few adjectives that end in –*ly* (such as *friendly*, *lonely*, *miserly*); these do not have an adverb form.

The use of adverbs is explained in Adding Modifiers (Unit 3, pages 71–73).

## Distinguishing Word Classes

Many students find it difficult to identify the part of speech even for words they know and use every day. Even if they struggle with the terminology, they should have a word sense that allows them to separate nouns from verbs. Students who have had some grammar instruction and who have learned other languages are usually more successful at classifying words. It is worthwhile to learn the major word classes because this fundamental knowledge will make both vocabulary learning and sentence construction easier.

The previous sections have explained the four main word classes of content words—what nouns, verbs, adjectives, and adverbs essentially are. Each also has a list of common suffixes, but this list is not foolproof. For instance, −en is both an adjective suffix and a verb suffix.

Another complication in English is the flexibility in the part of speech categories. We can use nouns as adjectives and make nouns verbs and verbs nouns. For instance, the popularity of social media has led to the formation of new words and new uses of old words. We now accept as verbs the words *friend* and *unfriend* (even though we already had a verb form of *friend*—*befriend*). Similarly, the verb *like* has become a countable noun, as in "it got 300 likes."

To figure out its part of speech, it is easier to think of the word in relation to other words. For instance, nouns often follow articles like *the* and *a*. If you are not sure whether a word is a verb, say it with *to* and see if it makes sense as an infinitive. For example, "to discuss" makes sense whereas "to discussion" does not, so *discuss* is the verb.

Here are some simple sentence patterns that can help you:

> The NOUN was gone.
> It is a NOUN.
> He wants to VERB.
> It is ADJECTIVE.
> They did it ADVERB.

With the word family *success/succeed/successful/successfully*, we can see how each word would fit in the blanks to reveal its part of speech:

> The <u>success</u> was gone.
> It is a <u>success</u>.
> He wants to <u>succeed</u>.
> It is <u>successful</u>.
> They did it <u>successfully</u>.

Note that the first sentence does not work as well for the meaning, but the structure can still help you to identify the noun of the group of words.

## Exercise 2.1

Decide which type of word goes in each blank—a noun, verb, adjective, or adverb. (There will be only one word per blank.) After you have labelled each blank underneath, fill in appropriate words to fit the sentence:

1. A _____ book lay on the _____, next to the black _____.

2. The student _____ his homework. He went back to his _____ to get it.

3. The _____ child _____ went back to her _____ .

4. His job was _____ . He wanted to _____ .

5. He said that _____ is a _____ .

## Exercise 2.2

In each grouping, find the word that is not the same part of speech as the other three:

| | | | | |
|---|---|---|---|---|
| 1. | a) walk | b) slow | c) run | d) hike |
| 2. | a) stare | b) glance | c) look | d) watchfully |
| 3. | a) gossip | b) chatty | c) talkative | d) communicative |
| 4. | a) friendly | b) nicely | c) lovely | d) lively |
| 5. | a) difficulty | b) confusing | c) dilemma | d) complication |
| 6. | a) observant | b) attention | c) watchful | d) alert |
| 7. | a) oppose | b) resist | c) contradict | d) antagonism |
| 8. | a) emotion | b) feeling | c) excitement | d) sentimental |
| 9. | a) advantage | b) gain | c) achieve | d) acquire |
| 10. | a) quiet | b) peaceful | c) relax | d) tranquil |

## Understanding Word Formation

Many words can be divided into identifiable parts. The main part of the word is the **root**, also referred to as the "combining form." A group of letters attached to the beginning of the word is called a **prefix**. Prefixes include letter combinations such as *in-* and *un-* that make words negative. **Suffixes** are letter combinations that are attached to the end of the word. Suffixes such as *−hood* and *−ly* show the part of speech of the word. (Many of them have already been introduced in this unit on pages 25, 27, and 28.) Word endings can also show plurals, possessives, and verb endings (*−s, −ed, −ing*). The word *affix* is used to refer to both prefixes and suffixes.

Many roots and affixes come from Greek and Latin. For instance, the word *multilingual* is an adjective that can refer to someone who speaks several languages. It comes from the Latin words for many (*multi-*) and tongue (*lingua*) and has the adjective ending *−al*. Similarly, *polyglot* is a noun referring to someone who speaks several languages, but it is based on Greek words: *poly* (many) and *glotta* (tongue).

Prefixes and suffixes are often given as separate entries in the dictionary. For example, you can look up *ante-* and learn that it means *before*, as in *anteroom*, and that it is not the same prefix as *anti-*, which means *against*.

Another type of word formation is shown in **compound nouns**, like *keyboard*, *toothpick*, *season pass*, and *mother-in-law*. They may be written as one word, hyphenated, or as two words. Check your dictionary if you are not sure which way to write the word. Often, more than one way is accepted. Sometimes there is a gradual change over time as the word gets more accepted. For instance, *website* started out as two words and is now commonly written as one. **Compound adjectives** (such as *accident-prone*) are usually hyphenated.

Examining the parts of a word can often help you to figure out what unfamiliar new words mean. However, this is complicated by the fact that there are so many affixes and roots to learn—many with the same function and meaning. Moreover, it can be difficult to ascertain whether a letter combination is actually a prefix or just the start of the word. For example, *in* is a negative prefix in *inactive* but not in *interest*.

Although word dissection can be a great help in identifying meaning, it can also sometimes be misleading. There are many inconsistencies. For example, *impossible* is the opposite of *possible*, but *impertinent* is not the opposite of *pertinent*. If you are not familiar with the word *slaughter*, you could be tempted to divide the word *manslaughter* as *mans-laughter*.

Learn some word formation patterns, but keep your eye out for words that do not make sense.

## Negative Prefixes and Suffixes

A number of negative prefixes change words to the opposite meaning. They are mostly used with adjectives and sometimes verbs. The most common negative prefix is *un-*: *unclean, unaware, uncommon, undo, unlock*.

Another common prefix is *in-*, but it is trickier because it undergoes spelling changes and has two meanings. The negative prefix *in-* (as in *inactive*) can also be spelled *il-*, *im-*, and *ir-*: *illogical, impossible,* and *irregular*. It depends on the next sound. *Impossible* is easier to say than "inpossible" would be. Also, sometimes *in-* is not a negative; it simply means "in," as in *inhale, input,* and *indent*.

The prefixes *dis-, mis-, mal-,* and *non-* also commonly make negatives: *dishonest, misunderstand, malformed, nonconformist*.

The suffix *−less* shows a lack of something: *careless, soulless, worthless*. Some of these words have an opposite formed with *−ful* (*careful, soulful*—but **not** *worthful*.) (Note that the word *full* is spelled with two *l*'s but the suffix only has one *l*.)

In English, some full words (*bad, evil, ill, wrong*) are used to make hyphenated compound words that are negative: *bad-tempered, evil-doer, ill-advised, wrong-headed*.

---

### Exercise 2.3

Use prefixes or suffixes to make the negative forms of these words:

able, appetizing, behave, competent, continue, finite, interesting, literate, manage, nourished, readable, relevant, sufficient, visible, wise

## Common Prefixes

Some prefixes refer to a numeric quantity: *uni-* (unicycle), *mono-* (monogamy), *bi-* (bilingual), *tri-* (triangle), *dec-* (decathlon), *cent-* (centennial).

Some prefixes refer to size: *mini-* (minimum), *maxi-* (maximize), *ultra-* (ultrasound).

Some prefixes have the same meaning as prepositions, as this chart shows:

| Prefix | Meaning | Example |
|--------|---------|---------|
| co- | with | co-worker |
| ex- | out | exit |
| inter- | between | intermix |
| sub- | below | submarine |
| syn- | with | synchronize |
| trans- | across | transportation |

Here are some other useful prefixes:

| *cyber-* | computer | cybercrime |
|----------|----------|------------|
| *neo-* | new | neo-Nazi |
| *re-* | again | renegotiate, renew |

## Exercise 2.4

Identify prefixes and suffixes in the words below. Give the part of speech and the meaning of the root word.

| | |
|---|---|
| unforgettable | inedible |
| information | premarital |
| irrecoverable | malfunction |
| breakage | bilingual |
| underestimated | substandard |

## Learning Word Families

Words that have different prefixes and suffixes but the same root and basic meaning are said to belong to the same family.

Examples of word families:

success, succeed, successful, unsuccessful, successfully, unsuccessfully

development, developer, develop, developmental, developmentally

supervision, supervisor, supervise, supervisory

It is useful to know other words in the same family because:

• It increases your vocabulary.
• You can use the words for paraphrasing and for varying your wording in essays.

- You can determine the meaning of less common words in the family by recognizing the relationship.
- You can recognize patterns that can be helpful for spelling or meaning.

   Word families are not usually highlighted in the dictionary. You have to look at neighbouring entries to determine other words in the family. Be sure to check the meanings to see if the words are actually related. For instance, *organ*, *organism*, *organize*, and *organza* all start with the same letters and may have similar origins, but the words have very different meanings and so would not be put in the same word family. For negative prefixes, take a guess—for example, whether it is *inefficient* or *unefficient*—and look for the word in the dictionary.

## Exercise 2.5

Complete the word families in this chart (the first is completed for you as an example):

| NOUN | VERB | ADJECTIVE | ADVERB |
|---|---|---|---|
| richness<br>riches | enrich | rich | richly |
| advice | | | |
| | | believable<br>unbelievable | |
| | | bright | |
| | | clear | |
| | endanger | | |
| identification | | | |
| | | | imaginatively |
| | prove | | |
| | | recognizable | |
| | | soft | |

## Exercise 2.6

Use words from the chart to fill in the blanks in the following sentences:

1. Security was tight. Everyone had to show _____ to enter the hall.

2.  Her job is to _____ students on their course selection.

3.  He had changed so much that she didn't _____ him.

4.  He walked _____ close to the edge of the cliff.

5.  The _____ of the light bothered him.

6.  The most important quality of good writing is _____.

7.  When you read a book, you see the characters and setting in your

    _____.

8.  I would never have imagined that. Her performance was

    _____ bad.

9.  She had to provide _____ of her identity.

10. It made a big difference when the screen was _____. We

    could see more _____.

## Using Different Members of the Word Family

Note the changes in sentence structure that are required when you use a different part of speech:

> He worried that the whales would become <u>extinct</u>. [adj]
> He worried about the possible <u>extinction</u> of the whales. [n]
>
> There was no <u>agreement</u> among the committee members. [n]
> The committee members did not <u>agree</u>. [v]
>
> The explosion made Eric <u>deaf</u>. [adj]
> The explosion <u>deafened</u> Eric. [v]

Using different parts of speech can help you to vary your expression and sentence structure and make your sentences more concise. For example, given the writing topic "What is the key to success in college?" students often repeat the same phrase "the key to success" throughout the essay. One step to varying the wording is to choose a different "family member" for your sentences. Note the sentence variety below:

> Attendance is the key to <u>success</u>. [n]
> Students must attend class to be <u>successful</u>. [adj]
> Students who attend class <u>succeed</u>. [v]

You can see more on this subject in the section on Paraphrasing in Unit 8 (pages 240–43).

## Exercise 2.7

Rewrite the following sentences by changing the underlined word to another word in the same family, as in the examples above.

1. The puppy has so much <u>curiosity</u> that it gets into everything.
2. One student from each class was a <u>participant</u> in the project.
3. I liked that the material was <u>soft</u>.
4. Elizabeth enjoys being <u>solitary</u>.
5. They tried to hide that they were <u>disappointed</u> with the results.
6. Jason only felt more <u>confusion</u> when the teacher explained it again.
7. When all the guests arrived, Tracey made the <u>introductions</u>.
8. There was no <u>verification</u> for the story.
9. When the bomb went off, there was <u>chaos</u> in the city.
10. The committee is waiting for the president's <u>arrival</u>.

## Understanding Word Meaning

Word meaning should never be considered a straightforward equation—that this word equals that meaning. As in any language, one word can have a range of meanings or several different meanings. The word *jerk*, for example, can describe a tug on a rope, a type of Jamaican chicken dish, or a person whom no one likes. It is clear which meaning is meant by the context.

**Synonyms** are words that have similar meanings, while **antonyms** are words that have opposite meanings. However, it is important to remember that synonyms are not interchangeable. There may be slight differences of meaning and usage. For instance, you can tell someone to *concentrate* or *focus* on an assignment; the two words are synonyms in this context. However, *concentrate* is also used in chemistry to talk about concentrations in solutions, and *focus* is used for cameras; in those cases, the two words are no longer interchangeable.

**Thesauruses** (dictionaries of synonyms and antonyms) are useful tools for reminding writers of other possible word choices. Thesauruses are available in book form, online, and even within many word processing programs. However, you should not just blindly choose a synonym from a thesaurus. First make sure you know how the word is used and whether it applies to that context.

Words may have both a **literal meaning** and a **figurative meaning**. For example, the word *lion* literally refers to an African animal, but it could mean a leader, as in the phrase "a lion among men." Such metaphorical meanings are common in written language and are often difficult for students to understand if the reference is not clear to them. As in all vocabulary learning, reading also helps you to learn figurative meanings.

## Exercise 2.8

Replace the underlined words or expressions with other words or expressions that have similar meanings. Try coming up with a synonym yourself, but use a thesaurus if you get stuck. You might have to adjust the sentence structure by, for example, adding prepositions with verbs.

1. He made a <u>rookie</u> <u>error</u> by <u>expecting</u> his <u>staff</u> to <u>correct</u> the <u>problem</u> on their own.

2. Newspaper <u>articles</u> are <u>constantly</u> <u>warning</u> <u>readers</u> about some health <u>hazard</u> of common foods. It is not surprising that people become <u>skeptical</u> after a while.

3. The stranger's act of <u>kindness</u> <u>astonished</u> the <u>beggar</u>, who was <u>accustomed</u> to <u>abuse</u>.

# Understanding Connotation

It is not enough to know the meaning of a word (its **denotation**); you must know its **connotation**—the emotional impact it makes. Essentially, words have a positive or negative connotation. For instance, a person is complimented when he is called *brave* but insulted when he is called *reckless* even though the words mean essentially the same. A real estate agent will refer to a *house* as a *home* to highlight the positive connotation. There is also the strength of the emotional content. For example, the verb *murder* is much stronger than the verb *kill*.

The term **euphemism** refers to a nicer, more polite way of saying something. It is a word or expression that has a less negative connotation. For instance, someone might say, "my grandmother passed away" instead of "my grandmother died." Instead of asking, "Where is the toilet?" people use a number of different words and expressions, such as "the ladies' room" or "the facilities."

Words have a lot of power and must be used carefully. Make sure you understand the connotation of the words you use in your writing. As you expand your vocabulary, pay attention to the connotation of the new words and expressions.

### Activity

With a partner, consider the connotation of the following groups of words. Do they have the same meaning? Which are positive, and which are negative? Which are stronger?

1. arrogant, confident, bossy, aggressive, argumentative, fearless, self-reliant

2. thrifty, stingy, economical, prudent, miser, Scrooge, cheap, careful with money

3. secretive, sneaky, uncommunicative, close-mouthed, guarded, trustworthy

4. slender, thin, slim, anorexic, skinny, scrawny, emaciated, svelte, underweight

## Recognizing Idioms

An idiom is an expression in which the **figurative** meaning is different from the **literal** meaning. *Figurative* means that the whole expression gives a picture that is different from the meaning of the individual words (the word *literal* is related to the word *letter*; think of it as letter by letter or word by word). For example, the idiom *let the cat out of the bag* does not literally refer to a cat and a bag; it means reveal a secret. To *kick the bucket* means to die; this idiom has led to the expression *bucket list* (a personal list of things someone wants to do before he or she dies).

Idioms are generally more conversational in style. For example, "Same-sex marriage is a political hot potato" is more informal than "Same-sex marriage is a controversial issue." You can use some idioms in formal, academic essays, but select them carefully and use them judiciously. If there is another, more standard way to express the same meaning, use that if you want to be more formal. The more idiomatic language you use, the more conversational your writing becomes. This is not always appropriate in academic essays.

Idioms are generally explained in dictionaries. It's important to be able to identify a phrase as an idiom. You can find it in the dictionary under the main words (usually nouns or verbs). For instance, the idiom *it went in one ear and out the other* is probably in your dictionary under the word *ear*.

**Activity**

With a partner, discuss the following idioms. Do you know what each one means? Do you both agree on the meaning? Look up the idioms in your dictionary.

> to jump the gun
>
> to be caught red-handed
>
> the black sheep of the family
>
> a piece of cake
>
> in hot water
>
> to keep tabs on someone

**Activity**

In small groups, make a list of 10 idioms that you know. Compare it to the other groups' lists, looking for common ones. Which ones would be most useful for students to learn?

## Using Jargon

Jargon is technical language, such as medical terminology, legalese, and computer terms. The word *jargon* often has a negative connotation because it is extended to mean wording that is not clear. Writers are often told to avoid jargon, but it actually depends on the audience. If the intended readers or listeners have the right background to understand the technical language, then jargon is not only appropriate, it is necessary. It allows professionals within that group to communicate effectively and concisely with each other. For example, a doctor can tell another doctor that a patient has a *subcutaneous haematoma* but would tell the patient that it is a lump.

Jargon is not always easy to identify. It can include simple, everyday words that have a more specific meaning in a technical field, such as *cookies* in computer terminology. Some words start out as jargon and move into common usage. Computer terms like *input* and *output* are now used for non-computer purposes.

**Acronyms** (like AIDS and NIMBY), **initialisms** (like CD and USA), and other short forms are also common in jargon. (Acronyms are pronounced as words, while initialisms are pronounced as individual letters.) If you must use such an abbreviation, use the long form first, give the abbreviation in brackets after it, and then continue by using the abbreviation. (Note that most people just refer to all abbreviations that consist of initial letters as "acronyms.")

Avoid using jargon if your audience would not understand the words. If it would be easier to explain your points with the jargon, make sure you explain it for your readers first.

### Activity

Identify the fields these groups of words come from:

1. IV, contusion, ICU, carcinoma, septicemia

2. plaintiff, subpoena, writ, affidavit, pro bono

3. boot, blog, mouseover, CPU, data compression

4. escrow, tenancy in common, lien, title search

5. vehicle trespass, B&E, complaint, disorderly conduct

## Recognizing Inappropriate Language

Some words and expressions are not suitable for academic essays and other formal writing. Academic style is explained in Unit 1.

**Colloquialisms** are informal, conversational words and expressions. Dictionary entries may label these words as informal. The word *kid*, for example, is not suitable for more formal speaking or writing situations. It would be more appropriate to use *children* instead of *kids*.

**Slang** is a type of language, common in casual speech, that is generally characteristic of a specific group (such as teenagers or rap musicians) and sounds odd when used by non-members. For example, middle-aged parents are ridiculed when they try to sound like their teenaged children: "Yo, bro, 'sup?"

In addition, slang changes over time—it is like fashion. In the 1920s, young people would have called something really good *the cat's pyjamas* or *the bee's knees*. In the 1950s, they would have described it as *neato* or *swell*, then *groovy* in the sixties. At the end of the twentieth century, teens used *awesome* and words like *bad*, *sick*, and *wicked* to describe something that was in fact very good. Slang also varies region-ally: A British teenager is more likely to say, "Brilliant!" whereas a Canadian might say, "Sweet!"

**Obscenity** is another kind of language that is more common in spoken language than in written. Again, attitudes have changed. In 1939, audiences were shocked when Rhett Butler said to Scarlett O'Hara, "Frankly, my dear, I don't give a damn" in the film *Gone with the Wind*. Today, movies and even television shows are filled with profanity. Newspapers often do not print obscene words; if they have to quote someone who used a swear word, they print only some of the word (for example, "f***"). Note, however, that even swear words that do appear in print are not usually appropriate for academic writing.

**Overly formal** language is also not appropriate in your writing. A real estate agent talking about the *purveyance of a domicile* instead of the *sale of a house* would confuse and put off most clients. Remember that the primary purpose of writing is to give information clearly and concisely to the intended audience. Write to communicate, not to impress.

### Activity

In small groups, make a list of current slang expressions that would be inappropriate in an essay, and choose some replacement words or expressions.

## Dealing with Unfamiliar Words

As you read, you will come across unfamiliar words. If you stopped to look each one up in the dictionary, reading would become tedious. It is faster to try to guess the meaning from the context when possible. If you understand the gist of what is being said, you can keep reading. If you think the word is vital, look it up. How you read also depends on the material and the purpose. If you need to know the material well for your studies, look up the new vocabulary. (See Unit 8 for more on dealing with different types of reading.)

Readers learn words by seeing them many times and gradually working out the meaning in their own minds. They use their knowledge of the language and of the world to help them. The more they read, the more words they learn. And the more they encounter the words, the more complete their word knowledge becomes. For example, they will learn about different meanings and uses the words have.

### Figuring out Meaning

#### Looking around the Word

Here are some examples of how context can help you understand words:

> As we passed the rotting garbage, we tried covering our noses to keep out the vile stench.

If you do not know what the words *vile* and *stench* mean, you can figure out from this sentence that they refer to the awful smell of the garbage. And, in fact, *vile* means "terrible, really bad," and *stench* means "bad smell."

> When his father asked, "And where do you think you're going?" the teenager looked back at him <u>sullenly</u>.

*Sullenly* is an adverb, describing the way the teenager looked at his father. The father is challenging his son, so chances are that the son is not too happy. From what you know about the relationship between teenagers and their parents, you can guess that it is not a pleasant expression on his face. The adjective *sullen* means "resentful, unsociable, and sulky."

## Looking inside the Word

Besides looking around the word to the context to figure out its meaning, you can look inside the word. You can look for familiar prefixes, suffixes, and roots, as in these examples:

**indeterminate**
This word has an *in-* prefix, which is probably negative. The root *determine* is recognizable as the verb meaning "to find out the facts about something," and the *-ate* ending is an adjective ending, so *indeterminate* means "impossible to know exactly."

**naysayer** [used in "A Global Warming Deal to Do Nothing Still Possible," page 15]
has three parts: *nay* (meaning "no"), *say*, and *-er* (a suffix showing someone who does something), so a naysayer is someone who says no.

When you come across an unfamiliar word, keep reading and see whether the meaning of the sentence is clear enough. Use context clues and your knowledge of language to help you figure out the word. Go to the dictionary when you need to.

When you do the Definitions exercises for the reading selections in Part 2, try to use context clues to match the words with the definitions.

## Exercise 2.9

Use context clues and word form to help you figure out the meaning of the underlined words:

1. It was <u>serendipity</u> that I came across that article. I wasn't even thinking of my research project when I found it, but it has just what I need.

2. They were <u>at loggerheads</u> over the proposal. In the end, they couldn't work together and had to submit separate proposals.

3. The leather sofa was comfortable, but it was <u>cumbersome</u> every time he had to move.

4. They were surprised at his decision to donate the proceeds of the sale because <u>altruism</u> had never been one of his qualities.

5. Simplified novels are <u>abridged</u> versions of the books that also have changes in vocabulary and sentence structure to make them easier to read.

6.  I am <u>famished</u>. I only had a cup of yogurt for lunch.

7.  I love to watch professional soccer because the players have such speed and <u>agility</u>.

8.  Ever since I started taking that medication, I feel so <u>listless</u> that I don't get enough of my work done.

9.  She presented some <u>cogent</u> arguments and managed to get the opposition to back her plan.

10. Unlike his shy sisters, he is very <u>gregarious</u> and makes friends easily.

## Recognizing Collocation

Some words go together, and some do not. The word *collocation* (made from *co*, for "with," and *location*) refers to words that tend to be together in the same place—in other words, probable word combinations. For example, *say*, *speak*, *talk*, and *tell* have the same basic meaning but collocate with different words. We can "tell a secret" but not "speak a secret." We "speak a language" but "say a word." We "talk tough" but "tell the truth." We "say thank you" but "talk over a problem."

Collocation can include adjectives that go with nouns (*antique furniture* but not *ancient furniture*), verbs that go with nouns (*to offer advice* but not *to award advice*), prepositions or particles that complete verbs (*to depend on* someone but not *to depend for* someone), and noun combinations (*time management* but not *price management*).

Not only do the words go together, they often go together in a specific order. It would sound odd to hear "a matter of death and life," "through thin and thick" or "cold and hot."

Even if they have never explicitly learned about the concept of collocation, native speakers of a language are likely to feel that certain words sound better together than others. English language learners, however, often use improbable combinations, especially if they translate from their native language or use a bilingual dictionary that does not explain usage. Some dictionaries list collocations in their word entries, and the *Oxford Collocations Dictionary for Students of English* specializes in this feature of English.

To learn collocations, pay attention to how specific words are used, and look for common word combinations. It is important to get a sense of which words sound right together. The Language Study notes for the reading selections in this book contain a list of expressions and collocations in order to draw your attention to them. You can practise correcting collocation errors in Exercise 7.3.

## Exercise 2.10

In the following list of verb + noun combinations, cross out the unlikely ones, leaving the collocations:

*Example:* take a course, ~~study a course~~, ~~make a course~~, pass a course

1.  take a test, work a test, follow a test, run a test

2. ask a request, make a request, want a request, grant a request
3. conduct research, make research, carry out research
4. drop a hint, take a hint, see a hint, have a hint, give a hint
5. get experience, make experience, lack experience, acquire experience
6. run up a debt, make a debt, settle a debt, take a debt
7. do a method, adopt a method, work a method, follow a method
8. follow a reason, give a reason, take a reason, hold a reason
9. show a risk, follow a risk, run a risk, make a risk, take a risk
10. gain support, take support, run support, provide support

## Exercise 2.11

From each list of adjectives, choose the ones that collocate with the noun. You are looking for adjectives that often describe the noun. For example, the adjectives *lengthy* and *unavoidable* could be used to describe the noun *delay*, but the adjectives *heavy* and *accidental* would not be likely collocations. There may be more than one good choice in the list.

| Adjectives | Noun |
|---|---|
| light, pale, thin, weak | tea |
| alarming, dangerous, hazardous, nasty | material |
| accurate, careful, close, dense | examination |
| bad, firm, good, nasty, ugly | rumour |
| momentary, slight, stopping | hesitation |
| gainful, reasonable, seasonal, trustworthy | employment |
| broken, faulty, healthy, sound | reasoning |

## Appreciating Language Change

As you study vocabulary, you may wonder why English is such a crazy language—it has a huge vocabulary, with many words meaning almost the same thing, and the spelling and pronunciation can be chaotic. Most of the characteristics of English are explained by its history. Essentially, English is a mix of languages—like a stew of different ingredients. As different peoples invaded and settled in England, their languages affected English. For instance, many synonyms have come from other languages. In addition, the evolution of the language has caused divergence between spoken and written forms.

The capsule history below gives you an idea of some of the forces that have influenced English. If you are interested in learning more, you can search online for the history of the English language or read a book like *The History of the English Language* by Brigit Viney (Oxford University Press).

## A Capsule History of English

- English is a Germanic language that came to Britain from Europe 1500 years ago (after the Romans left), displacing the old Celtic language. Old English from this period is called Anglo-Saxon.
- Soon afterwards, Christian missionaries brought the Roman alphabet to Britain. They also caused church vocabulary to enter the English language from Latin.
- The Viking raiders in the sixth and seventh centuries settled in the east of England. Common English words that originated in the Vikings' Norse language include *skin* and *thing*.
- Then in 1066, the invasion by William the Conqueror brought Norman French to England. For two centuries, the nobility spoke French, while the common people spoke English. While the use of French gradually died out, the language left its mark on the vocabulary of English, practically doubling its size, leaving English/French pairs of synonyms like *help/aid*, *ask/demand*, *wedding/marriage*, and *pig/pork*.
- The printing press in the fifteenth century led to the standardization of spelling just as the sounds of the language were shifting, so spelling did not reflect the actual pronunciation.
- The advances of science and technology required new words, and European scientists and inventors looked to Latin and Greek to make new words like *television*, *microscope*, and *psychology*.
- The British Empire spread English all over the globe, and regional varieties and accents developed. Some countries use English as an official language instead of one of their native languages and make new varieties such as Singlish (Singaporean English).
- English has become the world's most useful language. It is the most studied second language and is often used as a medium of communication between people who do not share a native language. It is the international language of air traffic, business, and the media.

English is a flexible language, readily accepting words from other languages and allowing words to change part of speech or meaning. It's a free-for-all with no official institution trying to control the language (as there is in French). New words are coined every day, and lexicographers (dictionary writers) can barely keep up with the linguistic innovations.

## New Words in English

Words enter the language every day. Many are coined by writers (including ad writers and songwriters). If the words catch on, they eventually enter the language. The term *McJob* (for a menial, low-paying job), for example, was coined by Canadian writer Douglas Coupland, who also brought *Generation X* into English. Rap music has created words like *bling* and *peeps*.

Some words are blended (called **portmanteau** words):

> brunch: breakfast + lunch
> chillax: chill + relax
> ginormous: gigantic + enormous

Some words are short forms:

> to diss: disrespect
> selfie: self-portrait photograph

Brand names become generic:

> xerox machine: for any photocopier
> to google: to look for information using a search engine on the Internet

### Activity

In groups, make a list of five words that you think have entered the language in the past 30 years. Research the origin of the words to see whether they are as new as you think they are.

### Activity

News organizations, dictionary publishers, and other institutions often choose a "word of the year." Their choices may be neologisms (new words), existing words that acquired new meanings, or words that were just very much in the public consciousness that year. For example, the verb *vape* was chosen as 2014 Word of the Year by Oxford Dictionaries.

In an online search, find out what words were featured as a Word of the Year for last year. Which is your favourite? Explain why.

Choose a year in the past, perhaps 10 years ago, and find out which words featured as a Word of the Year. How have these words fared since then? Are they established in the English language, or have they died out?

## Using Dictionaries

Dictionaries are extremely powerful tools for learning vocabulary. The information given extends beyond definitions; it includes the part of speech, pronunciation, different forms of the word, and even the etymology (the word's history—where it comes from). You can check the different meanings, the spelling, and the usage of a word you want to write.

Dictionaries speed up the vocabulary learning process. You can learn a new word without consulting a dictionary, but you need to read it or hear it many times to learn the meaning from the context. A dictionary provides the information you need to understand the word and know how to use it.

Many different kinds of dictionaries are available. Second-language learners often use **bilingual dictionaries**, which translate words to and from their native language. While these dictionaries are good for lower levels, advanced students are usually encouraged to use monolingual (one language) dictionaries because translation is a different process from using the language. **Dictionaries for language learners**, such as the *Oxford Advanced Learner's Dictionary*, guide students in how to use the words with example sentences and lists of collocations—they are useful for anyone who wants to increase their word knowledge. A **thesaurus** is a dictionary of synonyms and antonyms. It does not replace a regular dictionary, but it is useful as a secondary reference book—to remind users of words they know.

Students today are likely to use **electronic dictionaries** in the form of online dictionaries, phone apps, or dedicated devices. As with any dictionary, they can vary widely in quality. It is important to watch out for false information online, especially on wiki sites (those written by contributors). For instance, some students doing research came back with the plural of *moose* as *meese* because of a deliberately false entry in urbandictionary.com.

**Print-form dictionaries** are far from dead, however. Many schools allow students to use book dictionaries for tests and exams; electronic formats are prohibited because there is no way to limit them to just a dictionary function. Bibliophiles (look that word up if you don't know the meaning) love the look and feel of a beautiful dictionary. Moreover, print dictionaries are often better for browsing: You can flip through pages and come across words you may never have found otherwise. Using electronic formats is like looking through a small window, whereas a book offers you a view of the whole panorama.

### How to buy a print-form dictionary

- Don't just pick the cheapest or smallest one. A dictionary is a good investment—it will last you for years. Mini-dictionaries will not give as much information.
- Shop in your campus bookstore. It usually has selected the better books, and there may be special deals.
- Ask your instructor for recommendations.
- "Test drive" the dictionaries by looking up a few words. Look up the same words in several dictionaries, and compare the entries. Look up common words that may have many definitions (such as *set* and *like*) and more academic words (*enumerate*, *repatriate*).
- Check for the clarity of the definition and how much information is given. Look for a clear, legible typeface and a format that is easy to handle.
- Check the date of the dictionary to make sure it is a recent edition, not just a reprint. Check for current slang (words like *bling*, *geek*, and *diss*) to see whether the dictionary is up-to-date.

One common question about dictionary use is how to find a word in a dictionary if you do not know how to spell it. One technique is to concentrate on the beginning of the word. Even electronic dictionaries that guess at your word work much better if the first few letters are correct. Get to know possible letter combinations for sounds. For instance an *s* sound could be spelled with an *s*, a *c*, an *sc*, or even a *ps*.

Students who use only electronic dictionary formats may have to learn how to use a book dictionary. It takes practice.

## What You Can Learn from a Dictionary Entry

This excerpt from the dictionary has four main entries: *riot*, *riot gear*, *riotous*, and *riotously*:

---

**riot** /'raɪət/ *noun, verb*

■ *noun* **1** [C] a situation in which a group of people behave in a violent way in a public place, often as a protest: *One prison guard was killed when a riot broke out in the jail.* ◇ *food/race riots* **2** [sing.] **~ of sth** (*formal*) a collection of a lot of different types of the same thing: *The garden was a riot of colour.* **3 a riot** [sing.] (*old-fashioned, informal*) a person or an event that is very amusing and enjoyable

**IDM** run 'riot **1** (of people) to behave in a way that is violent and/or not under control **SYN** rampage: *They let their kids run riot.* **2** if your imagination, a feeling, etc. **runs riot**, you allow it to develop and continue without trying to control it **3** (of plants) to grow and spread quickly ↻ more at READ *v.*

■ *verb* [I] (of a crowd of people) to behave in a violent way in a public place, often as a protest ▶ **riot·er** *noun*: *Rioters set fire to parked cars.* **riot·ing** *noun* [U]: *Rioting broke out in the capital.*

'riot gear *noun* [U] the clothes and equipment used by the police when they are dealing with riots

**riot·ous** /'raɪətəs/ *adj.* [usually before noun] **1** (*formal or law*) noisy and/or violent, especially in a public place: *riotous behaviour* ◇ *The organizers of the march were charged with assault and riotous assembly.* **2** noisy, exciting and enjoyable in an uncontrolled way **SYN** uproarious: *a riotous party* ◇ *riotous laughter*

**riot·ous·ly** /'raɪətəsli/ *adv.* extremely: *riotously funny*

---

- The entry for the headword *riot* is subdivided into three sections: one for the noun, one for the idiom *run riot*, and one for the verb.
  - » Noun: The noun *riot* is designated countable with a [C]. Two of its meanings (2 and 3) are for its use in the singular—"a riot." Also, the first example sentence shows you the phrase "a riot broke out," so you know that you can use the phrasal verb *break out* with the word *riot*.
  - » Idiom: The first entry for the idiom *run riot* includes a synonym for it, *rampage*. The instruction "more at READ v." directs you to the entry for *read*, where you can find another idiom *to read somebody the riot act*.
  - » Verb: This entry starts with the designation "I," which means that *riot* is an intransitive verb. Note that it tells you that the verb is usually applied to the behaviour of a crowd of people. The entry also gives two nouns, *rioter* and *rioting*, which are derived from the verb.
- In a dictionary, often the adverb form is just given in the adjective entry, but if it has a different meaning, the adverb gets its own entry. Therefore, *riotously* is separate from *riotous*.

**Activity**

In small groups, discuss these entries from the *Oxford Advanced Learner's Dictionary*, 8th edition. Oxford University Press, 2010. First, be sure you understand all the terminology. If your group is not sure of something, ask your instructor. Then discuss how useful the information is. For example, why do you need to know whether a noun is countable or uncountable? How would this information help you to write a grammatical sentence using the word *riot*?

If group members have different dictionaries in class, compare the entries for *riot*. How do the dictionaries differ in the information they give and the way it is presented? Which dictionary is the most useful? Why?

## Building Vocabulary

Although you will not have a chance to look up every unfamiliar word you come across in your reading, it is a good idea to make a vocabulary list for any reading you study in class. Write down any words your instructor specifically teaches. Look up unfamiliar words in the dictionary. Write them in your notebook, along with a definition and any other useful information (part of speech, irregular forms, usage label—such as colloquialism, synonyms, collocations). Even if you do not go back and memorize this information, the fact that you have gone to the effort of writing it down means that you will remember it better. If you just look up a word in the dictionary and continue with your reading, you will not retain it as well.

### How to expand your vocabulary

- Read a lot to increase your exposure to words and how they are used.
- Read a variety of types of material (newspapers, books, websites), on different topics, to widen the fields of words you encounter.
- Pay attention to the language when you read. Look out for new words.
- Try to guess the meaning of words from the context.
- Pay attention to how the words are used in a sentence and which words accompany them.
- Use a dictionary to find out more about unfamiliar words.
- Keep a notebook for vocabulary you encounter. Notes can include grammar and usage notes, such as the part of speech and the collocation. Write down the phrase or sentence the word appeared in so that you can put it in context.
- Learn words in small groups. For example, if you use a dictionary to look up the meaning of an unfamiliar word, check out the derivatives, collocates, and any synonyms or antonyms given. Make sure you understand differences in usage.
- Remember that the more you read, the more you will encounter the words, and then you will get a clearer picture of their meaning and usage.

# Sentence Writing Skills

Words are combined to make sentences, and sentences are combined to make paragraphs. Sentences are the most important structure for meaning. They are the basic units of grammar because the grammaticality of writing is determined by the correctness of the sentences.

Essentially, a sentence starts with a capital letter and ends with a period (or question mark or exclamation mark). The reader must be able to tell where each sentence begins and ends. When you are writing by hand, make sentence boundaries obvious with clearly formed capital letters and periods. Take care that sentences in typed documents are also clearly delineated. It is essential that a sentence look like a sentence.

This unit reviews the major parts of a sentence, starting with the core and moving through the various elements—such as modifiers and clauses—that can be added to the sentence. If you need more detail about specific grammatical rules of English, consult guides such as the *Oxford Practice Grammar*. Problem areas in sentence structure, such as run-ons and fragments, are dealt with in Unit 7, Editing and Correcting Skills.

## A Note about Grammar Terminology

To explain sentence structure, we must use technical labels for the word forms and structures. Sometimes the terminology can vary, depending on which grammar resource you consult. For example, the words *progressive* and *continuous* are both used to label the same aspect of the verb. The technical explanations here have been kept as simple as possible.

In this unit, many grammatical terms are in boldface when they are first introduced and defined. (You can search for the first uses of the term in the index.) Knowing the proper terminology is useful if you need to find out more about the grammar point, but for the most part you can get by on just a few commonly used words. For instance, you do not need to know the term *copula verb* to do the work in this unit, but you do need to understand what a verb is. If the grammar term is only mentioned once, you can assume it is not important to memorize, but if the word is used frequently in the unit, you do need to know it. As with any new vocabulary item, grammar terminology often becomes clear through context.

## Recognizing Basic Sentence Structure

A sentence needs a **subject** and a **predicate** to qualify as a grammatical sentence. The subject is what you are talking about, and the predicate is what you are saying about it. The subject is essentially a noun or a stand-in for a noun (such as a pronoun or a noun clause) along with any determiners or modifiers. The predicate is the verb along with objects, complements, determiners, and modifiers. (A **complement** completes the verb; for instance, an adjective can complete the verb *to be* in a sentence such as "He is tall.") In English sentences, the subject tends to come before the verb.

Verbs often encompass more than one word because they can include **auxiliary verbs** (also called **helping verbs**). These auxiliaries are usually forms of the verbs *be*, *have*, and *do* (which can also stand alone as main verbs). **Modal auxiliaries** (*can, could, may, might, must, ought to, shall, should, will, would*) never stand alone; they must be completed by a main verb. **Phrasal verbs** (such as *get by* and *sleep in*) include one or two particles. These verb forms are explained in the next sections.

In the following examples, the bare subject (without determiners and modifiers) is underlined once, and the verb (without objects and modifiers) is underlined twice.

> The children slept.
>
> The sleeping children looked very peaceful.
>
> The children in the next room woke up at the sound of the alarm.
>
> The alarm woke the children.
>
> They were disturbed by the noise.
>
> The horrible noise echoed throughout the house.
>
> It was loud.
>
> We had never heard that noise before.
>
> It may have been caused by the furnace.

The use of *and* can make a compound subject or a compound verb:

> The children and their parents were invited to a special lunch.
>
> They laughed and sang.
>
> Kelly, Megan, and Annie were all considered for the promotion.

Identifying the verb first can make it easier to determine the subject. Although English does have some reverse sentences, such as questions, the subject usually appears before the verb. Remember that verbs are actions or states. The subject is usually the person or thing doing the action. You can ask a "who/what question" with the verb to find the subject. (In the example sentences, the subject is underlined once; the verb twice.)

| For the sentence . . . | Consider . . . |
|---|---|
| <u>Eliza</u> <u>saved</u> the drowning boy. | Who saved the boy?<br>Eliza did, so *Eliza* is the subject. |
| <u>Swing dancing</u> <u>is</u> a lot of fun. | What is a lot of fun?<br>*Swing dancing* is the subject. |
| <u>Kate and I</u> <u>went</u> to the dance together. | Who went to the dance?<br>*Kate and I* is a compound subject—<br>two subjects joined by *and*. |
| <u>Did</u> the <u>students</u> <u>understand</u> the assignment? | Who understood (or did not understand) the assignment?<br>*The students* did (or did not). |
| <u>Taking that course</u> <u>was</u> a mistake. | What was a mistake?<br>*Taking that course* is a noun phrase subject. |
| There <u>were</u> two <u>raccoons</u> in the tree. | What was in the tree?<br>*There* is an adverb—it cannot be the subject. This is a case where the subject comes after the verb. Notice that the verb *were* is plural because it agrees with the noun *raccoons* and not the word *there*. |

A subject cannot be inside a prepositional phrase (see pages 74–75).

| | |
|---|---|
| The <u>students</u> in the advanced class <u>were allowed</u> to join the field trip. | The word *class* is in the phrase starting with the preposition *in*, so *class* cannot be the subject. |
| <u>One</u> of the students <u>was</u> late. | *One* is the grammatical subject. |
| Unfortunately, the adorable little <u>puppies</u> in the window of the pet store <u>come</u> from a notorious puppy mill. | *Puppies* is the grammatical subject. |

## Exercise 3.1

Identify the subjects and verbs in the following sentences:

1. Tina baked a pumpkin pie for Thanksgiving dinner.
2. The bird in the tree is a blue jay. Can you hear its distinctive call?

3.  The chess pieces were scattered across the room. The boys were asked to pick them up.
4.  Tomorrow we can go to the museum. There is a new Egyptian exhibit that I want to see.
5.  There is a new student in the class. Her name is Maya.
6.  Swimming is my favourite exercise. I find it very relaxing.
7.  My cellphone was stolen in Paris even though I was very careful with it.
8.  Each of the books was autographed by the author.

## Understanding Verb Tense and Aspect

Verbs are categorized by **tense** and **aspect**. *Tense* refers to time, essentially past, present, and future. The terms *continuous* and *perfect* refer to **aspect**: *continuous* (also called *progressive*) denotes an ongoing action, while *perfect* refers to a completed action.

Tense and aspect are usually considered together when we categorize the verb tenses of English:

| to walk | Present | Past | Future |
|---|---|---|---|
| Simple | she walks | she walked | she will walk |
| Continuous | she is walking | she was walking | she will be walking |
| Perfect | she has walked | she had walked | she will have walked |
| Perfect continuous | she has been walking | she had been walking | she will have been walking |

Of these 12 tenses, half of them you will rarely use. The six most important tenses to learn are the simple tenses, the present and past continuous, and the present perfect.

Note the formation of these verbs. The simple present and simple past are formed without any auxiliary verbs. The simple future uses *will* as an auxiliary. Note that an −*s* ending is used in the third person singular (*he, she, it*) in the simple present. Continuous forms are formed with the auxiliary verb *to be* and the −*ing* form of the verb. Perfect verb forms are made with the auxiliary verb *to have* and the past participle (which ends in −*ed* in regular verbs).

The basic uses of the tenses are explained below. Common errors in verb tense use are explained in Unit 7, page 215.

### Present

To express general facts, you use the simple present tense, as in the sentences on the next page.

| | |
|---|---|
| The earth is round, and the sky is blue. Astronomers study stars. | facts |
| I walk to work every day. Students often come late for early morning classes. | habit |

To describe actions that are occurring now, use present continuous (also called *present progressive*):

| | |
|---|---|
| I am studying Japanese as a third language. She is waiting in the cafeteria. | activities that are currently going on |

To express past ideas that are relevant to the present, use the present perfect tense or present perfect continuous:

| | |
|---|---|
| Ellen has lived in Edmonton for six years. | She still lives in Edmonton. [If she doesn't live there now, you would say "Ellen lived in Edmonton for six years."] |

Note this use of the present perfect:

| | |
|---|---|
| Have you ever been to Paris? | The present perfect is used because the question does not specify a time. It is referring to the person's experience up to the present time. |

The simple present tense is often used to tell a story. For example, we could say, "Shakespeare tells the story of two star-crossed lovers in *Romeo and Juliet*" or "In the 2012 movie, the Avengers fight aliens in New York City." This use of the present tense is also heard in sports broadcasts, as in the famous line, "He shoots, he scores."

## Past

Actions that happened in the past and are complete are described with the simple past tense:

| | |
|---|---|
| They opened the store three years ago, but this was the first time they made a profit. | Simple past tense is used because a specific time period ("three years ago") is given. |

Actions that took place over a period of time are expressed with the past continuous:

| | |
|---|---|
| Naomi was cleaning up the mess when her supervisor walked in. | *Cleaning up* reflects a continuous action, while the verb *walked in* is in the simple past because it is a definite past action—not continuous. |

Actions that occurred before another past action are in the past perfect:

| | |
|---|---|
| He had studied Arabic for several years before he went to Egypt. | *Had studied* is in the past perfect to show that it happened before he went to Egypt. |

The past perfect form is used less frequently today. People tend to use the simple past for past actions, even if one happened beforehand:

> After he washed the car, it rained.

However, in formal writing and for clarity, it is better to use the past perfect.

### Future

The simple future (with *will*) can be used for most actions that will take place in the future:

> The band will take the bus to Halifax.

The present continuous and *going to* also express future actions:

> The band is taking the bus to Halifax.
> The band is going to take the bus to Halifax.

The difference in meaning is slight, but the *will* form tends to be used with decisions just made, whereas the other forms refer to already-decided-upon events.

Note that the simple present is sometimes used for future scheduled events, often regular events:

> The bus to Halifax leaves at nine.

## Recognizing Different Verb Forms

As we have seen, English verbs often encompass more than one word. In addition to the main verb, auxiliary verbs and particles become part of the verb form. Besides forming continuous verb tenses, the auxiliary verb *be* is also used to form the passive voice. Modal verbs are another type of auxiliary. Multi-word verbs include particles, prepositions, and adverbs. These verb formations are explained below, followed by a review of the auxiliary verbs. Common verb form errors are explored in Unit 7 on page 215.

### Passive Voice

In an active sentence, the grammatical subject does the action of the verb, while in the passive, the subject is acted upon. Only transitive verbs (verbs that require a direct object) can be used in the passive voice because the direct object becomes the subject of the sentence in the passive.

**How to make a sentence passive**

- Move the direct object before the verb, making it the subject of the verb.
- Use the correct form of the auxiliary *to be* to keep the verb tense and subject–verb agreement.
- Change the verb form to the past participle (the –*ed* form).
- Put the original subject in a *by* phrase if it is necessary to the meaning of the sentence.
- Delete the original subject if it is unnecessary.

Here's how it would work with this example sentence:

Anita painted the landscape.
[subject] [verb] [direct object]

1. Move the direct object (*landscape*) before the verb, making it the subject of the verb.
2. Use the correct form of the auxiliary *to be* (*was*) to keep the verb tense and subject–verb agreement.
3. Change the verb form to the past participle (the –*ed* form) (*painted*).
4. Put the original subject (*Anita*) in a *by* phrase if it is necessary to the meaning of the sentence.

Here's the sentence in the passive voice:

The landscape was painted by Anita.

Only use the passive voice when you want to emphasize the action itself rather than who performed the action.

Here are examples of active and passive sentences:

| | |
|---|---|
| Ivan opened the package.<br>The package was opened by Ivan. | The first sentence is active—*Ivan* is the subject, doing the action, *package* is the direct object.<br>The second sentence is in the passive voice; the auxiliary *was* shows the past tense. |
| Someone spilled the wine.<br>The wine was spilled. | We do not know who did the action, so it can be left out in the passive voice. |
| They rewrote the report.<br>The report was rewritten. | In the passive voice, the focus is on the report rather than who rewrote it. |

For the passive voice, a form of the verb *to be* is used (*is, am, are*), and the main verb is in the past participle form, which ends in *–ed* for regular verbs. There may also be modal verbs in the structure (*will be, would be, may be*) or other verb forms (*have been, is being*).

> The show will be cancelled if it rains.
> The painting could have been forged.
> The documents were shredded accidentally.
> The exhibit was seen by thousands of people.

The active voice is preferred because it is easier for readers to understand, but the passive is useful when you want to de-emphasize who or what did the action. It is therefore common in technical writing. For example, lab reports are often written in the passive because it does not really matter who did the action.

> The water was heated to the boiling point, and the solution was added.
> The company was founded in 1845.
> The parade was postponed because of the accident.

A general guideline is that if you need a "*by* phrase" to show the actor, the sentence should probably be in the active voice.

### Exercise 3.2

Determine whether the following sentences are active or passive.

1. She bought all her textbooks online.
2. The manager corrected the mistakes and reprimanded the staff.
3. The car bomb exploded, killing five.
4. The interview was scheduled for 11:15.
5. His story was not believed by anyone.
6. The lawyer advised the client to stay quiet.
7. Finally, the winner was chosen.
8. I can't remember the last time we spoke.
9. Everyone enjoyed the concert.
10. The game was lost by a slim margin.

Go back over the sentences, and decide whether the voice can easily be switched. If so, make active sentences passive and passive sentences active (you may have to add an agent doing the action for some of the passive ones).

### Modal Auxiliaries

Modals (*can, could, may, might, must, ought to, shall, should, will, would*) are used as auxiliary verbs and do not stand alone. They can be tricky because each of them can be used for more than one purpose—expressing the ideas of permission, ability, necessity, or possibility. However, the verb forms themselves are simple; modal verbs have only one form, and they must be followed by a main verb, which is always in the base form (that is, with no endings).

Here are examples of the most common uses:

| | |
|---|---|
| Can I borrow your pen? | informal request |
| She cannot swim. | ability |
| When I was younger, I could speak German fluently. | past ability |
| Could I please see you for a minute? May I have Friday off, please? | formal requests |
| It may rain tomorrow. He might be able to help you. | possibility |
| I sent that package last week; it must have arrived by now. | strong probability |
| You must quit smoking. | strong obligation, with speaker having some authority |
| You ought to quit smoking. You should read this article—it's really interesting. | advice |
| She should be back tomorrow. | probability |
| He would go to the café every morning. | regular action in the past |
| Would you please stop it? | polite request |

## Phrasal Verbs

English has many two-word verbs and some three-word verbs, commonly referred to as phrasal or multi-word verbs. These combinations consist of a verb and one or two particles. The phrasal verb has a different meaning from that of the verb by itself. For example, *to blow up* means to explode, and *to drop out* means to quit school.

Grammarians make a distinction between **particles** and **prepositions** even though they are essentially the same words (*at, by, for, from, in, off, on, to, up,* etc.). How the words are labelled depends on their function in the sentence. A particle is considered part of the verb—the two words work together both grammatically (in sentences) and semantically (in meaning). A preposition, on the other hand, is generally followed by a noun, making a prepositional phrase such as *on the bus* or *up the street.*

Compare the phrasal verbs with the regular verbs in these example sentences:

| | |
|---|---|
| He had to wake up early. | wake up is a phrasal verb |
| She walked up the staircase slowly. | *up the staircase* is a prepositional phrase |
| Hold on a minute. | *hold on* is a phrasal verb meaning to wait |
| Hold onto this rope. | *onto this rope* is a prepositional phrase |

Because some phrasal verbs are transitive (followed by a noun), it can be difficult to distinguish particles from prepositions:

| | |
|---|---|
| I can't put up with his behaviour any longer. | *put up with* is a phrasal verb meaning to tolerate |
| They have to set up the room for the meeting. | *set up* is a phrasal verb; *the room* is the object |
| They went up the room to collect donations. | *up the room* is a prepositional phrase. |

However, distinguishing particles and prepositions is a grammarian's job, and you do not have to worry about proper labelling. You just have to know what the phrasal verbs mean and how to use them correctly in a sentence. Check your dictionary if you are unsure. Phrasal verbs are often listed along with the entry for the main verb. Example sentences show the sentence structure as well as make the meaning clear.

It is also worth noting that some phrasal verbs are separable, with the object coming before the particle:

| | |
|---|---|
| It is simple to look up the address on the Internet.<br>It is simple to look the address up on the Internet. | Either order is possible here. [However, when a pronoun is used, only one order is possible: "to look it up": It is simple to look it up on the Internet.] |
| Aggressive drivers often cut people off. | While it is possible to say "cut off people," it does not sound right with this phrasal verb. |

Finally, phrasal verbs tend to be idiomatic and therefore more common in conversational speech than in academic writing. For instance, your instructor may ask a student to "hand out the test papers" but may write that someone "distributed the test papers."

## Review of Auxiliary Verbs

The different auxiliary (helping) verbs were introduced in the previous sections. To help you with the various uses and corresponding verb forms, here is a reference chart:

| Auxiliary verb | Verb form that follows | Uses | Examples |
|---|---|---|---|
| be (am, is, are, was, were, being, been) | present participle (–ing form) | continuous tenses | He is reading. I was cleaning. |
| be (am, is, are, was, were, being, been) | past participle (–ed form) | passive voice | The decision is made. The car was stolen. |
| have (has, had) | past participle (–ed form) | perfect tenses | He has left. They have stopped. |
| do (did) | base form (no endings) | emphasis; negatives; questions | She did find it. We did not ask. Do you know the answer? |
| will | base form (no endings) | future tenses | They will leave on Friday. |
| modal verbs (can, could, may, might, should, would, etc.) | base form (no endings) | to express ability, possibility, etc. (see pages 56–57) | They can walk there. She might be late. We should go now. |

The auxiliary verb determines which form of the verb follows it. If the sentence has several auxiliary verbs in a row, the last verb is the main one (underlined in the examples below):

> He should have been <u>paying</u> attention in class.
> He should have been <u>elected</u> president.

Unlike modal verbs, which can never stand alone, the auxiliary verbs *be*, *have*, *do*, and *will* can be the main verb (but *will* is rarely used in this way):

> Richard <u>is</u> a hard worker.
> They <u>have</u> $50 to spend on the gift.
> He <u>did</u> the dishes right after dinner.
> She was exhausted, but she <u>willed</u> her eyes to stay open.

## Exercise 3.3

Use the verbs in the list to fill in the blanks. Change the verb form to make it fit the sentence: You may have to add an ending (*–s, –ed, –ing*) or use an irregular form of the verb (for example, *be, been, is, are*), but use only one word for each blank. Verbs from the list can be used more than once, and not all of them have to be used.

| attend | pass |
|--------|------|
| be | prefer |
| believe | read |
| figure | tell |
| miss | want |

1. Students should _____ class regularly in order to _____ their courses. They also need to _____ punctual so that they do not _____ anything important.

2. Even when he _____ them the truth, they did not _____ him.

3. Marta _____ to buy a modern house in the suburbs, but Rick would _____ an old fixer-upper close to downtown.

4. He couldn't _____ out how to install the sink, so he finally _____ the instructions.

5. It _____ hard to catch Ryan in a lie. He _____ a good poker face.

## Recognizing Verbals

When is a verb not a verb? Verb forms such as gerunds, participles, and infinitives never function as the main verb of a sentence or a clause, so they are not really verbs. Instead, they are referred to as verbals. They function as nouns, adjectives, and adverbs.

A **gerund** is the *–ing* form of the verb acting as a noun:

> Seeing is believing.
> Understanding English verb forms can be difficult.
> I hate shopping for shoes.

The **present participle** is the *–ing* form of the verb acting as an adjective:

| | |
|---|---|
| <u>Running</u> water does not freeze readily. | *Running* is an adjective describing water. |
| The boys <u>running around the room</u> are my nephews. | *Running around the room* is a participle phrase describing the boys. |

The **past participle** is the third principal part of the verb, the *–ed* form for regular verbs. An *–en* ending is also common for the past participle (e.g., *begun, broken, chosen, written*). (You can find the simple past form and the past participle of irregular verbs in the dictionary.) The past participle is used for the passive voice, and it can be used as an adjective:

> Some politicians would like to see an <u>elected</u> Senate.
> I love <u>freshly baked</u> bread.

An **infinitive** is the bare form of the verb, with or without *to*, such as (*to*) *eat*, (*to*) *sleep*, and (*to*) *understand*. It is usually a verb complement following the main verb, but it can be used as a noun:

| | |
|---|---|
| To love is to live. | *To love* and *to live* function as nouns. |
| To lose that file after so much work was disheartening. | *To lose that file after so much work* is the subject of the verb *was*. |
| They want to hire more staff. | *To hire* completes the verb *want*. |
| To fail is not a disaster. | *To fail* functions as a noun.* |

*In modern English, infinitive subjects are not common. Instead, it is preferable to use a gerund subject or an *it* structure:

> Failing is not a disaster.
> It is not a disaster to fail.

---

It can be difficult to figure out exactly what function a verbal is fulfilling in a sentence. Do not worry too much about proper labelling. You just need to develop a "sentence sense" so that you can identify the subject and verb in a sentence and determine which words work together in phrases.

---

Here are some example sentences to consider. The main verb is underlined twice and the subject is underlined once:

| | |
|---|---|
| The <u>children</u> <u>are skating</u> on the backyard rink. | present continuous tense of the verb *to skate* |
| <u>Skating</u> <u>is</u> good exercise. | *Skating* is a gerund, the subject of the sentence. |
| Their precision skating <u>team</u> <u>won</u> the competition. | *Skating* is an adjective describing the subject *team*. |
| <u>He</u> <u>is trying</u> to make the team. | present continuous tense *To make* is an infinitive completing the main verb *is trying*. |
| <u>Trying to make the team</u> <u>is</u> futile. | The gerund *trying* is part of the subject. *To make* is the infinitive form, also not the main verb. The subject is *trying to make the team*. |
| The first-year <u>students</u> trying to make the team <u>are having</u> trouble. | The verb *have* is in the present continuous tense; *trying* is an adjective describing the students; *to make* is an infinitive completing the verb. |
| The <u>woman</u> watching the dancers <u>is</u> a talent scout. | The participle *watching* describes the woman. |
| <u>Watching the dancers</u> <u>is</u> a good way to learn the choreography. | The gerund phrase is the subject. |

## Understanding How Verbs Determine Sentence Structure

The verb is the most important word in the sentence. A sentence does not exist without a verb. Moreover, the verb shapes the sentence. Once you choose the verb, you must use the sentence structure that the verb dictates. The verb determines the type of object or complement that follows. It can even determine which verb tenses and aspects can be used.

Some verbs (like *buy* and *spend*) are **transitive**. This means they must be followed by an object, which is either a noun or a noun stand-in (pronoun or noun phrase or clause). Only transitive verbs can be put into the passive voice (pages 54–56).

| He bought a car. | Saying "he bought" by itself would be incomplete and ungrammatical. *Buy* is a transitive verb. |
| He spent a lot of money. | Again, because the verb spend is transitive, "he spent" by itself would be illogical to the audience, who would ask "He spent what?" |

**Intransitive** verbs do not need an object:

> She slept.
> She walked.

Sometimes a verb can have both transitive and intransitive uses:

> He whistled.
> He whistled a happy tune.

---

Dictionary entries label verbs as transitive or intransitive.

---

With some intransitive verbs, the grammatical subject can be affected by the verb instead of doing the action. Look at the differences here:

| I broke the glass.<br>He ended the relationship.<br>Alan Turing cracked the code. | subject did the action; transitive verb |
| The glass broke.<br>The movie ended at six.<br>The paint cracked. | subject affected by the action; intransitive verb |

Some verbs can take an indirect object as well as a direct object:

| She gave them the clothes. | direct object = clothes<br>indirect object = them (*to* them) |
| They offered him the job. | direct object = job<br>indirect object = him (*to* him) |

Some verbs have a second direct object, called an **objective complement**:

| They named the baby Lily. | two nouns as objects: *baby, Lily* |

In some verbs describing emotions, the person is the grammatical subject, while in others the person is the object:

| | |
|---|---|
| I fear snakes.<br>Snakes scare me. | These two sentences have a similar meaning, but in the first sentence, the person is the subject of the sentence; in the second, the object. |
| I like math.<br>Math interests me. | These also have a similar meaning but a different sentence structure. |

Most verbs describe actions, but some actions occur over a period of time, such as *grow* and *develop*, while others describe an accomplishment, such as *decide* and *solve*. The type of action can affect how the verb is used, as shown in these examples:

| | |
|---|---|
| He was working on the problem, but his colleague solved it. | The verb *work* can be continuous. |
| He worked on the problem, but his colleague was solving it. | **incorrect:**<br>*Solve* describes an achievement, so it cannot be used in the continuous aspect. |
| They decided to take the train. | The verb *decide* describes an achievement. |
| They stopped deciding to take the train. | **incorrect:**<br>The verb *decide* cannot be used with *stop*. |

Some verbs are **stative**—they describe a state, not an action. Stative verbs include *be*, *seem*, and *feel*. These verbs (also called **linking** or **copula verbs**) are followed by a noun or by an adjective:

> Ian is an engineer.
> The children were happy.
> Elizabeth seemed tired.

Some verbs can be either action or stative verbs, depending on how they are used:

> He looked around the room.
> He looked angry.

Verbs may require specific prepositions before the noun:

| | |
|---|---|
| Harry depends <u>on</u> the income from his parents' trust. | You can't say *depends to* or *depends by* or use any other preposition. |
| Immigrants must adapt <u>to</u> a new way of life. | Do not get *adapt* mixed up with the transitive verb *adopt*. |
| They couldn't deal <u>with</u> the new situation. | *Deal in* and *deal out* both exist but have very different meanings. (Look them up.) |

Some verbs are followed by an **infinitive form** (*to* + base form) of a second verb, while others are followed by a **gerund** (*–ing* form of the verb used as a noun):

| | |
|---|---|
| I enjoy skating. | *enjoy* + gerund. |
| I enjoy to skate. | **incorrect** |
| He wanted to change programs. | The verb *want* is followed by an infinitive. |
| He wanted changing programs. | **incorrect** |

Some verbs can take both infinitives and gerunds. Sometimes there is a meaning difference:

| | |
|---|---|
| I like to swim.<br>I like swimming. | Both sentences are possible. Both mean essentially the same thing. |
| James stopped to talk. | This means that James stopped what he was doing in order to talk with someone. |
| James stopped talking. | This means that James was talking, but then he stopped. |
| Stephen remembered to leave the key with the concierge.<br>Stephen remembered leaving the key with the concierge. | Stephen remembered that he had to leave the key, and so he did it.<br>Stephen remembered the action of doing it. |

There is no grammatical rule to explain why some verbs take an infinitive and others take a gerund. You have to learn the pattern for each verb. Here are a few common verbs as examples:

**Verbs that can be followed by a gerund:** avoid, delay, deny, enjoy, keep, miss, practise, risk, suggest

**Verbs that can be followed by an infinitive:** afford, appear, choose, decide, expect, fail, happen, hope, learn, need, pretend, promise, seem, threaten, want

Verbs can be followed by more than one kind of complement, but it is important to know which structures do not work:

| | |
|---|---|
| She suggested buying a second car. | *suggest* + gerund |
| She suggested (that) they buy a second car. | *suggest* + noun clause |
| She suggested them to buy a second car. | **incorrect** |

Recognizing the characteristics of the verb can help you to distinguish confusing pairs such as *adopt* and *adapt*:

| | |
|---|---|
| Immigrants adopt many customs from their new homeland. | *adopt* (to take on) is a transitive verb |
| Immigrants often find it hard to adapt to the cold weather in Canada. | *adapt* (to get used to) is often used as an intransitive verb followed by the preposition *to* |

Native speakers of English do not stop to think about how verbs determine sentence structure. They speak and write just what sounds right to them because they have heard and read the verb used many times. However, when they try to use a verb they are not as familiar with, especially in writing, they may form a faulty sentence. The same is true for English language learners, but they tend to make more mistakes because they have not heard and read enough English to develop an ear for the correct grammar.

It would be impossible to memorize the characteristics of all the verbs in English. What is possible, however, is to be aware that verbs behave in different ways. If you make a verb error in a sentence, check the meaning and usage of the verb in the dictionary. If English is not your first language, avoid translating when you write, because you are more likely to make such verb errors. An English verb might have the same basic meaning as a verb in another language, but it is unlikely that the usage of the two verbs is the same.

If you are having trouble using certain verbs correctly, study the sentence patterns that commonly go with the verb. Dictionaries like the *Oxford Advanced Learner's* often give example sentences. You can also look up lists of verbs (such as "verbs followed by infinitives") in grammar books or on the Internet to see which category the verb belongs to.

## Exercise 3.4

Rewrite each of the following sentences by substituting the verb in brackets for the verb underlined in the sentence. Make whatever changes are required in the sentence. Note that more than one option may be possible, and in some cases no sentence changes may be required.

*Examples:*

| | |
|---|---|
| Original: I don't <u>appreciate</u> having those photos posted online. [approve] Rewrite: I don't approve of those photos being posted online. | The word *appreciate* is a transitive verb, but *approve* usually takes the preposition *of*. |

Original: Harris <u>said</u> that the funding was running out. [tell]
Rewrite: Harris told them that the funding was running out.

The verb *tell* often requires a person as a direct object, so *them* was added to the second sentence (even though the first sentence does not specify whom Harris was talking to).

1. He <u>anticipated</u> getting the promotion. [hope]
2. They <u>arranged</u> for the delivery to come this afternoon. [order]
3. I <u>regret</u> giving him a recommendation. [be sorry]
4. Patrick <u>depends</u> on his wife's advice. [rely]
5. The orphans <u>were deprived</u> of adequate nourishment. [lack]
6. Richard <u>commented</u> on the errors in the report. [criticize]
7. They <u>trusted</u> his ability to get the job done efficiently. [believe]
8. The manager <u>considered</u> hiring a new assistant. [decide]
9. They <u>looked</u> like they were having fun. [seem]
10. Mr. Martinez <u>chose</u> Mrs. Simpson to be chair. [name]

## Using Determiners

Determiners are words that come before a noun to identify which person, place, or thing is being talked about. There are different kinds of determiners:

**articles:** a, an, the

**demonstratives:** this, that, these, those

**possessive pronouns:** my, your, his, her, its, our, their

**quantifiers:** all, any, another, both, few, many, more, several, some, one, first, double, half (and other words based on numbers)

The articles in English are *a*, *an*, and *the*. *A* and *an* are **indefinite articles**. They have the sense of "one," so they are not used for plural forms. No article is used for plural nouns used in an indefinite sense. *The* is a **definite article** and is used with both singular and plurals.

|  | Indefinite | Definite |
|---|---|---|
| Singular | a book<br>a student | the book<br>the student |
| Plural | books<br>students | the books<br>the students |

Generally, the first time a noun is introduced, the indefinite article is used, but once the reader knows which thing is being referred to, a definite article is used to refer to something specifically:

> I picked an apple off the tree. [one apple] The apple was red and juicy. [specifically, the apple I picked] I like apples. [apples in general] The apples in my uncle's orchard are especially good. [specific apples]

*A* is used before consonants, and *an* is used before vowel sounds. This usage depends on how the initial sound is pronounced, so both *a* and *an* can appear before *h* and *u*:

> a walk, a school, a book, a car, a dish, a fairy tale, a lovely scene
> an article, an elephant, an island, an octopus, an ugly hat
> an umbrella, a university, a hero, an hour
> a/an herb

Definite articles are generally not used with abstract nouns. When they are used, it indicates a meaning difference.

> It is important to have beauty in our surroundings.
> That new car is a beauty.
> Truth is important in a relationship.
> He needs to tell the truth so we can get this matter cleared up.

While these are the basic rules, article use is one of the most difficult aspects of English grammar for language learners. Many languages do not have articles, and even for those that do, the rules of article use in those languages are very different from those for English. For example, English does not use an article before people's names or before country names like Canada, England, and China; however, articles are used with country names that include a word that means "state" in its name, so we say the United States, the Republic of China, and the Kingdom of Saudi Arabia.

For demonstratives, it is important to know that *this* and *that* are singular, while *these* and *those* are plural. *This* and *these* refer to something closer to the speaker (in space, time, or reference) than *that* and *those*, as in these examples:

> Could you please hand me that brochure? The one on the desk over there.
> These questions seem difficult. Perhaps we should change them.

For more examples of determiner use, see the note on *few* (page 349) and Correcting Determiner Errors (page 208).

## Exercise 3.5

Fill in the blanks with articles or other determiners where required:

1.  They've decided to arrange _____ picnic for _____ park's

    anniversary. They are going to hire _____ clowns and _____

magicians. _____ neighbourhood high school band is going to perform

in _____ band shell during _____ afternoon, and _____ local

bands are going to play _____ more modern music in the evening.

_____ food vendors will sell everything from _____ hot dogs to

_____ ice cream.

2.  We had _____ wonderful trip to Halifax. We visited _____ museum at

_____ Pier 21. It told the story of European immigrants who disembarked

at _____ pier. Many travelled by _____ train to _____ final

destinations. I even found _____ name of _____ ship that _____

family came to Canada on. We also took _____ trip on _____ *Bluenose*

replica ship. I love any kind of _____ sailboat, so _____ tall ship was

_____ real thrill. We saw _____ display about _____ *Titanic* at

_____ Maritime Museum of _____ Atlantic. Many of _____ *Titanic*

victims are buried in _____ Halifax. _____ story of _____ 1917

Halifax explosion was really astonishing. _____ munitions ship blew up

in _____ harbour, levelling _____ entire downtown area, killing 2000

and injuring 9000.

## Using Pronouns

Pronouns take the place of nouns and refer back to them.

**Personal pronouns**

| | |
|---|---|
| first person singular | I, me, my, mine, myself |
| first person plural | we, us, our, ours, ourselves |
| second person | you, your, yours, yourself/yourselves |
| third person singular | he, she, it, him, her, his, hers, its, himself, herself, itself |
| third person plural | they, them, their, theirs, themselves |

A pronoun has to have a clear **antecedent** (the noun that the pronoun refers to) that agrees in person and number. This means that if you use *he*, for example, the reader must know who you are referring to and that *he* must refer to a male. Often the antecedent is a noun in the previous sentence:

| | |
|---|---|
| Jennifer had to do the assignment again. <u>Her</u> computer crashed, and <u>she</u> had not made a back-up. | *Her* and *she* are both pronouns referring to Jennifer. |
| The students could not understand the lesson on pronoun reference, so <u>they</u> asked the instructor to go over it again. <u>He</u> showed <u>them</u> some errors from <u>their</u> essays and asked <u>them</u> to fix <u>them</u>. | Note that the two uses of *them* at the end could be confusing—the first *them* refers to the students; the second *them* refers to the errors. However, because of context, this would be clear enough for the reader to follow: the verb *fix* would be completed by *errors* not *students*. |

While English nouns use the same form for subject and object forms, some personal pronouns have different forms for **subject** (*I, he, she, they, we*) and **object** (*me, him, her, them, us*):

| | |
|---|---|
| The <u>student</u> is in class.<br>ic<u>He</u> is in class. | The nouns *student* and *he* are the subjects. |
| They saw the <u>student</u> yesterday.<br>They saw <u>him</u> yesterday. | Here, *student* and *him* are the objects of the verb. |

*Whom* is the object form of *who*, but its use is considered formal and is dying out in English:

| | |
|---|---|
| To <u>whom</u> do you wish to speak?<br><u>Whom</u> did they visit? | grammatically correct but considered formal and old-fashioned |
| <u>Who</u> do you want to talk to?<br><u>Who</u> did they visit? | commonly heard |

It is sometimes difficult to identify exactly who a pronoun refers to. For instance, *we* can include the person being addressed—or not. The pronoun *you* can refer to one person or many, or it can refer to people in general.

Unlike other European languages, English has to make do with fewer pronouns. The language actually used to have more pronouns, but its evolution eliminated them. For example, *thee* and *thou* were the singular forms of *you*, but their use died out. In a similar way, the pronoun *they* is often now working as a singular to fill a gap in the language—the lack of a singular pronoun unmarked for gender—in other words, another way of saying "he or she." (See pages 202–3 for a more detailed discussion of the issue.)

Personal pronouns have different **possessive forms**. Some are determiners and therefore used before nouns (*my, our, your, his, her, its, their, whose*), and some stand on their own (*mine, ours, yours, his, hers, theirs*).

That is <u>my</u> bag. The other one is <u>yours</u>.

Note that the personal possessive pronouns do not have apostrophes. The pronoun *its* is often incorrectly written as *it's* (which is the abbreviation of *it is* and *it has*) or even *its'* (a word that does not exist). Similarly, *whose* is often incorrectly written as *who's*.

The use of **relative pronouns** (*that, who, which*) is shown in the section on Writing Adjective Clauses (pages 81–82).

For **reflexive pronouns**, *self* is the singular ending and *selves* is the plural ending: *myself, yourself, himself, herself, itself, ourselves, yourselves, themselves*. Reflexive pronouns refer back to the subject:

> My hand slipped, and I cut <u>myself</u>.
> She sees <u>herself</u> as a natural leader.

The **demonstratives** *this, that, these,* and *those* work as determiners (pages 67–68), but they can also be used as pronouns. The same basic rules apply: *this* and *that* are singular; *these* and *those* are plural; *this* and *these* refer to something closer to the speaker than *that* and *those*.

> I don't want to start with <u>these</u> problems. <u>Those</u> look easier.
> Use this hammer. That one over there is too heavy for you.

**Indefinite pronouns** include *anyone, everyone, no one,* and *somebody*. Unlike possessive personal pronouns, indefinite pronouns do take an apostrophe for the possessive form: *anyone's, everyone's,* etc.

While the basic rule is that pronouns have antecedents, *it* can appear in structures where it does not refer to anything specifically, where, therefore, it is not really a pronoun. This is called a **non-referential *it*** or a **dummy *it***.

> It is raining.
> It's time he got a job.
> It surprises me that she did not get the promotion.

See Unit 7, pages 201–07, for explanations and exercises on common errors made in pronoun use.

## Adding Modifiers

Adjectives and adverbs can be added to a sentence to describe nouns and verbs. Often, they are optional in the sentence structure, except for adjectives used with stative verbs:

| | |
|---|---|
| They bought a small house.<br>They bought a house. | The word *small* here is optional. |
| The house is small. | The word *small* cannot be left out of this sentence; it is needed to complete the verb *is*. |

More than one adjective can be used to describe one noun. Commas (or *and*) are used to separate adjectives that refer to the same quality, such as size:

| | |
|---|---|
| We lived in the small red brick house on the corner. | The adjectives *small*, *red*, and *brick* refer to different qualities—size, colour, and material (note that adjectives have a preferred order, so that size precedes colour—you would not say "red brick small house"). |
| People enjoy the sweet, salty taste of these chocolate pretzels. OR<br>People enjoy the sweet and salty taste of these chocolate pretzels. | The words *sweet* and *salty* both refer to taste. |

Adverbs can describe the action of the verb, but they can also describe adjectives and even a whole sentence. Adverbs generally describe how, when, and where something was done. Some adverbs are derived from the adjective—by adding *–ly*. Other adverbs are function words like *yesterday*, *nearby*, and *twice*. Adverbs are not as fixed in position as nouns, verbs, and adjectives are:

| | |
|---|---|
| He closed the door quietly. | *Quietly* is an adverb of manner describing how the door was closed. |
| She was very surprised. | *Very* is an adverb describing the adjective *surprised*. |
| Gradually, they filled the box of donations.<br>They gradually filled the box of donations.<br>They filled the box of donations gradually. | *Gradually* is an adverb describing how the box was filled—it can be used in different positions in the sentences. |
| Hopefully, we will get there on time. | *Hopefully* describes the whole action of the sentence. (Note that the use of *hopefully* as a sentence adverb is not accepted by some grammarians, but it is common usage.) |

**Adjective phrases** can be used as a unit to describe a noun. They are usually hyphenated:

| | |
|---|---|
| The technology is up to date.<br>They use up-to-date technology. | The phrase *up to date* is hyphenated when it is used as an adjective. |
| The boy is six years old.<br>A six-year-old boy made this. | When a phrase with a plural noun is converted to an adjective, that noun is made singular. |
| They watched the man eating shark.<br>They watched the man-eating shark. | Note the difference in meaning. In the first sentence, it is the man doing the eating—he is eating shark meat. In the second, the shark is capable of eating humans. |
| They use environmentally friendly products. | A hyphen is not used for an adverb + adjective combination. |

The hyphens make it easier to read the sentence because the hyphens make the adjective phrase one unit. However, do not overuse this structure because it can make the sentence confusing.

In addition to adjectives, other words can modify nouns, as in the following examples:

Nouns: library book, home country, mother tongue, luxury car
Active participles (*–ing* verbals): welcoming committee, steering wheel, dancing troupe
Passive participles (*–ed* verbals): elected representatives, toasted marshmallows, paid work

## Comparatives and Superlatives

Different forms of the adjective are used to make comparisons. For comparing one thing to another, the comparative form is used. It is formed by adding an *–er* ending to words of one or two syllables. For longer words, *more* appears before the adjective:

> She is <u>taller</u> than I am, but I have <u>longer</u> legs because I have a <u>shorter</u> torso.
> That is the <u>more expensive</u> of the two options.

The superlative form is used when the comparison is between one thing and two or more. It is formed with the *–est* ending or the addition of *most* before the adjective:

> He was the <u>brightest</u> child in the class.
> Of the three options, that is the <u>most cost-effective</u>.
> That is the <u>most ridiculous</u> idea I have ever heard.

*Less* and *least* are used as the opposite of *more* and *most*:

> She is <u>less experienced</u> than I am.
> They were <u>the least prepared</u> team in the competition.

## Exercise 3.6

Fill in the blanks with suitable adjectives or adverbs:

1. The _____ house was _____ and _____.

2. Several _____ children played around the _____ park.

3. The _____ robots completed the _____ work.

4. A _____ hat lay on the _____, _____ ground.

5. A _____ _____ toy was the last item at the _____

   auction.

## Using Prepositional Phrases

Prepositional phrases are a frequent add-in to the basic sentence structure. Most specify time or place (when or where); some show the manner—how something was done. They are formed with a preposition followed by a noun phrase (a noun along with any determiners and adjectives required):

| | |
|---|---|
| in the house | on the corner |
| at school | by the church |
| with the red hat | under the sign |
| in five minutes | about the argument |
| in a sloppy way | during the storm |

Prepositions:

about, above, across, after, against, along, among, around, at, before, behind, below, beneath, beside, between, by, down, during, except, for, from, in, inside, into, near, next to, of, off, on, onto, out of, outside, over, past, through, to, under, until, up, upon, with, within, without

Notice how the prepositional phrases (underlined in the sentences below) add meaning to the sentence:

The girl threw the ball.
After her brother's taunt, the girl from next door threw the ball into the street.
Jack sat at the back of the bus to avoid the family with the crying baby.

Being able to identify prepositional phrases is important because by eliminating these phrases from the mix, you can isolate the core of the sentence (the subject and verb) and check to see whether the sentence is grammatical. A grammatical subject never appears in a prepositional phrase:

| | |
|---|---|
| One of the soldiers was killed. | The subject is *one*, not *soldiers*. |
| The members of the choir were tired after the long rehearsals. | The subject is *members*, not *choir*. |

Prepositions themselves pose problems both for people learning English as a second language and for native speakers. The basic meanings are relatively straightforward, but usage can be idiomatic and vary in different varieties of English. For instance, it is possible to say "he lives on Main Street" and "he lives in Main Street," depending on the dialect of English you speak.

Prepositions also combine with verbs in idiomatic combinations. Some verbs are completed by a specific preposition. For instance, we say *to rely on* and *to contend with* someone or something. In addition, prepositions figure in phrasal verbs (see pages 57–58), although they are referred to as particles in such combinations. For example, we say someone is *getting by* on a reduced income and that someone is trying *to catch up*. A good dictionary includes phrasal verbs and gives the prepositions that go with the verbs.

## Exercise 3.7

Underline the prepositional phrases in the following sentences, and identify the main subject and verb of the sentence:

1.  Some of the best dinosaur fossils can be found at the Royal Tyrrell Museum in the Badlands area near Drumheller, Alberta.

2.  In Quebec City, you can visit the Plains of Abraham, the site of the 1759 battle where the English forces defeated the French, putting Canada under the control of the British.

3.  The corner of Portage and Main is the downtown heart of Winnipeg and is considered the windiest intersection in the world.

4.  Victoria, the capital of British Columbia, is located on Vancouver Island, whereas Vancouver is on the mainland and is a much larger city.

5.  Niagara Falls is not the highest waterfall in the world, but the Horseshoe Falls, on the Canadian side of the border, is the world's largest by volume of water.

## Exercise 3.8

Add prepositional phrases to the following sentences, as in this example:

The books were delivered.
The books for the advanced class were delivered on Friday.

1.  The house was demolished.

2.  The students are studying quietly.

3.  The wall needs to be painted.

4.  The band performed.

5.  The rugby team won the game.

6.  The movie is playing.

7.  The children are running.
8.  The man fell.
9.  The instructor gave the driving lesson.
10. Anna is taking Japanese classes.

## Using Coordinate Conjunctions

Coordinate conjunctions are used for connecting sentences or parts of sentences. The term *coordinate* indicates equality between elements being joined (unlike sub-ordinate conjunctions, which make one clause less important, or "sub-ordinate"). The elements can be single words, phrases, or clauses. It is important that the two elements being joined be the same type, however. For instance, you cannot use a coordinate conjunction to connect a noun and a verb.

**Coordinate conjunctions:** and, or, but, so, yet, for, nor

Study these example sentences:

Jesse <u>and</u> Kate were putting up new drywall.

The conjunction *and* connects two nouns (*Jesse, Kate*).

We arrived tired <u>yet</u> happy.

The conjunction *yet* connects two adjectives (*tired, happy*).

In Ottawa, they visited the Parliament Buildings and skated on the Rideau Canal.

Two verb phrases are connected (main verbs are *visited* and *skated*).

Marcus wanted to take fencing lessons, <u>but</u> he could not afford the gear.

Two full clauses are connected with *but*.

You could see the Friday show <u>or</u> go to the matinee on Wednesday.

Two verb phrases are connected (main verbs are *see* and *go*).

Martha installed a firewall and changed the passwords.
Martha installed a firewall, and Sylvia changed the passwords.

Note the punctuation. A comma is used in the second sentence because the *and* is connecting two clauses rather than two phrases.

Rob topped his hamburger with mustard, ketchup, and relish.
Rob topped his hamburger with mustard, ketchup and relish.

Both sentences are correct. In a list of three or more items, the comma before *and* is often considered optional. (This is called a serial comma.)

In informal writing, sentences often begin with a coordinate conjunction. (You can see many examples in the article "A Global Warming Deal to Do Nothing Still Possible" on pages 14–15.) This usage is conversational style and, technically, not grammatically correct, especially with a comma after the coordinate conjunction.

| Conversational style | Academic style |
| --- | --- |
| Students taking an online course can study in a homey atmosphere. And they can even do their work in their pajamas. | Students taking an online course can study in a homey atmosphere, and they can even do their work in their pajamas. |
| But they do not get the social interaction of the classroom. | However, they do not get the social interaction of the classroom. |
| And it is hard to discipline themselves to complete work on time. | In addition, it is hard to discipline themselves to complete work on time. |
| So it is not surprising that many do not succeed. | Therefore, it is not surprising that many do not succeed. |

Avoid starting sentences with coordinate conjunctions in formal writing: in essays, business communication, and technical reports.

## Exercise 3.9

Merge the two sentences into one, using coordinate conjunctions, eliminating unnecessary words, and making whatever other changes are required.

1. Peter had to get the transmission fixed. He had to get the brakes fixed.
2. Zach thought he passed his driver's test. He had to book another one.
3. Kate plays the piano. She plays the guitar.
4. My uncle was killed in a motorcycle accident. My mother won't allow me to get a motorcycle.
5. Erin's brother is an engineer. Erin's brother-in-law is an engineer.
6. Melissa could go to the University of Calgary. Melissa could go to the University of Alberta.
7. Ben thought he had a job on the oil rig. The job fell through.
8. We thought of holding my parents' anniversary party on a dinner cruise boat. We thought of holding my parents' anniversary party in the revolving restaurant.
9. Christine was supposed to pick Jim up at the train station. She forgot.
10. Suji couldn't understand the formula. She read the chapter again.

## Parallel Structure

When using coordinate conjunctions, you must ensure that each sentence part that you join has essentially the same grammatical structure, whether single words, phrases, or full clauses. Sometimes the structures are in a series of elements. This is called parallel structure:

| | |
|---|---|
| Marta likes dancing and singing. | Parallel structure—the *and* connects two gerunds. |
| Marta likes to dance and sing. | Parallel structure—the *and* connects two infinitives. |
| Marta likes dancing and to sing. | **incorrect:** not parallel |
| Marta likes to dance but hates to sing. | Parallel structure—the *but* connects two infinitives. |
| Marta likes to dance, but Dimitry prefers to sit on the side. | Parallel structure—the *but* connects two clauses. |
| On their vacation trip, they wanted to sit on a beach, eat great food, and they hoped to visit family. | **incorrect:** not parallel |
| On their vacation trip, they wanted to sit on a beach, eat great food, and visit family. | Parallel structure—the *and* connects three verbs (*sit*, *eat*, *visit*), all in the base form. |

Ensuring parallelism can be difficult. You have to figure out what parts of the sentence are being linked. Putting the sentence elements in a vertical list can help you see whether each element has the same structure and fits the sentence:

| | |
|---|---|
| When Eli lost his keys, he looked<br>    under the desk,<br>    beside the filing cabinet, and<br>    checked under the sofa cushions. | **incorrect:** not parallel—the verb in the third element does not fit |
| When Eli lost his keys, he looked<br>    under the desk,<br>    beside the filing cabinet, and<br>    under the sofa cushions. | parallel structure |

Parallel structure is especially important in thesis statements when three elements are often linked to show the three ideas explored in the body paragraphs. You can practise parallel structure with thesis statements in Unit 5.

## Exercise 3.10

For each list, identify which item is not parallel, and then make it parallel:

*Example:*    washing dishes
              setting the table
              to pour the drinks [not parallel—use *pouring the drinks*]

1. a good plot
   interesting characters
   kept the audience's attention
   exciting special effects

2. worried
   in a bad mood
   tired
   frustrated
   hungry

3. strolling through the park
   running around the track
   rollerblading down the path
   walk around the block

4. made some appetizers
   put the beer in the fridge
   set the table
   tidying the living room

5. tour the Parliament buildings
   the bike paths around the city
   visit the National Gallery
   shop in ByWard Market

## Exercise 3.11

Fill in the blank with a word or phrase that will fit the sentence and have parallel structure:

1. Marie topped the pizza with tomatoes, sausage, _____, and onions.

2. I was born in Edmonton, raised in Vancouver, and later _____.

3. College students can be high school graduates, mature students, or

   _____.

4. Her presentation was clear, concise, and _____.

5. To be successful, college students should attend class, manage their time,

   and _____.

## Writing Noun Clauses

A clause is part of a complex sentence and has both a noun and a verb. Noun clauses function as a noun would—in other words, as a subject or an object. The noun clauses are underlined in these example sentences:

> The inspector noticed <u>that the handle had broken off</u>.
> She asked <u>whether I could come</u>.
> They wondered <u>if it would rain</u>.
> <u>Who will win the race</u> is a mystery.

**Words that may begin noun clauses:**

that, if, whether, when, where, what, why, how, who, whom, which, whose

Noun clauses can function as both subjects and objects:

| | |
|---|---|
| <u>His behaviour</u> was inexcusable. | *his behaviour* is the subject |
| <u>What he did</u> was inexcusable. | *what he did* is the noun clause subject |
| I understood <u>his apology</u>. | *his apology* is the object |
| I understood <u>that he was sorry</u>. | *that he was sorry* is the noun clause object |

Many noun clauses begin with *that* (never *which*), but note that if the clause comes after the verb, *that* can be eliminated if the sentence is clear without it:

| | |
|---|---|
| She realized that he was late.<br>She realized he was late. | both sentences are acceptable |

Noun clauses that function as subjects should be relatively short. English doesn't like top-heavy sentences requiring the reader to wait for a long time to come to the verb, because these sentences are more difficult to understand. They can be revised by using an *it* phrase:

| | |
|---|---|
| That we could still negotiate a fair deal after so many false starts is amazing. | awkward but grammatical |
| It is amazing that we could still negotiate a fair deal after so many false starts. | better |

Be careful with the word order in noun clauses that deal with questions. The question structure (using the verb *do* and inverted word order) is not used:

| | |
|---|---|
| They asked what time did she finish. | **incorrect** |
| They asked what time she finished. | **correct** |
| They wanted to know did she have time for another project. | **incorrect** |
| They wanted to know if she had time for another project. | **correct** |

## Exercise 3.12

Complete the noun clause to fit the blank:

1. She asked whether _____.

2. That _____ was disappointing.

3. How _____ was Jane's main concern.

4. He didn't understand why _____.

5. Whoever _____ is fine with me.

## Writing Adjective Clauses

Adjective clauses, also called **relative clauses**, describe a noun. They usually come after the noun and begin with relative pronouns. In these example sentences, the adjective clauses are underlined:

> The woman <u>who led that protest march</u> is Jamie's cousin.
> The cottage road, <u>which is not paved</u>, is impassable in the winter.
> The DVD <u>that he ordered</u> is not available anymore.
> The tourist <u>whose luggage was stolen</u> spent hours filling out a report.

**Relative pronouns:** who, whom, whose, what, which, why, that, when, where

Adding clauses to sentences is a good way to give extra information to a sentence without changing its main idea or focus. For example, if you want to identify someone but you do not want that identification to be the main idea of the sentence, you can use an adjective clause:

> My friend Liz, who went to Europe with me, is travelling to New Zealand this summer.

As in noun clauses, *that* can be eliminated if the meaning is clear:

> The DVD <u>he ordered</u> is not available anymore.

The relative pronoun *whom* is the correct form when the pronoun refers to the object of the verb or of the preposition. However, as noted earlier, *whom* is dying out in English usage. In conversation and informal writing it is almost never used, but it is more common in academic writing:

| | |
|---|---|
| The woman whom I met last week is a set designer. | used in formal English |
| The woman who I met last week is a set designer. | commonly heard |
| The woman I met last week is a set designer. | The pronoun *who* is often dropped, especially in informal English. |

Punctuation is important in sentences that contain adjective clauses. Commas around the clause signal that the information is extra, that taking out the clause will not affect the meaning of the sentence. If there are no commas, the clause is essential to the meaning because it restricts who or what is being spoken about.

The first case is called a **non-restrictive (or non-defining) adjective clause**, while the latter case is a **restrictive (or defining) adjective clause**:

| | |
|---|---|
| The Class 2B students, who failed the test, have to attend a tutorial. | non-restrictive clause showing that all the students in Class 2B failed |
| The Class 2B students who failed the test have to attend a tutorial. | restrictive clause—only some of the students in Class 2B failed |

The relative pronoun *that* is used in restrictive relative clauses, while *which* is used for non-restrictive clauses:

> The course that she wanted to take is already full.
> The first year biology course, which is required in many programs, has several sections.

## Exercise 3.13

Identify the relative clause in each of the following sentences. Add commas where necessary (that is, for the restrictive relative clauses):

1. Nunavut which was created from the Northwest Territories in 1999 has an Aboriginal government and Inuktitut as an official language.
2. The spot where the cottage will be built has a nice view of the lake.
3. Janice whom I taught last year is planning to be a teacher herself.
4. The company where she worked part-time in high school offered her a scholarship.

5. The president of the college who uses a wheelchair has done much to improve the accessibility of campus facilities.

6. The apartment which I saw last week is still available.

## Exercise 3.14

Combine the following sentences using relative clauses. Change the word order as necessary:

*Example*:   We got married in the church. The church is being torn down.
The church where we got married is being torn down.

OR

The church that is being torn down is the place where we were married.

1. I worked at the company part-time as a student. The company offered me a full-time position when I graduated.

2. The students forgot to do their assignment. Those students had to stay after class.

3. The singers were trained in Europe. The singers were most familiar with classical tradition.

4. We are meeting at a restaurant. The restaurant is on campus, next to the biology building.

5. Children come to the community pool to learn to swim. Their ages range from seven to twelve.

6. Some people keep exotic pets such as tarantulas, rattlesnakes, and piranhas. These people want to be different and prefer to live dangerously.

## Writing Adverb Clauses

Adverb clauses (often called **subordinate clauses**) modify whole sentences and, like adverbs, tell when, where, why, or how something was done. Subordinate conjunctions allow you to combine two sentences to make one new one:

He studied hard for the test. He didn't get a passing grade.
Although he studied for the test, he didn't get a passing grade.
Marie was late for the interview. The car broke down.
Marie was late for the interview because the car broke down.

**Subordinate conjunctions:** after, although, as, because, before, even though, if, since, unless, until, when, where, whereas, whether, while

The adverb clause that begins with the conjunction is also called a **subordinate clause**, or **dependent clause**, and the other half of the sentence is the **main**

**clause**, or **independent clause**. The clause is dependent because it cannot stand on its own; it depends on the main clause to make a complete sentence:

| | |
|---|---|
| Although he studied for the test. | **incorrect:** incomplete sentence |
| He didn't get a passing grade. | complete sentence |
| Because the car broke down. | **incorrect:** incomplete sentence |
| Marie was late for the interview. | complete sentence |

For most sentences, the subordinate clause can come either before or after the main clause, but notice that the sentence is punctuated differently for each:

| | |
|---|---|
| If you remove the cover first, it is easier to access the parts. | You need a comma after the subordinate clause in order to signal the end of the clause to the reader. |
| It is easier to access the parts if you remove the cover first. | A comma is unnecessary when the subordinate clause comes after the main clause because the conjunction signals the beginning of the subordinate clause. |
| Although, he was tired of hearing her complaints, he finished the job. | **incorrect:** There is no comma after the conjunction. |

Often, you have a choice whether to use a coordinate or subordinate conjunction. Some express the same meaning:

| | |
|---|---|
| Although Takeshi hates playing golf, he never misses the company golf day. | subordinate conjunction used (*although*) |
| Takeshi hates playing golf, but he never misses the company golf day. | coordinate conjunction used (*but*) |
| Although Takeshi hates playing golf, but he never misses the company golf day. | **incorrect:** You cannot use both conjunctions in a sentence with two clauses. |

A sentence with a coordinate conjunction is considered a compound sentence; in that case, both clauses have the same weight. A sentence constructed with a subordinate conjunction is considered a **complex sentence**. It allows you to express different levels of meaning. What is expressed in the subordinate clause is the less important (subordinate) idea; the main idea is in the main clause:

> Although school uniforms are often hideous, it is comforting to know that everyone is dressed the same and your style can't be found wanting.

The writer is acknowledging the lack of fashion in uniforms but is stressing the positive side (the idea that is in the main clause).

If the sentence were to be flipped, it could be used in an essay discussing the disadvantages of uniforms:

> Although it can be comforting to know that everyone is dressed the same, it must be acknowledged that school uniforms are truly hideous.

As can be seen here, *although* can be used for conceding a point (further discussed on page 184).

You can write a sentence with more than one subordinate clause as long as you have a main clause to make it a grammatical sentence. But do not overload your sentence like this:

> While he was waiting for the train, wondering if it would ever come, he looked through a magazine because he was very bored, but even though the articles were interesting, he could not concentrate on the information given, as his thoughts kept coming back to the mistakes he had made in the job interview.

*Although, even though*, and *though* mean essentially the same thing, but there are slight differences:

| | |
|---|---|
| Although he had done his training, he could not complete the marathon. | |
| Even though he had trained hard for months, he could not complete the marathon. | *Even though* shows a stronger contrast, for something that is surprising. |
| Though he had trained hard for months, he could not complete the marathon. | Incorrect for academic writing: *though* as a conjunction is informal. |
| He had trained hard for months. He could not complete the marathon though. | Here, *though* is an adverb, not a conjunction. |

Remember that *even though* is always two words.

**Conjunctive adverbs** (also called adverbial connectives) such as *however and therefore* are often confused with subordinate conjunctions. The differences between the different kinds of sentence connectors are shown on pages 88–90.

---

### Exercise 3.15

Join the following pairs of sentences with a subordinate conjunction (page 83):

*Example:*   I tried to install the wireless router. My system crashed.
         When I tried to install the wireless router, my system crashed.

1. Tim Horton had a hand in starting the business that bears his name. Laura Secord had nothing to do with the candy-making business.

2. The candy store was named after Laura Secord. The founder wanted a Canadian heroine as a trademark.

3. The Canadian flag is such a recognized symbol today. It did not have an easy road to design and official acceptance in 1965.

4. The first explorers came to Canada seeking a route to the Orient. They came back for the valuable fish and furs.

5. British Columbia agreed to join Canada. A railroad would be built to connect it with the eastern provinces.

6. The Canadian Pacific Railway took many years to complete. It was so difficult to build through the rock of the Canadian Shield in central Canada and the mountain ranges in British Columbia.

7. The United Empire Loyalists came north to Canada after the American Revolution. They wanted to remain British subjects.

8. Lacrosse is one of Canada's national sports. It is not very popular, especially when compared to hockey.

9. Tommy Douglas became a member of Parliament. He wanted to extend Saskatchewan's medicare program to all of Canada.

10. The Acadians were expelled from Nova Scotia. They settled in Louisiana.

## Reducing Clauses to Phrases

When two clauses have the same subject, one clause can sometimes be reduced to make a phrase. Study these examples:

| Original sentence | Reduction | Comments |
|---|---|---|
| 1. While they were going over the lesson, the students discovered a new problem. | While going over the lesson, the students discovered a new problem.<br>Going over the lesson, the students discovered a new problem. | Because *they* and *the students* refer to the same people, the clause can be reduced to a phrase. |
| 2. Gillian, who is the former president of the club, stayed on to help her successor deal with the reorganization. | Gillian, the former president of the club, stayed on to help her successor deal with the reorganization. | The adjective clause can be changed to an adjective phrase because *Gillian* and *who* both refer to the same person. |

| 3. While the students were listening to the lecture, the lights went out. | While listening to the lecture, the lights went out. | **incorrect:** The reduction is ungrammatical because the two original clauses have different subjects, *students* and *lights*. The lights were **not** listening to the lecture when they went out. |
| 4. We ordered the meal for the group before we went to the restaurant. | We ordered the meal for the group before going to the restaurant. | The reduction works because *we* refers to the same group of people in both clauses. Note the change of wording in the reduction. |
| 5. The movie was sold out although it received bad reviews. | The movie was sold out despite having received bad reviews. | Note the change of wording in the reduction. |

## Exercise 3.16

In the following sentences, identify the adjective and adverb clauses. Then, where possible, reduce the underlined clauses to phrases, rewording the phrase where necessary.

1. When he was touring the house, Marc noticed that it needed a lot of work.

2. The house, which was located in a prime downtown area, had large rooms and original wood panelling that needed to be stripped.

3. The powder room, which was tucked under the stairway, had pink tiles and 1970s fixtures.

4. Because he had worked for his father's construction company, he had the skills to do most of the work himself.

5. He particularly liked the stained glass, which was almost 100 years old.

6. Elena, who was Marc's wife, was reluctant to take on the project because she didn't want to live in a construction zone for years.

7. Although she was handy with power tools and a paint brush, she preferred a place that required less work.

8. Because they both had demanding jobs, she wanted to have relaxing weekends, not more work.

9.  <u>If they did the work themselves</u>, they could afford to live downtown.
10. <u>After they weighed all the pros and cons</u>, they put in an offer on the house.

## Connecting Sentences

It is often necessary to show the logical connection between two sentences. This can be accomplished through the use of conjunctions or conjunctive adverbs. This section has some handy review charts contrasting different ways to connect sentences.

Here is a list of commonly used connectors:

| **Connector type** | **Function** |
|---|---|
| Coordinate conjunctions (and, or, but, yet, so, for, nor) | can join sentences (and can join parts of sentences with the same grammatical structure) [See pages 76–78, Using Coordinate Conjunctions.] |
| Subordinate conjunctions include: after, although, as, because, even though, if, since, when, whereas | can join sentences [See pages 83–85, Writing Adverb Clauses.] |
| Conjunctive adverbs include: consequently, for example, furthermore, however, in addition, moreover, nevertheless, then, therefore, thus | cannot be used as conjunctions to make one sentence from two sentences [See pages 119–20, Using Transition Signals.] |

It is relatively easy to keep these three categories separate. The list of coordinate conjunctions is complete—there are only seven short words to remember. To distinguish conjunctions and conjunctive adverbs, it is useful to remember that conjunctions can only be placed at the beginning of one of the clauses, whereas adverbs can be placed in different positions, as in this example:

| | |
|---|---|
| Their initial findings were inconclusive, but another attempt at the experiment was more successful. | There is only one possible placement for the conjunction *but*. |
| Their initial findings were inconclusive. However, another attempt was more successful. OR Another attempt, however, was more successful. OR Another attempt was more successful, however. | The adverb *however* can be placed in different locations in the second sentence. |

However, the word *so* is tricky because it can function as both an adverb and a conjunction:

| | |
|---|---|
| They were tired, so they skipped class. | *So* is used as a conjunction. |
| They were so tired that they skipped the class. | *So* is used as an adverb, modifying the adjective *tired*. |
| They were tired. So they skipped class. | This use of *so* is common in conversational English. It is not appropriate for essay writing. |

Here is a review of the ways sentences can be connected. Pay attention to the punctuation and capitalization.

| | |
|---|---|
| a) The students worked hard. They passed the test. | two grammatical sentences separated by a period |
| b) The students worked hard they passed the test. | **incorrect**: run-on sentence (specifically, a fused sentence) |
| c) The students worked hard, they passed the test. | **incorrect:** comma splice (a type of run-on sentence). A comma alone cannot be used to join two sentences. |
| d) The students worked hard; they passed the test. | two sentences joined by a semicolon |
| e) The students worked hard, so they passed the test. | two clauses joined by a coordinate conjunction (*so*) |
| f) The students passed the test because they worked hard. | two clauses joined by a subordinate conjunction (*because*) No comma is necessary between the clauses. |
| g) Because the students worked hard, they passed the test. | Subordinate conjunctions can also come at the beginning of the first clause, but then a comma is needed to show where the first clause ends. |
| h) Because, the students worked hard, they passed the test. | **incorrect:** There should be no comma after a subordinate conjunction. |

| | |
|---|---|
| i) Because the students worked hard, so they passed the test. | **incorrect:** Two conjunctions should not be used if there are only two sentences being joined. |
| j) The students worked hard. Therefore, they passed the test. | two separate sentences Because a conjunctive adverb (such as *therefore*) is not a conjunction, it cannot join two sentences. |
| k) The students worked hard; therefore, they passed the test. | The semicolon (not the conjunctive adverb) is joining the sentences. |
| l) The students worked hard, therefore they passed the test. | **incorrect:** Conjunctive adverbs cannot join sentences. |
| m) The students worked hard. They therefore passed the test. | Because *therefore* is an adverb, it is not restricted to the beginning of the sentence. |
| n) The students worked hard. So they passed the test. | **incorrect** in formal English: This structure is commonly seen in conversational English, but you should not use it in essays and other formal writing. |

## Exercise 3.17

Connect each pair of sentences given below. Show possible ways the sentences can be connected. You can switch the order of the two sentences.

1. Several classes had been cancelled. The students did not cover all the course material.
2. Several classes had been cancelled. The students managed to cover all the course material.
3. They did not take the proper precautions. An accident occurred.
4. They did not take the proper precautions. The experiment proceeded without incident.
5. A snowstorm was making driving hazardous. We postponed the meeting.
6. A snowstorm was making driving hazardous. The college did not close.
7. The essay had several errors. It lacked a recognizable thesis.

## Analyzing Sentence Structure

If you come across a long, complicated sentence in your reading, identifying the **core** (the subject and predicate) can help you to understand it. You can also check the core of the sentences you have written to make sure they are grammatical.

In this unit, we have reviewed the basics of sentence structure—what makes up the core and what are the possible modifiers, phrases, and clauses that can be added. Breaking down a sentence into its component parts is called *parsing*. Linguists and grammarians can go into great detail analyzing sentences and labelling the parts, but students who want to improve their reading and writing skills do not need to go into such detail. However, they do need to develop a basic "sentence sense"— knowing what words go together and what the core of the sentence is.

As you know, sentences are made of groupings of words called phrases and clauses. When you read or write a sentence, you should be able to identify which words go together. Because a phrase or clause will work as a unit, one test for whether a group of words is an actual phrase or clause is to move or delete the group.

Here are some example sentences from the readings. Each has been analyzed. Note that the grammatical subject is underlined and the main verb is underlined twice.

1.  "The distaste for true math often begins in high school." (Martyn, page 261)

                      **a**          **b**             **c**

     The <u>distaste</u> [for true math] [often] <u><u>begins</u></u> [in high school].

     a) a prepositional phrase describing the noun *distaste*
     b) an adverb modifying the verb *begins*
     c) a prepositional phrase functioning as an adverb, answering the question "where?"

2.  "Widowed for five years now, she lives alone in her own house except for the occasions when I come home to tidy her household affairs." (Engkent, page 353)

                   **a**                **b**      **c**        **d**

     [Widowed for five years now], <u>she</u> <u><u>lives</u></u> [alone] [in her own house] [except for the

                                            **e**

     occasions] [when I come home to tidy her household affairs].

     a) adjective phrase describing *she* [*widowed* is the adjective, and the rest of the phrase is a prepositional phrase]
     b) adverb
     c) prepositional phrase
     d) prepositional phrase

e) adverb clause [*when* = subordinate conjunction, *I* = subject, *come* = verb, *home* = adverb, *to tidy* = infinitive complement of the verb *come*, *affairs* = object of the verb *tidy*]

3.    "These companies are taking our tap water, which on average in Canada costs us less than one-tenth of a cent per litre, filtering it, although it is already perfectly clean, and selling it back to us at a markup that can be several thousand times its original price." (Petty and Trudeau, page 310)

                                            **a**

These <u>companies</u> <u>are taking</u> our tap water, [which on average in Canada costs us

                                          **b**

less than one-tenth of a cent per litre], <u>filtering</u> it, [although it is already perfectly

                                          **c**

clean,] and <u>selling</u> it back to us at a markup [that can be several thousand times its original price].

Note that this sentence has three main verbs in the progressive tense: *are taking*, *are filtering*, and *are selling*. The auxiliary verb *are* is not repeated but is understood.

a) adjective clause describing tap water [*which* = relative pronoun, *costs* = main verb of the clause]
b) adverb clause [*although* = subordinate conjunction, *it* = pronoun subject, *is* = main verb, *clean* = adjective complement for the verb]
c) adjective clause describing markup [*that* = relative pronoun, *can be* = main verb]

As you work on specific readings in Units 9–16, you will be asked to do further sentence analysis like this. What is important is not that you learn the specific grammar terminology but that you can group words that go together and identify the core of the sentence.

## Building Complex Sentences

Good writing has a variety of sentence structure and length. It is important to be able to write complex sentences with clauses and phrases. Too many simple sentences can be tedious to read. Moreover, complex sentences allow you to layer information, with the main idea in the main clause and additional information in subordinate clauses. Too many complex sentences, however, can be tiring to read or too convoluted to follow.

In this unit, we have reviewed the essential elements of a sentence. The core of a sentence is the subject and predicate. The addition of adjectives, adverbs, and prepositional phrases modifies the basic nouns and verbs. Adding clauses makes the sentence complex, as shown on the next page.

| | |
|---|---|
| The one-cent coin was eliminated. | simple sentence in the passive voice |
| a) In Canada, the one-cent coin was finally eliminated in February 2013. | addition of two prepositional phrases and an adverb |
| b) In Canada, the one-cent coin, which was commonly called the penny, was finally eliminated in February 2013. | addition of adjective clause to a) |
| c) Even though many people predicted problems, the one-cent coin was easily eliminated. | addition of adverb clause to original sentence |

## Exercise 3.18

Alter the simple sentences below by adding modifiers (including phrases and clauses). Try out different structures, as shown in the example sentences above. You can make alterations to the base sentence, such as changing the article, when necessary.

1. The students played soccer.
2. A student centre was built.
3. The helicopter crashed.
4. The manager sent a message.
5. The instructor cancelled the class.

## Using Punctuation and Capitalization

Punctuation is an important part of sentence structure. Readers rely on capital letters and end punctuation to tell them where sentences begin and end. Commas show the different parts of a sentence. Because sentences in academic English are more complex, the punctuation is crucial to the reader's ability to follow the sentence. The basic uses of different punctuation marks are introduced here. Correcting common errors in punctuation is addressed in Unit 7, pages 216–17.

### End Punctuation

The end of a sentence is marked by a period, question mark, or exclamation mark. In essay writing, almost all of your sentences will end with a period; you should have very few questions and no exclamations at all.

Sentences should not end with three dots (an **ellipsis** mark). It gives the impression that the writer is not committed to the sentence and is just trailing off. (Ellipsis marks are used in academic writing in quotations to show that some words have been left out.)

Periods are also used with some abbreviations, such as shortened words (Prof. for Professor) and university degrees (M.B.A.). **Initialisms** (abbreviations formed from the first letter of words, such as ESL for English as a Second Language) and **acronyms** (like initialisms but pronounced as words, such as AIDS for Acquired Immune Deficiency Syndrome), rarely have periods between the letters. Check your dictionary or style guide if you are unsure of the usage.

## Space

Space is an element of punctuation because it shows readers where words, sentences, and paragraphs begin and end. Space contributes to the readability of the document. A text that is too jammed with words is harder to read. Your resumé, for example, should have enough white space to make it attractive and readable.

There should be no space between the end of the word and the punctuation. A comma, for instance, should never appear at the beginning of the next line.

In the old days of typewriters, typists were taught to leave two spaces at the end of a sentence. This is no longer the convention now that people use computers and proportional fonts; one space is sufficient.

Space defines paragraphs. Generally, paragraphs are indented with five spaces, or a half-inch tab space. Block-style paragraphing uses no indent but rather a blank line between paragraphs. Readers should be able to easily see where a new paragraph starts. Avoid sloppy, misleading spacing, such as indenting at the beginning of a page where there is no new paragraph.

Proper margins are important for all your documents—leave an inch on each side. Use left justification with a ragged right margin so that you will not have gaps in your lines of text or have to figure out where to properly split a word with hyphenation. Double-space assignments so that your instructor has room for corrections and comments.

Do not use full justification for your work, because that creates uneven and unattractive spaces between words. Some people do not like the ragged right edge caused by left justification, but documents formatted that way are easier to read.

## Commas

Commas are placed in sentences mainly to separate different parts of the sentence. Commas generally appear:

- after initial adverbs: Thankfully, we hailed the rescue team.
- between items in a list: We ate roast beef, mashed potatoes, green peas, and squash. OR We ate roast beef, mashed potatoes, green peas and squash.
- after adverb clauses: Because it was raining, we cancelled the picnic.
- before clauses introduced by coordinating conjunctions: I took a nap, and then we left.
- before and after modifying phrases or clauses: John, who is this year's president, gave a welcome speech.

The second example in the list above shows the optional use of a **serial comma** (also called an Oxford comma), a comma before the *and* in a list of more than two items. Use of the serial comma is often just a matter of preference, but it is mandated in both MLA and APA style (see Unit 8, pages 236–37). Whether you choose to use the serial comma or not, be consistent.

Commas appear in lists of adjectives where the two adjectives have a similar function and could be replaced with an *and*:

> She told a strange, sad story about a beautiful Mexican dancer.

A missing comma can change the whole sentence:

> Students come to class to learn not to have fun.
> Students come to class to learn, not to have fun.

Commas differentiate restrictive and non-restrictive adjective clauses (see page 82).

| | |
|---|---|
| The band members who did not get their permission forms signed could not join the field trip. | only some of the band members |
| The band members, who did not get their permission forms signed, could not join the field trip. | all the band members |

Comma usage is sometimes a matter of style rather than a grammar requirement. The best general rule to follow is to use a comma when it helps the reader understand the sentence. For example, a comma after an adverb clause helps the reader separate the two parts of the sentence.

| | |
|---|---|
| When he was going out to exercise the dog started barking. | This sentence is confusing because the verb *exercise* can be both transitive and intransitive, so "to exercise the dog" makes sense. The reader does not know where the clause stops until after he has read the whole sentence. |
| When he was going out to exercise, the dog started barking. | The comma helps the reader to see the two separate clauses. |
| The dog started barking when he was going out to exercise. | No comma is necessary because the conjunction *when* serves as a sentence divider. |

### Exercise 3.19

Insert periods, commas, and capital letters where needed in the following paragraph:

> cleaning out my grandmother's cluttered musty old house after she died was a monumental task like many old people who had lived through unspeakable war and famine she was an incurable hoarder she kept old newspapers plastic bags and cardboard boxes she did not trash out-of-date calendars she just tacked up a new one in a different spot on the wall we found new clothes that had been saved for a special occasion and never used her husband's clothes still hung in the closet even though he had passed away a dozen years earlier in the cold cellar were jars of pickled food that must have been 20 years old two full-size freezers were crammed with food some of the packages were many years old she felt safe with all her possessions and never wanted to let anything go

## Apostrophes

Essentially, apostrophes are used for contractions and for possessive forms.

A contraction is a shortened form of words, such as *he isn't* for *he is not*. In a contraction, an apostrophe takes the place of dropped letters. For example, in verbs contracted with *not*, the apostrophe replaces the *o* (*isn't, doesn't, can't*). The auxiliary verbs *be*, *have*, and *will* are sometimes contracted: *I'm going, they've noticed, she'll see, I could've done it.* Apostrophes can also show dropped numbers, as in "The radio station played hits from the '70s." Apostrophes are **not** used in non-contracted verbs (*she tries, he listens*). Do not confuse the verb form *lets* ("he lets me take the car") with the contracted form *let's* (*let us*, as in "let's go").

Possessives are words that show that something belongs to something else (for example, *Jim's car, the students' pet rabbit*). The possession can be a loose relationship, as in such phrases as *a day's work* or *a summer's day*.

There seems to be an epidemic of apostrophe overuse and misuse today, not only in students' writing but also on printed signs and even in some published works. Some people incorrectly bestow apostrophes on words ending in *s* and between *nt* letter combinations. As a result, we see miswritten words such as "chair's" and even "he wan't's." A sentence such as "Were in trouble now" can be impossible to read without the apostrophe in *we're*.

An apostrophe can change the meaning of a sentence:

| | |
|---|---|
| The drill sergeant called the recruits names. | In other words, he called them names, mocking them. |
| The drill sergeant called the recruits' names. | This means that he called out their names. |

Apostrophes are **not** used before most plurals (*many ways, two different techniques, a dozen tomatoes*). The very few exceptions are plurals when an −*s* alone would be confusing:

> He got all A's and B's on his report card.
> She dots her i's with circles.

Sometimes apostrophes are used in plurals of shortened words (for example, *reno's* for *renovations*) and plurals of number and letter combinations, but these are unnecessary:

> He ordered CDs of hits from the 1960s and 1970s.
> They booked two limos for transportation to the prom.

## Exercise 3.20

Insert apostrophes where needed in the following sentences:

1. Susans brother has been living in his grandfathers house to help take care of him. Hes missed some classes but hes planning to make them up with night classes. The universitys online program lets him follow many different options.

2. Lets go to the Johnsons cottage this weekend. Weve had an open invitation for ages. Ill just give them a call to see if its okay. Itll be good to get away, and if we dont go now, who knows when well be able to get away?

3. James always listens to his teachers instructions because he knows how important following instructions is to getting good marks.

4. Unlike his siblings, hes willing to take over his fathers business selling antiques.

5. The students work needed to be completely redone. I dont know why there were so many mistakes.

## Colons

Colons (:) are used to show illustration of an idea. They can be used to introduce a sentence or a list. They should not be used after *are* or *such as*. Note these examples:

| | |
|---|---|
| The pizza dough requires few ingredients: flour, water, sugar, salt, oil, and yeast. | **correct:**<br>The colon comes after a full sentence and before a list. |
| My favourite sports are: soccer, swimming, and squash. | **incorrect:**<br>The colon is unnecessary. |
| There was only one thing left to do: He had to contact his friend's parents to let them know what happened. | **correct:**<br>The capital on *he* is optional. |

## Semicolons

Semicolons (;) are used between two related sentences and to distinguish items in a complex list where commas are needed within some of the items in the list:

> The soccer game was exciting to watch; the teams had each been previous champions.

> Dave was the strongest member of the team; however, he was let go because he could not get along with anyone.

> Canadian coins show a number of national symbols: the maple leaves on the penny; the beaver, the animal that brought many Europeans to Canada, on the nickel; the dime's *Bluenose*, a famous racing schooner from Nova Scotia; the caribou on the quarter; the loon on the dollar coin; and the polar bear on the two-dollar coin.

## Quotation Marks

Quotation marks ("..." or '...') are used to show that you are using someone's exact words (North American usage favours double quotation marks instead of single.)

> Emma Teitel concludes that we have lost "the art of public confrontation." (page 298)

For a quote appearing within a quote, you should use quotation marks different from the ones you used for the main quote (for example, single quotation marks instead of double).

> Peter Martyn points out that "George Orwell decried his contemporaries' 'lack of precision' in their use of words." (page 261)

Quotation marks are also used around the titles of short stories and articles, while the titles of books or newspapers are printed in italics. For example, "If the artists starve, we'll all go hungry" was one of Elizabeth Renzetti's columns in *The Globe and Mail*; it is reprinted in *Skill Set*.

## Hyphens and Dashes

A hyphen is used within a word (such as *co-author* and *self-discipline*), while a dash is used between words in a sentence. Some words have two accepted spellings—with a hyphen and without. Sometimes the word loses the hyphen over time. For instance, the word *e-mail* is now usually written *email*. Check your dictionary if you are not sure of the spelling.

If a word cannot fit on a line, a hyphen is used to break the word into two parts. The hyphen must appear between syllables (syllable breaks are shown in dictionaries). You will see this use of the hyphen in publications because the text is written with full justification (both the right and left margins). If words were not split, there would be annoying white spaces in the lines. You can avoid this use of the hyphen by simply writing the whole word on the next line. Use only left justification with a ragged right margin in your documents.

A dash is used to set words off from the rest of the sentence. These words can be extra information or a comment. The same function can often be met by commas or parentheses (round brackets), which can set off a clause or phrase that is not part of the main idea—but the dash gives more emphasis. Notice the usage of each parenthetical dash in this section.

A parenthetical dash is also called an "em dash" (because of typesetting—it is the same width as the letter *M*). There should be no space before or after the dash.

While a hyphen can be found on a standard keyboard, dashes are not. Word processing programs may replace two typed hyphens with a long dash. Otherwise, it is a symbol that can be inserted, along with the "en dash." The en dash is used with numbers such as dates (for example, 1947–63) and is the width of the letter *N*, thus not as wide as the em dash.

## Capitalization

Capital letters appear at the beginning of sentences and on proper nouns (official names):

> Maria is planning a trip to Saskatoon to visit her grandmother.
> In 2012, James Burton earned his M.B.A. at the Haskayne School of Business at the University of Calgary.

The names of school subjects are capitalized if they are official titles but not if they are general subject names. The names of languages, however, are always capitalized.

> He wanted to take another biology course, so his advisor recommended BIOL 130, Introduction to Cell Biology. To fulfill his requirement for another English course, he is taking Creative Writing.

The capital letter has been dropping from such common phrases as "French fries," but the word *French* should be capitalized because it is a proper noun—the name of a nationality.

The use of capitals in the titles of books or articles depends on the citation style used. In MLA style, for example, the title of this book would be written *Skill Set*, and Emma Teitel's article (page 297) would be "Turning the Dinner Table on Instagram," with the first and the main words capitalized. In APA style, the titles would be *Skill set* and "Turning the table on Instagram," with the first word and proper nouns capitalized. Newspaper headlines tend to be written with only the first word (and proper nouns) capitalized.

## Exercise 3.21

Capitalize the words that need capital letters in the following sentences:

1. the marine museum of the atlantic in halifax, nova scotia, has exhibits on the 1917 halifax explosion and the response to the sinking of the *titanic* in 1912.
2. sainte-marie among the hurons is a recreated seventeenth-century jesuit mission headquarters in midland, ontario.
3. sir john a. macdonald was canada's first prime minister. his picture is on the 10-dollar bill.
4. remembrance day honours canada's war dead. two minutes of silence commemorates the end of world war I at 11 a.m. on november 11.
5. john mccrae wrote the poem "in flanders fields," which is often recited on remembrance day.

## Exercise 3.22

Add capitalization and punctuation where necessary:

1. mr peterson requested the review of the department because of its poor performance the manager thought it was unnecessary
2. shakespeares play romeo and juliet tells the story of two teenagers in love in sixteenth century italy its a tragic tale because the lovers are from two feuding families
3. i dont know what to buy as a gift for joannes baby shower shes having twin boys
4. if youre worried about fitting the english course into your schedule why dont you take it online
5. lets take the train to montreal so we dont have to worry about driving and parking the citys subway system which is called the metro is an efficient way to get around town
6. a man who grew up not having to do housework is less likely to help his wife out around the house
7. to bake a cake you need to assemble the following ingredients butter sugar eggs flour baking powder salt buttermilk baking soda and vanilla
8. i asked him to leave me a copy of the report but he forgot he finally emailed it to me and i had to print out a copy
9. we went over every word of the report however we missed several errors so it didnt look very good when we gave it to the supervisor
10. she asked whether i could take over her shift on saturday night i wanted to go to jacks party so i said no

# Paragraph Writing Skills

A paragraph is a unit of discourse, the building block of meaning for documents—for essays, articles, and business and technical reports. A paragraph is defined by the space around it—in other words, it has to look like a paragraph to be a paragraph, no matter what it actually says or what the function of the paragraph is.

Readers depend on the space to see where each paragraph begins and ends. Usually, a paragraph begins with an indentation and may end in the middle of a line. In publications, the first paragraph after a title or subtitle is not generally indented (as in this book). In business writing, block style is common: paragraphs are not indented, but a blank line appears between paragraphs. Indenting the beginning of paragraphs is the most common style for student writing. Whichever style is used, it should allow the reader to distinguish the paragraphs easily.

The length of a paragraph depends on the purpose and the format of the document. Most modern writing tends to be in short paragraphs. Newspapers and magazines are printed in narrow columns, and long blocks of unbroken text are difficult to read. Modern novels have a lot of dialogue, and the convention is to start a new paragraph with each speaker. Websites also avoid long paragraphs because short blocks of text are easier to read on screen. Moreover, modern readers have a shorter attention span and so prefer shorter paragraphs. You can see much longer paragraphs in books published more than 50 years ago.

Academic writing favours longer, more structured paragraphs, as shown in the sample paragraphs and essays in this book. A single paragraph writing assignment may be 150 to 200 words, but in an essay the paragraphs tend to be about 100 words each (with the introduction and conclusion slightly shorter than the body paragraphs). In contrast, the explanation paragraphs you are reading now average 50 to 100 words. Some of the non-fiction reading selections in Part 2 have even shorter paragraphs because the articles were originally published in newspapers and magazines.

A paragraph is a unit of meaning, as is a sentence. Each paragraph puts forth an idea and supports it. What is in a paragraph depends on the function it serves. It may introduce or conclude an essay or provide a transition between sections of a long essay. It may be a definition, description, or comparison.

Most academic-style paragraphs start with a topic sentence, which introduces the main idea. The rest of the paragraph is essentially composed of arguments supporting the idea in the topic sentence, with supporting details supplied to prove those arguments.

This unit isolates the paragraph as a writing assignment. Many writing courses focus on paragraph structure first before moving onto essay writing. If your course focuses on the essay, it is still important to review the basics of paragraph structure in this unit.

---

To make sure your paragraphs are identifiable as paragraphs, indent the beginning of the first sentence by five spaces (half an inch—one default tab space). For handwritten essays, indent each paragraph about one to two inches.

---

## Writing Independent Paragraphs

Sometimes students are required to write single, expository paragraphs for assignments. These independent paragraphs tend to be longer than the paragraphs that would appear in an essay or report. The stand-alone expository paragraph may have 8 to 12 sentences and range from about 150 to 200 words. These paragraphs begin with a topic sentence, have two to four supported points, and end with a concluding sentence. In essence, they are a shorter version of an essay, and they allow students to practise the basics of making arguments and supporting them before moving on to the complexity of a longer piece of writing.

Here is a typical outline for an independent, developed paragraph:

Topic sentence, giving the main idea
  Elaboration of topic sentence (if necessary)

Point 1
  Support for Point 1 (explanation, example, illustration)

Point 2
  Support for Point 2 (explanation, example, illustration)

Point 3
  Support for Point 3 (explanation, example, illustration)

Concluding sentence

This is not the only way to develop an independent paragraph, but it is one way that will lead you to success and help you to build your essay-writing skills. This pattern of development can also be applied to body paragraphs of an essay.

Here are examples of developed paragraphs following this pattern. The word count is included to show you typical length. Note that the first paragraph has an elaboration sentence and four points. The second and third sample paragraphs are different viewpoints on the same subject; note how the opposing arguments are presented.

Assignment prompt: *What is the value of taking notes in school?*

> Students should take notes when they are attending lectures or reading. Note-taking is a skill they can develop in their high school years and is especially vital in college and university. First, by the very act of writing, they are engaging in active, not just passive, learning. Research has shown that students retain less if they only listen or read, but by writing and talking about the material, they retain it better because these actions require more of the brain. Second, note-taking forces students to process the information. Because they cannot write down every word, they have to choose the most important points, paraphrase, and summarize information. Even if the notes are lost, the action of note-taking means that the material is better understood and more firmly fixed in the brain. In addition, college and university classes rely on the lecture to transmit information. The professor might have a different take on the subject from the one offered in the textbook and only explain it in class. Finally, students can use the notes they have taken for review for tests and exams. It is easier to reread notes than to reread the whole textbook. Thus, note-taking is a valuable practice for students. [202 words]

Assignment prompt: *Should cursive still be taught in school? ["no" answer]*

> It is not surprising that handwriting has been dropped from many elementary school curricula. One reason is that cursive is difficult to master. Many schoolchildren, especially those who are left-handed, can only produce a nearly illegible scrawl nowhere near the model handwriting they are copying. Writing by hand is so torturous that students in the past were given lines to write as punishment for bad behaviour. Second, learning to write takes hours of practice. These precious hours of school time could be used for something else, such as math, reading, and physical education. Most important, widespread use of computers has displaced most of the reasons to write by hand. Students can type on a keyboard, or even speak out loud, and end up with a neat and legible product. With laptops, tablets, and smartphones, students always have an input device close at hand. Even the need for a signature is disappearing as biometric data such as thumbprints will soon be widely used to identify people. Writing by hand is another old-fashioned skill that has justly met its end. [178 words]

Assignment prompt: *Should cursive still be taught in school? ["yes" answer]*

> Despite the growing use of communication technology, elementary school teachers should not give up teaching students to write in cursive. First, writing by hand is good physical and mental exercise. Children

develop fine motor skills by using a pen. It is also a calming exercise—people doodle to help them think, for instance. Writing by hand fires up different parts of the brain than typing does. For instance, students develop the rhythm and muscle memory that helps them to remember the spelling of words through the flow of one letter to the next. Taking lecture notes by hand helps people remember the material better. In addition, people have more of a connection with documents that are produced by hand. Handwriting is personal, individual, and artistic. These qualities make a handwritten letter more special than any electronic message. Finally, despite the proliferation of electronic devices, cursive is still useful. A signature is still called for on legal documents. Moreover, students often have to write tests and exams by hand, and cursive is much faster to produce than printing. Students who do not learn to write handwriting also cannot read it, leaving inaccessible many documents, both historical and personal ones, such as their grandparents' letters. For these reasons, handwriting is vital, not a relic that should be tossed. [216 words]

## Writing Topic Sentences

In academic writing, the topic sentence is generally the first sentence of the paragraph. A topic sentence states a supportable idea that can be explained and explored in the rest of the paragraph. All the other sentences in that paragraph relate to the topic sentence; these sentences are more specific than the topic sentence, which is quite general.

Topic sentences are particularly important in expository paragraphs that argue or explain an idea. In essays, they are found in the body paragraphs but not in the introduction or conclusion. Note too that narrative paragraphs and process descriptions may open with the first event or step, so they might not have a topic sentence introducing the paragraph. In an essay, the topic sentences of the body paragraphs take their cue from the thesis statement. A good topic sentence should tell the reader what to expect in the paragraph. For example, for a paragraph that starts, "Editing is an important step in writing an essay," the reader will expect that the paragraph shows why editing is so important. The topic sentence also limits the paragraph—all the sentences should fit under the umbrella of the topic sentence. This is called unity—the paragraph should have one main idea. For example, "Students should brainstorm their topic first" would not fit in the paragraph about editing.

It is important to distinguish a topic from a topic sentence. A topic is what the paragraph is about, such as "living in residence." In a topic sentence, there is a controlling idea that says what idea the writer is going to explore about living in residence, such as "living in residence is the best choice for first-year students."

## Exercise 4.1

Consider these topic sentences, which have a different focus but on are on the same topic. Discuss how they differ and what each paragraph would say. Note when the focus is on the parents and when it is on their children.

(Note: *Empty nesters* are parents whose children have grown up and left home, and *boomerang kids* are adults who come back to live in the family home, usually after college or university graduation.)

1. Boomerang kids must make adjustments to their lifestyle in order to live with their parents.
2. Adult children who live with their parents should contribute financially to the household.
3. Adult children who still live at home must take on more responsibility for household chores.
4. Parents should treat boomerang kids as adults, not children.
5. Many college and university graduates are forced to return to their parents' home.
6. Empty nesters should downsize their homes once their children leave to prevent them from returning.

**The topic sentence**

- should be the first sentence of the paragraph
- gives the main idea of the paragraph
- is a full, grammatical sentence and not a question
- should state a supportable idea that can be explained in one paragraph
- should be in the writer's words (not repeating the wording of a topic question or quoting)
- should relate to the thesis (if it is the topic sentence of a body paragraph)

A well-written topic sentence serves as a guideline for the writer as well as the reader, so instructors generally insist that students start with a topic sentence. Practising writing topic sentences will also help students to write better thesis statements for their essays. The main difference between a thesis statement and a topic sentence is that a thesis statement gives the main idea of an essay while a topic sentence introduces just a paragraph.

Here are some examples of topic sentences for you to consider:

Assignment Prompt 1: *Choose one study skill, and explain why it is important for student success.*

| | |
|---|---|
| Students should preview textbook chapters before class. | **correct:**<br>As required by the prompt, this topic sentence identifies one study skill. The reader expects the rest of the paragraph to give reasons why this action is important. This intent would be clear even without the topic question to refer to. |
| They should preview textbook chapters before class. | **incorrect:**<br>The word *they* does not have an antecedent—that is, we do not know who *they* refers to. (Even if the paragraph is part of an essay, the topic sentence should not contain pronouns unless the antecedent is in the topic sentence itself.) |
| Students should preview textbook chapters and take notes in lectures. | **incorrect:**<br>A topic sentence should have one main idea, not two. |
| I am going to explain the importance of previewing chapters. | **incorrect:**<br>A topic sentence should not announce the main argument. |
| Students can do many things to increase their chances of success in a course. | **incorrect:**<br>This is too broad—you are not going to talk about "many things"—just one. |
| A student's life is hard. | **incorrect:**<br>This sentence is too general—it sounds as though it is introducing a topic rather than stating a main idea. |

Assignment Prompt 2: *Should fighting be banned in all levels of hockey?*

| | |
|---|---|
| Although many fans enjoy watching the fisticuffs, fights should not be allowed in hockey games. | **correct:**<br>The topic sentence clearly states the position and does not repeat the exact wording of the topic question. (Note that the first half of the sentence is a subordinate clause making a concession. See pages 83–85 and 184.) |
| Yes, fighting should be banned in hockey. | **incorrect:**<br>A topic sentence should not begin with *yes* or *no*. |
| Fighting should be allowed in hockey because the fans like it. | **incorrect:**<br>Avoid using *because* in the topic sentence; the rest of your body paragraph will explain the reasons, and giving one reason in your topic sentence may limit your paragraph. |
| Hockey is the only professional sport that allows its players to fight in a game. | **incorrect:**<br>This is a fact, not a supportable idea. |
| Why should fighting be banned in hockey? | **incorrect:**<br>A topic sentence should answer the question, not pose one (or repeat the topic question). |
| Many people want to stop hockey players from fighting during games. | **incorrect:**<br>This does not give the writer's viewpoint. |
| Hockey is Canada's national game and the fans are passionate about it so they like everything, especially when the players engage in an exciting bout of fisticuffs, so hockey should stay the way it is and keep fighting allowed. | **incorrect:**<br>This is an overloaded topic sentence. |

## Exercise 4.2

Here are three prompts for paragraph-writing assignments. For each prompt, consider each of the five options given for possible topic sentences. Explain why each sentence would work or would not work to begin a paragraph answer.

1. How should young adults deal with overprotective parents?
   a) There are many ways young adults could try dealing with their overprotective parents.

b) Young adults need to prove that they are responsible.

c) These days, young adults and parents seem to have many issues.

d) Many parents are too worried about their children and want to protect them in every situation.

e) No matter the age, parents will always be protective of their children.

2. Why is it important for students to prepare for lectures?

a) It is important for students to prepare for lectures.

b) Students can do many things to prepare for lectures.

c) Students can read ahead to prepare for lectures.

d) Why is it important for students to prepare for lectures?

e) By reading ahead to prepare, students can understand lectures more easily.

3. Should employees be allowed to bring dogs into the workplace?

a) Dogs are very important to humans.

b) It depends on the workplace.

c) Just as dogs have earned a place in people's homes, dogs should be welcomed in some workplaces.

d) I think dogs should be allowed in the workplace.

e) No, dogs do not belong in the workplace.

## Making Points

The topic sentence introduces the main idea that is being put forth in the paragraph. That main idea is argued with several points. In the paragraph below, three points (marked in boldface) support the idea that teenagers make a profitable movie audience:

> Teenagers are the most desirable market for movie producers. They are more likely than any other age group to spend their entertainment dollar on the cinema. **First, teenagers go to the movies as their main social activity.** They are old enough to go out on their own but too young for other social activities such as bar-hopping. They even go to see movies they are not that interested in simply because their friends are going, and they might see a movie more than once. **Moreover, teenagers prefer the theatre as a more enjoyable environment for movies.** They get out from under their parents' watchful eyes and appreciate the full effects of a large screen and superior sound system. Their parents, on the other hand, often prefer to cocoon at home and wait for the DVD. **Finally, teenagers have disposable income to spend at the cinema.** They often have allowances and part-time jobs but do not have to pay rent or tuition, unlike college and university students. It is not surprising that so many movies today are aimed at teenagers' tastes.

The points made should relate directly to the topic sentence and should have the same focus. The points should be supportable yet more specific than the topic sentence. For example, for the topic sentence "Part-time jobs can be very beneficial to students," your points should say **why** part-time jobs are good and should focus on the students' point of view, not the employers' or the parents'. Here are some examples of sentences created as points for a topic sentence for you to consider:

Topic sentence: *Part-time jobs can be very beneficial to students.*

a) Students generally work at low-wage jobs as servers in restaurants.

**incorrect:**
This does not show a benefit for students.

b) Students can gain many benefits from part-time jobs.

**incorrect:**
This does not make a point; it just repeats the main idea of the topic sentence.

c) Employers can pay students less money.

**incorrect:**
This is a benefit for employers, not students.

d) Students can develop good work habits.

**correct:**
This is a benefit for students.

e) Students have to learn to manage their time efficiently to balance both work and school.

**incorrect:**
This is a requirement, not a benefit. (Note, however, that a rewording would give a benefit, using "to balance both work and school": "Students learn valuable time management skills when they have to balance both work and school.")

f) Part-time jobs are an important source of income for students.

**correct:**
This is a benefit for students.

g) Handling customers is an important part of many entry jobs.

**incorrect:**
Though related to a benefit (students can learn people skills by handling customers), it is not the actual benefit.

h) Students eventually have to enter the work world.

**incorrect:**
This does not show the connection to part-time jobs.

i) Students who work develop useful skills.

**correct:**
This is a benefit for students.

j) It is difficult for students to afford tuition and the cost of living.

**incorrect:**
Though this shows the reason why students need money, it does not focus on the benefits of working.

### Exercise 4.3

For the following topic sentence, choose three sentences that would make the best points for that paragraph:

Cooking a meal from scratch is a worthwhile skill to acquire.
- a) Cooking is a lost skill.
- b) Home-cooked meals are more nutritious.
- c) People eat too much junk food.
- d) Cooking at home is less expensive than eating out.
- e) Many prepared foods are available in grocery stores.
- f) Cooking is useful for entertaining and impressing guests.
- g) Cooking is not very difficult to learn.
- h) Cooking at home is very important.

## Supporting Points

When you make a point, you have to support it. Support means giving the reader examples or explanations to make that point clear and to convince the reader of its validity. The supporting sentences are more specific than the point they are supporting. Note that restating a point is not supporting it.

Point: *Documents must be written for the intended audience.*

| Supporting Sentence | Type of Support |
| --- | --- |
| The level of vocabulary and the background given should reflect the knowledge the proposed reader has about the subject. | an explanation |
| For example, a computer user manual should have simple instructions with no jargon. | an example |

It is important that you give specific support and not make general statements as shown in the next example:

Assignment prompt: *What is the best sport to watch in the Winter Olympics?*

| | |
| --- | --- |
| Hockey is the best sport to watch in the winter Olympics. First, it is very exciting. The action is fast-paced. Fans can watch what is happening and be very entertained. Second, it is a surprise as to who will win. Fans watch because the game could have any outcome. They do not know who will eventually win the game. Finally, hockey players are athletes playing at the top of their game. They have trained for many years, and they have many skills. It is exciting to watch skilled athletes. For these reasons, hockey is the not-to-be-missed event of the Olympics. | This paragraph has weak support because it is too general. The statements could apply to most sports, not just hockey. |

Of all the impressive athletic contests that people can watch at the Winter Olympics, hockey is the one that most deserves viewers' attention. First, hockey is exciting because of its speed. Skaters can move faster than runners. A constant turnover of players as lines change on the fly means that the players are ready to go at full tilt. The puck shot across the ice can travel at 90 kilometres an hour—as fast as a car going down a highway. The speed of the game also means that players have to have quick reflexes. The audience has to pay attention to see all the action. Most important, hockey is a community-building sport. All Canadians have a patriotic duty to support their hockey team because it is our national sport. Canadians gather in sports bars, community centres, and schools to watch their team play. No contest is viewed more than the gold medal hockey game.

*This paragraph is better because the support is more specific to hockey.*

Note how the structure of a paragraph moves from general to specific. The topic sentence is general, the points are more specific, and the support given is more specific still. Study this example:

For the topic sentence "Canadians can reduce the amount of garbage going into landfills," here are three possible points:

1. They can reduce what they bring home.
2. They can find other uses for what they no longer need.
3. They can use recycling facilities.

In a developed paragraph, points such as these generally have from one to three sentences in support. For this example on the environment, a reader would expect that each of these three points be followed by statements that explain how Canadians can do this. Discuss how this is accomplished in the following deconstructed paragraph:

Topic sentence: *Environmentally conscious Canadians can reduce the amount of garbage going into landfills.*

Point #1:  First, they can shop wisely to buy less.
    a) They do not need to replace functional electronics, clothing, and furniture simply because they are not the latest style.
    b) They can choose products with less packaging, such as bulk food items.

Point #2:  Canadians can also find other uses for what they no longer need.
    a) For example, they can donate used clothing to thrift shops.
    b) If they are handy, they can refurbish furniture.

Point #3:  Finally, Canadians can use recycling facilities offered by their municipality.
    a) They can make sure that cans and bottles are placed in designated bins.
    b) In addition, they should separate recyclable paper and cardboard in their garbage collection.

Concluding sentence: All Canadians must do their part to protect the environment.

**Activity**

In small groups, come up with another supporting statement for each of the three points in the paragraph outline above.

---

### Exercise 4.4

Below is a topic sentence, followed by three points. After each point is a selection of sentences (labelled a, b, and c) written to support the point. Choose the sentence or group of sentences that makes the best support for each point:

Topic sentence: *Punctuality is important to success in college.*

1. First, when students arrive on time for class, they create a good impression.
   a) They are less likely to miss important information and tests, and so their marks will be higher.
   b) They impress the teacher. The teacher will be quite satisfied with the impression the students make.
   c) They show that they are interested in the class and are prepared to work hard. Teachers are more likely to give breaks to such hardworking students.

2. In addition, students who are late often miss important information.
   a) A lot of important information is given at the beginning of class, and latecomers will lose out. That will result in a lower mark.
   b) For example, they may not get the feedback from the last assignment, which is often handed back first in class. They will also miss the explanation for that day's lesson.
   c) Sometimes there is a pop quiz at the beginning of class. Latecomers who miss it will get a mark of zero.

3. Finally, late students miss out on time given for tests and assignments.
   a) They show that they don't care about the test, so the instructor is less likely to take their work seriously.
   b) These students get a lower mark if they do not complete a test. Sometimes they might even miss a test entirely since pop quizzes are often given at the beginning of class.
   c) Tests are very important, and students need to pass these tests to pass the course. Every test mark counts and can make the difference between passing and failing the course.

## Exercise 4.5

Academic writing usually moves from general to more specific statements. Pick the most general from the following statements:

1.  a) College students do not have parents shepherding them through their schedules.
    b) College students have to become self-sufficient when they strike out on their own.
    c) College students have to prepare their own meals.
    d) College students have to be responsible for rent, utilities, and transportation.

2.  a) She won our neighbourhood Monopoly challenge.
    b) She is good at all sorts of games.
    c) She cleaned us all out in poker last night.
    d) She was always the leader of the children in the playground.

3.  a) Smoking impairs your ability to breathe.
    b) Smoking is bad for your health.
    c) Smoking can lead to lung disease.
    d) Smoking makes your breath stink.

4.  a) Contract work can lead to abuse of workers.
    b) Contract workers often receive no benefits.
    c) Contract workers have no job stability.
    d) Contract workers get paid less for the same work.

5.  a) Some people put clothes on their pets.
    b) Some people sleep with their pets.
    c) Some people treat their pets like people.
    d) Some people pamper pets with spa treatments or doggie daycare.

## Exercise 4.6

For the following selection of points, determine whether the choices given are examples of good support or poor support, and explain why. For instance, an example or explanation is good support, whereas a repetition of the idea or a sentence that goes off-topic does not work as support.

1.  Some tattoos are memorials.
    a) A person may get a tattoo with the name of a friend, family member, or pet who has died.
    b) Some people get a tattoo representing their favourite sports team.
    c) Tattoos can be very beautiful artwork.
    d) Tattoos are permanent.

2. One advantage of destination weddings is that the couple and the guests get a vacation.
   a) They could spend a week at a luxury resort on a Caribbean island.
   b) Destination weddings also limit the number of guests that can attend.
   c) The wedding participants can enjoy a holiday away from home.
   d) Some people prefer destination weddings as something different.

3. Improving public transit benefits society as a whole.
   a) Less polluting exhaust is produced by buses or trains than by individual vehicles.
   b) Everybody can benefit from more buses and trains.
   c) More efficient transit means that people waste less of their workday sitting in traffic jams.
   d) The benefits not only accrue to transit users themselves but also to their employers and their families and to those who commute by car.

4. Although intern positions are supposed to help young people enter the workforce in their field, unpaid internships are not as beneficial as they are considered to be.
   a) Many employers take advantage of the system and use interns as unpaid labour.
   b) With so many interns and so few jobs, the odds of getting a paid position are not good.
   c) Many graduates take internships to gain experience in their field.
   d) Unpaid internships do not benefit young people even though they are supposed to be an entry into a good job.

---

### Exercise 4.7

In pairs or small groups, write one or two sentences to support each of these general statements. Compare your answers with your classmates':

1. Students need good study habits to succeed in college. (What habits?)
2. Job candidates need to prepare for an interview. (How?)
3. Hiking in the wilderness can be dangerous. (Why?)
4. Board games can teach children valuable skills. (What skills?)
5. Students can furnish their first apartment very cheaply. (How?)

## Giving Examples

Examples make good support for points because they make it easy for your reader to see what you mean. However, sometimes students struggle using examples effectively in paragraphs. Many students have three common problems: not making the example specific enough, misusing the words and expressions that indicate examples, and dragging out an example into a story.

UNIT 4: PARAGRAPH WRITING SKILLS

## Specific Examples

A good example is specific, not general. Study these sentences:

| | |
|---|---|
| Exercise can be incorporated into everyday activities. For instance, people can take the stairs instead of the elevator. | **correct:** The second sentence gives an example of a specific activity—taking the stairs. |
| The story of Laura Secord warning the British troops of an American attack includes many myths. For example, one version says she led a cow through the swamp. | **correct:** The second sentence gives an example of a myth—that she led a cow. |
| Swimming has many physical benefits. For example, swimmers get exercise. | **incorrect:** This example (getting exercise) is too general. |
| Swimming has many physical benefits. For example, swimmers enjoy full body movement without putting pressure on their joints. | **correct:** This example is more specific. |
| In order to succeed, salespeople must be outgoing. For example, they cannot be shy. | **incorrect:** Instead of actually giving an example, the sentence repeats the same idea in different words. |

## The Language of Examples

The transition signals *for example* and *for instance* are generally used to introduce a sentence example. The two expressions mean essentially the same thing and so are usually interchangeable. They usually appear at the beginning of the sentence, but they can be in the middle or at the end:

> People can cut down on unnecessary trips with their vehicles. For example, they can walk or bicycle to the corner store.

> Students can build their reading skills gradually. They can read children's books, for instance, to develop their abilities with simpler vocabulary and sentence structure.

Make sure you have a complete sentence:

| | |
|---|---|
| Children learn many useful skills when they play board games. For example, counting skills. | **incorrect:** This is a sentence fragment. |
| Children learn many useful skills when they play board games. For example, they practise counting. | **correct:** This is a full sentence. |

You can also use *example* as a noun:

> The homeowners came across several setbacks as they were finishing their basement. One example was the leak they uncovered in the back of the house.

If you are giving a list of examples within a sentence, use the verb *include* or the phrase *such as*:

> My courses this semester include biology, psychology, and chemistry.
> I like to play team sports, such as baseball and hockey.

Both *include* and *such as* tell the reader that these are only some of the examples, so do not end the sentence with *and so on*, *etc.*, or an ellipsis (. . .). (Note that the comma appears before *such as*, not after.)

Finally, do not use abbreviations such as *e.g.*, *i.e.*, and *etc.* in your paragraphs and essays. These abbreviations are useful for note-taking but are not suitable in academic writing.

## Avoiding Narrative Examples

A common writing problem among students is launching into a drawn-out story of a real or hypothetical person when they want to give an example to support a point. This use of narrative in examples leads to wordiness and distracts from the main point:

> People who live in a messy environment have many problems. One of them is wasting time looking for things that are misplaced. For example, Tom has a job interview. As he is getting ready, he starts looking for a clean white shirt and a copy of his resumé. He digs through all his stuff at home but without any success. As a result, he loses time and arrives at the interview too late. Thus, he lost a good chance to get a good job.

**incorrect:**
Five sentences are used to give the example about Tom—the reader will lose track of the main point.

> People who live in a messy environment have many problems. One of them is wasting time looking for things that are misplaced. For example, a job candidate who arrives late for his interview because he could not find a clean shirt may lose his chance at the job.

**correct:**
This example is given in one sentence.

To avoid giving narrative examples, try to give your example in one sentence (usually a complex sentence), and focus on the important information that relates to the point you are making.

You can practise rewriting narrative examples in Exercise 7.22 on page 225.

## Writing Concluding Sentences

If you are writing a single-paragraph writing assignment, your paragraph should have a concluding sentence to tie it all up. Generally, the concluding sentence echoes the topic sentence—giving essentially the same main idea but not repeating it in the same words. (Note that in an essay or report, a body paragraph does not necessarily need to be wrapped up in a concluding sentence; shorter paragraphs do not need a concluding sentence because the topic sentence is probably still fresh in the reader's mind.)

Note the concluding sentence at the end of the following stand-alone paragraph:

> Although working part-time can create a serious time crunch, high school students should consider the many advantages of having a job. The most important consideration is the money. The cost of such desired items as a cellphone or designer clothing can exceed a teenager's allowance. More important, however, many students must start saving for their post-secondary education. In addition, part-time jobs give students a taste of the working world. With this taste, they can find out what jobs suit their personality and talents. For instance, they can learn whether they like dealing with the public. They also learn how hard it is to work, especially in minimum-wage jobs. This gives them a greater appreciation for the work itself and for the education required to get a better job. Finally, in the workplace students gain valuable skills. These skills include practical ones, such as working with cash or answering the telephone, and soft skills, such as communication strategies and working as a team. **Therefore, students who can handle the load should work part-time to reap the many benefits of a job**.

**Activity**

Examine the concluding sentences in the sample paragraphs in this unit. Consider how they differ from the topic sentences.

## Exercise 4.8

Here are six topic sentences, some of which are from previous exercises in this unit. Write a concluding sentence that could complete the paragraph. Use the same basic idea as in the topic sentence, but do not use the same wording.

1. Punctuality is important to success in college.

2. Adult children who live with their parents should contribute financially to the household.

3. Students should preview textbook chapters before class.

4. Survival swimming skills should be taught to all children.

5. Cooking a meal from scratch is a worthwhile skill to acquire.

6. The weather is a safe topic of conversation for small talk.

## Achieving Unity

A paragraph should have unity—it should have one main idea. The topic sentence sets out this main idea, and all the other sentences should fit under the umbrella of the topic sentence. For example, a paragraph that begins "Part-time jobs can be very beneficial to students" should only have sentences that explain why part-time jobs are good for students. It should not contain sentences that give the disadvantages of working or explain how to find a job.

### Exercise 4.9

Identify the two sentences that do not fit in this paragraph:

> ESL students can benefit from reading children's fairy tales. First, reading is the best way to improve general language skills because it exposes students to both language and ideas. The simpler vocabulary and sentence structure of children's books make them accessible to ESL students and allow them to build their reading skills gradually. Modern novels are also good reading practice because students have to follow a complex plot with a variety of characters. Second, fairy tales are part of the culture, and ESL students need to be familiar with these stories to understand references in film and other literature. For example, psychology books may refer to a person exhibiting a Cinderella complex. The characters are well known and can appear in movies, in modern novels, or even in newspaper articles. For instance, a politician's situation might be described as "the emperor's new clothes," a reference to a story by Hans Christian Andersen. Andersen was a Dane who had an unhappy childhood but gained a measure of fame with the stories he wrote. Furthermore, the fantastical worlds of magic, witches, and elves can be entertaining. The popularity of these tales has survived over centuries to modern incarnations such as the Harry Potter books. Rather than dismissing fairy tales as juvenile reading, ESL students should seek them out as supplemental reading.

### Exercise 4.10

Choose which of these 12 sentences would fit under this topic sentence:

Topic sentence: *The economics of professional sport is detrimental to the fan base.*

1. Games often start later in the evening so that they can be broadcast in the more lucrative prime-time spots even though that is often too late for younger viewers.

2.  Violence should be better controlled in games so that it does not set a bad example for children.

3.  Amateur athletes are struggling to survive on very little money.

4.  Free agents switch teams as they chase bigger salaries, so fans have trouble staying loyal to certain players.

5.  Games are paused so that broadcasters can insert commercial breaks.

6.  Professional athletes often sign multi-million-dollar endorsement contracts.

7.  High salaries of players are often reflected in higher ticket prices.

8.  Athletes demand higher salaries not because they need the money but because it is part of a competition—the best-paid athlete is considered the best athlete.

9.  Games are less interesting to watch when the team with all the high-priced talent is generally the one that wins.

10. Fans of small-market teams are often in danger of losing their teams to bigger cities.

11. Expansion of leagues requires more players, diluting the talent pool.

12. Only billionaires can afford to buy sports franchises.

## Using Transition Signals

Writers need to help readers follow the development of their ideas. To this end, they use transition markers or signals—words and expressions that introduce a sentence to show how the sentence relates to other sentences.

For example, a phrase such as *for example* tells readers that the sentence is an example of the point made in the previous sentence. Just as signals on a car tell the drivers behind where the driver is going, the signals in a paragraph tell readers where the ideas are going so they can follow them.

Common transition signals

**Addition:** also, finally, first, furthermore, in addition, moreover, next, second

**Cause and effect:** accordingly, as a result, consequently, therefore, thus

**Comparison:** likewise, similarly

**Contrast:** however, in contrast, instead, nevertheless, on the contrary, on the other hand, otherwise

**Emphasis or clarity:** in fact, indeed, in other words, of course, that is

**Special features or examples:** for example, for instance, in particular, mainly, specifically

**Summary:** in brief, in closing, in conclusion, in short, on the whole, to conclude, to summarize

**Time relations:** afterwards, at that time, earlier, in the meantime, lately, later, meanwhile, now, then

Most of these expressions function as adverbs and are sometimes called conjunctive adverbs or adverbial connectors. It is important to distinguish them from conjunctions such as *although* and *but* so that you join sentences correctly. (This grammar point is discussed in Writing Adverb Clauses in Unit 3.)

Here are some examples of transition signals at work. Note that in the following pairs of sentences, the second pair includes a transition signal making it easier to follow the meaning:

1.  a)  I went through the paper files to scan the older documents into the system. I weeded out the out-of-date papers and checked the accuracy of the information in the system.

1.  b)  I went through the paper files to scan the older documents into the system. At the same time, I weeded out the out-of-date papers and checked the accuracy of the information in the system.

2.  a)  Essay writing helps students to develop their thinking skills. They have to understand the relationship between a general idea and a specific example.

2.  b)  Essay writing helps students to develop their thinking skills. For instance, they have to understand the relationship between a general idea and a specific example.

3.  a)  Smokers should have the right to decide whether they poison their own bodies or not. They cannot make that choice for the others whom they affect with second-hand smoke.

3.  b)  Smokers should have the right to decide whether they poison their own bodies or not. However, they cannot make that choice for the others whom they affect with second-hand smoke.

## Exercise 4.11

Write an appropriate transition signal in each blank:

1.  Computer games can give children an opportunity to exercise their problem-solving skills. _____, in a strategy game, children have to work through different scenarios to make the most advantageous move.

2.  Many drivers exhibit unnecessary aggressive behaviour on the highway. Some tailgate trying to make other drivers speed up or move out of the way. _____, some drivers weave in and out of lanes looking for any space to advance.

3.  Disney movies often have "happily ever after" endings even when the source material is a tragedy. _____, in the Hans Christian Andersen story "The Little Mermaid," the mermaid dies at the end, while in the Disney cartoon she marries the prince.

4.  We worked together to paint the room efficiently: Jack used the roller to cover the large surfaces. _____ I used a brush to cut in around the trim and the corners.

5.  I missed the class when our instructor taught us how to do a summary. _____, I did not do well on the summary test.

6. The Canadian team was considered a favourite for the championship. _____, the odds changed when a few of the top players were injured.

7. The United States is the most powerful country in the world. _____, it is understandable that many underdog countries feel resentment toward Americans.

8. Many parents solve their children's problems, which does not help their children's self-confidence. _____, when the children grow up, they depend on other people to solve their problems.

9. A post-secondary education costs students thousands of dollars. _____, graduates can expect greater income.

10. Reading children's books is good reading practice because the stories have simpler ideas, structures, and vocabulary. _____, children's books teach about the culture.

11. First, he went to the bank to withdraw some cash. _____ he went to bargain with the person selling the bike.

12. Modern technology is supposed to improve communication between people. _____, people tend to email strangers across the world rather than actually talk to their next-door neighbour.

13. People sleep better if they wind down before they go to bed. _____, instead of watching television or using the computer, they should read or listen to restful music.

14. In an ice hockey game, five players try to shoot a rubber puck into a goal net against a goaltender. _____, ringette has five players on the ice with a goaltender. _____, ringette is played with a straight stick and a rubber ring.

## Achieving Coherence

The sentences in a paragraph must fit together in a logical, coherent manner. The word *cohere* means "to stick together."

Readers can follow a paragraph better when the ideas are in an order they are familiar with. For instance, a paragraph describing the history of something would most likely be in chronological order. Subtopics should be dealt with one at a time. For example, in the paragraph on the benefits of part-time jobs on page 117, both financial reasons are dealt with together, at the beginning.

Another way to achieve coherence is through the use of transition signals, like *for example* and *in addition*. The use of these signals was shown in the previous section.

In addition, pronouns refer to a specific noun and help to link sentences:

> Andrew had to get his project approved. It [refers to the project] was an orientation film in which he [Andrew] needed to interview first-year students. They [the students] would discuss the problems they had faced.

Demonstrative pronouns (such as *this* and *these*) also help to link sentences:

> Fairy tales, folk tales, and myths are important parts of children's books. **These stories** teach a cultural heritage that is built upon in other kinds of literature.

Remember that in English, an indefinite article is usually used the first time something is mentioned, and then a definite article is used thereafter. This grammatical structure also helps readers follow the ideas:

> We wrote **a report** at the end of our project. **The report** summarized our problems and how we overcame them.

Repeating key words, or using synonyms to refer to them, is another way to ensure coherence in a paragraph:

> Luxury **cars** are a waste of money. While these **vehicles** are comfortable and well made, they are too expensive to purchase, maintain, and insure. Drivers really just need a car to get them safely from point A to point B. The powerful engine of a **luxury automobile** is useless when a driver is stuck in a traffic jam or restricted by speed limits.

---

**How coherence is achieved**

- in the order of the sentences
- by the use of transition signals to show the reader how the ideas connect
- by the use of pronouns to refer back to nouns in a previous sentence
- through the repetition of words and ideas

---

## Studying Sample Paragraphs

Examine the paragraphs below, reviewing the features of a good paragraph as you read. Compare the topic sentence and concluding sentence of each. Identify the points made to prove the main idea and the specific examples or explanations used to support the points. Identify transition signals and other methods used to achieve coherence.

### Sample Paragraph: Choosing a College Program

*Should students choose a college program based on what they like to do or on what they think will get them a job?*

> Students who enrol in college should choose a career path based on their own interests and talents rather than on a job's earning potential. One reason is that people spend a large part of their lives at work, and it is wrong to waste precious hours of life doing something they do not enjoy. Second, if they choose a career in an area where they are talented, they will probably achieve more. For example, an accountant who wishes she had followed her passion for music will probably not be as successful in her job as someone who actually enjoys working with numbers. Finally, the job market

is unpredictable. For example, a diploma in computer programming used to be considered a guaranteed ticket to economic success, but with the high-tech bust, many programmers found themselves unemployed and forced to reinvent themselves in other fields. Thus, high school graduates should follow their passions when they choose a career.

## Sample Paragraphs: English Names

The following two paragraphs on English names have different purposes and styles. The first is cause/effect, explaining reasons. The second is a process paragraph; it explains how to do something. Note that this paragraph uses *you* because it addresses readers directly. It is not a general *you* referring to all people.

Assignment 1. *Why do Chinese students often adopt English nicknames?*

Choosing an English nickname is a common practice among Chinese students. This practice starts as a fun activity in class, often initiated by their teachers. However, the students may go on to use this name in their dealings with English-speaking people, whether in business, travel, further studies, or eventual emigration. While many immigrants are reluctant to anglicize their names, the Chinese are used to being called by different nicknames rather than their official given names. Therefore, they do not see adopting a nickname as losing their identity—just as adopting yet another one. Moreover, they find an English name practical when they move to countries such as Canada. English speakers generally find Chinese names more difficult to pronounce and remember than names from other languages. Chinese students and immigrants may decide it is easier to adopt a new given name than to hear their name regularly mangled. It is important, therefore, to make a wise selection so that the name is suitable for use in the future.

Assignment 2. *In a paragraph, give advice to someone choosing an English name.*

If you decide to choose an English name, it is important to choose a suitable one. The most important criterion is the sound of the name. Ideally, your new name should share some sounds with your actual given name, such as "Julia" for "Jun-Lu." Most important, the sounds should be ones that come across clearly when you pronounce them. Avoid difficult sounds in English, such as the "th" sound. Two-syllable words are easier to hear than monosyllables, so "Jason" comes across more clearly than "Fred." Because the name is supposed to make your life easier, stick to fairly common given names. Search online baby name sites, which give information such as the popularity of names over time. For instance, old-fashioned names like Ethel and Wilbur would sound out of place today. Finally, choose a name for its practicality. You may be attracted by what the name means or the fact that it is the name of your favourite movie character, but you may have to say and answer to your English given name every day. Having a name such as "Money" and "Bambi" will not make it easier for a person to fit in. Choosing an English name requires thought and research—and many second opinions, so try out your name with English native speakers before you settle on it.

## Sample Paragraphs: Family Dinner

The following paragraphs are all on the same topic—the family meal. Read the paragraphs, and examine the structure and language of each paragraph. Look at the main idea in the topic sentence, and identify the points made and the supporting sentences. Determine the approach of each paragraph. For example, is the paragraph discussing causes, effects, or solutions? Is it descriptive? Is it a comparison? Does it describe a process? Determine the style of each paragraph—is it personal, conversational, or academic?

Compare Paragraphs A to F. See how the same information can be given differently for a different purpose. You can also compare these paragraphs to an essay on the same topic on pages 150–51.

With a partner or in a small group, write a possible topic question for each paragraph. You have to imagine what question would have generated the paragraph—in essence, you are working backwards by extrapolating the question from the paragraph.

### Paragraph A

The shared family meal is yet another casualty of the hectic modern lifestyle. We do not take the time to sit down to dinner together. One reason is our complicated schedules. Children's after-school and evening hours are filled with sports and music lessons. When they reach the teenage years, these activities are replaced by part-time jobs. Parents not only work long hours, but their return home may be delayed because of a long commute. As a result, family members often eat separately. Moreover, a sit-down meal requires time to prepare and to consume. People do not want to devote that much time to what they consider a simple act of fuelling their bodies. Finally, many lack the culinary skills to make nutritious and appealing meals. They rely on restaurant take-out and processed foods from the supermarket. It is not surprising that suppliers of ready-to-eat food are doing such good business, and it does not look as though this trend will reverse itself any time soon. Family dining is obviously a thing of the past.

### Paragraph B

As our family sat down to Thanksgiving dinner, I enjoyed the sight of the gathering of the clan for the traditional meal. The whole extended family, all 17 of us, came dressed in Sunday best. My grandfather sported his favourite bowtie, and the younger girl cousins had new dresses to show off. The main table was set with the best linen, china, and crystal, and the centrepiece of gourds and autumn foliage proclaimed the season. The children's table was at the end of the formal dining table, but it looked festive even with the orange polyester tablecloth and everyday dishes. After saying grace, we passed the dishes around the table. Everyone had contributed to the meal: Grandma had cooked the turkey, and Grandpa had carved it. Uncle Garth had brought his special wild cranberry sauce. Aunt Judy's vegetable medley tempted even the most determined of broccoli haters. My mother's pumpkin pie topped with dollops of whipped cream was the traditional dessert. It was a scene played out every year, but I never got tired of it.

## Paragraph C

A shared meal is an important family ritual, worth nurturing and keeping alive even in the fast-paced lives of the twenty-first century. First, families who take the time to dine together are generally eating healthier foods. They are not gobbling down a slice of pizza before running off to a night class or music lesson. Families who value mealtime usually take care with the food itself—making sure it is nutritious and tasty. In addition, the family meal is an opportunity for learning. Children can help to prepare and serve the meal, thus acquiring practical cooking skills. They can also learn social skills, such as proper table etiquette, that will serve them well in their future business lunches. Finally, a family meal is above all a time for family members to touch base and talk about what is happening in their daily lives. At the end of the school- and workday, the family can sit down together and share what happened that day as they eat their evening meal. Families that eat together have stronger bonds because the shared meal is a uniting element in family life.

## Paragraph D

Although experts say that the family meal fosters communication skills and intimacy, dining together does not work for all families. Some people are just not good cooks. A pizza pocket heated in the microwave may be better than what can be produced in the home kitchen. Families that lack cooking skills may also find it stressful to try to produce edible meals. In addition, having dinner together may not be worth the time and effort involved. Shopping, meal preparation, and cleaning up all take valuable time. Coordinating schedules to clear a mealtime for everyone can be impossible. Finally, many people find eating with their families stressful. Instead of casual conversation, children may be subjected to grilling—having to explain their failing grades or account for a call from their teacher. Parents may nag their children about their eating habits or their manners. The picture of the family dining together is as old-fashioned as a Norman Rockwell painting, so families should not worry too much if they cannot achieve that ideal.

## Paragraph E

Over the past three generations, the eating habits of Canadians have changed dramatically. In the past, mealtimes were generally regular, and families often sat down to share a meal together. Today's busy families rarely find the time to eat together; people grab a bite to eat when they can and often eat alone, sometimes taking their food to their bedrooms or eating in front of the TV. Instead of home-cooked meals, Canadians today eat more processed foods and restaurant meals. Supermarkets stock a variety of prepared foods—from frozen dinners to deli meals. The growth of fast-food restaurants shows how important they have become to family life. The types of foods Canadians eat have also changed because of the greater variety of ethnic food available. They used to have very conservative tastes, sticking to the food they knew from home. Now Canadians of all ethnic backgrounds consume Italian pasta, Chinese stir fry, Greek souvlaki, Thai noodles, Tex-Mex tacos, and Middle Eastern hummus. Moreover, fruits and vegetables are shipped in from all over the world, so Canadians are not restricted by what is locally in season. Our food and the way we eat it is in line with the way we prefer to live our lives.

*Paragraph F*

Even with today's hectic lifestyle, it is possible to reap the benefits of a shared family meal. First, it is important to acknowledge the importance of the family dinner and to schedule time for it. This may mean cutting down on some activities. At the very least, Sunday dinner should be set aside as family time. Second, if the meal is planned ahead of time, it will go more smoothly. The menu should be decided on, and groceries should be bought beforehand. In addition, the work should be shared. If it is up to only one person to do all the preparation, the meal does become more of a chore. Children can start helping with food preparation at a very young age—washing vegetables, for example. Working together not only lessens the workload, it allows family members to talk together and to acquire cooking skills. Furthermore, for the meal to be an important part of family life, it must be acknowledged as a time for discussion. Parents should be careful not to nag but to listen to their children's concerns. Talk about political and social issues can pass on moral values and increase awareness of current events. Proper table etiquette can be taught at the same time. Finally, the family should share cleanup responsibilities. By working, talking, and eating together, families can forge strong bonds and foster communication.

**Activity**

Here are some suggestions for paragraph-writing topics. Narrow your topic so that it will be workable in 150–200 words. Be sure to make your focus clear in your topic sentence.

1. Boomerang children (you can use the ideas from the topic sentences on page 105 or use a different focus).

2. Should children be paid for household chores? Support your answer.

3. How should adult children deal with overprotective parents?

4. Choose a skill, and explain why it is useful or why it is not. Here are some skills you could write about: playing a musical instrument, changing a tire, touch typing, mending clothing, driving a car, skating, painting walls. You can refer to the paragraphs on cursive writing (pages 103–4) as examples.

5. Choose one specific sport, and explain why it is a good sport to participate in or why it is good to watch.

6. What are the advantages or disadvantages of living in a campus residence?

7. Is shopping a good leisure activity, or is it just a chore that has to be done?

---

### Writing a developed paragraph

- Start with a topic sentence that clearly delineates the main idea of your paragraph.
- Give two to four arguments for that main idea.
- Support each argument with explanation or examples.
- Use transition signals to show the relationship between ideas.
- Write a concluding sentence for your paragraph.
- Make sure your paragraph has unity (one main idea).
- Make sure your paragraph has coherence (all the ideas flow logically from one sentence to the next).
- Check your paragraph for grammar, spelling, punctuation, and style.

# Essay Writing Skills

Essays are essentially arguments. The word *essay* comes from the French word meaning *to try*. The writer tries to show or prove something to the reader. The audience for students' essays is their professor or teacher. The purpose is purely academic; instead of giving new information (the purpose of most written communication), student essay-writers are charged with the task of showing what they have learned, synthesizing information, and explaining the thesis in a way that shows their understanding of the subject. Students are being tested on both their thinking and their communication skills, so essay-writing requires logical organization of ideas.

Even though students may never be asked to write essays outside school, the skills that are developed in essay-writing are applicable to most work communication tasks—communicating clearly, organizing ideas, and giving relevant arguments.

## Understanding Essay Structure

The essay structure often taught in school is the five-paragraph essay of about 500 words in length. It has an introduction, three body paragraphs, and a conclusion. Even though this type of essay is rarely seen outside the classroom, the form is adaptable to other kinds of writing. Business reports, for example, are longer than five paragraphs, but they too have an introduction, a body divided into different ideas, and a conclusion. Moreover, the five-paragraph essay model can be expanded by simply adding paragraphs to the three basic sections.

In a five-paragraph essay, the first paragraph is the **introduction**. It provides background for the reader, gets the reader's attention, and prepares the way for the thesis statement. The thesis gives the main argument of the essay and comes at the end of the introduction.

The thesis statement is supported in the **body paragraphs**. The arguments are divided so that each paragraph has a different main idea. The body paragraphs start with a topic sentence giving the main idea of that paragraph. A good body paragraph has support for the points made, has unity (only one main idea), is coherent (the sentences flow and follow logically), and has transition markers (to signal the relationship between ideas). These features are explained in Unit 4.

The **conclusion** generally starts with a restatement of the thesis and goes on to present a "so what?" idea to lead the reader back out of the essay. The conclusion should not provide new ideas to support the thesis. In a short essay, the conclusion should not summarize the essay: that would be too repetitive.

Sometimes this type of essay is referred to as a "hamburger essay," with the introduction and conclusion serving as the bun holding the meat of the essay (the body) together. This analogy simply tells students that the introduction and conclusion hold everything together and that the body of the essay is the most important part.

## Comparison of the Paragraph and the Essay

Unit 4 focuses on the structure of a paragraph. An independent, developed paragraph is like a mini-essay. Instructors often start by having students write paragraphs to practise the important skills of making points and supporting them before moving on to full essays. Moreover, this type of paragraph is similar to the body paragraph of an essay, so what students learn from writing a developed paragraph can be applied to essay writing.

A developed paragraph can be expanded to essay length. You need to expand on the ideas and write introductory and concluding paragraphs. Compare the independent paragraph below and the five-paragraph essay on the same topic that follows (the word counts are supplied to give you an idea of comparative length). You can consider the questions and examples that follow the essay to guide your analysis.

Topic question: *In the modern world, is cooking still an important skill?*

> Even with the wide variety of prepared foods available today, cooking is a worthwhile skill for anyone to have. The most important reason is that home-cooked foods are more nutritious than processed foods, which contain high amounts of salt, sugar, and fat. People who cook at home have control over the ingredients. They can tailor the dishes to their family's tastes and avoid allergens. Second, being able to cook is a useful social skill. Inviting friends over for dinner is a time-honoured way to entertain. In Canada, home-cooking has an added dimension when immigrants can share food from their native country with people of a different ethnic background. For example, many Canadians would enjoy trying home-cooked Chinese food, especially if all they know is the food-court version. Finally, knowing how to cook is important for self-sufficiency. As much as possible, people should be able to take care of themselves and not have to rely on others. It costs money to have others do the work, and cooking is not that difficult. People should start learning to cook when they are children, but it is never too late to start acquiring the skills required. [193 words]

### The Value of Home-Cooking

With the modern busy lifestyle, people seek to save time in meal preparation. They often eat out, whether at fast-food places or upscale restaurants. They buy prepared foods from the deli counter of the supermarket or frozen meals that just have to be warmed up in the microwave. Today it is possible to survive without knowing one end of a chef's knife from the other, so cooking is becoming a lost skill. However, the ability to prepare a home-cooked meal is a valuable skill.

The most obvious benefit of home-cooking is the ability to control the quality of the food. Processed foods contain high amounts of sugar, salt, and additives, while fast food is high in fat. Cooks choose their own raw ingredients and control the seasonings, so they can ensure freshness and make the dishes to their taste. This is especially important for people with allergies or restricted diets. Furthermore, cooks supply their own labour and can thus spend their food budget on superior ingredients. The same quality of food would not be found in most affordable restaurants.

Cooking is also a valuable social skill. Hosting a dinner party is a time-honoured method of entertaining guests. Even for casual get-togethers, it is gratifying to be able to serve food that is homemade. In the dating game, moreover, cooking is useful. It is said that the way to a man's heart is through his stomach, and women also find competence in the kitchen an attractive quality. Parents may also expect their adult children to cook well enough to contribute to holiday dinners and to carry on their family traditions. For immigrant families, preparing ethnic foods is a way to keep their native culture alive.

In addition to the social rewards, cooking has psychological benefits. People can feel personal satisfaction when they produce a delicious meal. Self-sufficiency is a goal in itself because it is humiliating to have to admit to an inability to provide the basic necessities of life. Cooks can also exercise their creativity: They can tweak recipes and even develop new flavour combinations. The simple tasks of working with food can be pleasurable, especially when people avoid modern gadgets in favour of working by hand. For example, kneading bread dough and whipping cream can relieve stress as well as give muscles a workout.

These many benefits of cooking show that it is still an important skill despite the proliferation of restaurants. Even people who grew up in homes devoid of the heady aroma of home-cooking are turning to the kitchen. The popularity of cooking shows on television, how-to videos on YouTube, and expensive, illustrated cookbooks shows that cooking is not entirely disappearing from modern life. If foodies can convert more people to the benefits of home-cooking, everyone will live better.

[462 words]

## Analyzing Essay Structure

1. Consider the thesis statement: "the ability to prepare a home-cooked meal is a valuable skill."
   - Note that the thesis is the last sentence of the introduction. It is a full sentence.
   - The adverb *however* at the beginning of the sentence links the thesis to the rest of the introduction.
   - The thesis answers the topic question ("In the modern world, is cooking still an important skill?"). The answer is essentially *yes*, and the essay explains why cooking is important. (For a yes-or-no essay question, you must choose one answer and explain the reasons for your choice.)

- Note that the thesis is similar to the topic sentence of the developed paragraph ("Even with the wide variety of prepared foods available today, cooking is a worthwhile skill for anyone to have."). A topic sentence is essentially a thesis for a paragraph, but we use the term *topic sentence* when we are discussing paragraphs.

2. Examine the introductory paragraph. It gives background for the reader by explaining why the topic is an issue at all. A hundred years ago, no one would have asked this question, because cooking was vital to everyday life. You could not readily order pizza delivery or buy frozen meals in the supermarket.

3. Note that the topic sentence of each body paragraph also answers the question, giving one reason. The topic sentence is fairly general. It tells the reader what the main idea of that particular body paragraph is. The third topic sentence ("In addition to the social rewards, cooking has psychological benefits.") starts with a transition referring to the argument of the second body paragraph (the social rewards).

4. Each body paragraph expands on the main idea given in its topic sentence. For instance, the first body paragraph explains the different nutritional benefits of home-cooking.

5. The conclusion starts with a restatement of the thesis. It goes on to consider the future by saying that the skill is being kept alive in society.

## Planning an Essay

An essay requires more planning than an independent paragraph. Writers must make sure that the essay is well balanced. For example, the three body paragraphs should be approximately the same length. Each paragraph should have different ideas with no repetition or overlap.

Writing is generally a three-stage process: planning, drafting, and editing. The planning stage includes researching, thinking about the topic, brainstorming ideas, and putting together an outline. The drafting stage is when the actual writing is done. The final stage involves rereading the draft, revising, editing, proofreading, and correcting. However, writing does not always proceed in such a clear-cut way. For instance, writers may revisit the outline once they start writing because they think of a better way to organize it. People who compose on a computer may find they move between the three stages, adding ideas and editing as they write.

Students often spend too little time in the first and third stages; they rush to get words on paper without thinking about how they want to develop their ideas, and they are too easily satisfied with what they have written, reluctant to delete sections that do not work or to proofread carefully to catch mistakes. Granted, students are often put into writing situations in which they do not have the luxury of time to plan or edit. If they are required to write a 500-word essay in an hour, they must concentrate on getting words down as quickly as possible. However, if they have practised writing an essay with the three stages, they can work more efficiently when they are under tight time constraints.

## Choosing a Topic

The first step is choosing a topic. Usually, teachers give their class a choice of topics, perhaps related to assigned readings or current events. Often, the topics are discussed in class before students have to write about them. Some topics focus on general knowledge, while some require background reading and research.

Students should pick the topic they are most comfortable with. They probably have choice within the topic, such as agreeing or disagreeing with a statement (for example, "Assisted suicide should be made legal in Canada. Agree or disagree"). They may have to narrow down the topic, perhaps talking about a specific immigrant group in Canada instead of immigrants in general.

Sometimes students are asked to come up with their own topic, but this is usually done as part of a process, not out of thin air. For instance, students may start with a subject they are interested in, do some background reading, and then consult with their instructor to narrow in on a topic.

### Activity

In groups, make a list of essay topics you would like to write about. Exchange your list for another group's, and rate the other group's list as to which topics you would want to write about. Discuss different possible approaches to the topics and ways they could be narrowed.

## Understanding the Essay Question

It is important to understand what the topic is asking you to do. Essay prompts can be in different forms.

**Yes-or-no essay questions** (such as "In the modern world, is cooking still an important skill?" or "Should religious schools be funded in Canada?") require you to choose one side and give reasons to support that position. It is important not to waffle or sit on the fence. You need a clear position to argue from.

Sometimes essay prompts require some **set-up**, so they might begin with a few sentences of explanation before the actual topic question or direction:

A secondary school education is the minimum requirement in today's world. Even for physical labour, workers may need a high school diploma. However, many students do not finish secondary school. They drop out because of a lack of motivation, poor grades, or personal problems. Educators try to keep such at-risk students in school long enough to graduate. What changes can they make to keep such students in school?

This essay prompt explains what the problem is; your job is to offer solutions.

Sometimes instructors give a quote from a reading and ask you for your take on it. This makes for a more difficult topic because it is open-ended.

| | |
|---|---|
| Peter Singer quotes Andrew Carnegie's dictum: "The man who dies rich dies disgraced." Agree or disagree with this statement. | In this essay, you need to take a position and support it. If you agree, you would argue in favour of philanthropy, that the rich need to give to charity. If you disagree, you would probably say that the rich deserve to keep their money. |
| Peter Martyn says, "Words matter. They indelibly colour our perceptions." Discuss. | This topic hinges on finding good examples of the power of language. It is not a topic you can actually disagree with. |

As mentioned in Unit 1, most academic essays are impersonal. Essay topic questions will generally show whether a more personal response is required:

| | |
|---|---|
| What are the benefits of doing volunteer work? | Here you can talk about the benefits that anyone can experience, with examples of specific kinds of volunteer jobs. |
| What have you learned from doing volunteer work? | This question is asking you to recount your own experience. |

A standard five-paragraph essay is about 500 words. Some topics are wide in scope—too wide to be adequately treated in an essay. Instructors usually leave room for students to **narrow a topic** to focus on what they are comfortable discussing. For instance, an international student writing about high school students preparing for college can write about students in his or her native country—this focus would be made clear in the introduction and thesis. An essay question may ask, "What support should parents give children who are in college or university?" but instead of using unwieldy phrases such as "college or university" or "post-secondary education," a college student can just write about college and a university student can just write about university.

For the question "What are the advantages or disadvantages of online courses?" you are being asked to take one position in your essay—either for or against online courses. However, you could easily narrow this topic down further by looking at it either from the students' point of view or the administration's. Thus, you could focus your essay on the advantages of such courses for the school or the disadvantages for students. These are just two of the possible approaches. If you wanted to talk about advantages for the school, you could even focus on the administration or on the instructor.

**Activity**

In small groups, look over a list of essay topics, and discuss what you would write to answer the question. You can use the list you generated in the Activity in the previous section, Choosing a Topic (the list of questions for Essay-Writing: Practice Topics on page 155), or another list you may have. For instance, you can search "essay topics" online and get lists of sample questions from standardized tests like the TOEFL test.

## Generating Ideas

Before you start writing your essay, be sure you have enough to say. We use the term **brainstorming** to refer to the act of coming up with ideas. Brainstorming involves writing down preliminary thoughts about the topic. It can be accomplished alone, in consultation with an instructor, or in a group with other students.

One of the best ways to brainstorm is just to jot down point-form ideas about your topic:

> *What should parents teach teenagers to prepare them for living on their own?*
> - budgeting
> - cooking nutritious meals
> - keeping track of their bank balance and credit card purchases
> - saving money on food purchases
> - cleaning rooms (bathroom, kitchen, living areas)
> - doing their own laundry
> - dealing with utilities (hydro, gas, cable)
> - dealing with emergencies in their home, such as toilets flooding and power failures
> - using basic tools (hammer, screwdriver, paint brush)
> - performing first aid
> - taking care of a car

With the ideas you have generated in your brainstorming, you have the raw material for your essay. Without the brainstorming, you might write your essay on the first three ideas that come to your mind, but it would be difficult to write a whole paragraph on just doing laundry, for instance. However, once you have many ideas listed, you can see what goes together and organize the ideas in paragraphs (as shown in the next section). For example, a paragraph on household chores can include cooking and cleaning tasks; laundry would be just one example in the paragraph.

If you have a controversial issue that has two sides, the topic question usually asks you to choose one. However, it is best to brainstorm for both sides. One reason is that it helps you to generate more ideas; coming up with one argument often reminds you of the counterargument. Moreover, you can actually write your essay for the side for which you have more to say.

*What are the advantages or disadvantages of online courses?*

| Advantages | Disadvantages |
| --- | --- |
| – no commuting time for students and teachers | – lack of human contact |
| – no transportation costs | – no real socialization with other students |
| – can do the work on their own schedule (especially good for parents and disabled students) | – hard for students to motivate themselves without regular classroom routine |
| – convenience | – high failure rate |
| – cost-effective for administration— no classroom required | – easier to discuss course material in person than to write in discussion boards |
| – course could be cheaper | – some students do not have the equipment or the knowledge to use online material |
| – more students in one class | – students might find it difficult to work at home because of distractions |
| – with fewer instructors, more standardization of course delivery and examination | – some students may lack the reading skills required |
| | – easier to have someone else do the work for the student (cheating) |

Brainstorming in this manner is an efficient way to start your essay-writing process, but there are other ways of generating ideas. People who think visually may use bubble diagrams for their points with lines to connect related ideas. Free-writing is a method in which students just write what comes into their heads and then look through the writing for an argument they can develop. Some writers ask themselves questions about a topic ("Why does this happen?" "What can this lead to?" "Who is affected?") to generate ideas. Asking questions can also be used within the other methods.

You may need to experiment to find out what works for you. Whichever method you use, it's important to think about the topic thoroughly to generate enough ideas to choose from and not just use the first three arguments that come to mind. Effective brainstorming requires critical thinking about the subject. Consider the topic from different viewpoints. For instance, if you are asked to come up with a solution to a problem, make sure you spend enough time considering the problem itself and the different ramifications.

In brainstorming, there is no such thing as a bad idea. You do not have to worry about using every idea you come up with. You do not have to worry about correct grammar or spelling. It is just a matter of getting ideas on paper or on the screen. However, if you find you do not have enough to say on one topic after you have brainstormed using the suggestions mentioned, then it is a good idea to go back to the topic choices and consider doing a different one.

**Activity**

With your instructor and classmates, discuss the techniques you have found helpful for getting started with an essay or for getting past writer's block. Consider different ways of brainstorming.

## Organizing Ideas

Once you have enough ideas to work with, you need to organize your ideas into paragraphs. Think of it as packing belongings in boxes. You want to put the items that fit together in one box and then label the box. The box is like a paragraph, and the label is the topic sentence.

Consider this example:

How can at-risk students be encouraged not to drop out of high school?
a) tutoring for students who are failing
b) alternatives to regular courses (co-op, independent study)
c) visits to post-secondary schools, work sites
d) speakers from the work world, former drop-outs
e) counselling
f) arts courses (music, drama, art)
g) variety of courses, both academic and hands-on
h) extracurricular activities to engage the students
i) mentoring with graduates who have gone on to post-secondary education
j) financial support so they will not have to work long hours part-time

First, look for ideas that go together. For instance, points a), e), and i) all deal with offering personal support with academics. Points f) and h) focus on offering other activities in the school to attract students.

Just as there is not one right way to pack your belongings, there are different ways to organize ideas. For example, point i), mentoring, could go with tutoring and counselling, but it could also fit with c) and d) in a paragraph on how students need inspiration from others. It would depend on how you want to develop your ideas.

Furthermore, you do not have to use all your generated ideas. Some good ideas may just not fit in your essay. Therefore, just as you may have to abandon a piece of furniture that would not fit in your new apartment, you may have to leave out some of the ideas from your brainstorming.

**Activity**

Choose one of the three examples of brainstorming given in this section and the previous one (on preparation for living alone, online courses, or at-risk students). With a partner, discuss possible ways to organize an essay from the point-form ideas.

## Writing a Title

A title is not always necessary, but writing one can help you start your essay. It gives you a perspective and helps you to limit the scope of your paper. If you need a title for your essay, make sure it is appropriate and relatively short. Do not just put the essay topic question on your cover page.

Generally, titles are phrases, not full sentences or questions. For example, a story in this book is called "Why My Mother Can't Speak English" rather than "Why Can't My Mother Speak English?"

Newspaper articles have headlines rather than titles. They generally give the main idea. Short forms are common to save space. Often a telegraphic style is used, leaving out grammatical words such as articles and auxiliary verbs. The only words capitalized are the first word and proper nouns. This style is not appropriate for essay titles.

### Activity

In small groups, look over the titles of the sample essays in Units 5 and 6. In addition, look at the titles of the readings in Part 2 as listed in the table of contents. Discuss the titles. Which ones give you a good idea of the contents of the essay or article, and which do not?

### Exercise 5.1

Write some appropriate essay titles for the following topics (you may have different titles for one topic, depending on the point of view of the essay):

1. Would self-driving cars make the roads safer?
2. Should religious schools be funded by the government?
3. Why do people get tattoos?
4. What can people do in their everyday lives to lessen environmental damage?
5. What kind of adjustments do adult children and their parents have to make when the children move back home after college or university?

### Writing an Outline

An outline is a plan for an essay. Following the plan keeps you on track as you write. An outline can be very detailed or very simple. It can be written in full sentences or in point form. A basic outline for a five-paragraph essay would give the thesis and the three topic sentences; these sentences could be revised as you write the draft. You can also include the supporting points in your outline.

Instructors may ask you to complete an outline and submit it for feedback before you write your essay. Sometimes they prescribe a format, with a specific numbering system. They may give you a printed sheet to fill out. They may assign part of your essay grade to the outline.

Here is an example of an outline for the essay "The Value of Home-Cooking" (pages 128–29):

Topic question: *In the modern world, is cooking still an important skill?*

Thesis: The ability to prepare a home-cooked meal is valuable.

1. food quality
   a) processed foods contain sugar, salt, fat
   b) cook chooses raw ingredients
   c) avoid allergens
   d) cheaper

2. social skill
   a) hosting dinner parties
   b) attracting opposite sex
   c) keeping immigrant cultures alive

3. psychological benefits
   a) personal satisfaction
   b) self-sufficiency
   c) creativity
   d) satisfying physical activity

An outline is a map for you to follow. It makes writing the essay easier. However, it does not have to be set in stone. You can revise your outline as you write.

**Activity**

Choose one of the sample essays at the end of this unit. With a partner, write the outline for the essay.

## Writing a Thesis Statement

The thesis statement is the most important sentence in the essay.

A thesis statement should

- answer the topic question
- be a supportable idea, not just a fact
- show the point of view of the writer
- be one sentence
- be a statement, not a question
- be the last sentence of the introduction
- be concise
- have parallel structure

Study these examples of poor and good thesis statements:

Topic question: *Should exotic pets be banned in Canada?*

| | |
|---|---|
| Many people keep exotic pets such as monkeys, pythons, and tigers. | **poor thesis:** This is a fact, not a supportable idea. |
| Exotic pets should be banned in Canada. | **poor thesis:** This just repeats the wording of the topic question. |
| In this essay, I will talk about exotic animals as pets in Canada. | **poor thesis:** This is called an announcement thesis—one that uses *I* and the word *essay*. |
| Should we be able to keep exotic pets in Canada? | **poor thesis:** A thesis should **answer** the question, not ask one. |
| I like my pet tarantula. | **poor thesis:** While this is an opinion, it cannot be argued; it is also too narrow. |
| Pets are important to human life. | **poor thesis:** too broad |
| Exotic animals make dangerous pets. | **poor thesis:** too narrow; gives one reason |
| All jurisdictions in Canada should have rules severely restricting the keeping of exotic animals. | **good thesis:** clearly states the position (Note that the word *should* indicates an opinion. Without this modal verb, this statement would be a fact, not an opinion.) |
| Canadian law should allow people to keep exotic animals as pets. | **good thesis:** clearly states the position |

## Writing a Three-Pronged Thesis Statement

For a five-paragraph essay, students may be asked to write a focused thesis statement that lists the three arguments that will be explored in the essay. This type of three-pronged thesis only works for short essays; the statement would become unwieldy if it had to include more than three arguments. Moreover, this kind of thesis statement can be difficult to write because it has to be concise and have parallel structure. However, some instructors prefer that students use a three-pronged thesis statement.

To see how the three-pronged thesis statement works, we can revisit the essay "The Value of Home-Cooking" (pages 128–29):

Thesis statement: *However, the ability to prepare a home-cooked meal is a valuable skill.*

Topic sentence #1: *The most obvious benefit of home-cooking is the ability to control the quality of the food.*

Topic sentence #2: *Cooking is also a valuable social skill.*

Topic sentence #3: *In addition to the social rewards, cooking has psychological benefits.*

To write a three-pronged thesis, you need to incorporate the ideas of the three body paragraphs into the thesis:

The ability to prepare a home-cooked meal is a valuable skill because it gives the cook the ability to control the quality of the food, because it is a valuable social skill, and because it has psychological benefits.

first draft of a thesis: We can see that this thesis statement, while grammatical, is long and hard to follow; moreover, the words *skill* and *valuable* are repeated.

Cooking is a valuable skill because it gives the cook the ability to control the quality of the food and because it has social and psychological benefits.

second draft: The repetition of "valuable skill" has been eliminated and the words *social* and *psychological* have been linked because they are both adjectives referring to an advantage.

Cooking is a valuable skill because it has nutritional, social, and psychological benefits.

third draft: By paraphrasing the idea in the first topic sentence, we can find an adjective that is applied to food quality and balances with "social and psychological benefits"

Sometimes students write a four-sentence thesis. This should be revised to make one statement:

Swimming pools in school are a good investment for three reasons. First, swimming is so important that all children should learn how to swim. Second, having pools on-site is very convenient for lessons. Third, the community can use the pool after school hours, making it more economical.

**incorrect:**
A thesis statement should be one sentence.

Swimming pools in school are a good investment because of the need for basic swimming skills, the convenience of the on-site facility, and the potential for community use.

**correct:**
Note that this thesis is one sentence with parallel structure: *because of* connects the three nouns *need*, *convenience*, and *potential* (which are each completed by a prepositional phrase).

A thesis statement may have to be revised to ensure that it is concise, with parallel structure:

| | |
|---|---|
| The family meal means that people can share food, spending time together, and good behaviour can be learned at the table. | **incorrect:**<br>The structure is not parallel. |
| The family meal provides people with an opportunity to share food, spend time together, and learn good behaviour at the table. | **correct:**<br>The parallel structure here can be seen in the series of verbs in the infinitive form: *share*, *spend*, and *learn*. |

In a five-paragraph essay, the thesis statement may state the three main ideas to be discussed in the body, but in a longer essay this is not practical and a less specific thesis is presented:

| | |
|---|---|
| Teenagers often conflict with their parents on their social life, appearance, and household responsibilities. | This is a three-pronged thesis statement; it's good for a five-paragraph essay. |
| Teenagers' relationship with their parents is often full of conflict. | This is a more general thesis statement; it works for a longer essay. |

Whether you use a focused thesis statement or a more general one depends on the topic, the length of the essay, your personal preference, and the assignment instructions. For instance, if the topic question asks "why?" it is often better to give your three reasons in the thesis:

Topic question: *Why do people eat fast food?*

| | |
|---|---|
| People eat fast food for many reasons. | **incorrect:**<br>"for many reasons" is the type of vague phrase that should not be used in a thesis. |
| People eat fast food because of its taste, price, and convenience. | **correct:**<br>This three-pronged thesis gives a clear idea of what the essay will argue. |

If you do use a thesis statement that gives the three arguments, keep the same order of presentation of arguments in the body of the essay.

Study the sample essays at the end of this unit. Identify the thesis statement.

## Exercise 5.2

For each topic, choose which sentence would work best as a thesis statement. Explain why. Look for the statements that actually answer the question. Discuss why the statement is appropriate or not for a thesis.

1. Topic: What factors determine how readily immigrants assimilate into Canadian society?
   a) Canada is a country of immigrants.
   b) Immigrants should learn the language, participate in social activities, and learn about their new country.
   c) Some immigrants do not assimilate into Canadian society because they are too shy, too attached to their native culture, and too busy working.
   d) How well immigrants settle into life in Canada depends on their background, their environment, and their personality.
   e) Immigration is a difficult process.

2. Topic: What support should parents give children who are in college or university?
   a) Parents are very important to the learning process.
   b) Parents of university students should help with finances, give general academic advice, and provide moral support.
   c) This essay explains the role of parents of college students.
   d) Parents should let their children make their own decisions about college or university.
   e) Students should choose a good program, establish a network of friends, and enjoy the experience to succeed in college.

3. Topic: In Canada, single adults now outnumber married ones. There is less pressure to get legally married today. Women are not financially dependent on men, and religious and social pressure to marry has diminished. Can marriage survive as a vital social institution?
   a) Today people do not get married or stay married long.
   b) In this essay, I will show that marriage can survive as a vital social institution.
   c) Despite its usefulness, marriage is unlikely to continue to be essential in Canadian life.
   d) Marriage is a social institution in Canada.
   e) People get divorced because they fall out of love, they change their outlook on life, or they get tired of staying with one person.
   f) Today there is no reason to get legally married in North American society.
   g) People get married because of financial, social, and religious reasons.
   h) Marriage will remain important in Canadian society because of tradition, legal incentives, and the human desire to mark life events.
   i) People do not have to get married anymore because our society accepts unmarried couples.

### Exercise 5.3

Here are incorrect four-sentence theses. Rewrite each into one concise, grammatical thesis statement. Make the sentence concise by deleting any information that can be explained in the body paragraphs.

1. For students who are at a loss during a teachers' strike, these are things they can do. They can read their textbook and review their notes. They should complete any assignments given before the strike so they will be up-to-date and maybe even ahead when the strike is over. They could do extra reading on the subject material to truly master it.

2. There are three main reasons for leasing a car. First, the monthly payments are lower. Second, you can always drive a new car after the three-year lease is over. Third, I don't have to worry about breakdowns as usually everything is covered under warranty.

3. There are several basic types of TV commercial. One is the lifestyle ad where advertisers want consumers to think they will have the kind of life depicted in the commercial if they use the product. Another kind is the humorous commercial that tries to make the consumer laugh and therefore remember the product. Third, there are straight information commercials that tell the consumer what he needs to know.

4. The transportation system can be fixed if everyone co-operates. First, the public transit system needs to be improved to make it more convenient to use. Second, more goods need to be shipped by rail instead of by truck. Finally, use of personal vehicles needs to be controlled with fines or incentive programs.

## Writing an Introduction

The function of an introduction is, of course, to introduce the topic to the reader. In a five-paragraph essay, the first paragraph is the introduction, while in a longer essay or report, the introduction may extend to several paragraphs or a whole section or unit. The introduction leads the reader gradually to the thesis, provides any background information the reader may need, and narrows the topic. In an essay, the introduction generally ends with the thesis statement.

What is actually in the introduction depends on the topic. For instance, an essay discussing solutions to a problem should have an introduction that explains the problem for the reader. In an essay discussing one side of a controversial issue, the main opposing arguments can be mentioned briefly in the introduction as a lead-in. If a reading (for example, a book, a story, an article) is a point of departure for the essay, the point of view of the reading's author may be mentioned before the essay writer goes into his or her own thesis.

In addition to examining the sample introductions in this section, you should look at the full essays in this book and in other essay resources you may be consulting. Look at the introductions you like, and think about why they work.

## Sample Introductions

Sample A. In an essay that discusses the effects of overwork, it would be appropriate to explain the causes first:

> Although it was once predicted that technology would result in too much leisure time for workers, the opposite seems to have happened. Instead of working fewer hours, we are working harder than ever. Downsizing has put pressure on surviving employees. Smartphones keep workers in contact with clients and their work at all times. As a result, stressed-out workers are showing signs of physical, mental, and social problems.

Sample B. In an essay in favour of euthanasia, the main arguments against it could be mentioned in the introduction:

> Even though euthanasia is already practised in Canadian hospitals, many people do not want the procedure legalized and controlled. They fear that it would lead to the "murder" of the terminally ill, the elderly, and the disabled. They think that life and death should be in the hands of God. However, mercy killing can mean a more humane way of dying, a return to a natural lifecycle, and a measure of control for those whose life spans are at an end.

Sample C. This introduction establishes that starting college is both exciting and challenging, before explaining the difficulties:

> Graduating from high school and going off to college is an exciting time. Students look forward to being on their own and pursuing the studies that will lead them to a career. However, many find that this is not as easy as they thought it would be. First-year students may even drop out when they find they cannot make the transition to college successfully. College students have to adjust to living on their own, being responsible for their studies, and coping with financial limitations.

Sample D. In an essay that responds to a reading, it is useful to recap the author's arguments:

> In "If the Artists Starve, We'll All Go Hungry," Elizabeth Renzetti points out how artists are suffering in the new economy. The Internet has created an environment where people expect to get videos, music, and books for free. It is not surprising that artists are giving up creative work, knowing they cannot make a decent living from it. However, the work they produce is vital to our economy and the health of our society. In order to save it, we have to devise a whole new way of paying artists for their work.

Students often struggle writing the introduction. It is helpful to remember that an introduction does not have to be written first—it appears first in the essay, but it might be easier to write it when the body of the essay is drafted, as long as the writer has a thesis as a beginning point. Because the introduction and conclusion often contain ideas that do not fit the body, writing the introduction later can work. Moreover, writers who are blocked at the introduction might find that drafting the body can cure this block.

One common mistake is starting the introduction with the thesis—this leaves no room to do anything else but proceed to the arguments of the essay. Here is an example for the topic "What are the benefits of studying abroad?"

When it comes to the benefits of studying abroad, it is often said that people who have an opportunity to study abroad will have a new life and a bright future. Because of the development of the global economy and education, an increasing number of students choose to study abroad. This phenomenon has become more common than it was 30 years ago. Studying abroad can help students to learn a new culture, have friends from different countries, and acquire an advanced education.

This introduction lacks a linear progression of ideas; it zigzags, giving an advantage of studying abroad, then explaining that the phenomenon is increasing, and then going back to advantages. Note also that the writer keeps repeating the phrase "studying abroad."

Choosing to take a university year in another country is an increasingly popular option. Even though it can be expensive and difficult to arrange, many students take advantage of the opportunity to study overseas. They realize that the benefits are worth the effort. Studying abroad can help students to learn a new culture, make friends from different countries, and acquire an advanced education.

This improved introduction ends with the thesis statement. It uses synonyms for "studying abroad." It starts with a general fact about the phenomenon before moving to the benefits.

Study these examples—two unsuccessful introductions followed by a third one that works better:

Technology has advanced greatly through the years. We rely on technology. We cannot live without it. Banning cellphone use in class is unfair.

This introduction starts with too broad an idea because "technology" can refer to anything from a pencil to a supersonic jet.

Smartphones are vital to everyday life. They are much more than a phone. Students can use them to communicate, to find information, and to take notes. Therefore, a ban on cellphone use in class is unfair.

While this introduction starts with a narrower topic, it is also unsuccessful because it gives the reasons that the ban is unfair. In other words, it starts arguing the thesis before the body of the essay.

Smartphones have come under a lot of criticism from educators, who say that students are addicted to the devices, that they use them to cheat on tests, and that the phones distract them from the real world. Therefore, teachers want to ban them in class. The ban is short-sighted, however, because the phones are useful in the education process.

This is a better introduction because it prepares the reader for the essay by giving background information—that educators want to ban the phones and why. Now the writer is set to argue against this.

Another problem students sometimes have with introductions is that they try to say too much. For instance, they want to give the whole history of the subject as background. However, an introduction should not be too long; it should be shorter than a body paragraph. It should catch the readers' attention and prepare them for the essay, and that is enough.

Examine the introduction paragraphs for the sample essays at the end of this unit. What kind of background information is given? How does the introduction lead to the thesis?

---

**An introduction should**

- gradually lead the reader to your thesis, which is the last sentence of the introduction
- give background information to the reader or prepare the way for your thesis
- not mention arguments in support of your thesis (i.e., it should not repeat statements that are in your body paragraphs)
- not be longer than a body paragraph, in most cases

---

## Writing Body Paragraphs

Body paragraphs in an essay are similar to the developed paragraphs discussed in Unit 4. Each starts with a topic sentence giving the main idea. The rest of the paragraph explains that idea with supporting points (usually two to four points). A body paragraph, however, is generally shorter than an independent paragraph, and it does not require a concluding sentence.

In an essay, the topic sentences of the body paragraphs take their cue from the thesis statement. In other words, they should relate to the thesis by taking the same general idea but narrowing it down for the focus of the paragraph. The wording should be different so that the sentences are not repetitive. If the three arguments are listed in the thesis, the body paragraphs should be in the same order.

Study this example:

Thesis statement: *Public transit is a worthwhile investment because it is good for citizens' health, finances, and quality of life.*

Topic sentence #1: *Public transit leads to health benefits for the whole population.* [health]

Topic sentence #2: *Investing in a better transit infrastructure ultimately saves money for everyone.* [finances]

Topic sentence #3: *Citizens' quality of life improves as more people use public transit and the number of cars on the roads decreases.* [quality of life]

A common problem found in essays is the use of a topic sentence that does not focus on the arguments of the thesis:

| | |
|---|---|
| **Cars produce a lot of pollution.** | This topic sentence does not directly state a reason why public transit is worthwhile. Instead, it mentions a problem. This sentence could work inside the body paragraph as part of the explanation, but it is not a good topic sentence because it does not relate directly to the thesis. |
| **Public transit leads to health benefits for the whole population.** | Note that this topic sentence directly states an advantage, giving a reason why transit is worthwhile. |

One of the problems students have when they are writing a body paragraph is that they write an introduction of one or two sentences before they give the topic sentence:

| | |
|---|---|
| **Cars produce a lot of pollution. Their exhaust is made up of toxic gases that lead to respiratory problems. Therefore, cutting car use by increasing public transit makes a healthier environment.** | The topic sentence idea is actually the third sentence here. Moreover, the idea that cars cause pollution is well known and does not need to be stated. |

The topic sentence of each body paragraph should be clear on its own. Use nouns, not pronouns, in the first sentence of a paragraph. For example, Topic sentence #1 above cannot read "It leads to health benefits for the whole population" because the "it" cannot refer back to a noun (public transit) in the previous paragraph. Each paragraph is a new beginning, so nouns should be clearly identified.

The topic sentence sometimes links to the previous paragraph. For example, an alternate topic sentence for the second body paragraph of the essay outlined above could be, "In addition to health benefits, public transit has financial advantages."

Do not overload your topic sentence. Remember that you have a whole body paragraph to explain the idea.

A successful life is one that also makes a mark on society. People can do this through their work but also through other achievements, such as participating in political movements or doing volunteer work. Raising children to become valued members of society is a way of making a difference in the world. Having friends and helping those in need are important aspects of human existence. Human beings are social animals above all else, so lives spent in isolation cannot be viewed as valuable as those that involve reaching out to people.

This body paragraph is from the essay "The Definition of Success" on pages 151–52. The topic sentence is relatively short. It introduces the idea, but does not try to explain the idea—that job is left to the body paragraph.

Body paragraphs in an essay do not need concluding sentences, especially concluding sentences that just repeat the topic sentence. However, you can use a concluding sentence in the paragraph if it is necessary and works well, as in this example:

The skills I learned in the food service industry carry over to everyday life. . . . These may not be skills vital to my existence, but I take pride in them.

This is the beginning and end of a body paragraph from "What McJobs Have Taught Me" (page 154). Note that this body paragraph does have a concluding sentence, but it does not just repeat what was said in the topic sentence—it adds the idea of pride.

Explore the sample essays at the end of this unit. Analyze the structure of the body paragraphs. See how the topic sentences relate to the thesis. Identify which topic sentences have links to the previous body paragraph. Determine which body paragraphs have concluding sentences.

**A body paragraph should**

- begin with a topic sentence that relates to the thesis statement and introduces the main argument of the paragraph
- give two to four points in support of that main argument
- have each point explained and/or illustrated with examples
- have coherence and use transition signals to logically connect ideas
- have one main idea that supports the thesis (in other words, it should have unity and not go off topic.)
- have a concluding statement only when necessary to add something to the general idea

**Exercise 5.4**

Here is an introduction with a thesis statement. For each possible body paragraph that could follow, choose the best topic sentence of the four choices given. Explain your choice.

> Personal vehicles have long been recognized as major sources of pollution. While it is relatively easy to give up driving a car in major cities that are well served by public transit and have other initiatives such as car-sharing, a personal vehicle is a necessity for most Canadians. Even if they must drive, however, they can reduce the harm caused by their car by changing what, when, and how they drive.

1. a) Bigger vehicles such as SUVs burn more gas and therefore emit more toxic gas.
   b) Canadians should choose a more fuel-efficient vehicle.
   c) All Canadians should buy hybrid cars because they produce less pollution.
   d) People should take public transit instead of driving.

2. a) Most Canadians can reduce the number of trips they take by car.
   b) Car-pooling is a good method to reduce the use of personal vehicles.
   c) The government should improve the public transit system.
   d) When should people use a car?

3. a) Most people drive too fast and too far, so they burn too much gas.
   b) In addition to using public transit, Canadians should walk and cycle more.
   c) Using a GPS system can prevent getting lost and driving too much.
   d) Good driving habits can also lead to a reduction in the polluting effects of cars.

**Exercise 5.5**

Write three topic sentences for each of the following thesis statements:

1. Students should pick a post-secondary program based on their interests, their skills, and the job prospects.

2. History courses are important because they teach critical thinking skills, explore life lessons, and inform students about their heritage.

3. How easily immigrants adapt to their new country depends on their educational background, their language skills, and their personality.

## Writing a Conclusion

Conclusion paragraphs are similar to introductions in that they are not developed as body paragraphs are. Like an introduction, a conclusion should not contain ideas that support the thesis. Essentially, a conclusion is like an upside-down introduction, starting with a restatement of the thesis and then moving on to broader ideas.

A conclusion can give the "so what?" idea, showing the significance of what has been argued in the essay. It can offer suggestions for improvement or predict the future. It is the last thing said to the reader, so the conclusion should have a memorable idea.

Here are sample conclusions for the same topics as the sample introductions on page 143:

### Conclusion A

With all these harmful effects of working long hours, we should make a change in our work habits. Even though cutting hours would result in lower pay, we have to value our health above anything else. We need to make sure we lead a balanced life and not work ourselves to death.

### Conclusion B

Euthanasia must be considered now that life and death is no longer a simple matter. Society must come to grips with the issue, and people must acknowledge that it already happens. Physicians play an important role, as does technology. We cannot turn back the clock, so we must accept dealing with a complex issue in a complex world.

### Conclusion C

If students can make these adjustments to college life, they will be successful in school. Moreover, they will have gained maturity and learned to deal with responsibility. This will be as valuable as their education in their future life.

### Conclusion D

These different ways of paying artists will have to be combined. It should not be left to one sector of the economy to insure that artists have enough to live on. With a stable income, artists can focus on creative work and not have to worry about the commercial value of what they produce. In this way, we will gain symphonies rather than jingles and public art installations rather than company logos.

The conclusion starts with a restatement of the thesis, but that is the only repetition, and it should not be in the same words.

In longer essays, you can write a short summary in a conclusion, but this is not advisable in short essays because it is too repetitive. Similar to the introduction, the conclusion should be shorter than the body paragraphs.

A conclusion should not suddenly reveal a preference or point of view to the reader, because this should have been clear in the thesis statement. A conclusion should not apologize for brevity (for example, "These are only some of the problems teenagers face") or make new points to support the thesis.

Study the conclusions in the sample essays in this book.

A conclusion should

- start with a restatement of the thesis statement—one sentence
- go on to give a "so what?" idea—showing the relevance of what has been proved, predicting what will happen in the future, or suggesting a plan of action, for instance
- not mention arguments in support of the thesis (it should not repeat statements that are in the body paragraphs)
- not be longer than a body paragraph, in most cases

## Studying Sample Essays

Read the following sample essays, examining the structure. For each, identify the thesis statement, and see how the topic sentences relate to it. Look at the support given for the points made in the essay. Examine the introductions and conclusions. You can also make a point-form outline of the essay to help you see the structure.

Other sample essays to study can be found in Unit 6, at the end of each non-fiction reading unit (Units 9–15), and in Appendices C and D.

Essay 1 Prompt: *Why is dining together as a family so important for children's development?*

### The Family Meal

In today's hectic lifestyle, many meals have become little more than pit stops. People grab something on the run, often fast food or processed foods, and rarely take the time to sit down and enjoy a meal together with the most important people in their lives—their families. However busy their lives become, people should take the time to gather together for meals. The family meal provides people with an opportunity to share food, learn good behaviour, and spend time together.

Because a meal is primarily about the food, a shared dinner offers many health benefits. The food is generally more nutritious, since it is more likely to be home-cooked. It is usually consumed more slowly—which is also good for the digestive system. In addition, children are introduced to foods they might not eat if they are accustomed to having individual meals. Shared dinners often feature food that is traditional to the family and its ethnic culture. Moreover, children may learn how to appreciate and prepare such foods.

The family meal also offers opportunities to learn good behaviour. Children can practise proper table etiquette when they share a relaxed meal at home rather than grabbing a burger at a drive-through. These good manners will serve them well later when they are attending business lunches or wedding receptions. The meal also offers a good opportunity for family members to share the chores of preparing and serving the meal and cleaning up afterwards. Children who have learned to work together in this way grow up to be more considerate and less likely to sit around expecting to be waited on.

Finally, dinnertime is an occasion for enjoyable, relaxed conversation. Because the meal is at the end of the day, everyone will have news to share, so it is the best time for conversation. Children can describe what they learned at school, and parents can relate events from their workday. They can discuss current events and exchange opinions. They can even discuss problems and find solutions. Not only will they practise communication skills but also problem-solving techniques. With everyone leading such busy lives, a shared meal is a uniting element, giving family members an opportunity to communicate with one another.

The benefits of a shared family meal are so profound that people should not eliminate it from their lives, no matter how busy they get. Modern families must take a good hard look at their schedules and take some time off from business meetings, extracurricular activities, and clubs to spend time together as a family sharing a meal. Even if they find it impossible to arrange to eat together every evening, they should schedule a family meal once a week at the very least.

(You can compare this essay to Paragraph C on page 125.)

Essay 2 Prompt: *What is the meaning of success?*

### The Definition of Success

Many people equate success with wealth. They think that if someone has a mansion and a fleet of luxury cars, that person must be successful. However, few people ever attain that degree of affluence. Nevertheless, many people can look proudly upon their many achievements. Success means making worthwhile contributions in work, finding a place in society, and gaining contentment in life.

Because work is so important in human life, people need to do a worthwhile job to be considered successful. It does not matter whether the job is running a global corporation or cleaning the streets; all work contributes something to society and needs doing. Some work may not pay very well, such as artistic endeavours, but it should still be recognized as valuable. Artists contribute memorable performances, written works to educate and entertain, and sculptures and paintings to satisfy the aesthetic needs of their audiences. People need to take pride in their work and do it to the best of their ability to be deemed a success.

A successful life is one that also makes a mark on society. People can do this through their work but also through other achievements, such as participating in political movements or doing volunteer work. Raising children to become valued members of society is a way of making a difference in the world. Having friends and helping those in need are important aspects of human existence. Human beings are social animals above all else, so lives spent in isolation cannot be viewed as valuable as those that involve reaching out to people.

Aside from what they contribute to society, people are not successful if they have not achieved some measure of contentment in their own lives. This may not involve vast sums of money or numerous possessions but enough to have their basic needs met, such as a home and a family. Studies have shown that people in poorer countries actually have more joy in their lives than those in rich Western countries. Moreover, people who gripe and complain about every facet of their existence must be judged as failures.

When people want to evaluate the success of their lives, they must look at what they have accomplished through work, through their contributions to society, and in their individual existence. A life well-lived is one that has made a mark as well as one that satisfies the person living it. People only get one chance at life—they must do what they can with the time they are given.

Essay 3 Prompt: *Why do people get tattoos?*

## Body Art

Human beings have been tattooing their skin for thousands of years, mainly as a tribal practice. In North America during most of the twentieth century, tattoos were sported only by rebels, such as bikers and criminals. A sailor might get inked at the end of a night of drinking and carousing. Tattoos had an element of freak show to them, and they were viewed as not quite respectable. Today, however, tattoos are everywhere—on lawyers, teachers, and grandmothers. The reasons that body art is so popular stem from artistic pursuits, personal expression, and group affiliation.

Tattoos can simply be viewed as another form of human decoration, one that is permanently inscribed on the skin. Body art has its place beside makeup, hairstyles, jewellery, and fashion—ways that people enhance their physical attributes. Tattoos can be elaborate works of art, such as dragons breathing colourful flames stretching over the back. On a smaller scale, an inked hummingbird on an ankle can be considered just a pretty picture. Tattoos draw attention to the body, something people have sought to do since prehistoric times.

Some people get tattoos to express their personal interests and attachments. For example, a tattoo can show the name and image of a loved one who has passed away and thus serve as a permanent memorial. A chef might have an image of his favourite food inked on his forearm. People can get tattoos to show their hobby or their favourite rock band. On a more spiritual side, Chinese characters are popular tattoos, usually ones that express a concept the person admires, such as "joy" or "wisdom." The tattoo shows what the person believes in.

Tattoos can also show group membership. This is probably the most traditional of reasons to get inked. Certain tribes or religious groups would have specific symbols that branded members. Biker gangs and criminal groups sported tattoos that showed permanent affiliation. A marine might get the motto "Semper Fi" inscribed on his arm. Even teenagers rebelling against their parents or trying to look cool are showing that they are part of their peer group.

The motivations behind tattoos vary, but they are currently very much in style with no signs of the fad waning. However, anyone contemplating a tattoo should think long and hard about it. Many people later regret getting their tattoos. Their body art may not look as crisp with the passage of time, or their interests and passions may change. Removal is a complicated, expensive, and often painful process, and anyone who invents a simpler way to accomplish it can look forward to booming business.

Essay 4 Prompt: *How are reality television shows made?*

### Reality, Manipulated

Unscripted television is dominating the program schedule for many networks. Lifestyle shows give lessons on cooking, decorating, or buying real estate. Competition shows have contestants battling it out using their wits, athletic ability, or performance talents. Some of these programs are informative time-wasters that fill up the daytime schedule for networks, while other shows carve out high ratings in prime-time spots. No matter what the format, unscripted shows have to succeed as good television. Even though these programs are called "reality television," the reality they portray has been staged and manipulated through the casting, filming, and editing process.

The first step in creating reality television is casting. The participants in the program have to be telegenic, as do the locations. The audience wants eye candy— to watch attractive people on lush tropical beaches. Good television also depends on conflict. For instance, the survivors on the island have to be a mix of characters that are naturally going to butt heads. The researchers casting the show go through hours of video of prospective participants, looking for those who are good-looking, articulate, and unreserved. A good back-story also makes for good television. A contestant who has overcome trauma is someone the audience can root for.

Even though the participants have no script to read from, they are manipulated during the filming process. The director stages situations to get the reactions he needs. For example, he may delay part of a participant's home renovation to see how the participant copes. In addition, participants often do confessionals during which they talk directly to the camera to explain what has been happening in the action part of the show. In these confessionals they are answering leading questions from the director, who is off camera. For instance, the director will try to extract negative statements about the other participants. All of this is to try to get emotional reactions to make the story more dramatic.

Editing is an essential part of making reality television. The producers go through transcripts and hours of video to put together a few minutes of television. They have to find a story to tell and make sure that all the elements needed to tell that story have actually been captured by the camera. The editors cut together the footage, choosing the best shots to illustrate the story, and show reactions from the participants. The end product has to tell a clear, entertaining story that fits the time limits.

The process of making reality television shows how much the programs are crafted—unlike real life, television reality does not just happen. Even though critics deride such programming as cheap television, they are the result of many hours of work by skilled artists. Moreover, there is no sign that the popularity of such shows is waning.

## Personal and Impersonal Essays

Some instructors assign personal topics to their students in an effort to engage them more in their writing. Others want students to practise writing objectively and impersonally as training for the work world. You should be able to handle both kinds of essays and know what is called for. The topic question usually indicates whether it requires a personal response.

Here are two essays on the same topic, the first personal and the second impersonal. See pages 10–11 for more on writing impersonally.

Essay 5 Prompt: "McJob" is the term coined by author Douglas Coupland to refer to low-paying, often menial jobs that frequently involve serving the public, based on the model of working at McDonald's. *What have you learned from working at McJobs?*

### What McJobs Have Taught Me

As a high school and then university student, I had my share of McJobs. I worked as a waitress, a cashier, and tour guide. Although some of my friends sneered at my jobs and chose to get into debt with student loans instead, I found that working like this was a good experience. My jobs taught me valuable skills in time management, food and drink preparation, and speaking to the public.

My work experience taught me how to use my time and energy profitably. Not only did I have to balance my studies, work hours, and social life, I learned how to get the most out of my work hours. In the restaurant, I never went anywhere empty-handed; I had enough miles to walk without having to do them twice. If I took plates of food or drinks to the tables, I went back to the kitchen with empty plates from other tables. Even today, as I clean house, I find that I work as efficiently as I did in my days as a server, making sure I am carrying something both coming and going.

The skills I learned in the food service industry carry over to everyday life. Sometimes I had to mix drinks, so I picked up some bartending skills that still come in handy at parties. At times I had to help the kitchen staff, so I learned to cook and plate food. I did not even know how to cook eggs before I had to help prepare breakfast at a truck stop restaurant where I worked. When we have large family dinners, my skill at balancing plates is impressive and useful. As a cashier, I became adept at handling money for everyday transactions. These may not be skills vital to my existence, but I take pride in them.

Probably the most important skills I acquired were people skills. As a waitress, I had to deal with rude and picky customers. Serving food for a catering company took me to formal functions at embassies and government buildings where I had to contend with a demanding clientele including celebrities and dignitaries such as the prime minister. As a tour guide, I learned to project my voice and keep my audience interested—skills that later helped in my career as a teacher. Because I worked in Ottawa, I had to be bilingual, so my fluency in French increased.

Even though working part-time made it difficult to spend enough time on my school work, I do not regret the hours I worked because of all I learned. I probably would have wasted more time if I had not had those jobs, and my marks would not have been much better. Moreover, I gained much more than just the income.

Essay 6 Prompt: "McJob" is the term coined by author Douglas Coupland to refer to low-paying, often menial jobs that frequently involve serving the public, based on the model of working at McDonald's. *What can students learn from working in such jobs part-time and during the summers?*

### The Benefits of McJobs

Students often work at part-time or summer jobs to pay their way through school. These positions are usually "McJobs"—low-paying labour, often involving serving the public. While many people disdain such menial work, students can actually benefit from such jobs in more than monetary terms. Students can learn time management, practical skills, and personal skills.

By working part-time, students learn to manage their precious time. First, they have to balance their school and work responsibilities. They know they cannot procrastinate with their academic assignments because they have little time to waste. They cannot spend free time on video games. Moreover, students learn to be punctual because bosses are less accepting of tardiness than teachers are. Finally, they learn to get their work done efficiently and use their time productively. McJobs often require that a number of tasks be accomplished even during downtime. For example, servers have side duties cleaning equipment, stocking supplies, and preparing plates, so they are busy even when the restaurant is almost empty.

Students can acquire a wide range of practical skills on the job. These skills can be carried over to other jobs or even to everyday household chores. For example, students who work as landscapers will be able to take care of their own yard and garden when they become homeowners. Restaurant cooks learn how to run a kitchen and can serve their future families good meals. Cashiers become adept at handling money and learn the physics of packing groceries into bags or boxes. Even if such abilities are not used in future careers, no skill is useless.

Since so many McJobs involve dealing with the public, student workers develop valuable people skills. They learn how to be polite and cheerful and how to listen to a complaint without losing their temper. Because they deal with such a wide range of people, they have a better understanding of humanity. For example, a cashier in a fast-food restaurant will see people struggling to come up with a few dollars to pay for a meal. Camp counsellors learn how children develop and learn. As a result, students develop the compassion and emotional intelligence that will serve them well throughout life.

Part-time and summer jobs allow students to grow and acquire skills. Students have to make sure that they do not take on too many hours, because their school work is still the priority. However, learning does not stop at the classroom door, and students should be open to these experiences that they may not have a chance at again.

## Essay-Writing: Practice Topics

Essay-writing, of course, requires practice. All the reading selections in Part 2 have Discussion questions and Assignment topics that can be used as a base for essay-writing. Here are some general essay topics, some of which you may have already done some work on in this unit:

1. Write an essay on one of the topics your group generated in the Activity Choosing a Topic on page 131.
2. What are the benefits of doing volunteer work?
3. Would self-driving cars make the roads safer?
4. Should religious schools be funded by the government?
5. What kind of adjustments do adult children and their parents have to make when the children move back home after college or university?
6. Should textbooks be replaced by e-books?
7. Why should students study history?
8. What are the advantages or disadvantages of being famous? (Note: Focus on fame alone, not wealth.)

### Essay checklist

- A five-paragraph essay has an introduction, three body paragraphs, and a conclusion.
- The introduction provides background information and leads the reader to the thesis.
- The thesis statement is the last sentence of the introduction. It is one sentence. It states the main argument, which is a supportable idea. It can be a general thesis, or it can give the three arguments of the essay (concisely and in parallel structure).
- Each body paragraph starts with a topic sentence that relates directly to the thesis and gives the main focus of that paragraph.
- Each body paragraph contains points that are supported by specific examples or explanation.
- The arguments in support of the thesis are only in the body paragraphs—not in the introduction or conclusion.
- The conclusion starts with a restatement of the thesis. For a short essay, this restatement is the only summary required.
- The conclusion ends with a "so what?" idea, explaining the relevance of the argument or taking the idea to a possible future but not giving more arguments in support of the thesis.

# UNIT 6

# Rhetorical Skills

*Rhetoric* is the art of speaking or writing to make an argument or impress someone. Communicating effectively involves knowing the structures of language—the way words, sentences, paragraphs, and essays are put together—and the way language is manipulated to have an effect on the reader. As always, what is said depends on the audience and the purpose of the document.

Writing instructors generally speak of different rhetorical forms, such as narration and comparison. Each form has its particular use in communicating ideas. For example, if you are asked to tell a story, you will use the narrative form to tell what happened. If you are asked to explain a word or idea, your rhetoric technique is definition to explain what something is.

While you may be called upon to write an essay in one specific mode, most writing is a mix. For instance, an author might start with a short narrative and then proceed to argumentation. Of course, there may be an emphasis of one form over another. Most essay-writing fits under the general umbrella of exposition—making points and supporting them.

This unit deals with the specific modes of writing. Each is explained and illustrated with sample paragraphs and short essays.

## Explaining and Illustrating

Essay topics assigned to students in college or university often require the writer to show and tell. This is the essence of illustrating as a rhetorical form. Instructors want the students to be able to explain an idea, a concept, a thought. Illustrating then is the ideal mode. Often, merely stating something is not enough; it requires showing.

All essays require explanation and illustration. We may label an essay an illustrative essay when its main purpose is to explain something without a pronounced argument. Examples of illustrative essays in this book include: "Body Art" (page 152), "What McJobs Have Taught Me" (page 154), "The Benefits of McJobs" (page 155), and "The Lure of Costumes" (pages 351–52).

Here is an example of an illustrative paragraph, followed by an illustrative essay:

> Excessive hoarding is a psychological disorder. Hoarders are obsessive about collecting things. Some of these items might be quite useless. For example, some people keep every flyer that is delivered to their house or every plastic bag they bring home from shopping. In addition, hoarders

cannot bear to throw things out. They are emotionally attached to their collections. Attempts to clear out items make them feel like a part of them is being ripped away. Finally, hoarding is clearly an illness because sufferers cannot live normal lives. Their homes become huge messes that are unsanitary and unsafe. One famous hoarder, Langley Collyer, died in 1947 when some of the mountains of junk in his home fell on top of him. It took a month to find him because literally tons of stuff had to be removed from the house to clear the way. Most people do not understand the complexity of the hoarding mentality and do not perceive it as a serious illness.

### The Hazards of Tree Planting

Every summer, thousands of Canadian university and college students head north to plant trees. Logging companies reforest a certain percentage of their cut land, so they subcontract to tree-planting companies. The goal of a tree planter is simple: plant as many trees as possible. Tree planters are paid per tree, so their fortunes rely on the speed with which they can put seedlings into the ground. It seems, however, that every aspect of the job—the weather, the animal life, and the rough living and working conditions—is designed to slow the planter's pace.

Planters work in the rain, during thunderstorms, and even in snow at the beginning of the tree-planting season. At the end of the day, home is a thin nylon tent, which can be crushed in a spring snowstorm. Later in the season, they have to endure the kind of searing heat that sparks forest fires. A clear-cut has no place for hiding from the sun, and the pace that kept planters warm in May can bring heat exhaustion in June.

The bug situation is like a video game in which increasing levels of difficulty bring new enemies to fight. Level 1 would be early May, easy and relatively bug-free. Level 2 would introduce the blackflies, a few at first and then a psychotic swarm of tiny, persistent flies getting into the planter's eyes, ears, and nose. Level 3 would be blackflies and mosquitoes. After mosquitoes come other bugs, such as friendly flies, deer flies, sandflies, and horseflies. Each has their own deadly weapon and method of attack. Unlucky planters have even found wasp nests with the thrust of their shovel. It's not enough to be suffering from the bites themselves; every planter is in constant danger of self-inflicted bug-swatting-related injuries.

In addition to bugs, tree planters have larger threats from the animal world. For instance, bears are attracted to the food and garbage around camp and become a terrifying nuisance. Hungry bears, undeterred by such defensive systems as noise-makers and flares, sometimes come right into the camp. On the job, planters must make enough noise to warn off any bears that happen upon their assigned planting plot.

Dirt is a constant companion in the bush. It is inhaled, eaten, and ground into a tree planter's flesh. A planter's hands will not be completely free of dirt until a few weeks after the return to civilization. Locals in "day-off" towns know how to spot a planter: A planter's shovel hand has rough calluses that become havens for dirt and sand. Tree planters generally go into town once a week to get a decent shower, do laundry, and pour a couple of beers down their throat to chase all that dirt they swallowed.

The job itself entails bending over to put a seedling in the ground 2000 times a day, scrambling over obstacles and unfriendly terrain. Trees cannot be haphazardly shoved into the ground; quality is of the greatest concern to the crew boss. The plug must remain unbent and completely in mineral soil, while the tree itself must be straight, at the proper depth and spacing. A planter has to satisfy several tree checkers as well as his or her crew boss. In a 10-hour day, allowing for breaks and bag-up times, 2000 trees means a tree planted every 10 seconds. Good planters often plant three or four thousand a day, working quickly because the money earned depends on how many trees get planted. At eight to 10 cents a tree (depending on the terrain), a planter can make $250 a day and earn enough for tuition in the first month.

Because of the repetitive and high-impact nature of the work, planters are prone to injuries. For example, tendonitis strikes ankles, knees, elbows, and wrists. Kicking the ground to expose soil causes a numbness in the toes that can last for months after planting. Bruises and scrapes are inevitable in the rocky, "slash"-covered landscape. A nasty spill is often the consequence of moving at the necessary speed. Rainy or icy conditions are especially hazardous. The weight of three to four hundred seedlings in a planter's tree-bags makes every step an awkward balancing act.

Tree planting is no summer vacation. It is hard, miserable, competitive work, and those who enjoy it are certifiably insane. Do not go for the experience, to save the environment, or to make money. In fact, do not go at all. As for me, I will be there again next year.

(Note: This student essay has a little personal twist at the end, with a humorous effect. Therefore, it is not a pure academic essay.)

## The Language of Explanation and Illustration

Because the concept of explaining and illustrating is so fundamental to essay-writing, the expressions used in this mode of writing have already been covered. See Giving Examples in Unit 4 (pages 114–17).

### Writing Assignments
1.  Choose a current fad or fashion, and explain its popularity.
2.  Write an essay explaining the duties in a job that you have held.

## Narrating

Storytelling is the most ancient of human arts, serving as both entertainment and a teaching tool. Researchers have shown that facts are remembered better if they are delivered in the context of a story. In other words, you may recall the facts of events better if you read them in a historical novel rather than in a history textbook.

Narration is simply telling a story, saying what happened, whether it be a true story or a fictional one. How much detail is in the story, however, depends on the audience and purpose. You may be spinning out a story of something funny that happened to you, perhaps even exaggerating for effect. You may be writing a fantastical children's story to entertain your young nephew. Or you may be relating what happened in a traffic accident for a police report, as in the following account:

> I was driving northbound on Chapel Road, going through an intersection that had no traffic lights or stop sign. A car in the southbound side was in the left turn lane. The car turned left before I cleared the intersection and hit the front of my car, on the driver's side. It pushed my car up onto the snow bank.

Here is another simple narrative:

> My tree-planting crew members all know the dangers of bears. I've told them to make a lot of noise when they are out in the bush. Many of them sing as they plant trees. This bear, however, came upon me suddenly. I was unloading the seedlings from the back of the truck. The other crew boss had gone to check on one of her planters. This black bear came around a thicket. I don't know who was more surprised—the bear or me. After a moment's hesitation, it charged at me, knocking me down. It bit on my steel-toed boot but didn't break through to my foot. With my free foot, I kicked it in the snout, and I yelled at it. It backed off and then charged again. I kicked it again, and it turned back and loped off into the bush. Fortunately, I wasn't really hurt.

Some people are gifted storytellers, enthralling listeners and keeping their attention. Others have trouble telling a story, confusing their audience by skipping back and forth relating the events that happened or boring their audience with too many unnecessary details.

It is important to keep your audience and purpose in mind. A story for entertainment is generally longer and more detailed. A narrative that simply states the facts of the events would be used in a business report. In addition, how much information you give depends on what your audience already knows. For example, if you are telling what happened to Uncle Joe when he was fishing, you do not need to give as much information to your family members, who already know Uncle Joe, as you need to give to your friends, who may not know the personal quirks of your extended family.

Narratives can be found in many types of writing. Journalistic essays often start with a narrative—an account of something that happened to the author or someone else. The author uses the narrative to get the reader's attention and to serve as an introduction to the topic. This is the technique used in "White Tops, Grey Bottoms" (pages 339–40). Some essays, such as "No Hyphen for Me" (pages 325–26), use narrative as the primary mode. Stories are told in fiction, so the reading selections in Unit 16 are all examples of narrative.

Be sure to make the point of your narrative clear. For example, if you are writing a complaint letter to a company and are telling a long, involved story of what happened, you should have an introductory paragraph that succinctly tells what your complaint is and what action you want. The narrative can then support your point.

Sequence is an important consideration in narration. An audience can follow a story better if it is told in chronological order (with the events in the order that they occurred). Use time transition signals such as *then* and *as a result*.

Here are two versions of the same story, a well-known Aesop's fable. The first uses dialogue to spin the story out. The second is a simple reporting of events.

## The North Wind and the Sun

The North Wind was a boisterous and blustering fellow. His breath blew cold and strong, and he liked to shake leaves from trees and push the waters of the sea into billowing whitecaps. In particular, he liked to wreak havoc on the people below.

He would send their hats flying off their heads, tie their laundry into knots on the clothesline, and scatter important papers across the yard.

"I own the sky, and I rule the Earth," he boasted.

One fall day, as the North Wind was up to his usual mischief, he came upon the Sun, who was covered behind some clouds. The North Wind blew them away so that he could see the Sun clearly.

The Sun smiled. "Thank you, North Wind. I'm sure the people down there appreciate what you have done too."

The North Wind sensed that the Sun was making fun of him with his easy smiles. And he didn't like it. "I'm stronger than you are, you know."

The Sun smiled again. "I'm sure you are, North Wind."

The Wind looked below and saw a traveller walking along the road. The man wore a heavy cloak and a wide-brimmed hat.

"We should have a competition. Do you see that man below? The one who can take his cloak off will be considered the stronger. Do you want to go first?"

"No, you can have the first go at it."

The North Wind came behind the traveller and suddenly burst forth a wintry blast. He caught the traveller unawares—momentarily. Then the man grabbed his cloak and hat tightly against his tiny frame. The North Wind twirled about and sent a powerful gust in front of the man. More determined than ever, the traveller wrapped his clothing about him.

Now, this went on for quite a while, but no matter which way the wind blew, the traveller held onto the hat and cloak for dear life. Finally, the North Wind exhausted all his tricks and withdrew.

When it was the Sun's turn, he merely kept beaming brightly, and soon the traveller felt not only the warmth but the heat of the day. The man began to remove his clothing: first his hat and then his heavy cloak. Pretty soon he was loosening his other garments.

"Sometimes," the Sun said, "gentle persuasion works better than force."

Note that in this version of the story, the present tense is used:

> One day the North Wind and the Sun decide to have a competition to see who is the strongest. They spy a traveller below and agree that the one who is able to get the man's cloak off will be deemed the winner. The Wind blows harder and harder, but the man holds on to his cloak very tightly. Then it is the Sun's turn. As the rays of the Sun beat down on the traveller, he grows very warm and takes off his cloak. The moral is that sometimes gentle persuasion works where force does not.

## Exercise 6.1

Here is another Aesop's fable, told in the past tense. Rewrite it, changing it to the present tense. Or rewrite it adding details to expand the story:

> There once was a hare who wanted to race with a tortoise. He believed it would be an easy win since the tortoise crawled on all fours and carried his home on his back. The hare had powerful hind legs, and he could spring

forth in great leaps and bounds. The race was unfair, of course. Surprisingly, though, the tortoise said yes to this competition. So on the day of the race, both hare and tortoise agreed that the first to reach the pond across the meadow would be the winner. The hare graciously gave his competitor a head start. In two hops, the hare caught up with the tortoise and in another two leaps he was far ahead, so far ahead that he decided to rest and take a nap. The tortoise, however, steadily plodded on, one leg after another, until he passed the sleeping hare. By the time the hare woke up, the tortoise had reached the pond. The moral of this story is that slow and steady wins the race.

## The Language of Narrative

Traditional storytelling has some standard expressions, such as the opening "Once upon a time" and the ending "and they lived happily ever after." Native speakers of English have generally grown up hearing fairy tales, Aesop's fables, and the stories of Greek myths, so the language of narrative is familiar to them. English language learners may wish to check out books of these stories; not only are they a way to improve language skills, but they are also a way to learn about cultural references.

## Verb Tense: The Narrative Present

When you relate a story, it is important to keep verb tense in mind. In English, the simple present tense is often used to tell a story since it makes it more immediate. For example, even though Shakespeare has been dead for 400 years, you could say, "Shakespeare tells the story of two lovers in *Romeo and Juliet*." The past tense is also used for narration. It is important, however, not to mix the two tenses unnecessarily. Whether you decide to tell your story in the present tense or in the past, do not switch.

In Unit 16, "Why My Mother Can't Speak English" is told in the present tense, while the other stories in the unit are told in the past tense.

### Writing Assignments

1. Write a one-paragraph account of something interesting that happened to you recently.
2. Write the story of a folk tale or fairy tale that you know. Add dialogue to make the story more detailed.
3. In small groups of two to four students, each group should start a short story, writing the first sentence. The paper should then be handed to another group to continue the story. Afterwards, the whole story can be shared with the class. The stories can be read aloud or projected onto a screen.

## Describing

Description paints a picture in the reader's mind. Sometimes you need to add description to clarify what you are talking about. Sometimes you want your audience to practically feel and sense it themselves. You may not be called upon to write a descriptive essay, but you may have to include description in other forms of writing. Remember your audience and purpose. For instance, the amount of detail you include will vary, depending on whether you are trying to entertain your audience with a story or just trying to make something clear on the way to explaining something else.

Here are three examples of descriptive paragraphs:

Everybody needs a private place to think, dream, and just escape life. When I was younger, I spent a lot of the summer at our family cottage. It was a chalet-style building, and my bedroom was under the roof. Outside my room was a little balcony, which had a ramp that led to the rocky hill right next to our cottage. The ramp meant that I could leave my room without going through the main door of the cottage and alerting the whole family to my movements. That balcony exit was my personal escape. I didn't really get into mischief, but I liked to go out and climb to the top of the hill. It was mostly rock, but there was an indentation that provided a not-too-uncomfortable seating area. I could look down at the roof of the cottage to one side, deep into the woods on the other, and in front of me was the lake, which I could see between the trees. I often did not see any other people even though I was only a few feet from our neighbour's lot. I loved to sit there and smell the pine, feel the warm sunshine and the cooling breeze, and hear the lapping of the waves. It was my little piece of heaven.

My roommate's brother Ammar is a giant. He's not just tall; he's also as broad as a linebacker. He tends to wear clothes two sizes too big for him in a style generally seen in a rap video. His unkempt hair and perennial five o'clock shadow add to his unfriendly giant appearance. If you saw him coming down the street, you'd probably surreptitiously get a better grip on your purse or cross the road outright. However, if instead of doing either of those things, you offered him some ice cream, you'd probably end up being best friends forever and have play dates to watch Disney movies. He once came over specifically to watch *Finding Nemo* with me, while his sister rolled her eyes and stayed in her room. I don't think she appreciates his particular charms.

Sao Paolo, founded in 1554 by Jesuits, remained relatively unimportant until it became the key port for the export of coffee in the late nineteenth century. Today it is the financial and industrial capital of Brazil. Growth has been accompanied by distinct spatial expressions of class. Working-class areas arose close to industrial sites, while elite areas developed on higher ground; in some cases elite areas are enclosed by security fences and patrolled by guards. Squatter settlements, known as *favelas*, are common on the city's outskirts. About one-third of the *favelas* are on riverbanks and subject to flooding; one-third are on steep slopes and may be subject to landslides and erosion; and about one-tenth are located on waste dumps or landfill sites.

Excerpted from *Human Geography*, 7th edition, by William Norton, Oxford, 2009, p. 546

Look for descriptive passages in the readings in Part 2. For instance, Peter Singer describes different watches in "Why Pay More? To Be Conspicuous" (pages 284–85), and Salim Sachedina describes the Toronto of the 1960s in "No Hyphen for Me" (pages 325–26). Discuss the techniques the authors use for description.

> **Some pointers to keep in mind for description**
>
> - As with all writing, clarity is vital.
> - Organize your details so that your reader can follow you.
> - Keep in mind your audience and purpose.
> - Use adjectives and adverbs, but don't overload your sentences with them.

### Writing Assignments

1. Write a one-paragraph description of your favourite place in your hometown.
2. Write a description of an interesting person you know.
3. Describe an object (such as a can-opener) for someone who has never seen one. You can pretend you are describing it for an alien from another planet.

## Defining and Classifying

Sometimes in your writing you have to explain the meaning of a term. You might have to write a short paragraph to define a technical term in a report, or you might have to write a whole essay, such as "The Definition of Success" (pages 151–52). Classification involves defining something using various categories. For example, you might write about the kinds of customers you have as a server in a restaurant or different types of marketing approaches that can be used with a product. Another kind of classification is division in which the different parts of one thing are described. For instance, you could write about the main components of a 3-D printer.

Dictionary definitions can be used effectively in an essay. Peter Martyn offers an *Oxford English Dictionary* definition in his essay "Fear Math, Not Numbers" (Unit 9, pages 260–61). He is using the authority to make a point, and the dictionary definition is only a small part of this explanation of the difference between mathematics and arithmetic. Less skilled writers sometimes fall back on a dictionary definition to fill up space or to provide an introduction when they are at a loss; sometimes the definition is unnecessary because the word is clear on its own.

Here is an example of a definition paragraph:

> Narcissism is defined as self-love. The word comes from Narcissus, a character in Greek mythology who was handsome and vain. He fell in love with his own reflection in a pond, staring at it for hours, while the lovesick nymph Echo looked on and tried to call out to him. His name was later given to the flower that tends to grow by lakes and ponds. Narcissists can be vain, like Narcissus. Mainly they think they are special and privileged and no one else in the world matters. For instance, students who interrupt the class to demand attention to their needs may be showing this kind of behaviour. Many

narcissists are charming and attractive, so they get away with lording it over others. They generally have an exaggerated view of their abilities. For example, some contestants on televised talent shows often react with disbelief when informed that they have no talent. Unfortunately, narcissism has been fostered in modern society with its emphasis on individual wants and needs.

Here is an example of a classification essay:

### Three Kinds of Bad Drivers

Driving to work or school is one of the most risky activities people undertake in their daily lives. The possibility of getting hurt or killed in a traffic accident is actually higher than getting killed by a terrorist, but people do not take the dangers of the road seriously enough, whether they are pedestrians, cyclists, or drivers. Much of the danger on the roads is caused by poor driving habits. Three of the worst kinds of drivers are those who are overcautious, distracted, or aggressive.

Some drivers are so afraid of driving that, ironically, they create more hazards trying to be careful. Overcautious drivers insist on going very slowly. They may go down the highway below the speed limit or below the speed of traffic. It would not be as dangerous if they restricted their movements to the slow lane, but sometimes they take the middle lane to avoid the truck traffic or even clog up the fast lane. If they do not know where they are going, they may crawl down a street looking at street signs, or even reverse if they miss their turn. Overly careful drivers delay making left turns, waiting for the road to be completely clear, thus causing the drivers behind them to become impatient and perhaps even do something rash, such as pulling around them.

Other bad drivers are those who try to do two things at once. The most common transgression today is using a cellphone while driving. Even using a hands-free set does not prevent a driver from being distracted. Cellphone users often weave in their lane or drive more slowly because they are concentrating on their call. Some drivers try to consult a map while they are actually moving. Some use traffic jams to catch up on their reading, even when the traffic is stop-and-go. Other activities include eating or personal grooming, such as putting on makeup. Any of these actions distract the driver from the most important task—driving. Preoccupied drivers put everyone at risk since it takes only a split second to cause a crash.

Aggressive drivers are probably the worst kind of driver. They drive quickly and take risks because they are always in a hurry. They think the speed limit is for wusses, and they tailgate drivers in the fast lane on the expressway, even if those drivers are driving 120 kilometres per hour in a 100-kilometre zone. Aggressive drivers are also annoying because they follow so closely that they have to hit the brake lights often, confusing drivers behind, who think there is a traffic slowdown. These drivers have Type A personalities—they are competitive and do not want to be behind anyone. They weave in and out of lanes and take chances. It is only luck and the attentiveness of other drivers that save them from more accidents.

The most dangerous hazards on the road are other drivers, so careful drivers have to watch out for those who are overly cautious, preoccupied, or aggressive. All drivers have to understand the characteristics of bad drivers in order to be able to predict their behaviour on the road, and they have to be vigilant for signs of these driving behaviours.

## The Language of Definition and Classification

Writers have different techniques available to add information to help readers understand what something is.

| | |
|---|---|
| "It worked well for the baby boom generation (1946–1965). But their children (born 1972 to 1992) entered a very different labour market." (Goar, page 270) | In this case, just giving the birth years in brackets is enough to define the generation. |
| "...ways of spending money that had no other objective than the display of wealth itself. He termed this 'conspicuous consumption.'" (Singer, page 284) | Here, Singer gives the definition before giving the term itself. Note that he uses the verb form of *term*—the word is more commonly used as a noun. |
| "When asked what he thought about 'food instagramming'—photographing your meal at a restaurant and uploading the pictures onto social media—he explained that while he does this 'all the time,' he isn't particularly fond of the practice." (Teitel, page 297) | Teitel sets the definition off between parenthetical dashes (see page 99 on Punctuation). |
| "But this month, the United Nations Environmental Programme (UNEP) released a major report on marine waste which cited garbage cleanups along the Mediterranean Sea showing plastic bags accounted for just 8.5 per cent of total marine litter." (Taylor, page 318) | A common practice is to give the full name of an organization and then the short form in brackets. After the first mention in the document, the organization is referred to by its short form. |
| "...she cannot understand that you don't give government officials *lai-shi*, the traditional Chinese money-gift given to persons who do things for you." (Engkent, page 354) | In his short story, Engkent uses Chinese words and expression that he knows his audience is not familiar with. In this quote, he explains what *lai-shi* is. Note that non-English words are in italics and that the definition comes after the comma. |
| "'You didn't live long enough in *hon san*, the sweet land, to understand the fears of the old. You can't expect the elderly to renounce all attachments to China for the ways of the *fan gwei*, white devils. How old is she, 70 now? Much harder.'" (Engkent, page 354) | For the two Chinese terms here, Engkent gives the translation instead of a definition. From the context, the reader knows that *hon san* refers to China and that *fan gwei* refers to non-Chinese. Note the use of commas to set off the translations. |

**Writing Assignments**

1. Write a paragraph defining an abstract term, such as *beauty*, *heroism*, *intelligence*, or *leadership*.
2. New words are coined every day; many come from developments in technology. Write a paragraph defining a new word or expression (such as *phishing*, *selfie*, *phablet*). Include information on how these words were developed.
3. What is a Canadian? Write a definition paragraph or an essay.
4. Write a classification essay on three kinds of people you encounter in your everyday life. For example, if you work as a salesclerk or restaurant server, you can describe three different kinds of customers or three kinds of supervisor.

## Showing Cause and Effect

Academic essays often explain the causes or effects of something. Sometimes an essay can discuss both causes and effects, especially if there is a domino effect or a chain reaction in which one event leads to another, which in turn leads to another. For example, you could explain how trying a drug could lead to addiction and how addiction may lead eventually to crime.

You can read many examples of cause and effect writing in this book. In Unit 4, Paragraph A (page 124) discusses the reasons that the family meal has become less common, and Paragraph C (page 125) explains the effects of having a regular meal together. The essay "Body Art" (page 152) explains causes (reasons for getting tattoos), while "False Economy" (pages 295–96) focuses on the effects of cheapness in our society. "White Top, Grey Bottoms" (pages 339–40) mentions both the reasons for choosing school uniforms and the effects of having them, and "The Case against Bottled Water" (pages 309–11) explains results of buying bottled water.

Study these examples of cause/effect writing:

Prompt: *Explain the effects of driving while using a cellphone.*

Even though many drivers claim that they can use a cellphone safely while behind the wheel, the effects of using a cellphone, even a hands-free device, while driving can clearly be seen. Researchers have found that the effect is equivalent to driving under the influence of alcohol, while talking to a passenger or listening to the radio does not have the same effects. Talking on a phone takes the attention away from the road, even when the driver has both eyes on the road and both hands on the wheel. This often results in a driver slowing down or weaving. Most important, cellphone users are prone to "inattentional blindness" whereby people do not process what they are seeing. This effect has been amply shown in tests like the gorilla test in which observers fail to see something in the picture when they are concentrating on something else. The human brain cannot multi-task, and laws prohibiting cellphone use while driving should include hands-free devices.

Here is an other example of cause/effect writing:

## Causes of Modern Incivility

Complaining about other people's behaviour is nothing new in any society. Ancient Greek writings show that even in those times, people were concerned that teenagers were disrespectful and impolite. Today, people point to such phenomena as road rage, the lack of formal manners, and vulgarity on television to make their claim that incivility is on the rise. Whether people are in fact ruder today than before is debatable. However, changes in technology, politics, and society in the late twentieth century have influenced human behaviour, making people less considerate of others.

The use of new technologies such as computers is the most obvious influence on behaviour. While technology does open up new ways of communicating with our fellow beings, it also cuts us off from real human interaction. It is much easier to be rude sitting in a car or at a keyboard than it is face-to-face. In road rage incidents, aggression and violence escalate between drivers, acts ranging from cutting other drivers off to obscene gestures to even physical confrontation between drivers who get out of their cars to fight. Psychologists say people feel dehumanized in their vehicles and therefore freer to act aggressively. Similarly, Internet users can send angry, obscene messages because they feel anonymous and not responsible for their actions.

Another problem is that new gadgets usually come into widespread use before the social rules for using them can develop. Cellphones offer convenience but also intrude on public space as people talk loudly on their phones in restaurants and let them ring in the middle of a lecture. Sometimes the use of a technology affects behaviour in other situations. People used to chatting with their family while they watch a movie at home sometimes behave the same way in a theatre.

Technology has also sped up our world, making us less considerate of others. With instantaneous communication possible, people do not take the time to reflect on their words. Moreover, this hurry-up world causes stress. People have a lot of information to digest and deal with—and little time to do it. Thus, it is not surprising that the courtesies people generally pay each other have fallen by the wayside.

The late twentieth century also brought a political shift that indicates a change in attitude that fosters selfishness. The right-wing conservative viewpoint preaches lower taxes, fewer social programs, and the rightful dominance of the marketplace. This is, in effect, an every-man-for-himself philosophy. People have to be ruthless to succeed, and they cannot consider others' welfare. Consequently, they behave inconsiderately.

The emphasis on individual needs has many manifestations in behaviour. The 1980s was called the "me" decade. Education became child-centred, and self-esteem was promoted. Parents and teachers were encouraged to praise children so that they could grow up to be confident and content; even poor results were given good marks for effort. However, this overemphasis on self-esteem resulted in a false sense of entitlement. People educated in this way may think too highly of themselves and may figure that they deserve special treatment, that what they want is more important than anyone else's needs.

In addition, deference to authority is less than it used to be. In traditional families, ideal children were those who were seen but not heard, because parental authority was absolute. Not only do present-day parents get less respect, but other authority figures, such as doctors, politicians, supervisors, and teachers, are also frequently challenged. Some of this is due to the media revealing the weaknesses of such figures. This lessening of deference to authority can be positive because it leads to such actions as questioning doctors and not just accepting everything they say, but it has also led to increased incivility, as protestors smack cream pies into the faces of prime ministers and teachers are harassed.

The media can, of course, be blamed for some of this rudeness and vulgarity. Bad behaviour gets featured on the news—whether it be politicians heckling each other in Question Period, hockey players beating each other to a pulp, or drunken celebrities landing in jail. People get a taste of fame and want to hold onto it. They crave the publicity—even if it is negative. Reality television stars find their 15 minutes of fame is not enough and cook up media stunts, such as pretending a child is aloft in a balloon, to extend the media coverage. While we pretend to be horrified, it is our appetite for celebrity news that feeds the paparazzi and schlock TV.

Although we can find many reasons why people behave with less consideration for others today, we should not be too quick to conclude that society today is uncivil. We have to recognize other truths. First, social rules are cultural. As our world brings people with different values together, some adjustments have to be made, leading to new standards of behaviour. We must also be careful to distinguish between casual and rude. A few decades ago, people dressed up to go on an airplane trip and never called an older person by a first name. Does this mean a decline of civility or merely a more relaxed style of behaviour? Finally, our society has made improvements in the way we treat those who have lesser status. Overt racism is less accepted today, and we make fewer class distinctions. Women are no longer considered the possessions of their husbands and relatives. In those respects, we can say modern behaviour is better.

## The Language of Cause and Effect

Here are some words and expressions used to show cause/effect relationships:

**Causes**
because, since, as, for, to result from, to be the result of, due to, due to the fact that, because of, the effect of, the consequence of, as a result of, as a consequence of, one reason that, caused by, attributed to, on account of, owing to

**Effects**
so, as a result, as a consequence, therefore, thus, consequently, hence, to result in, to cause, to have an effect on, to affect, the cause of, the reason for, thereby, cause of

Watch out for the different prepositions used. *Affect* is a transitive verb (it has an object), so there is no preposition afterwards; however, the preposition *on* often follows the noun *effect*. Both *in* and *from* can follow the verb *result*, but the noun *result* is generally followed by *of*. *Because* is followed by a clause; *because of* is followed by a noun or a noun phrase.

Analyze the following sentences. Identify the causes and the effects in each sentence and the words that point to this:

1. In Canada, education is under provincial jurisdiction. Consequently, the school system varies from province to province.
2. Because students in humanities courses have to write more essays, they develop their critical thinking skills more than students in the sciences.
3. Due to the changes in the curriculum, students have fewer electives to choose from.
4. Because of the construction of the school addition, noise was a distraction during tests.
5. The inclusion of arts and sports programs affects the drop-out rate as more students stay in school to participate in these activities.
6. One reason why the course has such a high success rate is the strong motivation of the students.
7. Their quick progress had a negative effect on the other teams, who had to scramble to catch up and so became careless.
8. Following up on the cases with nurses' visits results in fewer rehospitalizations.
9. This medication can have serious side effects. It can trigger migraine headaches.
10. Doctors looking into the causes of cancer have found that lifestyle can affect some rates of the disease.

**Writing Assignments**
1. In a paragraph, explain how the poor choice of a given name can affect a child.
2. In an essay, explain the reasons that young people start smoking.
3. In an essay, explain how traffic jams affect our society.

## Reviewing

When you write a review, you evaluate and give your opinion of a work. You could review a book, a movie, a CD, a concert, or a product. Your review might include comparisons to similar works. You can summarize the story, but remember that your audience might not yet have seen or read it, so do not reveal too much of the plot—especially the ending. Everyone is entitled to his or her own opinion, but this opinion should be clearly and logically supported.

Reviewing is also a base for critical analysis. The word *review* means to look over or look at something again. In short, reviewing is a critical evaluation or the close examination of materials. From an academic point of view, reviewing is not just a synopsis of what has been said or written, but rather it gives a perspective, or expresses an opinion, on the content. In a book review, for instance, you state the reasons for liking or for not recommending it and then back those reasons up with relevant details.

Here is an informal movie review:

> In the winter of 2009, movie audiences raved about James Cameron's *Avatar*, entranced by the flashy and innovative special effects but sadly blind to the movie's shortcomings. First is tragically mundane dialogue: The "I see you" line is supposed to pass for something both romantic and profound. It's amazing that with such a high budget, none of it could be put toward finding a decent screenwriter. Second, not only is the plot utterly predictable, it is a rip-off of Disney's *Pocahontas*, or *Dances with Wolves*, or any story in which our hero finds love with an exotic yet sympathetic native girl and learns to renounce his wicked ways and embrace the environment. With all the hype over the amazing technology used to make the film, it's impossible to avoid the conclusion that Cameron came up with the software first and then decided that blue cat people were a great way to showcase it. *Avatar* is yet another example of technology being deployed for the sake of, "Look how cool this is!" rather than to service a story.

Reviewing readings and writing personal responses is covered in Writing about Readings in Unit 8 (pages 249–52).

### Writing Assignments
1. Collect some reviews from the local newspaper or the Internet. It is easy to find reviews of movies, concerts, plays, books, and restaurants. Look at the techniques used. Choose two different reviews about something you are familiar with, such as a movie you have seen. Write a paragraph on how effective the reviews are. Would they have influenced your decision to see that movie?
2. Write a brief review (about 150 words) of a book, movie, computer game, concert, or CD.

## Describing Process

Process description is often found in technical writing. It is generally "how to" writing, common in instruction manuals. There are two basic kinds of process writing—instructional and descriptive. Instructions can be written in a list or in prose paragraphs. They are directed at the reader, so they use *you* and command sentences. The other kind simply describes the process objectively, without giving instructions. For example, if you explain to a gardener how to plant a flower, you are giving instructions. If you give an account of how a plant grows, you are writing a process description without being instructional.

Good process writing is clear and concise. You have to give enough information for your reader to understand the process being described but not too much information. You have to know your audience. If you are describing a technical process, much will depend on how comfortable the reader is with the jargon of the particular field.

It is important to break the process down into the different steps. Sometimes you will have to subdivide, with some general phases of the process broken down into various steps. For example, the planning stage of essay writing includes researching and thinking about the topic, jotting down ideas, and preparing an outline.

Paragraph F on the family dinner (page 126) describes process, as does the essay "Reality, Manipulated" (page 153).

The following examples show different kinds of process writing.

1.  Instructions:

    How to take notes:
    1.  Prepare for class ahead of time—do the assigned homework and preview textbook chapters.
    2.  Come to class on time with your tools—whether they are traditional (pen, paper) or electronic (laptop or tablet).
    3.  Choose a seat where you can hear the lecturer and see the board or screen.
    4.  Listen carefully to the lecturer, paying close attention.
    5.  Write down, in point form, the main points of the lecture.
    6.  Listen for cues, when the lecturer stresses specific points.
    7.  Use short forms for common words and the terms of the field.
    8.  After class, review notes, completing any missing sections to make sure they will be clear later.

2.  Instructional Process Paragraph:

    Note-taking is one of the skills you must learn in college or university, especially if you did not master it in high school. First, you have to come to class prepared, having read whatever chapters are required for that lecture. You need to bring your note-taking tools—your pens and notebook or, if you prefer, a laptop or tablet. Choose your seat so that you can hear the lecturer and see the board and screen. Listen carefully and pay attention to everything the lecturer says. Your goal is to write down the main points. To do that, you have to follow the lecturer's cues. For example, if the professor says something like "most important," you know that she is stressing something. Similarly, you can ignore any small talk, like the chat with students about the movies they saw on the weekend. To be efficient, use point-form notes and abbreviations. In addition to the standard short forms, you can develop your own system. Be sure to have short forms for the technical terms that are often repeated in that subject area. After class, go over your notes. If the notes are not clear, add information or rewrite illegible bits while the lecture is still fresh in your mind. If you take notes faithfully, you will remember your lectures better and have study notes ready.

3.  Descriptive Process Paragraph:

    Note-taking is one of the skills college students must learn since it is not usually taught in high school. The first step is proper preparation. Students need to have done the assigned reading. They must bring their note-taking tools, whether they prefer the tried and true pen and paper or use an electronic device. They should choose a seat where they can hear and see everything. Once the lecture begins, careful attention is required. Professors usually stress the important points. Students need to develop their own system of point-form notes, including abbreviations for technical terms common in their field. The last step is one that many students neglect. Notes have to be cleaned up and added to after class to make sure they are legible even after the material of the lecture is no longer fresh in the mind. The act of note-taking helps students retain the information better, and good notes serve as useful study guides.

Process description is also found in the description of biological or geological processes:

### Tsunamis 101

*by Jan Dutkiewicz*

Say *tsunami* and up pops a mental image of a single, giant wave rising out of the ocean to swallow cities whole. In reality, tsunamis (meaning "harbour wave" in Japanese) are a series of waves that start small and grow as they approach land. They are the result of oceans attempting to smooth out their surface after a disturbance.

Tsunamis are triggered by any phenomenon that causes a large part of the water's surface to rise or drop relative to normal sea level. These events are usually the result of earthquakes occurring along undersea fault lines, the cracks in the Earth's crust between tectonic plates. When these plates collide or grind against each other, they can elevate, lower, or tilt major sections of the ocean floor, suddenly offsetting the level of water at the surface. The displaced water then rushes to level out, causing a tsunami. The waves travel outward in all directions from the place where the earthquake occurred, just like the ripples created when a stone is thrown into a lake.

Tsunamis can also be caused by undersea volcanic eruptions, landslides, or explosions on the surface, such as the 1917 Halifax harbour explosion that sent 10-metre-high waves crashing into the city. It has also been suggested that asteroids or other extraterrestrial bodies could cause tsunamis if they plummet into large bodies of water, but there have been no examples of this in recent history.

A popular misconception is that tsunamis are monstrous waves that scour the ocean destroying everything in their path. The displacements caused by earthquakes and other cataclysms move huge masses of water, but they do not dramatically shift the surface level. Tsunami waves travelling in the open ocean can travel hundreds of kilometres per hour, but they are usually less than one metre high, and their crests can be up to 100 kilometres apart. They can be virtually invisible from the air and, for ships, be indistinguishable from the normal movement of the ocean. It is when these waves make landfall that they achieve their destructive potential. There are stories of fishermen who had no idea that a tsunami had struck their villages because they were too far out in the ocean to see or feel any waves at all.

As the ocean becomes shallower near the coast, tsunami waves slow down, compressing and directing their energy and volume upward, some rising to amplitudes of over 50 metres and annihilating whatever they encounter. Depending on the depth and slope of the coastline, it is also possible for the tsunami waves to wash over the shore like a flood or rapid current, as they did in the widely televised video footage taken in Thailand during the recent disaster in Southeast Asia.

Generally, coasts and islands with steep fringes or surrounded by barrier reefs are safer than those with gradually rising fringes or those that are exposed to open ocean. This is because reefs can absorb much of the oncoming waves' impact and deep coastlines do not allow tsunamis to slow down and grow into deadly towers of water.

Describing how to find a job is normally instructional, but the essay below shows how it can be written as a process description (in third person, avoiding the use of *you*).

### Looking for a Job

The job hunt is a formidable task that everyone has to face many times. Not only is one's livelihood dependent on the outcome, but the hunt can be frustrating and demoralizing. There is no avoiding it, however, and it can be more easily tackled as a step-by-step procedure. Finding a job requires preparing documents, searching for openings, and contacting employers.

The first step is writing the documents required for the job search. The most important one is the resumé, which defines the potential employee. Job seekers must summarize their education, experience, and skills. They have to write a search objective that encapsulates what they are looking for in a position. Second, cover letters need to be drafted. They are important because they can bring the resumé to life and can be tweaked for specific job requirements. A third useful document is a list of references to present at interviews. While the list itself is not difficult to assemble, it does take time to contact the people listed and ask them whether they will serve as references. Applicants may also need to make copies of their credentials such as degrees and certificates.

Once the required documents are assembled, job hunters must start looking for possible openings. The first step is networking. They must let friends, family, and acquaintances know that they are looking for work because more jobs are found through contacts than through actual advertising. Using connections may gain them a foothold they might not otherwise be able to get. Then, employment ads in all media need to be scoured for suitable positions. Job seekers must also identify companies that they would like to work for even if there are no positions currently advertised. A visit to a campus or community employment centre can also prove helpful in identifying potential jobs.

All this preparation leads to actually contacting and meeting potential employers. Applicants need to send in their cover letters and resumés to the employers and perhaps follow up with a phone call. When they are called in for an interview, they move on to another step in the job-hunting process. Applicants must prepare for the interview by practising answers to possible questions and by researching the company. They must also give attention to their appearance so that they make a good impression.

Following these steps will make the job hunt a manageable task. Looking for a job is never easy, but with a positive attitude and good preparation, job seekers should be able to find work that suits their qualifications and provides them with a livelihood.

**Writing Assignments**

1. Find a process description in a textbook for one of your core courses. Look for an example of point-form instructions, prose instructions, and a prose passage that describes how something happens or is done. Jot down notes comparing the three.

2. Write a process description of a task that you are familiar with. For example, you can write about painting a room, cleaning a kitchen, making a pizza, or taking an inventory.

3. In a paragraph, describe the process of getting a driver's licence.

## Making Comparisons

Comparison is an important technique in writing. Sometimes writers must compare two things to show which is preferable. Sometimes they use an analogy, a type of comparison, to explain something. The word *compare* itself is problematic because it actually means to show similarity. Writing teachers refer to "compare/contrast essays" in order to be precise, but common usage is just to talk about comparison with the understanding that it refers to both similarities and differences, with the stress on differences.

There is a common expression in English that says you cannot compare apples and oranges, which means you cannot compare two very different things. The two things you are writing about in a comparison essay should have some basis for comparison. It would not be logical to write an essay comparing a sock to a tree, for instance. Often, a comparison essay shows a preference for one or the other. For example, in an essay comparing life in a big city to life in a small town, you would probably take a stand that one is better than the other.

It is also important to remember that in an essay, the writer does the work. It is the writer's job to make the comparison clear; the reader should not have to infer it. For example, you cannot write an essay talking about one movie and then another and then say to your reader, "As you can see, these two movies are very different." You need to show how they are different. For instance, you could say something like "The new film shows the director's growth. He uses fewer cheesy special effects and instead relies on character development."

Four-paragraph comparison essays are not recommended because they usually end up as two separate descriptions with little explicit comparison. In a five-paragraph essay, in contrast, each body paragraph gives a different point of comparison and refers to both things being compared.

Comparison paragraphs are tricky to structure. You have to make sure that your reader can follow the points without getting confused. In block form comparison paragraphs, you talk about one item, then the other, keeping the elements in the same order. In a point-by-point comparison, however, you go back and forth like a ping pong ball, but you make sure that you maintain order. In an essay, you can have both kinds of paragraphs. However, instructors may prefer that you use the block style since the point-by-point can be tricky.

Here is an example of the point-by-point style of comparison paragraph:

When Canadian students graduate from high school, they have the choice of two different kinds of post-secondary institution: university or community college. Colleges are vocational, preparing students for specific careers. Graduates may work as aestheticians, computer technicians, paramedics, or videographers. University studies are more academic, with undergraduates studying in such fields as history, mathematics, and philosophy. These studies may lead to a profession, such as law, medicine, or engineering. Moreover, colleges give more practical, hands-on instruction. Future paramedics can be seen practising CPR on fellow students in the hallway, while other students are creating window displays or building models. In contrast, university students are more likely to be found at their computers, hunting for references for essays. Finally, college and university require different investments, with different results. College students have shorter programs, pay lower tuition, and usually study closer to home. In one to three years, they graduate with a diploma or certificate. University students, on the other hand, go to school longer, pay higher tuition fees, and sometimes have the additional costs of living far from home. However, their degree ultimately has more earning potential than a college diploma. While these are the traditional differences between colleges and universities, both institutions are changing, and the distinction is blurring: colleges are forming partnerships with universities, and some even offer degree programs.

Point 1 – orientation    - college (A)
                         - university (B)
Point 2 – instruction    - college (A)
                         - university (B)
Point 3 – value          - college (A)
                         - university (B)

Compare it to this block style of comparison paragraph:

When Canadian students graduate from high school, they have the choice of two different kinds of post-secondary institution: university or community college. Colleges are vocational, preparing students for specific careers. Graduates may work as aestheticians, computer technicians, paramedics, or videographers. Consequently, colleges give more practical, hands-on instruction. Future paramedics can be seen practising CPR on fellow students in the hallway, while other students are creating window displays or building models. In addition, college students have shorter programs, pay lower tuition, and usually study closer to home. In one to three years, they graduate with a diploma or certificate. In contrast, university studies are more academic, with undergraduates studying in such fields as history, mathematics, and philosophy. These studies may lead to a profession, such as law, medicine, or engineering. On campus, university students are more likely to be found at their computers, hunting for references for essays. Finally, university students go to school longer, pay higher tuition fees, and sometimes have the additional costs of living far from home. However, their degree ultimately has more earning potential than a college diploma. While these are the traditional differences between colleges and universities, both institutions are changing, and the distinction is blurring: colleges are forming partnerships with universities, and some even offer degree programs.

A) college     - orientation (Point 1)
                   - instruction (Point 2)
                   - value (Point 3)
B) university   - orientation (Point 1)
                   - instruction (Point 2)
                   - value (Point 3)

In the comparison paragraphs and essay below, examine and identify the structure of each paragraph.

Destination weddings offer couples something different from traditional weddings. A destination wedding takes place in an exotic location such as a tropical resort. A couple can have a romantic ceremony on a beach. The style is casual, to fit the environment. The wedding is usually small because only the couple's closest family and friends attend. Costs are also kept down because resorts often offer special package deals for the ceremony and reception. The destination wedding is also a vacation for the guests (who pay their own way) as well as a honeymoon for the couple. In contrast, traditional weddings take place in the couple's hometown, with the ceremony in a church and the reception in a hall. While these weddings can be casual, many are very formal, with the bride in an elaborate gown and the groom in a tuxedo. The size of the reception often gets out of hand as more guests get invited to fulfill social obligations. Therefore, the price can skyrocket to the $50,000 range, and that is before the honeymoon costs figure in. When couples consider these differences, they see the advantages of going away, so it is not surprising that destination weddings have become a popular trend.

### The Disney Version

In recent years, fairy tales have changed considerably. Children today are more familiar with the sanitized version, the Disney version, than with the raw tellings of the Brothers Grimm or Hans Christian Andersen. The classic tales of Beauty and the Beast, Sleeping Beauty, Snow White, Cinderella, and the Little Mermaid have been transformed into politically correct, cutesy renderings. The hard edge in the originals has been so softened that they have become cotton candy. The three dramatic differences can be found in fairy tale animals, in the level of violence, and in plot resolution.

Animals, big and little, populate the world of the fairy tale and contribute to the plot, but the cartoon versions are softer and more pet-like. For example, in Disney's *Beauty and the Beast*, the "beast" prince is a cute rendering of an animal. He has a bad temper, but his bark is worse than his bite. In the classic Brothers Grimm version, however, the petulant prince is transformed by a witch into a raging, ugly beast with little compassion for Beauty. Similarly, the little animals such as cute mice and twittering birdies become helpful domestic servants in the cartoons, helping Cinderella sew a dress and Snow White to clean the house. In the classic version, Cinderella has no use for mice, and the birds that separate the lentils from the sand are spiritual manifestations of her dead mother.

The original fairy tales are much more violent than the cartoon versions. Characters are asked to sever limbs, serve up pulsating hearts of virgins, and commit other gory acts. For example, Cinderella's stepsisters each cut off part of their foot to make the glass slipper fit. At the wedding ceremony, their eyes were pecked out by avenging birds befriended by Cinderella. In the Hans Christian Andersen version, the mermaid had to actually cut out her tongue to make herself mute. Moreover, she plotted to murder the prince's bride. The cartoon versions lack this type of violent act. There is no blood spilled in *Cinderella*, and the stepmother is not even very wicked. While the sea witch in *The Little Mermaid* is menacing, she does not actually kill anyone.

Finally, the story lines are softer in the new cartoon versions of the old stories. Sometimes the ending is even changed. Andersen's Little Mermaid kills herself at the end of the story, while Disney's mermaid has a happily-ever-after wedding with the prince. Cinderella's stepsisters are maimed in the original, just jealous and unhappy in the cartoon. Sleeping Beauty was raped by the prince in the Grimm version but awoken with a kiss in later stories. In the story of the three little pigs, the first two pigs are eaten, and the wolf gets his due in a pot of boiling water, while modified versions have no one getting killed.

Fairy tales have changed a lot over the years. Sometimes, change is good to keep in tune with the times, but in fairy tales, politically correct retellings have made the stories insipid. The desire to keep young viewers safe from the realities of life has emasculated the power of the classic stories.

## Analogy

An analogy is a comparison in which a situation is compared to something well-known in order to make it clear. In the following excerpt, see how the writer uses an analogy to help you understand an abstract concept:

> Canada has been described as a patchwork quilt of cultures, religions, etc., and is justly praised for making this work. But to continue the analogy, a patchwork quilt needs a backing to hold it together, and our public schools play part of this role. They provide all of our children the opportunity to interact with people from very different religious and cultural backgrounds, thus providing an opportunity to develop tolerance and understanding.

Excerpted from "The Religious Schools Dilemma," by Wayne Cook, *Toronto Star* 20 January 2005, p. A20

The basic analogy here is that a quilt is stitched together with separate pieces of fabric, just as Canada is a country of different ethnic groups. In a quilt, you can see the individual pieces. Canada has also been compared to a mosaic in which individual pieces are also visible. In comparison, the United States has been referred to as a "melting pot" because its ethnic groups have been all stirred together and come out as one entity—American. Discuss these comparisons. Are they valid today?

Here is another analogy:

> The English language is like a huge pot of stew. Old English, or Anglo-Saxon as it is known, is the base, a Germanic language. To this base many ingredients have been added. Words from Old Norse were brought to England by the Viking invaders. When William the Conqueror won the Battle of Hastings in 1066, he became the first of many kings of England who did not speak English. Their language, Norman French, gradually blended in with English, changing some of its structures and practically doubling its vocabulary. Another ingredient added to this stew was the huge vocabulary based on Latin and Greek words, used mainly for scientific and technical terms. As these ingredients cook in the stew, they become less distinct, and the flavours blend together.

## The Language of Comparison

An important thing to remember is that the comparison must be clear. For instance, if you use the word *more* in a sentence, the reader has to understand what comparison is being made.

## Comparatives and Superlatives

The comparative and superlative forms of adjectives and adverbs are used in comparison writing. The comparison form is used when two people or things are being compared; the superlative form is used when one is compared to all the rest. Comparative forms are formed with the addition of −*er* for adjectives of one or two syllables; *more* is used with longer words. Superlative forms are formed with the addition of −*est* for adjectives of one or two syllables; *most* is used with longer words. One-syllable adverbs have −*er* and −*est* endings; the rest use *more* and *most*.

|  | Positive form | Comparative form | Superlative form |
|---|---|---|---|
| 1- or 2-syllable adjectives and adverbs | cheap<br>fast<br>sleepy | cheaper<br>faster<br>sleepier | cheapest<br>fastest<br>sleepiest |
| longer adjectives and adverbs | expensive<br>successful | more expensive<br>more successful | most expensive<br>most successful |
| irregular forms | good<br>bad<br>less | better<br>worse<br>lesser | best<br>worst<br>least |

Note the use of comparative and superlative forms in the following sentences:

> Jane is taller than her brother.
> The more expensive model has a lot of bells and whistles.
> He works better when the background music is better.
> That is the best falafel I have ever eaten.
> He is one of the most successful jazz musicians in North America.
> Of the three options, this one is the least practical.

## The Verb *compare*

The prepositions *to* and *with* are often used with the transitive verb *compare*. A frequent error is using the active participle *comparing* instead of the passive participle *compared*. *Comparing* has to refer to whomever or whatever is making the comparison, while *compared* refers to what is actually in the comparison.

> They compared the options available. In order to make a valid comparison, they had to look at the manufacturer's specifications.
> Compared to the deluxe model, this one is a better buy. Those features are unnecessary.
> She put together a chart comparing the features of the two cars.
> Comparing the prices, she found the upgrades were not worth the cost.

## Making Comparisons: Examples

Here are some excerpts from the readings that illustrate words and expressions used to make comparisons:

"throwaway plastic bags might simply be better than the alternatives" (Taylor, page 318)

Do not confuse *than* (used in comparisons) with *then* (an adverb of time)—the two words sound the same in sentences.

"Wouldn't you laugh . . . at someone who pays more than 200 times as much as you do" (Singer, page 283)

Note the use of *as much as*.

"a new study was released showing that manual labourers and the unemployed are significantly more likely to play the national lottery" (Stern, page 290)

The word *likely* can be confusing for English language learners. It is an adjective (despite the –*ly* ending) which means probable.

"One Canadian study found that the highest rates of compulsive gambling show up in aboriginal communities" (Stern, page 290)

Note the use of the superlative form *highest*. The definite article *the* must be used with the superlative.

"one of modern life's most common social practices, or . . . one of its biggest transgressions" (Teitel, page 297)

Here are two examples of superlative forms: *most common*, *biggest*. Instead of a definite article, possessive determiners (*life's*, *its*) are used.

"if more and more of its Canadian-born citizens . . ." (Griffiths, page 330)

Note that the use of "more and more" is informal style. Some students overuse the structure, so use it only when you need to show progression.

"When clothing started to become less formalized . . . dress codes started to seem more like the universal dad's way of spoiling the fun" (Everett-Green, page 345)

Note the use of *less* and *more*.

**Writing Assignments**

Write a paragraph or an essay comparing:

- two places you have lived in or visited
- two schools or two education systems
- two vehicles, two computers, or two items you have contemplated purchasing
- two people you know

## Persuading

Most essays are a type of argument because you are putting forth ideas and supporting them, but when you are arguing a controversial issue, you need a persuasive argument. Unlike a quarrel, in which you have an emotional dispute with someone, a persuasive essay offers reasoning. You try to make someone understand your point of view or to move someone to an action that you recommend. You must be objective, logical, and forthright to win your case. You must connect and support your ideas.

Most of the essays in the reading section (Part 2) argue for a point of view. As you read the essays, pay attention to the author's thesis, and see how it is argued. For example, "The Case against Bottled Water" (pages 309–11) is a strong argument essay that presents three main arguments. Here are two more persuasive essays for you to examine:

### Why We Need to Pay Taxes

Canadians often grumble about paying taxes. They think the government is picking their pockets and wasting their money. They maintain that they pay too much and look longingly south of the border at the lower tax rates. They claim businesses are better run than the government—even when shown evidence of corruption and wastefulness in large corporations. They ignore the fact that Canada is an expensive country to run because it is a huge area with a small population. Most important, however, they do not realize that the services Canadians get with their tax money are a necessary and sound investment.

Taxes fund vital social services such as health, education, and welfare that all people benefit from, either directly or indirectly. For example, higher education levels mean better trained workers for the whole society. Schools train our doctors, architects, plumbers, and barbers. Business costs are reduced when graduates have the skills to do the job and do not need extensive training. Welfare for the less fortunate lessens the gap between the rich and the poor, an inequity that can lead to social problems such as crime. Governments that invest in recreation services for children will have a fitter populace and therefore save money on health care.

Second, taxes mean that the costs are shared by society and are therefore not an unreasonable burden for individuals. In the past, when individual citizens paid doctor and hospital bills, not only did Canadians have a lower health standard but also a terrible debt load. The few dollars contributed in a tax bill to pay for medical care eases a burden that could bankrupt an individual. Moreover, many families would not be able to send their children to school if they had to pay thousands of dollars a year for their education. In addition, the cost is borne by those who can most afford it, since taxes are generally tied to income.

Furthermore, systems that are funded by taxes rather than user fees have lower administrative costs. Privately run agencies have overhead costs. For example, they have to compete with other companies for the business and thus need to spend on advertising. User fees require middlemen and collection services. For example, in the American system of health insurance from employers, billions of dollars are wasted in administration. Governments just have to worry about covering costs, not about making profits to satisfy investors.

Canadians should realize just how costly the alternatives are and pay their tax bill without so much grumbling. Of course, this doesn't mean allowing government spending to get out of hand. Canadians need to be informed voters just as they need to be informed consumers. They need to make sure they get good value from their tax dollars.

Here is the second example of a persuasive essay:

### Technology and Children

Technology devotees are not satisfied with having made adults hooked on technology; now they are marketing their products to younger and younger consumers. Television programs have been designed for small babies. Children start playing video games and computer programs as preschoolers. Elementary schoolchildren have smartphones. Although parents today are eager to buy their children the latest in electronic gadgetry, they should stop and think about the ramifications. A dependence on technology can prevent children from developing properly.

The more time children spend with electronic gadgets, the less healthy they are. If they go outside after school, they play, run, and jump. They get fresh air and sunshine and lots of exercise. They get the exposure to nature that the brain needs to refresh itself. If they plunk themselves down in front of a TV or computer screen, they are straining their eyes and not exercising their bodies. Moreover, TV watching may be accompanied by snacking on junk food. In addition, kids plugged into personal music players are destroying their hearing. Cellphone radiation may harm developing brains.

Children's creativity is also restricted by television and computers. While a reader has to exercise his or her brain to imagine the world described in a book, a television watcher is passive. Artwork done on a computer is limited by the restrictions of the program. Children need to get physical with their creations—to feel the clay between their fingers, to hold the pencil or paint brush. Today's children "interact" with electronic toys that "talk" and move, while in the past they would have built a fort from a cardboard box and acted out scenes with handmade puppets. Children today rely on their toys to entertain them instead of making their own entertainment.

Social development is also retarded in our electronic world. Even though the Internet and cellphones are supposed to make communication easier, they actually replace face-to-face interaction. Children do not play with children in the neighbourhood; they send email to strangers around the world. They are busy text messaging instead of talking to the person they are sitting next to. Their portable music players transport them to another space, not the one they are physically in. Today's children are growing up less able to communicate with people directly; they cannot read facial expressions and body language.

Even though technology is supposed to be making this a better world, it is hurting our children. While it is impossible to stop the technological advances, wise parents should limit the time their children spend with electronic gadgetry. It is important to let them experience the real world first. Then they will appreciate and understand their technology better.

## Logical Fallacies

In argument, the term *logical fallacy* is used to explain a mistake in reasoning. Sometimes a fallacy is an unfair or improper method of arguing. Other times, it is a flaw in the process. Here are some common logical fallacies with examples:

| Example | Type of Logical Fallacy |
|---|---|
| You shouldn't listen to such an idiot. Even using all his fingers, he can't count to 10. | **Against the person:** Instead of focusing on the idea, the writer mocks the person. |
| This idea is good because it is fitting. There's nothing bad about a good idea when you know it is right. | **Circular argument:** The writer goes in circles rather than advancing the reasoning. |
| If you know what's good for you, do as I say. I have a third-degree black belt in karate. | **Appeal to force:** The writer becomes angry and threatens the opponent with harm. |
| Don't expand the welfare system. I know a panhandler downtown making $100 a day. These people are making a decent living off the streets. | **Hasty generalization:** The writer uses only one piece of evidence and draws a grand conclusion. |
| Sir, I broke my arm in a fall when I helped my sick grandmother to the hospital for emergency surgery today, so can I have an extension on my essay that was due yesterday? | **Appeal to pity:** The writer makes the opponent feel sorry for him. |
| His grades started slipping when he moved to the new apartment. | **Faulty chronological reasoning:** The writer draws a relation between one incident and another illogically. |
| Instead of frowning all the time, smiling wins friends. Many people are afraid of the dentist. | **Non sequitur:** One idea does not logically follow another. |

Make sure that your arguments are sound when you are writing a persuasive essay. Do not fall into any of the traps of logical fallacy.

## Conceding a Point

In spoken language, when you are having a discussion over an issue or arguing points of view, you often agree with the other person's arguments but add a counterargument. It is a "yes, but" strategy. Writers do the same thing when they concede a point but focus on what they perceive to be a stronger argument.

One reason that writing is so difficult is that you have to see your work from the reader's point of view and imagine what is going on in your reader's head. What you are saying may be perfectly obvious to you, but it may not be clear to the reader, so it is important that your arguments follow logically. Moreover, if there is a strong argument against your point of view, it is like the elephant in the room—there is no sense ignoring it. Your persuasive essay can become stronger if you anticipate and acknowledge some of the obvious counterarguments.

One of the easiest ways to make a concession in your argument is to use an *although* statement:

| | |
|---|---|
| Although computers have many educational benefits, they stifle children's creativity. | main argument is against computer use by children |
| Although computers may limit children's interaction with their immediate surroundings, they open up the whole world for their exploration. | main argument is in favour of computer use by children |

The main idea is in the main clause. By using a subordinate clause, you are saying that the statement in the subordinate clause is less important (therefore subordinate) to the idea in the main clause. Make sure that the idea you want to emphasize is in the main clause.

A concession can appear right at the beginning of a paragraph. Note these examples of topic sentences from paragraphs in Unit 4:

> "Although working part-time can create a serious time crunch, high school students should consider the many advantages of having a job." (page 117)
> "Although experts say that the family meal fosters communication skills and intimacy, dining together does not work for all families." (page 125)

You do not have to mention all the counterarguments in your essay, but if there is one that stands out as an obvious choice, concede it.

## Qualifying Statements

A good argument has to be reasonable, so it must acknowledge that the world is not black or white, all or nothing. When you write an essay, you have to choose your words with care so as not to alienate your readers. You do not want to overstate your case.

Readers can accept qualified statements better than absolute statements. In the following pairs of statements, the first is absolute while the second is qualified and therefore easier to accept:

| | |
|---|---|
| Women do well at language-related tasks while men are good at spatial tasks.<br>Women generally do better at language-related tasks while men tend to perform better on spatial tasks. | The addition of *generally* and the aspect of comparison makes the second statement more acceptable. |
| All teenagers work part-time.<br>Many teenagers work part-time. | Avoid using words like *all*, *always*, and *never*. They are rarely true. Instead, use *often*, *some*, and *many*. |
| All smokers develop lung cancer.<br>Smokers have a higher risk of developing lung cancer. | The expression "have a higher risk" shows that not all smokers get cancer. |
| She is the best film editor in the world.<br>She may be the best film editor in the world. | Modal verbs (e.g., *may*, *might*, *could*) are another way to qualify statements. |
| He has no knowledge of physics.<br>He seems to lack knowledge of physics. | Verbs such as *seem* and *tend* can also make statements less absolute. |

Remember also that the simple present tense expresses the idea of a general statement, so it does not need additions to express the idea of a common occurrence. Students sometimes try to show the idea of generality by using a future tense or adding *always*:

| | |
|---|---|
| First-year students always find it difficult to make the adjustment from high school. | This statement is not true. |
| First-year students will find it difficult to make the adjustment from high school. | This statement uses a future tense, which does not show generality. |
| First-year students find it difficult to make the adjustment from high school. | This statement has the simple present tense, so it is the best choice to show a general tendency. |

Be careful not to overuse qualifying statements. You still have to take a stand. You do not want to appear wishy-washy and uncommitted.

**Writing Assignment**

Write a persuasive essay on one of the current issues in the news. For example, take a stand on safe injection sites for drug users, year-round schooling, or the right-to-die movement.

# Editing and Correcting Skills

Perfection in writing is a lofty goal, one that is difficult to attain. Even professional writers have editors to catch their slips and errors—ones that they missed even after they have carefully proofread and edited their work. While some errors are based on a lack of knowledge (such as the misuse of a word), others are careless slips (like typographical errors). Some are major errors (those that can cause communication problems) while others are relatively minor. Sometimes what looks like a minor error can have major consequences—one misplaced comma in a contract famously cost Rogers Communications more than a million dollars.

Checking what you write is important. You should develop the habit of quickly proofreading your work before you press Send or Print. Even a simple text message can be transformed by quirky software, so casting an eye over it is important.

Why error-free is better:

- Sending out documents full of mistakes can cause miscommunication.
- Error-filled documents create a bad impression, indicating that you do not care about your work.
- If the organization you work for has to have your documents corrected and edited by someone else, you are a less valuable employee than you could be.

Unit 1 introduces the basic principles of good writing, such as clarity and conciseness, and of academic writing, such as answering the question and using the appropriate style. This unit focuses on the editing and correcting processes required to fulfill these requirements. Units 2 and 3 go over the basics of vocabulary use and sentence structure that you need to apply when editing and correcting. While this unit contains exercises to help you understand the specific points being explained, the real editing and correcting that you have to do is with your own writing. Doing a grammar exercise is much easier than fixing your own work—but it is correcting your own writing that is ultimately the most valuable exercise.

## Understanding the Process

**Correcting** your work involves looking for errors like spelling mistakes and punctuation errors and fixing them. **Editing** is a more involved process: you have to take a critical look at what you have written to see where it can be improved in structure, style, or expression. This distinction, of course, is not absolute; correcting and editing overlap. **Proofreading** is the final step—when you read over what you have written to check for mistakes.

When you read your work, you are not just looking for errors to fix, you are looking for ways to improve the way you express your ideas. All writers need to strive for clarity and conciseness. Writers hate deleting chunks of text they have toiled over, but that is what editing may require. Professional writers spend most of their time rereading, checking, and changing what they write.

Here are some examples of what you can accomplish with careful editing:

- cutting out repetitious phrases and sentences
- ensuring that your writing is in the appropriate style (no conversational expressions in an academic essay, for instance)
- varying your vocabulary
- varying your sentence structure
- adding specific examples to clarify your points

For in-class writing tests and exams, you often have very little time to go over your work, but you should give it at least a quick reread. For writing assignments, on the other hand, you may have several weeks to complete the work, so you should take advantage of the time to improve it. It is best to let a piece of writing sit for a day or two and then go over it with a fresh eye.

The only one who can actually improve your writing skills is you. While you can have your documents cleaned up by someone else, the goal is to make fewer errors in the first place. Therefore, you need to learn from the correcting process. Your instructor can show you where you need to improve and explain any problems you do not understand, but you must be motivated to fix the errors. Spending time on correcting and editing improves your writing skills, so what you write next time should have fewer errors in the first draft.

### Learning from Your Marked Work

People learn more from failure than from success. Even if your paper comes back to you covered in circles and comments, view it as valuable feedback you can use to improve. Some students only look at the grade they achieved and spend little time going over the paper. Some get frustrated and treat every marked error as a personal slight. However, even professional writers get their work edited and corrected, so you need to accept correction as part of the writing process.

Just as students have different ways of looking at their returned assignments, instructors have different ways of marking papers. Some write very few comments on the essay except for the grade itself; this often leaves students wondering why they received that particular grade. Some instructors mark only the specific mistakes they want the student to focus on correcting. While some instructors circle or underline errors and expect students to take the time to figure out what is wrong, other instructors actually correct the mistakes. Some instructors may use a rubric to break down the grades, with a point system for individual requirements such as proper essay structure and language use.

You should also take into consideration the time restrictions that instructors have—they cannot write detailed, explanatory comments on each paper. Moreover, they may be reluctant to do this because many students do not read them. However, instructors are generally willing to go over papers with you in person to explain anything that you do not understand.

Take the time to read over your instructor's comments. If you still cannot understand why something is wrong, ask the instructor or a tutor. Be an active learner. For instance, if you do not understand what a "run-on sentence" is, look it up. (For example, you can find run-ons listed in the index of this book. You can also do an Internet search for more explanations, examples, and even exercises.)

## Making Your Own Checklist

In order to improve your writing, you need to know where you tend to make mistakes. You can make a list of your own problem areas by looking at the feedback your instructor gives you from your assignments. Most students have a good understanding of their strengths and weaknesses. You can write down a reminder list of what you should check before you hand in an assignment. Focus on mistakes you can tackle.

For in-class assignments, you have to rely on a mental checklist rather than a written one. Commit to memory a few crucial items to check before you hand in your work.

Sample checklist:

| What to look for: |
| --- |
| – make sure thesis is at the end of the introduction |
| – check for parallel structure in the thesis |
| – check that words have not been accidentally shortened (*the* for *they*, for instance) |
| – check spelling of *to/too/two* |
| – check singular and plural references |

You can gradually eliminate items from your list as you learn to fix the problem. At first, the mistake will be one you have to carefully check for in your work. Gradually, you will learn to catch the error as you write without interrupting the flow of your ideas. For example, if you tend to misspell *there/their/they're*, you should check every use of those words before you hand in your work. You can also briefly pause before you write one of the words and do a quick review of the rules in your head to see which one you need. Mnemonic devices can help: think of the expression "here and there" to help you spell the adverb *there*—just add a *t* to *here*, but don't confuse *here* with *hear* (which is something you do with your *ear*). You can also replace *they're* with *they are* to reduce one potential error. Your writing will improve as you tackle individual problems that you have.

## Using a Dictionary Effectively

Your dictionary gives more than definitions. You can check for spelling and other word forms. A good dictionary, such as the *Oxford Advanced Learner's Dictionary*, gives example sentences that allow you to see how the word typically works in a sentence, along with common accompanying words such as prepositions. (See pages 44–47 in Unit 2 for more on using a dictionary.)

When you are working on an assignment at home, you have the time to check words as you write your draft. For instance, you can verify whether a verb like *expect* is transitive and requires a direct object. Dictionary checks should not interrupt the flow of ideas; use the natural pauses in the writing process for such investigations.

Dictionary use is different for in-class tests and assignments. If you are allowed to use a dictionary, you are probably not allowed electronic formats. Using a book-form dictionary can be time-consuming if you are not used to it, so you must use it judiciously. For example, look up any unfamiliar words in the test questions—they are crucial. Otherwise, check your spelling and word use after you have finished your writing.

## Using Computer Tools

Word processing software has spelling and grammar checkers. These tools have improved over the years, but they are not perfect. They can even make mistakes worse when they "guess" at what word you want. To use the tools effectively, you need to understand what the program is suggesting and why.

Auto-correct will usually catch typographical errors as you make them, but you should still run a spelling and grammar check of your document when you are finished. Be careful not to just automatically take the program's suggestions—consider each one. You must also proofread your work afterwards—don't rely on the program to fix all your mistakes. Spell checkers often verify that you have correctly spelled words but not that the words are the ones you actually wanted to use. Even though they are not perfect, you should use these tools for your documents.

### Proofreading tips

1. Let your work sit for a day or two. Look at it with fresh eyes.
2. Make sure that you have finished your editing and that you are satisfied with the content and the expression of your ideas.
3. Give the work your full attention. Turn off music. Close other applications on your computer. Put your phone on mute. Avoid distractions.
4. Work from a print-out. It will look different from the way it looks on the screen.
5. Read slowly, paying attention to each word.
6. Try reading your work aloud to see if it sounds right.
7. Block out sentence by sentence to focus your attention on each word.
8. Have your personal checklist ready. You can check for each error individually.
9. Use the computer's Find function to look for words you may have trouble with.
10. Use the spell check function in your word processor, but do not accept its suggestions blindly. Use your dictionary to check anything you are unsure of.
11. Double-check details, like the spelling of an author's name or a date.

## Submitting Drafts and Rewrites

In some English courses, you are given the opportunity to hand in multiple versions of an essay. You may have to hand in an outline before you write your first draft. You may write an essay in class and then be asked to rewrite it at home. Sometimes the assignment will ask you to build on what you have, adding references or other elements. Often instructors assign grades for each stage of the work. They give you feedback that you can use to improve your essay in the next stage.

Some students do only minimal corrections for rewrite assignments, but it is better to spend the time to go over all your errors carefully. Make sure you understand all your instructor's comments. Take advantage of the learning opportunity afforded by the assignment.

### Activity

Go over your previous writing assignments to see what kind of errors you tend to make. Correct the errors. You can get help from a classmate, a tutor, or your instructor. Make your own checklist to use for your next assignment.

## Examples of Correction and Revision

1. Original sentence: There are more than 7000 students in China choose to study in a foreign country in 2009.

| | |
|---|---|
| There <u>were</u> more than 7000 students in China <u>who chose</u> to study in a foreign country in 2009. | **Corrections:** The verb tenses are aligned; the missing relative pronoun is supplied. |
| In 2009, more than 7000 Chinese students chose to study abroad. | **Revision** is clearer and more concise. |

2. Original sentence: The employers blame the graduates do not have the right skill to find the job they are looking for.

| | |
|---|---|
| The employers blame the graduates <u>for not having</u> the right skills <u>for the job</u> they are looking for. | **Corrections:**<br>The verb *blame* is completed with the preposition *for* and a gerund; note that the original "right skill to find the job" talks about the job search rather than doing the job itself. |
| The employers blame the graduates for not being qualified for the jobs. | **Revision** is clearer and more concise. |

3. Original thesis statement: Some positive effects that divorce may have on the lives of children whose parents choose not to stay married are children become more mature, less stressful, and more freedom.

Some positive effects that divorce may have on the lives of children whose parents choose not to stay married are that children become <u>more mature, less stressed, and freer</u>.

**Corrections:**
The parallel structure is fixed; there is a vocabulary change—a person can be *stressed*, but an activity is *stressful*; the addition of *that* makes the sentence easier to follow.

Some positive effects that divorce may have on the lives of children are that they become more mature, less stressed, and freer.

**Revision:**
An unnecessary phrase is removed.

Divorce can have a positive effect on children by making them more mature, relaxed, and independent.

**Revision:**
The sentence keeps the sense of the original but uses adjectives that can have the same form; it's now more concise (shorter by six words)

4.   Original essay introduction: How come some teen don't attend school? Does the child lack support/understanding/motivation needed to attend school, or is it fear? But then again should society really force child to school if he/she don't want too. During this essay I'll like to talk about why or why not, its a good idea to force a child to attend school.

Why do some teenagers not attend school? Do they lack the support, understanding, or motivation to attend school? Are they afraid? However, should society really force children to go to school if they don't want to go? In this essay, I would like to discuss why or why not children should be forced to attend school.

**Corrections:**
The grammar errors and verb forms are fixed; the plural and singular forms are aligned (*some teen* becomes *some teenagers*).
It is not correct to use slashes between words—this shows a lack of commitment to a specific word, especially when they are synonyms. "But then again" is removed—it is a conversational sentence opener.

Students may choose to skip class for many reasons. Some lack the motivation to learn, while others need additional support to cope with the demands of the courses. Some students suffer social problems such as bullying, making them afraid to attend school. With so many underlying problems, it is a mistake to force high school students to stay in school.

**Revision:**
The original introduction has too many questions; the focus of an essay should be on answering questions, not just posing them. Most important, the writer does not have a clear thesis—he or she does not commit to one point of view; moreover, it is an announcement thesis. Because many statements are left unclear in the original, the revision has to be a bit of guesswork as to what the writer is trying to say.

## Recognizing Types of Errors

In order to improve your writing, it is useful to know the different categories of errors. If you can understand what they are and why you are making them, you can learn how to deal with them. You should be able to identify the different types of errors when you look at your returned assignments.

When you know the right spelling, but your fingers just hit the wrong keys, you make **typographical errors ("typos")**. The computer may auto-correct them before you even realize you made them. If you do not use or do not have an auto-correct feature, be sure to use the spell checker. Although you cannot rely on a word processor's spell checker to find all the errors, it does provide one of the easiest ways to find typos. (And if you are using an auto-correct feature, make sure it does not make changes you do not want.)

**Careless slips** are common. For handwritten work, you may drop the endings of words, turning *they* into *the*, for example. When you edit on the computer, you may accidentally leave a part of the first version of the sentence in the new sentence, making it ungrammatical and sometimes incomprehensible. The only fix is careful proofreading. When you are cutting and pasting or deleting sections, be sure to reread the whole sentence to make sure the change fits. Knowing what types of slips you commonly make allows you to find them more easily and may even prevent you from making them in the first place.

**Copying errors** are the ones that are easiest to avoid. Pay attention. Make sure you have written names, dates, numbers, and titles correctly. Imagine how your resumé would be received if you misspelled the name of the recipient.

Everyone makes **spelling mistakes**. The English language is a minefield of potential spelling errors, so spelling is addressed in a separate section in this unit (see pages 195–97).

**Grammatical errors** cover a wide range of different kinds of mistakes, including:

- singular/plural agreement
- pronoun use
- verb forms
- use of verb tenses
- parts of speech
- article use
- possessive forms
- sentence fragments and run-on sentences
- phrase and clause structure
- misplaced modifiers

The basics of sentence structure are dealt with in Unit 3, and some grammatical errors are further explained in this unit.

If you make **punctuation mistakes**, review the section on individual punctuation marks at the end of Unit 3. Make sure you know how to form and position punctuation marks correctly—whether you are writing by hand or using a keyboard. Different languages have different punctuation. For example, some languages begin quotation marks at the bottom of the line of text.

**Vocabulary errors** (also called errors in **diction**) include using the wrong word for the meaning you wish to express or using a word incorrectly in a sentence. They are often more serious than grammatical errors because they are more likely to cause misunderstanding. For example, in a sentence such as "He use a teeth stick daily," the incorrect verb form (*use* instead of *uses*) does not cause problems, but the term *teeth stick* will make the reader stop and wonder what was meant (the student was looking for the word *toothpick*).

Avoid vocabulary errors by expressing your ideas with words you know well and checking the words you are not sure of. Developing writing skills requires extending those skills, so it is important that you experiment a bit with vocabulary, but you can do most of your experimentation when the stakes are lower, as in practice writing assignments or essay drafts that you expect to revise.

If English is your second language, you may have trouble learning some of the features of English if they are completely different from the way your language works. Using the rules of your own language may result in **language interference errors**. Articles (*the, a, an*), prepositions, and verb forms often give ESL learners problems. The way certain words are used can be different in two languages. For example, the words *easy* and *hard* are generally used to describe tasks, not people, in English; a common ESL error is to say something like, "He is easy to learn English." Usually, students learn the trouble spots early on, but sometimes these errors become fossilized (see below).

**Fossilized errors** are essentially bad habits that are hard to break. Although the term *fossilized* expresses the idea that they are set in stone, they are not impossible to fix. You must be motivated to tackle them, however. The best way to deal with fossilized errors is to concentrate on one area at a time.

Often, writers recognize the fossilized errors they make and may even know how to fix them, but they make them anyway. They can fix them in a grammar exercise but not in their own writing. Common fossilized errors are subject–verb agreement (for example, writing "people thinks"). One student had a habit of putting a comma before every *and* that he used; even after he was taught about comma use, he still made the mistake consistently. Teaching does not fix fossilized errors; the writer has to consciously work to break the habit.

People who do not read enough are not as comfortable with the forms of Standard Written English, so they use spoken English to guide their writing. They make **"writing by ear" mistakes** because they try to write down what they commonly hear. Unfortunately, the English language is not written phonetically, so it is very hard to figure out the spelling of a word from the way it sounds. In speech, sounds are slurred together or dropped entirely. Unstressed vowels sound the same—like an "uh" sound, a sound called "schwa."

Here are some examples of "writing by ear" errors:

- sposta [supposed to]
- firstable [first of all]
- right from the gecko [right from the get go]
- madder-a fact [matter of fact]

These kinds of mistakes show the importance of regular reading in order to become familiar with spelling and written forms.

### Activity

Go over your previous writing assignments to see what type of errors you made. To categorize the errors, you have to determine why you made the mistake. For example, if you can easily correct the mistake, it may be just a careless slip or it may be a fossilized error—one that you make by habit.

## Correcting Vocabulary Mistakes

Mistakes at the word level can include spelling mistakes, part-of-speech errors, and word choice errors. Unit 2 reviews some basics of word use and form. Remember that word choice goes beyond knowing what a word means—you also have to consider how it is used in a sentence.

### Correcting Spelling Mistakes

English spelling is difficult. Even avid readers can be bad spellers. For some people, spelling is a problem that is part of a learning disability. However, anyone can become a better speller—it just takes work.

Check your spelling before you hand in your work. Make it a habit to run your eyes over anything you have written, looking for obvious errors. Know your weak spots, and look out for words you have problems with.

Use the tools you have, such as a dictionary and the spell checker built into the writing program you are using.

When you get an assignment back, correct the spelling mistakes you made, and write out the correct word several times. Muscle memory (from handwriting or typing) can help you to learn the word.

---

**Why you should work on your spelling**

- Just because English spelling is difficult, it is not acceptable to throw up your hands in defeat. Your spelling may not be perfect, but it can get better.
- Like it or not, you will be judged on your spelling. If you hand in a resumé with spelling mistakes, it will be rejected.
- Spelling mistakes are the most obvious writing errors and so make a bad first impression. Improving your spelling is one of the easier ways to improve your writing.

---

### Words Often Confused

Here are some words that are often misspelled because they are mixed up with another word, usually a homophone (a word that sounds the same):

accept (to receive, get), except (but not)

advice (noun), advise (verb)

affect (usually a verb), effect (usually a noun)

cite (to reference), sight (ability to see or something you see), site (place, location) desert (arid land), dessert (something sweet at the end of a meal)

hear (to listen), here (not there)

its (belonging to it—possessive form), it's (contraction of *it is* or *it has*)

loose (not tight), lose (be unable to find something you had)

passed (to have gone by), past (previous time)

principal (most important), principle (basic rule)

quiet (little or no noise), quite (rather)

right (correct), rite (ceremony), write (compose messages or documents)

than (comparative), then (adverb of time)

their (belonging to them), there (adverb of place), they're (they are)

to (preposition), too (also), two (the second number)

wear (to have clothes on), were (past tense of *to be*), we're (we are)

weather (climate), whether (if)

who's (who is, who has), whose (belonging to it—possessive form)

woman (singular), women (plural)

you're (you are), your (belonging to you)

## Words That Are Commonly Misspelled

| | | |
|---|---|---|
| accommodate | emphasize | preference |
| acknowledge | environment | prejudice |
| analyze | especially | proceed |
| argument | exaggerate | professor |
| athlete | exercise | pronunciation |
| beginning | fascinate | receive |
| believe | February | recommend |
| business | foreign | relevant |
| changeable | government | repetition |
| chosen | grammar | restaurant |
| committee | height | rhythm |
| competitive | immediately | schedule |
| convenience | knowledge | secretary |
| criticism | marriage | separate |
| definitely | necessary | sincerely |
| dependent | noticeable | studying |
| descendant | occasion | succeed |
| develop | occur | surprise |
| development | occurred | technique |
| embarrassed | parallel | tragedy |

## Word Boundaries

When we speak, there are no spaces between words. Speech flows from one sound to another, so it is hard to separate out individual words just from the sound of a sentence. As a result, some people often make spelling mistakes in which one word is written as two or two words are written as one.

Words that are often written incorrectly as one word:

> a lot
> each other
> even though
> in front

Words that are often incorrectly written as two or three words:

> nowadays
> nevertheless

Some words have different meanings if they are written as one word or two. Here are some examples:

| | |
|---|---|
| She has always been <u>a part</u> of the group. | This means that she does belong to the group. |
| She has always been <u>apart</u> from the group. | This means that she does not belong to the group. Note the preposition *from*. |
| <u>Maybe</u> he would prefer to work somewhere else. <br> It <u>may be</u> that he does not really want the job. | *Maybe* is written as one word when it means "perhaps" and as two words when it is the modal verb plus the verb *be*. |
| He wants to be left <u>alone</u>. <br> <u>A lone</u> man was walking down the street. | *Alone* is an adverb; *a lone* is a determiner and an adjective that needs to be completed with a noun. |
| He <u>already</u> packed the books. <br> He had the books <u>all ready</u>. | *Already* is an adverb describing the verb *packed*. In the second sentence, *all* refers to the books. |

## Activity

Look through your last marked assignments, and make a list of the spelling mistakes you made. Correct the mistakes. Write out each word 10 times, spelling it to yourself.

### Exercise 7.1

Correct the spelling errors in the following sentences:

1. Excercise should be apart of everyday life. Even a walk a round the neighbourhood can be benefisial.

2. Cloths that are not longer warn should be recycled as donations to chairity.

3. The imigrants' education level often determines weather or not they adopt to their new life easily.

4. The police pulled him over for wreckless driving. He had ran a red lite and almost hit a cyclist.

5. If the punishmint were more sever, may be fewer people would drive while texting on there smartphones.

6. After the acident, the car was a right-off. With the insuranse money, he bought a compac car so that he could save on gass.

7. Jill and her twin sister look alot a like, but its not hard to tell them apart. Jill smiles more then her sister.

8. They should definately contact the administration office to see if they can get an extention. They do not want to loose their chance at bidding for the projekt.

9. Employees prefer to higher collage graduates with some work exprience.

## Correcting Part-of-Speech Errors

Using the wrong part of speech in a sentence is a common mistake, especially for English language learners. The mistakes can be attributed either to a lack of knowledge about the word itself (not knowing the different forms used for different parts of speech) or to a lack of sentence sense (not knowing which part of speech is called for in that position in the sentence). In the first case, it is a lexical error, in the second, a grammatical one. This distinction is not evident to the reader, but if you often use the wrong part of speech in a sentence, it is useful to understand why you made the error so that you can work on that weakness, either with a dictionary or a grammar book.

### Activity

Look at the examples of such errors on the next page, and discuss different ways to rewrite the phrases.

| In the <u>nowadays</u>, with the <u>progressive</u> of <u>economic</u> and society . . . | a) The word *nowadays* is an adverb—the prepositional phrase requires a noun in that position.<br>b) The word *progressive* is an adjective—it does not fit with the preposition *with* and the determiner *the*.<br>c) The word *economic* is an adjective—what is the noun form? |
|---|---|
| In <u>additional</u>, <u>optimistic</u> in daily life can also bring <u>happy</u>. | a) The word *additional* is an adjective, so it does not work after the preposition *in*. It could be replaced by the noun form, or the whole prepositional phrase could be replaced by the adverb form of *additional*. Correct this phrase in these two different ways.<br>b) The word *optimistic* is an adjective—what part of speech is needed in this phrase?<br>c) The word *happy* is an adjective—what part of speech is needed in this phrase? |

## Exercise 7.2

Fix any errors in the parts of speech in the following sentences:

1. Although Canada is a safety country and the criminal rate is dropping, many people seem worry about dangerous on the streets.
2. Talk on the phone with their parents can decrease international students' homesick.
3. The team loss the game because of their star player's absent.
4. More trees and flowers can beauty our city. It's importance to develop more parks.
5. Technology ables people to get connected easy.
6. The most commonly use of cellphones is text messaging with people send hundreds of messages a day.
7. Parents' overprotective may cause their children to rebellion and get into trouble.
8. Because they want to success, they have to proceed very careful.
9. Immigrants might have to change their customs and believes to fit in with the cultural.
10. Students can improve their reading comprehend by practice more. They will become more confidence.

## Correcting Word Choice Errors

Choosing the correct words to express your ideas can be difficult. Sometimes two words express almost the same basic idea, but they are used differently. See Recognizing Collocation in Unit 2, page 41.

---

### Exercise 7.3

Correct the sentences below by changing the underlined words. You may have to make other adjustments to the sentence.

1. If the passport is lost or <u>robbed</u>, it is important to <u>communicate</u> the embassy.
2. She was so angry that she <u>hit</u> the door shut, but then she felt <u>shameful</u> about her outburst.
3. People who <u>visit</u> hockey games come to the <u>ice</u> <u>stadium</u> not only to see skating and goals but also fighting.
4. After she heard about the <u>stealing</u> in the neighbourhood, she got new locks <u>established</u>.
5. He is not very <u>true</u>; he will <u>say</u> the secret to someone.
6. He was caught <u>making</u> a crime and had to do community service.
7. His friend is planning to <u>make</u> a bachelor party for him.
8. He went to <u>tell</u> the accident to the police. It took him hours to <u>accomplish</u> all the forms.
9. The committee voted to <u>disagree</u> the plan.
10. While the girls were <u>jumping</u> in the schoolyard, most of the boys were <u>doing</u> soccer.
11. The young generation today is far too <u>reliable</u> on cellphones.
12. None of the <u>tellers</u> in the clothing store approached me offering help.
13. This assignment was <u>uneasy</u> at first.
14. People who choose <u>luxurious</u> cars often just want to show off their <u>richness</u>.
15. The author <u>narrated</u> a story of his youth, when he fell in love.
16. The problems we faced made the whole trip <u>unjoyable</u>.

## Correcting Grammatical Errors

Each sentence contains many elements that can trip up writers. Determiners and prepositions, the smallest of words, are especially difficult for ESL learners, but they can also cause problems for native speakers. In everyday speech, an incorrect verb ending can slide by unnoticed, but in writing, more care must be taken to use correct forms. This section highlights some common problem areas.

## Correcting Pronoun Errors

Pronouns stand in for nouns in sentences. They are among the smallest and most common words in English sentences—and yet they give writers no end of trouble. Both native speakers and ESL learners often make errors in pronoun use. Sometimes students try to avoid making the errors by repeating the noun—which can make sentences long and awkward.

The basics of pronoun use are explained in Unit 3, pages 69–71. This section highlights some problem areas.

## Pronoun Reference and Agreement

As explained in Unit 3, pronouns should have a clear antecedent (a noun that the pronoun refers to).

Here are some examples of common problems:

| | |
|---|---|
| Emma Teitel explains the problems of using Instagram. He says that it can be annoying. | The author is female; the pronoun should be *she*. |
| The company issued a recall. They claimed it was an easy problem to fix. | Neither *they* nor *it* has a clear antecedent. *They* is commonly used to refer to an institution, but this usage is grammatically incorrect. The institution is an *it*. |
| Each item requires their own catalogue number. | The possessive pronoun *its* should be used instead of *their* because *each item* is singular. |
| Sara told Rose that she had to attend the training session. | It is unclear whether it is Sara or Rose that has to attend; *she* can refer to either of the women. |
| We have to attend the Friday meeting. | The pronoun *we* can be inclusive or exclusive. In other words, for this sentence, the listener would not know whether he or she was included in the meeting or not. |
| You cannot expect to pass the course if you do not put in the effort. | The reference for *you* can be confusing because the pronoun can refer to one person or several. It can also refer just to the audience or to people in general. |
| Dan told his brother that he had found his keys. | The reference is ambiguous because *his keys* could belong to either Dan or his brother. |

## Pronoun Shift

One of the most common writing mistakes is pronoun shift in which the writer switches person using several pronouns in one paragraph, as in these examples:

> Parents should always continue to tell <u>them</u> how happy <u>you</u> are that <u>he/she</u> have made it this far, and that <u>you</u> believe in <u>them</u> and that <u>you</u> as parents is very proud of the accomplishments <u>they</u> made and that <u>they</u> can do anything <u>he/she</u> puts <u>their</u> mind to.

> Parents should always remember to tell <u>their</u> child that no matter what problems arise during their studies <u>you</u> will always be proud of the child because <u>they</u> have made it thus far.

> In addition, in order for a student to succeed, <u>he or she</u> must be persistent and patient. <u>One</u> must not give up when, for example, a failing mark hits <u>them</u> square in the face. Life is full of ups and downs. It's just reality, get over it and move on. Observe <u>your</u> mistakes and try not to do them again. No <u>one</u> is perfect.

Pronoun shifts are confusing to the reader. It can be unclear whether two different pronouns are referring to the same antecedent or to different ones.

## Singular *they*

English lacks a gender-neutral third person singular pronoun. Even though the pronoun *they* is grammatically plural, it is often used instead of *he* or *she* when the gender is not known. This widespread usage of singular *they* is technically ungrammatical, but it is common in spoken English and informal written English because it avoids the *he/she* problem, as shown in these example sentences:

| | |
|---|---|
| If a student misses a test, <u>he</u> needs to provide a valid excuse and documentation in order to write a make-up. | **incorrect** (unless referring only to male students): *He* used to be accepted as a standard all-purpose pronoun, but it is now considered sexist. |
| If a student misses a test, <u>she</u> needs to provide a valid excuse and documentation in order to write a make-up. | **incorrect** (unless referring only to female students) |
| If a student misses a test, <u>he or she</u> needs to provide a valid excuse and documentation in order to write a make-up. | **correct**, but awkward usage: *He or she* can be used for a single reference, but it becomes unwieldy when used repeatedly. |

If a student misses a test, he/she needs to provide a valid excuse and documentation in order to write a make-up.

**incorrect:**
Alternative words separated by slashes are unacceptable in academic English.

If a student misses a test, they need to provide a valid excuse and documentation in order to write a make-up.

**grammatically incorrect** (but commonly used):
This is a pronoun agreement error: *a student* is singular, but *they* is plural.

If students miss a test, they need to provide a valid excuse and documentation in order to write a make-up.

**correct:**
Both *students* and *they* are plural.

The use of singular *they* is so widespread that it is even used when the gender is known:

The winner will get a contract with a modelling agency, and they will get a chance to travel all over the world.

Since this is a reference to an all-female competition, the pronoun *she* should be used instead of *they*.

Using *they* as a gender-neutral, singular pronoun is gradually becoming acceptable in Standard Written English. Many writers and linguists argue that it should be accepted for historical and practical reasons:

- English needs such a pronoun—there is no way to express the idea of "he or she" concisely and elegantly.
- It is already in common usage, so English speakers are comfortable with it.
- Attempts to make up a new pronoun (such as *s/he*) have been unsuccessful and awkward.
- The usage has literary precedence—it has been used by such celebrated writers such as Charles Dickens and Jane Austen.
- It has grammatical precedence—the pronoun *you* used to be only used for the plural, but it is now used for both singular and plural.
- Singular *they* is the pronoun of choice in the transgender community.

However, the best advice for academic English is to avoid using singular *they* in your writing, unless you know your instructor approves of the usage. It will usually be marked as a grammar mistake.

## Use of *I* and *We*

Refer to the section on Writing Personally or Impersonally (Unit 1, pages 10–11) to review the differences in types of essays. If you are writing a personal essay, you can use *I*. However, most academic essays tend to be impersonal, so do not use *I*. This general guideline also depends on your instructor's essay requirements; some teachers have strict rules on using *I* and *we*—ask if you are unsure.

In most cases, *I* is unnecessary. You do not need to say "I think" or "in my opinion" because the ideas expressed in your essay should be your own, unless they are someone else's opinion, and then you should attribute them to that person.

| | |
|---|---|
| **Akerman says that schools are too strict with dress requirements.** | This statement summarizes Bev Akerman's opinion (in "White Tops, Grey Bottoms," pages 339–40). It is clear that this is Akerman's opinion. |
| **In my opinion, high school students should wear uniforms because of practicality, appearance, and security.** | The phrase "in my opinion" is unnecessary for this thesis statement. It is understood that in an essay, the opinion expressed is that of the writer. The thesis statement can stand on its own without this opening phrase. |

Once in a while, for purposes of emphasis and clarity, the use of *I* can work, but most students tend to overuse it. Sometimes they even overemphasize with a phrase like "in my opinion, I personally think that . . ."

Do not try to get around the use of *I* with phrases like "the author of this essay" to refer to yourself. This is awkward and ugly.

Do not use *we* in an essay when you mean yourself. Only the Queen can get away with that—it's called a "royal we."

*We* can sometimes be used in an essay—judiciously. It should refer to a group of which you are part—like students or Canadians. However, the *we* can be confusing as to whom it includes, and some instructors do not want to see it in academic essays at all, so it may be best to avoid it.

Keep your writing in the third person plural by using nouns such as *people*, *students*, and *Canadians* and following with the corresponding pronouns (*they*, *them*, *their*), and thus you can avoid using *I* and *we*.

## Use of *You*

Most European languages have more than one second person pronoun—they distinguish between singular and plural and sometimes between formal and informal. English now has only *you* as a second person pronoun. (English did have *thee* and *thou* for singular *you*, but those words have fallen out of use. You might come across them in older literature, such as the King James Bible and Shakespeare's plays.) Furthermore, *you* has replaced *one* to refer to people in general, as in "In that neighbourhood, you can hear the sound of airplanes flying into the airport." These different uses of *you* can make it confusing as to whom the pronoun actually refers.

Sometimes students run into problems with the *you* form because they switch references:

| | |
|---|---|
| When those children grow up, they will be very surprised to see that life is hard and you have to do things for yourself. If you don't baby your child, they will grow up to be adults who can think for themselves. | These sentences are confusing because the *you* in the first sentence refers to the children but the *you* in the second sentence refers to the parents. Moreover, the writer switches between *you* and *they* for the same people. |

The use of *you* has become common in many forms of writing, such as newspaper and magazine articles, where it gives a more casual, friendlier tone. In textbooks like this one, *you* is used to address the readers—the students—directly. Because writing today is generally less formal, *you* is used frequently.

Command sentences, also known as imperatives, are also considered to be *you* sentences. A statement like "Consider the differences between these two types of students" actually has an implied subject *you*, the person doing the action.

The use of *you* is considered inappropriate in academic writing, so students are asked to avoid it in their essays. Academic writing is impersonal, formal, and precise—three characteristics that do not allow for the use of *you*.

Students find it difficult to avoid *you*. One technique is to choose a noun that represents the group being discussed and to use the third person plural, as in these examples:

| Informal style (with *you*) | Academic style (without *you*) |
|---|---|
| When you are looking for a job, you should network and exploit your contacts. | Job hunters should network and exploit their contacts. |
| You should look both ways before you cross the street. | It is important to look both ways before crossing the street. Pedestrians should look both ways before they cross the street. |

When you do use *you* in some of your other writing, make sure that the pronoun reference is clear and consistent.

## Exercise 7.4

Rewrite the following sentences to eliminate *you*:

| | |
|---|---|
| *Example:* | You need to see the student advisor to change your timetable. |
| Possible rewrites: | Timetable changes must be approved by the student advisor. |
| | Students should see their advisor to change their timetable. |

1. The smallest problem with a luxury car will cost you a lot of money because the parts are harder to find and you have to pay the person for his or her time.

2. In order to pass the test, you must memorize the rules and road signs in the driver's handbook.

3. You can be successful at college if you attend class, pay attention to the instructor, and do your homework.

4. You could spend hours watching TV and YouTube videos and waste your whole day.

5. You do not have to include references on your resumé, but you should have a list of names and contact information prepared for when you get asked for it.

Why you should avoid using *you* in academic writing:

- It can be confusing as to who is being referred to.
- It is informal, conversational style.
- It is personal.
- Its use often involves pronoun reference shifts.

## Use of *One*

The pronoun *one* is used in formal English to refer to people in general. However, this use of *one* is considered very formal; *you* is generally used instead, in spoken English and in informal writing.

| | |
|---|---|
| One should read the chapter before class. | overly formal |
| You should read the chapter before class. | informal; commonly used in speech and writing |
| Students should read the chapter before class. | the use of the third person is suitable for academic writing |

Another problem with using *one* is that it is difficult to maintain throughout the paragraph, so many students end up shifting to different pronouns.

| | |
|---|---|
| One should take notes in class in order to learn more efficiently. When we come back from class, one should review our notes to help us remember them better. | **incorrect** pronoun shifts |
| One should take notes in class in order to learn more efficiently. When one comes back from class, one should review one's notes to help one remember them better. | **correct** but awkward |

Avoid using *one* in your writing. Use a plural noun, such as *people*, *students*, *Canadians*, so that the pronoun *they* works.

## Reflexive Pronouns

Reflexive pronouns can be difficult to use correctly:

| | |
|---|---|
| He sent the package to <u>myself</u>. | **incorrect:**<br>*He* and *myself* represent different people, so this is not reflexive. |
| <u>He</u> sent the package to <u>me</u>.<br><u>I</u> sent the package to <u>myself</u>.<br><u>She</u> bought <u>herself</u> a new laptop with her bonus money. | **correct** uses of pronouns |
| <u>They</u> wanted to do the work <u>themself</u>. | **incorrect:**<br>The reflexive for *they* is *themselves*. Note that *themself*, *them selves* (as two words), and *theirselves* are all incorrect forms of the reflexive. |

## Activity

Go through a piece of writing that you have recently done in class. Highlight each pronoun. Check to see whether each pronoun has a clear antecedent and reference. Check for pronoun shifts. Look for any errors you have made.

## Exercise 7.5

Correct any errors in pronoun use or form:

1. The student achievement awards were presented at the assembly. They deserved to be congratulated because they had worked so hard.

2. The zombies were attacking the armed survivors. They didn't stand a chance.

3. John and me worked on the project together. I was pleased that they turned out well.

4. The awards committee deliberated a long time. It was a surprise when they presented the trophy to myself.

5. The mayor rejected the solution that the committee had forwarded it. She preferred the old plan.

6. They say that you should not text and walk across the street. It can be dangerous for them. A car can hit one.

7. The Stockholm Syndrome is a term to explain how you can start to sympathize with your captors when they are put in an enclosed space for a long period of time.

8. When parents make sure that their children learn how to cook and do household chores, they are better equipped to look after theirselves when they live on their own.

9. Whoever completes the assignment first he can help the other students with his work.

10. John gave the flyers to Emily and I. He did not want to distribute them, but I did not mind doing the work.

## Correcting Determiner Errors

Review Using Determiners in Unit 3 on pages 67–68. ESL students often use the wrong article with a noun. Even if their native language uses articles, the rules of usage would not be the same as in English.

### Exercise 7.6

Correct the determiner errors:

1. Marilyn Bell was a first person to swim across the Lake Ontario.

2. There are many ways to access information through Internet.

3. Many of students enrolled in the College English have trouble writing an essays. They need to take it one step at the time.

4. Pete is considering going to University of British Columbia or Simon Fraser University.

5. Princess Diana was a most popular and famous woman in the world in 1980s.

6. Meaning of a gift can be misinterpreted and can cause problems in relationship.

7. He could be success if he took program seriously.

8. The honesty is one of most important traits she is looking for in an partner.

9. James wants to be doctor, but he is discouraged because it requires many years of a study.

10. The book on a table belongs to the student who usually comes in late.

11. I need to buy a umbrella. Mine broke in this huge storm we had last week.

12. A meeting has been rescheduled. Instead of starting a hour from now, we will have to meet these afternoon.

## Distinguishing Countable and Uncountable Nouns

As mentioned in Unit 2, page 24, nouns can be classed as countable or uncountable. Uncountable nouns often cause problems for ESL students; they may put them in plural forms or use indefinite articles (*a*, *an*) with them.

Here are examples and explanations of the use of uncountable nouns:

| | |
|---|---|
| I need some water.<br>Dieticians disagree on the value of drinking milk.<br>He stopped for gas before getting on the highway. | Liquids (*water*, *milk*, *gas*) are generally uncountable. |
| Would you like to go for a coffee?<br>Instead of a soft drink, I'd like a water. | These sentences (in informal English) show an ellipsis (a shortened form). Here, the speakers mean "a cup of coffee" and "a bottle of water." |
| She needs to cut down on salt.<br>The sand on the beach is very coarse.<br>I need to buy more flour. | Things that are in small grains (*salt*, *sand*, *flour*) are uncountable. |
| I need to buy some bread. A small loaf will do. I only eat a slice or two at breakfast. | *Bread* itself is uncountable, but *loaf* and *slice* are countable. |
| We need to buy some luggage. The airline has new restrictions on carry-on bags. | *Luggage* and *baggage* are uncountable nouns; *bag*, *suitcase*, and *backpack* (and other specific items of luggage) are countable. |
| They are shopping for furniture. They need a new sofa and a dresser. | *Furniture* is an uncountable noun; specific items of furniture (such as sofas, dressers, beds, and chairs) are countable. |
| She asked for advice, but she didn't take it. She said she found the information she needed on the Internet. | *Advice* and *information* are uncountable; you could say "a piece of advice" or "a piece of information" to refer to a specific point. |
| They need more time to complete the project. They had to redo the specs three times. | The noun *time* is uncountable when it is in a general sense but countable when it refers to specific instances. |
| He has a lot of work to do this month. He has to find more works for the gallery. | *Work* is almost always uncountable; the exception is when it refers to something like works of art. |
| Honesty is important in a relationship. There was no truth in what he said. Graduates have to accept hard truths about the current job market. | Abstract nouns are generally uncountable, but some of them have uses that are countable. |

## Exercise 7.7

Correct any errors in the use of determiners with countable and uncountable nouns:

1. I gave him an advice, but he refused to take it. He went ahead and bought the furnitures on delayed payments.
2. They suffered several setbacks in their plans. They didn't have the informations they needed at the start.
3. The teacher gave us many homeworks to do, but I got a head start on learning my vocabularies.
4. I bought new luggages for the trip—two suitcases and a rolling duffle bag.
5. She did not return the money but instead used them.
6. He restored the car. It's a real beauty now, but it took him a lot of time to do.
7. Many people who live on the street are addicted to alcohols and drugs.
8. The rehabilitation program gave them happiness and hopes.
9. Now that she has finished her assignment, she has another work to do.
10. I don't have the time or money to take on that project.
11. Students were having troubles with their reading and writing tasks.
12. Tattoos are like makeups, clothes, and jewelleries; they decorate the body.
13. I need to stop at the grocery store. I have to buy bread, a milk, a cheese, and some fishes.
14. The graduate students do many researches. The studies are often funded by pharmaceutical companies.
15. I asked him for an information package about the company.

## Correcting Singular and Plural Errors

Both verb and noun forms are determined by the concept of **singular** (showing one thing or one person) and **plural** (more than one). This sounds like a straightforward concept, but in practice singular/plural distinctions can cause problems. For instance, for subject–verb agreement, it is important to correctly identify the subject of the verb.

Here are some examples of common mistakes:

| | |
|---|---|
| The computers in the fourth floor lab <u>is</u> down because of a virus. | **incorrect:**<br>*Computers* is the subject and therefore requires a plural verb form (it should be *are down*). *Lab* is not the subject because it is in the prepositional phrase *in the fourth floor lab*. |
| Jennifer <u>walk</u> to school every day. | **incorrect:**<br>The verb should be *walks* because the third person singular verb form has an *–s* ending. |
| We should just save that problem for another <u>days</u>. | **incorrect:**<br>*Another* is singular and should be followed by *day*. |
| Everybody <u>have</u> to do the work. | **incorrect:**<br>*Everybody* is singular and should be followed by *has*. |
| <u>Researches show</u> that teenagers do not function well in the morning. | **incorrect:**<br>*Research* is an uncountable noun. This should be "Research shows . . ." |
| The <u>childrens</u> are waiting to go to the park. | **incorrect:**<br>The plural of *child* is *children*. |

## Exercise 7.8

Correct any grammar errors in the following sentences:

1. One of the band members are from Australia. He play the trumpet.

2. Working with John and Jane were a pleasure. They are very talented actor.

3. Anton was behaving like a six-years-old. I couldn't take it for another minutes.

4. Every day, the mother goose, along with its five goslings, go across the highway. The drivers all seems to be watching out for the geese.

5. Many people leaves the city on long weekends. The resulting traffic jams are an ordeal.

6. Each tool has their own place in the case. The compartments is very well organized.

7. Surveillance cameras does not help to make society secure. It only helps to capture criminals after the fact.

8. The number of candidates for the November elections have risen to 20. It should make for an interesting campaigns.

9. If any documents are misplaced, it can be found easily if the information are stored on computers. The search functions allow quick retrieval.

10. You should buy that laptop next week. They will probably go on sale.

11. The books in the hallway is donations for the charity books sale.

12. Emma take dance lessons every Tuesdays. She study Latin dancing.

## Showing Possession

Possession means that something belongs to someone or something. Nouns and pronouns have possessive forms. For nouns, an apostrophe with an *s* shows possession, as in these examples:

| | |
|---|---|
| John's car was stolen. | The apostrophe plus *s* is the possessive form of *John*. John owns the car. |
| The instructor's lesson plans had to be revised. | The lesson plans belong to the instructor. |
| The instructors' lesson plans had to be revised. | In this case, the lesson plans belong to more one instructor. The plural form of *instructor, instructors*, has an apostrophe after the *s* to show that the possessive is on a plural noun. |
| The Greens' house burned down. | *Greens* refers to the whole family—more than one Green. The apostrophe therefore comes after the *s*. |

Students sometimes confuse plurals and possessives and have trouble placing the apostrophe. For more examples and information, see the next section, Sorting out −*s* Endings (page 213), and the section Apostrophes in Unit 3 (pages 96–97).

Pronouns also have possessive forms (explained in Unit 3, Using Pronouns, pages 69–71). It is important not to confuse possessive pronouns that occur with nouns (*my, your, his, her, its, our, their, whose*) and the forms that are not used before nouns (*mine, yours, his, hers, ours, theirs*). Note that none of these possessives has an apostrophe.

| | |
|---|---|
| This is not my bike. That one over there is mine. | *My* is the form used with the noun *bike*, while *mine* is used when there is no noun afterwards. |
| They paid off their mortgage, so the house is now officially theirs. | Similarly, this sentence shows *their* with a noun and *theirs* without a noun. |
| Whose shoes are these? I thought they were yours. | *Whose* means belonging to whom. *Yours* is used instead of *your* because there is no noun following the word. |

Be careful not to mix up *it's* and *its*. The two words sound the same, but *it's* is a contracted form of *it is* or *it has*, while *its* is the possessive pronoun. Similarly, *who's* is a contraction of *who is* or *who has*, and *whose* is the possessive pronoun. Since contractions are generally not used in academic writing, you can avoid using *it's* and *who's* and thus avoid the mix-up.

## Exercise 7.9

Correct any errors:

1. I couldn't find out who's keys these are, so I took them down to the Security's Department.
2. Erin lent me her keys to the storage room's because I misplaced mines.
3. Her glasses broke when Tims brother stepped on them.
4. I didn't have a dictionary, so I borrowed Ron's. I had to go find mine later.
5. The childrens' babysitter needs a ride home if she babysits after midnight.
6. The Wilson's house was broken into last week. They're whole place was trashed.
7. I've been sitting here watching the puppy try to chase its tail. Who's dog is it anyway?
8. Helen and Andy left there backpacks near the bandshell's.
9. Sallys car was broken into, and her CDs were stolen.
10. If you don't have you're textbook, you can borrow Elizabeths, but make sure you don't mark it up because she is very fussy about her things.

## Sorting out *–s* Endings

Compared to most European languages, English does not have many word endings. However, many of them are multi-purpose. The *–s* ending, in particular, can be confusing, especially since apostrophes also play a part.

Here is a recap of the uses of *–s* endings:

1. **Plural forms of nouns:**

   They collected all the <u>books</u>, <u>toys</u>, and <u>puzzles</u> and put them into different <u>boxes</u>.

2. **Third person singular verbs in the simple present tense:**

   Peter <u>likes</u> to walk in the park. He <u>tries</u> to do it every day.
   She never <u>lets</u> her children watch television before they do their homework.

3. **Possessive forms (with apostrophes):**

   <u>Elizabeth's</u> car was stolen.
   The <u>driver's</u> side of the car was crushed.

   Remember that possessive pronouns (*his, hers, its, theirs, yours, whose*) do not have apostrophes.

4. **Contractions (with apostrophes):**

   <u>He's</u> reorganizing the department.
   <u>Let's</u> go to the park. [contraction of "let us"—do not confuse this with the verb form *lets* shown in the second example sentence for #2 above]
   <u>Who's</u> coming with us? ["who is"—do not confuse with *whose* (belonging to *whom*)]

   In most contractions, the *'s* stands for *is*, but it can also stand for *has* and *was*.

5. **Combining plural and possessive —s endings:**

   The <u>boys'</u> books were ruined in the rain.
   The <u>students'</u> timetables were not ready on time.

In these cases, the *—s* ending forms the plural, but only an apostrophe is added to show the possessive form (not an apostrophe plus *s*).

Remember that the possessive form of irregular plural nouns is similar to those of singular nouns: *the children's toys, the women's washroom, the men's clothing store.*

## Exercise 7.10

For each use of the *–s* endings underlined in the following sentences, determine which usage is being shown (Cases 1–5, as explained above). The first one is done here for you as an example:

<u>Nasir's</u> teacher <u>sorts</u> the <u>students'</u> work into <u>piles</u> before she <u>begins</u>.
  [3]          [2]          [5]               [1]            [2]

1. <u>Peter's</u> going to take over <u>Jenny's</u> <u>cases</u> while <u>she's</u> on vacation. The <u>clients'</u> <u>businesses</u> will be in good <u>hands</u>. Peter always <u>does</u> a good job because <u>he's</u> so conscientious.

2. The <u>Johnsons'</u> house is for sale. <u>It's</u> going to sell fast. <u>Joanne's</u> putting in an offer. She <u>thinks</u> she can get a good deal, but I think <u>it's</u> going to go for big <u>bucks</u>. And the <u>renovations</u> are going to be expensive too. <u>Jason's</u> <u>mother's</u> house would have been a better purchase.

3. The research <u>studies</u> showed that <u>children's</u> attention <u>spans</u> were suffering because of too much exposure to media. <u>Stephen's</u> trying to get his <u>kids</u> to read more <u>books</u>.

## Exercise 7.11

Correct any errors by adding, deleting, or changing any incorrect *–s* endings and apostrophes:

1. The student's want to delays the test. Simons going to talk to the instructor.

2. Its time to clean out that room. She need to get rid of those newspaper and magazines.

3. Its her boyfriends' fault. Hes so possessive that he never let's her go out with her friend's.

4. She want to change the reports conclusion. Its' not clear enough.

5. The boy's boat started sinking, but they made it to shore. They even rescued their belonging's.

6. A long time ago peoples had large families, but nowaday's people have fewer childrens.

7. There were many videos, CDs, and DVDs at Megans garage sale, but no one wanted to buy them.

8. On Tuesdays the instructors meet for lunch and discuss the students progress.

## Correcting Verb Tenses and Forms

The section Recognizing Different Verb Forms in Unit 3 (pages 54–59) explains the basic verb tenses and forms.

Here are some common errors to watch out for:

| Error example | Explanation of error |
| --- | --- |
| He walk to work every day. | leaving the −s ending off third person singular verb forms (should be *walks*) |
| They have took the wrong train. | incorrect past participle form (should be *taken*) |
| The manager could not running the machines at all. | incorrect verb form after modal auxiliaries (should be *run*) |
| The mistake is happened because he was not paying attention. | putting intransitive verbs in the passive voice (should be *happened* without *is*) |
| Polar bears will eat seals. | using the future tense instead of the simple present tense to express facts or general tendencies (should be *eat*) |
| He enjoys to ski in the winter. | using the wrong complement after a verb (should be the gerund *skiing*) |
| The team hopes advancing to the quarter finals at least. | using the wrong complement after a verb (should be the infinitive *to advance*) |

## Exercise 7.12

Correct any verb form errors in the following sentences:

1. Laptops are seemed to be useful in class, but they can being distracting.
2. The tour guide recommended to take the river route to getting a better view of the city.
3. Jack happened to see Eliza in the marketplace, so he will invited her to join us for dinner.
4. Many people enjoys travelling to other countries. Seeing historical sites can very interested.
5. Paulina has made the necessary changes last week. The program should works better now.
6. Jamie is used to work for his family. His family own a house renovation business. Jamie liked the work, but he wants to finished his business degree first.
7. The teachers in the promotion committee are concern about Marta's lack of progress. She is not able to concentrate on her work.
8. He keep telling me to invest more money in stocks, but I don't think I can afford taking the risk.
9. I have never been to Paris, but I am understanding it is a beautiful city.
10. The committee decides to postpone to repaint the clubhouse until after some much-needed renovations has been done.

## Correcting Errors in Punctuation and Capitalization

The basics of using punctuation and capitalization are explained on pages 93–100. Here are some common errors:

| | |
|---|---|
| The lifeguard's have a meeting before each shift. | **incorrect:** Do not use apostrophes for plurals. (See Sorting out *−s* Endings, pages 213–14, if you have trouble distinguishing possessives and plurals.) |
| Every spring he want's to clean out the basement, but it never get's done. | **incorrect:** Do not use apostrophes in uncontracted verbs. |
| They bought apples, peaches. | **incorrect:** Do not use a comma as a substitute for *and*. |

| | |
|---|---|
| Although, the whales are social creatures, they were removed from their family groups. | **incorrect:**<br>Do not use a comma after *although*. |
| They wanted to make several improvements to the park such as, adding more seating and flower gardens. | **incorrect:**<br>Do not use a comma after *such as*. |
| That it was his turn to be president, was totally forgotten. | **incorrect:**<br>Do not use a comma between a subject and a verb. |

## Exercise 7.13

Correct the punctuation and capitalization errors in the following sentences:

1. All student's entering huron college of applied art's and technology, must take the introductory writing course college english 101!

2. Although many students do not think they need a writing course College English prepares them to write research essays, and serves as a bridge to technical, and business writing.

3. Critical thinking skills are also developed, in writing courses, because essay-writing requires students to formulate a thesis organize idea's and support arguments.

4. Language course's are also popular at the college because students understand the value of speaking another language, courses are offered in french spanish mandarin and russian.

5. Language courses help students improve their Communication skills; something that employers' value.

## Improving Structure and Style

In addition to dealing with individual elements in a sentence, you may have to fix the structure of the sentence itself or edit it to be clearer and more concise. You may also have to consider the sentence in relation to the other sentences in the paragraph.

### Correcting Fragments and Run-on Sentences

Two of the most common types of sentence structure errors are fragments (incomplete sentences) and run-on sentences. Run-on sentences are commonly divided into categories according to different kinds of errors, such as **comma splices** (two sentences incorrectly separated by a comma), but they essentially have the same problem—they do not stop where they are supposed to stop. Fragments have too little in the sentence, and run-ons have too much. Fragments sound incomplete when you read them. Fragments and run-ons are sometimes used for effect in informal writing, but in academic writing, they are generally considered to be grammatical errors.

To fix a sentence fragment, you need to find out what is missing and supply it:

| | |
|---|---|
| Whale-watching off Vancouver Island. | **fragment:**<br>There's no main verb (*whale-watching* is a gerund). |
| Whale-watching off Vancouver Island was an incredible experience. | **correction:**<br>The sentence now has a complete idea. |
| When he saw the dinosaur bones in the Alberta Badlands. | **fragment:**<br>The word *when* is a subordinate conjunction, so this is a subordinate clause with no main clause. |
| When he saw the dinosaur bones in the Alberta Badlands, he relived his childhood dream of being a paleontologist. | **correction:**<br>The sentence now has a main clause. |
| The actor who was chosen for the lead role. | **fragment:**<br>The word *who* is a subordinate conjunction, so this is a subordinate clause with no main clause. |
| The actor who was chosen for the lead role had to leave the production. | **correction:**<br>The sentence now has a main clause. |
| The small red brick house down the street. | **fragment:**<br>This fragment lacks a predicate |
| The small red brick house down the street is for sale. | **correction:**<br>This sentence now has a predicate (a verb and whatever it needs to complete it). |

A run-on sentence, on the other hand, is essentially too much sentence:

| | |
|---|---|
| Graduates take entry-level jobs to get their foot in the door they do not want to be stuck there for years. | **run-on sentence:**<br>There is no punctuation or connector between the two sentences (the second one starts with *they*). |
| Polar bears live in the Arctic, they need the ice to live on. | **run-on sentence:**<br>This specific type of run-on is a comma splice in which a comma incorrectly divides the sentences. |

When the waitress took the orders, which was difficult to do because of the noise of the hockey game, which was the final game of the season, so the hockey fans were out in full force and full voice, she misunderstood the customers' orders, and the kitchen prepared the wrong food, so the customers were angry and complained to the manager, who blamed the kitchen staff, but the waitress admitted she could not hear the order very well, so new meals were prepared on the house.

**run-on sentence:**
This sentence is actually grammatical, but it is considered a run-on because it is overloaded with clauses.

There are three basic ways to fix run-on sentences: make two sentences, use a semi-colon, or add a conjunction:

The play had sold out its run was extended.

**run-on sentence:**
two full sentences with no connector

The play had sold out, its run was extended.

**run-on sentence:**
comma splice

The play had sold out. Its run was extended.

**correct:**
two separate, complete sentences

The play had sold out; its run was extended.

**correct:**
semicolon connects the sentences

The play had sold out, so its run was extended.

**correct:**
The coordinate conjunction *so* is used to connect the sentences.

Because the play had sold out, its run was extended.

**correct:**
The subordinate conjunction *because* is used to connect the sentences.

The play had sold out, therefore its run was extended.

**run-on sentence:**
The word *therefore* is a conjunctive adverb and cannot join two sentences on its own.

The play had sold out; therefore, its run was extended.

**correct:**
A semicolon connects the sentences.

The section Connecting Sentences on pages 88–90 in Unit 3 reviews sentence connectors that you can use to fix run-ons.

### Exercise 7.14

Decide whether the following sentences are fragments, run-ons, or correct sentences. Fix the fragments and run-ons:

1. Watching a soccer game on Sunday afternoon.
2. The goalkeeper came out to handle the ball the attacker managed to get a kick in to score a goal.
3. They managed another goal on a penalty kick, however the game was already lost.
4. Although they had been division champions. They could not get past the powerhouse teams.
5. I like to watch the young children play soccer. Because they all travel in a bunch following the ball.
6. She has become addicted to reality shows on television, she especially likes the ones where she can vote on who is the most talented.
7. Eating snacks in front of the television set and not exercising.
8. My children love to watch nature documentaries, which are a lot better than a steady diet of cartoons and music videos.
9. Infomercials, usually shown in the middle of the night, advertising a useless array of products.
10. Those infomercials, however, attract a large number of customers who cannot resist the sales pitch.

### Exercise 7.15

Fix the sentence structure errors to eliminate fragments and run-on sentences:

1. She's pretending to work. But she is just playing solitaire on the computer. And time is running out.
2. Including a list of references in the resumé. It is not necessary. Can be left for the job interview.
3. She lets Jake use the car whenever he asks. Even though he's a terrible driver. Last year he had three accidents.
4. We studied all the readings in class, however many of the students had trouble remembering the material for the test.
5. It's not hard to see what the problem is, the machine won't start because this piece is jamming it.
6. Because he had accumulated so much stuff in residence. He borrowed his parents' van when he was moving out.
7. Advantages of self-employment. Being your own boss and not having to answer to anyone. Choosing your own work hours.
8. I had to go to the bank. Before I could pay him back. Being in debt makes me uncomfortable.

9. He lets his employees have a say in the decision-making process, therefore their job satisfaction is high. Few of them moving on to other jobs.

10. Because of his success with the last project. He was promoted to assistant manager. After a while he was making much more money. So he asked his girlfriend to marry him.

## Correcting Parallel Structure

The basics of parallel structure are explained in Unit 3, page 78. Writing a Thesis Statement in Unit 5 (pages 137–40) explains the importance of parallel structure in three-pronged thesis statements.

### Exercise 7.16

Correct the errors in parallel structure in the following sentences:

1. Although many people think of Canada as being cold and snow, summer days can be hot and humidity.

2. Winter can be more enjoyable if people take up activities such as skiing, snowshoeing, or they could learn to skate.

3. First comes the thunder, and then it rained.

4. The flash flood damaged basements and causing sinkholes in the roads.

5. Potholes form in the spring due to the frequent changes in the weather. The pavement freezes and then cracked, stressing the asphalt.

6. Before the snow falls, we have to rake the leaves, plant some bulbs, and the mulch has to be spread.

7. At the cottage, Martin spends time on the lake canoeing, in his sailboat, and waterskiing.

8. An ideal job would have good financial compensation, a good work environment, and the co-workers have to be friendly.

9. For the make-over, her hair was coloured, cut, and a straightener was used.

10. The movie was R-rated because of excessive violence, the characters swore a lot, and nudity.

### Exercise 7.17

Rewrite these thesis statements so that they are concise and grammatical, with parallel structure:

1. The government should encourage young people to vote by teaching them about politics in schools, showing political news on television shows geared to them, and how easy voting is.

2. By reducing the workweek, the unemployment rate would be lower with more people working, productivity would go up, and more time for families and to enjoy life.

3. Parents can help their children go off to college by giving them money for tuition and living expenses, help them choose a school and program, and to encourage them when they are feeling discouraged.

4. The advantages of shopping online are that buyers can choose from a wide array of items, many of which may not be available in local stores, and they can do this shopping at home which is more convenient than going to the mall, and compare prices and read reviews before they buy.

5. Companies save on labour costs by hiring contract workers, they move production offshore, and customers have to do use automated and online ordering systems.

## Correcting Sentence Structure Errors

Unit 3 explained the various types of possible additions to basic sentence structure and showed how to add modifiers, phrases, and clauses. With more complex sentences, it is easy to make errors in sentence structure.

### Exercise 7.18

Correct the sentence structure errors:

1. Although running is a good way to keep fit, but it is hard on the knees.
2. By walking every day, it is a good way to keep healthy.
3. The team was the defending champions, however they failed to defeat a much weaker team.
4. Heading the ball into the open net, a goal was scored.
5. Even she was tired, she stayed late to help out.
6. What I do not understand is why are the plates broken but not the cups.
7. Amrita couldn't decide whether continue seeing him or not.
8. If he will take the bus he will be late.
9. After he had checked out everything in the store, and the clerk being no help to him at all. He left without make a purchase.
10. Children are overprotect by their parents grow up to being unable to take care of themselves.

## Editing to Improve Style

Good writing is clear and concise. It should be in an appropriate style; for academic writing, the style should be impersonal and formal. Editing for style requires rewriting the work, not just correcting errors. To eliminate wordiness, you must use precise vocabulary and delete repetitious phrases. If you need more explanation and examples, review Unit 1, especially the sections on Writing Concisely (pages 8–9), Writing Personally or Impersonally (pages 10–11), and Using Appropriate Style (pages 12–16).

## Exercise 7.19

Rewrite the following passages in a more academic style, and correct errors:

1. Look at residence for example. Residence is a licence to have fun, drink lots, and meet new people; basically a licence to party. Sounds like fun, but there are a few problems.

2. Well, in college it's a big difference. Now students have to budget their money well or they can get really screwed over. Which is the most important part of being on your own.

3. Parents should give help to their children when they asked you to. Otherwise, they will just yell at you for not giving them space. Sometimes they will say you're annoying and stuff like that.

4. No longer can you come home and have Moms home-cooking. Welcome to fast TV dinners and a life of Kraft dinner. Now that balanced diet has been thrown out the window to provide more time for homework and studying.

5. The rich people now-a-days have mommy and daddy's money pit to fall back on if they screw up once in university. But when poor students get in they know if they don't do well they'll be poor for years to come.

## Exercise 7.20

Rewrite the following personal statements to make them impersonal. You will have to generalize:

*Example:*   Now that my children have left home and I am approaching retirement, I would prefer to move to a bungalow. It would be easier to keep a smaller house, and I would not have to subject my arthritic knees to stair-climbing.

For empty-nesters approaching retirement, a bungalow is a good choice of house. The smaller size makes it easier to keep clean, and the lack of stairs makes it kinder to arthritic knees.

1. I like driving on four-lane highways. I don't have to worry about so many distractions. The traffic is all travelling in the same direction, so I only have to worry about lane-changers and the occasional traffic jam.

2. My friend wants a tattoo, but I think it's a mistake. She'll regret it when she gets older. She may no longer have the same interests, and the tattoo may not look as good later when the ink fades and her skin changes with age.

3. To cut down on my food preparation time, I often cook big batches of food on the weekend and freeze it. My family particularly enjoys the chilli, stews, and spaghetti sauce. I find that some soups also freeze well.

4. When I went to college, I decided to give up my car and rely on public transit. I would have good bus service from my apartment to the campus. By not having to pay for gas, insurance, parking, and maintenance, I could also save money from my meagre student budget. Finally, I could go partying without worrying about driving home.

## Exercise 7.21

Rewrite the following sentences to make them concise by eliminating repetition and unnecessary words:

*Example:*   When large factories are built, they invariably increase road traffic, which makes neighbourhoods far more dangerous places than they were before. [21 words]

Large factories invariably increase road traffic, making neighbourhoods more dangerous. [10 words]

1. Canadian streets and public spaces should have more surveillance cameras. Having more surveillance cameras can help police.

2. The key to success or the most important factor of success in college courses is time management. Managing time in a proper and effective way is the key to success at every part of life. Students all over the world in numerous colleges are facing the same problem of not coping with time.

3. I was shopping alongside with a friend of mine.

4. In college, students waste time on socializing and being with friends and waste their time on unnecessary things, such as talking on the phone, sitting in a café for hours, and lots of other things which affect their time.

5. I went to the mall that was close to where I reside. I walked into a store. It was a store only for watches. I was hoping I would definitely find what I was looking for because I spotted a store for watches.

6. What I would do next time would probably be to maybe start my research earlier so I would have extra time to spare if I ran into problems finding the resources needed to complete a complete research assignment.

7. Factors such as work, school, and other activities determine how much time and effort one can really put toward a relationship. To begin with, work can determine how much time someone can put into a relationship. For example, a couple where both people work a lot, less time would be put into the relationship but more effort should be put in to make up for the time.

8. In our modern-day society that we live in, it is understandable that materialism is equated with happiness because people are happy with material goods.

9. Grades should reflect actual student achievement. Giving students a grade that they do not deserve does not help them later in life. When students receive a grade, it should be earned and not given to them as a favour because it is not good for their future. Students need to learn how to earn a grade, rather than receiving a grade that they do not earn. The grade they receive should reflect their actual achievement and skill level. Marks should not be given to students who do not earn them. Later on in life it will not do any good for them due to the fact that they just received a mark instead of actually earning one. Marks should not be given to students just to do a favour for them because they would get credit for something they did not work for. Achievement should be the reason for receiving a good grade, not just being given one as a favour.

## Exercise 7.22

Some students launch into rambling narratives when they give examples in their academic paragraphs and essays. An anecdote can make something interesting, but it can also distract from the main task at hand—proving the points made. Rewrite each of the following examples, preferably in one sentence (see Giving Examples in Unit 4, pages 114–17):

1. Some people get a tattoo to remember someone or somebody. For example, a person showed his tattoo to me. He told me this tattoo means his girlfriend's name. When he and his girlfriend fell in love, he got the tattoo. Now they broke up, but he told me he would never erase the tattoo and forget his girlfriend because this is his first love.

2. People can edit their work faster and easier. For example, a student finishes an essay. He finds some mistakes and wants to edit it. If he writes his essay by hand, he needs to write it again. If the essay is in the computer, he can edit it using the cut and paste function.

3. Students should take advantage of their free time and seize the moment while they can. For example, the teacher has just assigned homework. At the end of the class, they know that they have a spare period next. Instead of taking the right step and completing that work, they waste time on something less important.

4. People will choose public transit if it is made more convenient and faster than driving. For example, a businessman has to get to work. There are traffic jams on the highway. The driving is all stop and go. But a train bypasses all the traffic. It moves more quickly. Moreover, the man can do work on the train.

5. Staying in contact with the professor and with the other students is crucial for students. For example, you missed a class and you want to know what you missed you can email your professor or your classmate to have them inform what you have missed and what you can do to make up for that class.

# Finding and Correcting Errors

It is easier to do grammar correction exercises when you are looking for a specific error. These exercises test your ability to spot and fix a variety of errors.

## Exercise 7.23

Correct the errors in the following sentences. Make minimal changes (adding, changing, or deleting words):

1. The student's completed the assignment quick, so they leave the class early.
2. The television is broke. I'll have to watching that episode online because, I want to know who was the killer.
3. Because he had took the wrong road. He was late for the meeting and miss the important details.
4. In winter, the children go skiing, skating. They don't mind the cold weather as long as their dressed proper for it.
5. I should not of change the date of the meeting the first one was more better.
6. When she reads slow and carefully, she can understand better and making less mistakes.
7. My purse is full of stuffs I don't need even I clean it out regular.
8. Each of projects have a difference advantage choosing one will be difficulty.
9. He is train to be a electrician. When he graduate, he will work for his uncle whom renovates and sell old house's.
10. The students had to redo there work because they're were to many mistake.
11. I find this grammar point very confused. May be the teacher could explaining it again.
12. Sylvia rather let Mike runs the workshops. So she can concentrate to the reorganization.
13. For every cases, the detective write's an official report for his client.
14. Even she disagrees about the decision, she try's to support the work the staff is done.
15. The programmers checked the code, ran some test case, and finally they find the problem.
16. The students' asked there teacher whether it was possible to schedule the tutorial for another days. They did not want to missing the career day presentation.
17. Maya didn't like the suggestion which Eric made it. She wanted to get more informations firstly.

## Exercise 7.24

With a partner, correct the vocabulary, grammar, and sentence structure errors in the following sentences:

1. Parents should understand that college students feel pressured everyday. But giving advices to them can make a differences.

2. He was expecting her to speak something good about his works.

3. Chinese culture emphasis on the importance of marriage life.

4. Not attending classes can be due to anything from bullying, unmotivated, distracted, lazy, etc.

5. Many people will consider getting a tutor for an extra help but now with technology there are many online websites and videos teaching almost every single course for free so students can successed.

6. Teenagers often brag each other with their smartphone, and compete on who gets first the latest smartphone in stores.

7. The huge different between Chinese and Canadian education system makes students going abroad be successful hardly.

8. Studying as a group it can be helpful to improve students knowledge through sharing ideas and debating on a topic.

9. Successful people have a schedule which let know exactly what time should do what.

10. Until now, I still like to playing piano very much, and music has become one of my favourite habits.

# Reading Skills

The importance of good reading skills cannot be overstated even in the modern world of emoji messages and online videos. It is impossible to become a good writer if you do not read a lot. Written English is different from the spoken variety of the language, so people who do not read much are not as familiar with the language—they are not comfortable with the complex sentence structures, the more sophisticated vocabulary, or the conventions such as using punctuation marks correctly.

Because students are often not sufficiently tested on their reading comprehension skills, some poor readers do not even realize that they have weak reading skills. After all, they know how to "read" the words, yet they may find it difficult to figure out the writer's main point or to detect tone, such as sarcasm and humour. Their vocabulary is limited, so they misunderstand what the writer is saying. They may read slowly and laboriously.

Reading skills, like all skills, are built gradually. The more you read, the easier it becomes. If you rarely open a book, it will be a chore when you do have to read something. With practice, you can increase your reading speed and level of comprehension. You will learn more words and be exposed to more new ideas. The more familiar you are with a subject, the easier it is to understand stories and articles on that topic.

Your choice of reading material also determines your comprehension and reading speed. Material is judged to be at a lower reading level if the words used are more common vocabulary and the sentence structure is relatively simple. For instance, newspaper stories are generally aimed at a high school reading level. The topic is also important—people are more comfortable with material on a subject they are familiar with even if the reading level is higher than they are used to.

How you read a text depends on why you are reading it. When you read a chapter of your textbook, you highlight important sections and make notes. When you read a novel for pleasure, you just read through it. You **scan** a newspaper, reading headlines, looking at pictures, and choosing interesting articles to read. You can **skim** a chapter in a textbook to get the gist of what is said. If you need to study a story or an article for school, you should do a more careful reading—making notes, highlighting important points, and looking up unfamiliar words in the dictionary.

This unit introduces some of the basics of reading. You can practise and build your skills with the readings in Part 2 of this book. You may also wish to review Dealing with Unfamiliar Words in Unit 2 (pages 39–40).

## Reading Textbooks

A good way to start any course is to become familiar with the course textbook as soon as you acquire it. Look over the table of contents to learn what the book covers. Read the introduction. Check out what the appendices have to offer. Look at the index, and be prepared to use it to find specific information.

Learn to navigate your textbook so that you can locate information quickly. Use the table of contents, page headers, and the index. You can bookmark any pages you might want to reference often.

A textbook makes a much better study tool if you mark it up as you read it. You can annotate the textbook with margin notes. Use highlighting judiciously— to emphasize only important sentences, not big chunks of text. Highlighting is used to draw your attention to something you might not easily find again, so you do not need it for tip boxes or lists that already summarize information for you.

If the textbook is borrowed or if you are planning to resell it, you probably want to keep the book itself fairly clean. You can use sticky notes for your annotations and bookmark important reference pages.

It is important to take notes as you read because you will remember the material better if you do so. Write notes summarizing each section of the book. This is more effective than simply underlining or highlighting because you have to process the information to paraphrase and summarize.

### Doing Assigned Readings

Students are often assigned reading to do before class. It could be an article, a story, or a chapter of the textbook. The instructor then organizes the class on the presumption that students have done the required reading. Students who come unprepared find themselves sitting in class not understanding what is being said. It is a waste of their time and money because they are not getting the value out of class that they have paid for in their tuition. The class discussion also suffers when students have not read the material to be discussed. Instead of having a lively discussion of the issues raised in the reading, students must endure listening to the instructor lecture for a long stretch.

If you have been asked to read an article or story from this text, you should spend time going over it as often as necessary for you to understand it. Some exercises may be assigned as homework, but even if they are not, you should read the notes, do the vocabulary exercises, and be prepared to answer comprehension questions and discuss the reading.

As you read, you may come across words and concepts that you are not familiar with. With the wealth of online information available at your fingertips, there is no excuse for not looking up these references. Many dictionaries have online versions. Proper names of people and places and historical references can easily be found with a search engine such as Google. A good student is a curious student.

## Reading from Paper and Reading from a Screen

As textbooks go electronic and more people buy e-books, educators have been examining the differences between reading on paper and reading on the screen.

E-books are convenient. They can be read on a tablet or a smartphone, devices people often carry around, so there is no need to carry heavy books as well. They are generally less expensive than paper versions. The information can be electronically searched, and notes on vocabulary and references can be accessed easily. E-books can also be annotated with margin notes.

Despite the convenience, reading from a screen has drawbacks. Studies show that readers remember more of what they have read from a traditional book than from an e-book. One reason is that people use spatial memory and can remember the location of information on a page. Another disadvantage is that reading from a screen can be more tiring for the eyes. The light from a screen can interfere with sleep preparation. Some people just prefer working with paper formats.

Most people probably use both electronic and paper reading materials. They may have a novel loaded on their phone to read on the bus and a paperback novel handy to read on the beach. Public libraries offer both electronic and paper books that can be borrowed. Whatever format you use, it is important to keep reading and to use your reading materials effectively.

## Distinguishing Fiction and Non-fiction

When you walk into any bookstore or library, you will find that the main division between books is fiction and non-fiction—in other words, between made-up stories and true stories. Even though this distinction becomes blurred when it comes to works such as autobiographical fiction, it is important to differentiate these two kinds of writing. Sometimes students get confused and refer to readings incorrectly. For example, they may refer to the actions in a non-fiction essay as happening to a character instead of to the author.

Even in the "real world" outside school, this distinction becomes important. Theologians and historians have argued about the fantastical theories presented in *The Da Vinci Code*, even though it is a novel, a work of fiction. Author James Frey was censured in the media because he fabricated part of his memoir (his life story); readers were expecting a "true" story. Journalists occasionally write about composite characters, combining characteristics of real people sometimes to conceal identities. We operate on this distinction between fiction and non-fiction even though "truth" is never as clear-cut as we would like. History, for instance, is subject to the interpretation of the writer, so different accounts about the same event can differ wildly.

| Fiction | Non-fiction |
|---|---|
| "made-up" stories | "true" stories |
| short stories, novels | articles, essays, columns, news stories |
| *I* ≠ author<br>*I* = narrator (usually a character in the story) | *I* = author |

We use the terms *short story* and *novel* to refer to works of fiction. Short stories can be anywhere from 500 to 5000 words. There are three short stories in Unit 16. Novels are usually 300 to 1000 pages. Sometimes books are made up of linked short stories—stories that share characters or place or both. Autobiographical fiction tells the life story of the author, but it is told in a narrative style, the events are not exactly as they happened, and the dialogue does not represent the actual words the participants used. Movies are usually works of fiction even if they are "based on a true story." Documentaries are non-fiction. Docudramas blur the line between fiction and non-fiction because actual events are dramatized. For instance, the film *United 93* recreates the hijacked flight on 11 September 2001 that ended in a field in Pennsylvania; the recreation is based on transcripts of cellphone calls and other recordings, but much of it is conjecture because no one on the plane survived to tell the true story.

It is best to have both fiction and non-fiction in your reading diet. One reason is that you will be able to distinguish between the two types of writing more easily. Fiction is sometimes dismissed because it is not "real." However, studies show that reading fiction has academic, mental, and social benefits. These advantages are explained in the essay "The Benefits of Reading Fiction" (pages 382–85).

## Referring to an Author

If *I* appears in the piece of writing (not in quotations), the identity of that person depends on what kind of writing it is—whether it is fiction or non-fiction. An *I* in a work of non-fiction refers to the author himself or herself. Thus, for example, for the article "No Hyphen for Me," you can say, "Salim Sachedina refers to his early days in Toronto in the 1960s." However, "Why My Mother Can't Speak English" is a short story based on true events; in other words, it is autobiographical fiction. You cannot say, "Garry Engkent's mother blamed her husband." Because the mother and the son have not been given names in the story, you have to refer to them as *the mother* and *the son*. They are characters, not real people. You can also refer to the son as *the narrator*.

Note that you can refer to fictional characters by their first or last names, depending on what they are called in the short story or novel. When you are discussing a non-fiction reading, however, you should refer to the author by his or her family name, or surname. For instance, in a research essay, you could say, "Trudeau and Petty explain why bottled water is not good for the environment." Sometimes the full name of the person is given for the first mention, and then the person is referred to by surname alone.

**Activity**

Scan through some of the reading selections in Part 2, looking for mentions of other writers. Note how the author refers to them. For example, Emma Teitel refers to the words of Anthony Bourdain; she calls him by his full name in the first reference and then just "Bourdain" (page 297). Compare this to Peter Singer's references (pages 283–84); because his article was printed in *The Globe and Mail*, it uses a different style.

## Identifying the Thesis of an Article

Most essays have one main idea that the author is trying to communicate to his or her audience. Sometimes the idea is stated directly, and sometimes it is not. The reader may have to infer the thesis. If the thesis is not immediately obvious to you, look at the organization of the reading. Remember that you are looking for the most general idea that is supported in the essay. Do not confuse the topic with the main idea. For example, "White Tops, Grey Bottoms" is about school uniforms (that is the topic), but the main idea is that schools are putting too much emphasis on dress codes.

One of the best ways to figure out the main idea of a non-fiction reading is to look at the title. This especially holds true for newspaper stories and columns because their titles are actually headlines, which are sentences with some of the function words (such as determiners) taken out. Take a look at the table of contents of this book, and read the titles of the readings in Part 2. The non-fiction articles are mostly from newspapers; most of the titles tell you clearly what the thesis is. For example, "The Case against Bottled Water" clearly shows the position of the authors. Compare these titles to the fiction pieces. It is not as obvious what "Soap and Water" is about.

A common organizational pattern for non-fiction writing, especially in newspapers and magazines, is to start with an anecdote—a story of something that happened to the author or to someone he knows. For example, Bev Akerman starts with a specific incident before she gives her arguments about school uniforms. The anecdotal introduction catches readers' attention because it is personal, something they can relate to.

Remember that in an academic essay, the thesis comes at the end of the introduction. This pattern is also sometimes used in journalistic essays and articles, except that the introduction may be several paragraphs long instead of the one-paragraph introduction you are used to writing for your essays. (Keep in mind that newspaper and magazine articles have many short paragraphs because they are written in narrow columns.)

In specific sentences, the main idea will be in the main clause. Look at the transitions the author uses. For example, expressions such as *however* and *it is vital to remember* point the way to main points.

Remember that the main idea will be supported by examples and explanations. When you read such specific statements, look for the point that is being made.

## Distinguishing Writers' Opinions

When you read essays and columns in newspapers and magazines, you have to be sure to follow different people's arguments. Often, authors mention some popular views before coming to their own. They start by relating these other views and then emphasize their own with a word like *however* or a phrase like *the truth is . . .*

Here are some things to watch for:

- expressions like *people think*, which automatically distance that view from the author's view
- words in quotation marks or expressions such as *so-called*, which show that the author does not agree with the word of expression
- verbs like *suppose, claim, purport*
- conjunctions such as *although* and *but* that show contrast
- transition signals such as *however* and *more important*, which show a shift in emphasis
- use of personal pronouns (*I, me*) to emphasize the author's point of view

Here are some examples:

| | |
|---|---|
| "an anonymous poster claiming to be a Manhattan restaurateur" | In this quotation (from page 297), Teitel uses the word *claim*, showing that she does not really accept what the poster is saying. |
| "Now, the received wisdom is quite different: uniforms are supposed to 'create an environment conducive to learning' and a sense of 'community among students.' Fair enough, I suppose, given the intense, competitive consumerism and cliquishness that plague many schools today." | In this quotation (from page 339), Akerman refers to a commonly held opinion (she calls it "received wisdom"). She uses quotation marks around phrases that are commonly used, although she does not reference a specific source for the words. Note that she gives a grudging acceptance of this view with the phrases "Fair enough" and "I suppose." |

The reading selections in this text have comprehension and discussion questions that ask you about the author's viewpoint. As you read the selections, look for the cues to the author's point of view, and discuss them in class.

## Recognizing Writers' Techniques

Writing is a craft. Writers use a variety of techniques to get their message across to their readers. Each word they put down is chosen from a vast array of possibilities.

The way they structure their paragraphs and sentences is part of their craft. They keep in mind their audience and purpose. They want to make sure that everything is clear to the readers. They try to entertain, inform, and convince readers.

The reading selections in Part 2 have notes on the authors' techniques. You can discuss structure and language as you take up the reading in class. Consider the decisions the author made. Look at the connotation of words. Consider how the topic is introduced and concluded. Are you caught up in the story the author tells? Are you convinced by the arguments? Reading attentively will make you a better reader, but do not forget that sometimes you can just sit back and enjoy the ride the author takes you on.

## Doing Research

Some of your reading will be research for your writing. You may be doing just general background reading to help you understand a topic, or you may be doing specific research for a paper.

Like most students today, you probably rely on the Internet for all your research. However, it is often difficult to tell where online information originates. Respected print newspapers, magazines, and professional journals often post articles online, and this material is reviewed, checked, and edited. Moreover, such publications stand by their work because they value their reputation. However, everything you read on the Internet does not go through that type of formal review. Anyone can start a website on any subject—he or she does not have to be an expert on that subject. Moreover, *Wikipedia*, an online encyclopedia, is open to editing by users and has misinformation deliberately posted in its entries. Even sites from reputable organizations can be hacked. Misinformation from one site can be copied to another and can go viral, infecting even reliable news sources.

You should try to authenticate any information you get from the Internet. See whether it fits what you already know. Take anything that sounds odd with a grain of salt. Look for independent sources that give the same information. Look at traditional print sources. Check where the websites are based. For instance, an *edu* at the end of the URL, or Internet address, usually denotes a school, and information on the official sites should be reliable—unless it is from student project pages.

The Internet is rife with information that is inadequate, incorrect, or even deliberately inflammatory (such as posts from trolls). Watch out for red flags that point to something wrong with the site. For example, some of the *Urban Dictionary* entries for *meese* as the plural of *moose* warn the reader not to trust English teachers and dictionaries and that *meese* is the only correct plural. (You can do a web search for "meese" to read these entries yourself.) *Urban Dictionary* is a wiki site—which means that anyone can post entries, even if they are not experts on the subject.

After you have researched your topic, you may use the information you have found in your writing. When you incorporate information from another writer into your essay, you need to cite it with a reference to the source of the information. General knowledge and historical facts do not have to be cited, but an author's interpretation of facts has to be cited. Any time you copy phrases and sentences from another writer, you must use quotation marks to show the copied words, and you must include a citation to show your reader where these words came from. Your essay should be essentially your ideas and words, with support from other writers' work.

## Referencing Sources

Referencing is essentially two different acts—using **in-text citation** and putting together the **bibliography**. The fundamental idea is that the in-text citation is a short form of the reference that points the reader to the full source information on the bibliography page. An in-text citation is essentially the author's name in brackets after the quote or paraphrase. The bibliography is usually the last page of the essay. The model essays in Appendices C and D show how to use and format references.

There are three common styles of referencing:

- **Chicago Manual** style (with a student version called Turabian style) is distinguished by its use of footnotes and endnotes instead of bracketed references.
- **Modern Language Association (MLA)** style is generally used for humanities subjects, such as English, in universities and colleges.
- **American Psychological Association (APA)** style is usually found in the sciences and social sciences.

The different citation styles can be confusing, and you may use different styles in different schools and even for different courses. Follow whichever guidelines your instructor gives you for research assignments. If your instructor does not specify a style, ask for one. Some instructors give detailed handouts with assignments, some direct you to your school library's information on citation style, and some point to an online reference site such as Purdue University's OWL (Online Writing Lab) website.

### The basic elements of referencing

- If you use the exact words of another author in your essay, you show that these are not your words by the use of quotation marks (or by using an indented block for a longer quote).
- You identify the author of these words—either with the author's surname in brackets or with a number leading to a footnote or an endnote that names the author. You must make it clear who said the words.
- If you include paraphrased ideas from another author in your essay, you show that these ideas are not yours in the same way that you would with a quotation, by stating the author's name and referencing the source.
- The in-text citation, whatever format you use, is a short form of the full reference on the bibliography page.
- The bibliography page is a separate page at the end of your assignment. It may be called "References" (in APA) or "Works Cited" (in MLA).
- Article and story titles are usually written between quotation marks, while the names of books, newspapers, and magazines are generally written in italics.
- The bibliography contains full source information so that the reader can locate the same resource you used.

Citations must refer to the source you actually used. An article may appear in print form in a newspaper, be online on the newspaper's website, get reprinted in a textbook or anthology, be reposted on another website, or appear in your school's library databases. Each of these citations would be slightly different. The title may also be different. In MLA style, the word *Print* is used to show that you read the print copy, and the word *Web* shows that you read an electronic copy, as shown in these examples:

| | |
|---|---|
| Mann, Doug. "Unplug the Digital Classroom." *Skill Set: Strategies for Reading and Writing in the Canadian Classroom.* By Lucia Engkent. 3rd ed. Don Mills: Oxford UP, 2016. 255–56. Print. | for the reading from this textbook |
| Mann, Doug. "Unplug the Digital Classroom." *Toronto Star.* 06 Oct. 2012. A.17. Print. | for the original article in the print version of the *Toronto Star* newspaper |
| Mann, Doug. "Let's Unplug the Digital Classroom." *Toronto Star.* 06 Oct. 2012. Web. 12 May 2015. | for the article online, in the *Toronto Star*'s website (read on May 12, 2015); note the difference in title |
| Mann, Doug. "Unplug the Digital Classroom." *Toronto Star.* 07 Oct. 2012. A.17. *Canadian Newsstand.* Web. 12 May 2015. | for the article online, in a school library's database (read on May 12, 2015); note the difference in date of publication |

Note that in MLA style, the references would appear double-spaced, with a hanging indent, and in alphabetical order. For websites, an access date is given at the end of the citation to show the date you looked at the site.

In contrast, here is what a reference to the Mann article (from this book) would look like in APA style:

> Mann, D. (2016). Unplug the digital classroom. In L. Engkent, *Skill set: Strategies for reading and writing in the Canadian classroom* (pp. 55–56). Don Mills, ON: Oxford UP.

Note that APA puts more emphasis on the date of publication: it appears for in-text citations (see the sample essay in Appendix D, pages 386–87), and it is more prominent in the reference list. APA does not use quotation marks for article and story titles, and only the first word of titles is capitalized.

Remember that citation is all about attention to detail. Be sure to copy information correctly. Proofread your work carefully.

## Avoiding Plagiarizing

Plagiarism is copying someone else's words or ideas and claiming them as your own. (Plagiarism also includes submitting your own work twice for different courses.) It is considered cheating or academic dishonesty. Usually, the punishment gets worse with each offence. For example, a first offence may mean a grade of zero on the paper and a notation on the student record. A second offence may mean failing the whole course, while the third may result in expulsion from the school.

Plagiarism is relatively easy to spot. Instructors get to know their students' writing styles and know what they are capable of. Generally, there is a noticeable difference between a student's writing style and a published author's. With modern technology, it is easy to cut and paste from other writers' works, but the same technology also makes the original sources easy to find.

Be careful when you take notes. Make sure you mark quotes accurately and keep references clear. It is also helpful to write your paper without constant consultation of your notes and sources so that you do not copy the wording. Make your points, and use your research to support those points. Quote only when necessary, and be sure to use quotation marks and include the reference. Follow the techniques for paraphrasing explained on pages 240–43.

Remember that a writing course is testing your ability to write, not to copy. It is dishonest to claim that the words on the page originated in your brain if they did not. In some cultures, writing does include copying phrases of well-known writers, but in Canadian schools, any such copying must be clearly shown with quotation marks and references. If not referenced otherwise, the words in the essay are assumed to have originated with the student writing the paper.

## Quoting

When you report what someone says, you put that person's words between quotation marks, but only if you are quoting the exact words used. Note the differences in these examples:

| | |
|---|---|
| Rhett Butler said, "Frankly, my dear, I don't give a damn." | This is a direct quote from the movie *Gone with the Wind*. |
| Rhett Butler said he didn't give a damn. | This is reported speech (also called "indirect speech"). It is not a full paraphrase of what the character said, and no quotation marks are used. |
| Rhett Butler exclaimed that he didn't care. | This is a paraphrase of what was actually said. |

Take note of the punctuation for a direct quote. The quotation marks curl around the quote and are found at the top of the line. A comma may separate the quote from the rest of the sentence. The period of the sentence comes before the quotation mark.

In research papers, you use two kinds of quotations. In one, you incorporate the words of the speaker in your sentences and show the exact words with quotation marks. Longer quotes are set off, separate from your paragraph and indented from the left margin. Both forms require a footnote or a parenthetical citation (the author's name and the page number in round brackets) to show where the reference comes from.

You can see examples of quotations in the two sample research essays in Appendices C and D. The first essay shows MLA style, and the second is APA style. Note how the quotations are integrated into the essay. They should not interrupt the flow of the writing.

Be sure to choose quotes wisely. Do not quote facts or straightforward, simple sentences. Instead, give such information in your own words. Choose quotes that express something in a unique manner. You should use quotes for impact, not to fill up space. They should fit your sentences smoothly.

**Using quotations in essays**

- Use quotations sparingly and wisely—don't quote to fill up your essay, and don't quote material that could be easily paraphrased.
- Do not quote factual statements. You can state the facts in your own words.
- Quotations should be integrated into your essay so that the ideas and sentences flow smoothly. (Do not introduce a quotation with an obvious phrase such as "Here is a quote from . . . .")
- Short quotations are set off with quotation marks and are inserted into the sentences you write.
- Long quotations (more than three lines) are usually indented in a block with no quotation marks.
- Use an ellipsis (. . .) to show left-out words if you have made the quotation shorter.
- If the author has not been mentioned in a signal phrase in the sentence, put the name of the author and the page number in parentheses after the quotation.
- If the article you are quoting from has no author, you can use the beginning part of the title in the reference after the quotation (but you can avoid this by mentioning the article in a signal phrase in your sentence).
- If you have paraphrased information from a source, indicate the author for the reference just as if it were a quotation.
- Be careful with your referencing if you are quoting a quotation; you need to use single quotation marks inside double ones to show this—make sure it is clear who said what.

**Activity**

Scan through some of the non-fiction reading selections in Part 2, looking for quotations. Note how the authors incorporate quotations in their writing. You can also check the referencing in the essays in Appendices C and D.

# Paraphrasing

Paraphrasing is the art of reporting what has been said by someone else. You must use different wording from what was used in the original. You express in a clearer, shorter, or different way what someone else has said or written. To be able to paraphrase well, you need a strong vocabulary and a good understanding of the original text, so paraphrasing is a test of reading comprehension.

The ability to paraphrase well is a skill that is often practised and tested in English courses. It is both a reading and writing skill. You will be called upon to paraphrase in reading comprehension tests, summaries, and essays. Some students have trouble accepting why they are asked to answer "in their own words" and are given no marks for copying the words from a reading in a test. Copying does not show understanding or a command of the language. Even people who know very little English can copy correctly. In addition, students have to paraphrase their own writing when they write an essay—they cannot repeat the same phrasing throughout the essay.

**What does "in your own words" mean?**

- words you "own"—part of your active vocabulary—words you would normally use
- not words that you came across for the first time in the article
- not phrasing that is unique to the author

Students sometimes ask what words from the original they can use in their paraphrase. You can use the same basic English words if they have no handy synonym. For example, you cannot avoid words like *language* and *immigrant*. You can also use expressions if they are Standard English, such as the phrase *supply and demand*. One test is that the words you use should be the ones you would normally use to say the same thing.

---

### How to paraphrase well

- Make sure you understand what is being said. (Look up the words you don't know.)
- Make sure you understand the context of the sentence(s) you are asked to paraphrase. (For example, if you have to paraphrase a quotation from a reading, read what comes before and after that quotation.)
- Before paraphrasing, put the reading aside for a minute, and think about the passage.
- Try to express the idea your own way, without looking at the original.
- Once you have used your own words, check the original wording to see if you missed any important parts.
- Use synonyms and different parts of speech, staying with words you know how to use in a sentence.
- Use a sentence structure different from the structure in the original quotation.

Imagine you were given this writing topic: "What is the key to success in college?" You would want to write about attendance, but you would want to avoid using the same wording as the question and repeating the same phrase throughout your essay. Here are different ways of saying the same idea. These examples illustrate some of the techniques used in paraphrasing.

| | |
|---|---|
| Attendance is the key to success in college. | This sentence uses the phrasing of the question, so it should be avoided in the essay. Instead, it should be paraphrased. |
| Attending class is important in college. | Just changing a part of speech can be a first step in paraphrasing. Here the gerund *attending* is used instead of the noun *attendance*. |
| Students need to come to class in order to pass their courses.<br>Students who come to class do well in their courses. | A paraphrase can be expressed in simple words completely different from the original. What is important is that the words express the same idea. Students are not specifically mentioned in the original topic question, but it is clear that the question is asking about student behaviour. |
| To achieve success, students must attend their classes.<br>Attendance is essential for students who want to succeed.<br>Successful students attend class. | Note how members of the same word family can be used to vary the sentences: *success* (n), *succeed* (v), *successful* (adj). |
| Absenteeism leads to failure.<br>Students who are often absent are in danger of failing their courses.<br>Students who skip class may fail their courses. | To add further variety, negatives can be used. However, it is important to make sure this does not change the meaning too much. |

What **not** to do in paraphrasing:

- Do not just manipulate the sentences by moving phrases around.
- Do not just copy the structure and swap words for synonyms or dictionary definitions.
- Do not use quotation marks around your paraphrase. (Once you put it in your words, it is no longer a quotation.)
- Do not use *I* in a paraphrase. Instead, refer to the author or speaker in the third person.

Study the good and bad examples of paraphrasing that follow.

1.  In a reading test, students are often asked to explain a statement from a reading:

| | |
|---|---|
| "Divorce can make children feel like damaged goods." | original words of the statement from the test question |
| This is saying that they are the goods that are damaged as a result of their parents' divorce. | **poor paraphrase:** The student's attempt to explain the statement is just a switch in the wording. |
| After a divorce, the children may feel worthless. | **good paraphrase:** It explains the expression "damaged goods." |

2.  Reading question: In the story "Why My Mother Can't Speak English" in Unit 16, what is the main reason the mother does not learn English?

| | |
|---|---|
| "For thirty-some years, my mother did not learn the English language, not because she was not smart enough, not because she was too old to learn, and not because my father forbade her, but because she feared that learning English would change her Chinese soul." | original quote from page 357, paragraph 65 |
| The mother did not learn English because she was afraid that it would change her Chinese soul. | **poor paraphrase:** "Chinese soul" is an expression unique to the author. |
| The mother did not learn English because she was afraid that she would lose her identity as a Chinese woman. | **good paraphrase:** It does not repeat author's words, and it shows the meaning of "Chinese soul." |

3.  In this example, the student's task was to paraphrase the quotation from an article in Unit 15:

| | |
|---|---|
| "Finally, I suspect the Uniformists have a secret motivation behind their fashion agenda: it makes public schools resemble, in the most superficial way, the exclusive private schools that pepper my Montreal neighbourhood." | original quote by Bev Akerman, page 340, paragraph 8 |

At last, I assume that people in charge of the uniforms have a secret ambition behind the dress code, to make public schools look like the exclusive private schools that hot-tasting berries of certain plants in the Montreal area.

The author thinks that those who support uniforms really want to make their schools look like elite private schools.

**poor paraphrase:**
- The student substituted synonyms for the original phrasing.
- The student incorrectly used *I*.
- It shows lack of understanding by using the dictionary definition of the noun *pepper* (which is used as a verb in the original).

**good paraphrase:**
It gets the main idea across, shows that the student understood the idea.

## Exercise 8.1

With a partner or in a small group, try to come up with as many different ways to express these ideas as you can. Compare your answers to those of another group.

1. Sean was fired for poor work performance.
2. An effective public transportation system is vital to any metropolis because it keeps the people moving efficiently and thus saves billions of dollars.
3. Clarity is the most important feature of good writing because the objective is to communicate information to the audience.
4. Students must paraphrase on tests and in essays to show their understanding of the material.

## Exercise 8.2

Paraphrase these passages:

1. Appearance is everything. We are constantly being judged by the way we look—to our advantage or disadvantage. Unattractive people may be viewed as inconsequential or ill-favoured, while very attractive people may be thought of as all beauty and no brains.
2. Although some people argue that people today are ruder and less considerate of others, it is easy to find examples of how we are better behaved than our ancestors. For example, our society has made improvements in the way we treat those who have lesser status. We make fewer class distinctions, and overt racism is not socially accepted today. Women are no longer treated as being nothing more than the property of their husbands or other male relatives.
3. It's hard to say who is more addicted to lotteries—the people who play them or the governments who depend on the revenue they generate. The money

goes to support many facilities that should be funded by taxes, such as hospitals and recreation centres. However, taxpayers seem to prefer putting their money toward lottery tickets than toward tax increases.

4. Women's sports have always gotten short shrift. Women golfers and tennis players would play for peanuts compared to the men's prizes. Women's hockey teams have trouble getting ice time. The poor media coverage for women's teams means that even their victories are buried in a few paragraphs in the sports section of the newspaper while losing men's teams get front-page coverage.

5. Halloween has become such a big holiday in North America that spending on it is second to that of Christmas. Houses are elaborately decorated to resemble haunted houses with ghosts and skeletons. Adults wear costumes to scare and delight trick-or-treaters or for parties. An interest in the supernatural is reflected in the current popularity of vampire books and movies.

## Using Reported Speech

Reported speech (or indirect speech) is a type of paraphrasing. It may not be a complete or true paraphrase, because often many of the original words are repeated. Reported speech is tricky because of the required changes, such as pronouns and time references. For example, the speaker's reference to *I* becomes *he* or *she*. If the speaker says *today* or *tomorrow*, you may have to change it to *that day* or *the next day*. Verb tense is also tricky. Often, you have to change the present tense verb to past tense. Here are some examples:

| Quotation | Reported speech |
| --- | --- |
| The director said, "Why isn't anyone listening to me?" | The director asked why no one was listening to him. |
| The actor said, "Why am I not getting more auditions?" | The actor wondered why he was not getting more auditions. |
| Peter said, "You have to do that scene all over again." | Peter said we would have to do the scene again. Peter told us to do the scene again. |
| John said, "Why don't you come with me to the game on Saturday?" | John invited me to the game on Saturday. |
| Ivana said, "Let's go to the 8 o'clock show, and then we can go for dessert." | Ivana suggested going to the 8 o'clock show and going for dessert afterwards. |

Note the use of different verbs such as *ask*, *wonder*, and *invite*, which show the function of the original statement.

## Exercise 8.3

Change these sentences from direct quotation to reported speech. You do not have to use all the words as long as you get the meaning across:

1. Susan said, "I'm going to work on that assignment tomorrow."
2. Raj said, "I will help you with the painting this weekend."
3. My sister asked, "What shall we get Mom for her birthday?"
4. Mohammed said, "Why don't we get tickets for the Great Big Sea concert?"
5. Lulu asked, "Will you help me prepare my oral presentation?"
6. He asked the TA, "Will Unit 6 be on the mid-term?"
7. Hans asked, "Do you know where Michael bought his Vespa?"
8. "I'm sorry. I forgot to call you yesterday," said Amar.
9. Brad said, "I think we should take up curling. It looks like a sport I could handle."
10. Lindy said, "Tomas should buy a new car. His is a piece of junk."

## Writing a Summary

Summarizing is a skill used every day. You summarize when you recount the plot of a movie or relate what happened to you in your day; summarizing textbook chapters is an excellent way to study for exams; journal articles are summarized in abstracts; and business reports often include an executive summary. Being able to summarize something concisely is a valuable skill worth cultivating.

When you summarize, you give the main ideas from a reading such as an article, story, or report. You do not include examples or specific details, such as dates, figures, and biographical data, unless they are important for comprehension. The points should be in the same order as in the original whenever possible. Make sure you cover the whole article. When students are faced with a strict word limit, they sometimes stop writing as soon as they reach this limit. Keep in mind that a summary by itself is objective. You do not give your opinion of what is said in the article or evaluate the author's writing. You just report what the author said.

The summary should be clear enough that someone who has not read the original text can still understand the summary and come away with the same basic information. Avoid vague statements such as "the authors talk about bottled water," which just state the topic and not the main idea. Usually the word *about* signals such a statement. One way to check clarity is to ask someone who has not read the original article to read the summary to see whether he or she has any questions.

Conciseness is important because the main purpose is to make something shorter. A summary can range in length from one sentence to one-third the length of the original article. For school assignments, you may be asked to write a summary that is one-tenth the length of the original so that a 100-word paragraph summarizes a 1000-word article. When you have a strict word limit, it may be easier to write a first draft without worrying about the word count. Then you can edit it, looking for ways to make it concise and eliminating unnecessary details.

Paraphrase is an important part of summarizing. Use your own words to express the ideas of the author. Copying sentences from the original is not acceptable. One good way to avoid copying phrases from the text is to draft your summary without looking at the original. You can check later to make sure you have covered all the ideas you need. Remember that if the article is in the first person (*I*), your paraphrase will use third person references such as "the author" and "she says."

A summary should follow good paragraph structure and start with a topic sentence. Just as the topic sentence of a developed paragraph gives the main idea (as shown in Unit 4), the topic sentence of the summary tells the reader that this is a summary. Usually, the author and title of the article are named, and the source information (the name of the newspaper, the date, and the page number, for example) may be given if necessary.

Here is an 88-word summary of an 830-word article that can be found in Unit 11 on pages 283–84:

> In "Why Pay More? To Be Conspicuous," Peter Singer criticizes conspicuous consumption—buying luxury goods just to show off wealth. He uses the example of the designer watches worn by Ukrainian government ministers to make his argument: the watches do not even work that well, they cost several times the average annual salary in Ukraine, and they indicate possible corruption. People do not need to give up all luxury items, but buying such high-end goods is immoral when the money could be spent instead on helping the poor.

Note that in this summary, the example of the watch is mentioned because it is a major part of the article, even though examples are usually not given in summaries.

## Steps for Writing a Summary

1. Read the entire article, story, or report, making sure you understand it all. You may have to read it a few times. Use a dictionary for unfamiliar words.
2. Put the article or story away, and think about what it said. Without referring to the original, write a quick draft of your summary, using your own words. Your draft can be in the form of jot notes.
3. Go over the article again, making sure you have covered all the main points in your draft.
4. Rewrite your summary, putting it in proper form.
5. Start a summary paragraph with a topic sentence that identifies the article (title, author's name, and source) and gives the main idea of the original reading.
6. Make sure your summary paraphrases the words of the author. Do not copy his or her specific expressions. Do not quote.
7. Check to see whether your summary says enough to be clear to readers who have not read the original.
8. Edit your summary to meet the required word length.
9. Correct grammar, spelling, and punctuation for your final draft.

## Writing the Topic Sentence for a Summary Paragraph

Just as the topic sentence of a paragraph often gives the main idea, the topic sentence of a summary tells the reader that the paragraph is a summary and identifies the work that is being summarized by giving the title and the author's name. (You may also be asked to give the source information in the first sentence, but that information could be given in a citation instead.) The first sentence gives an overview of the article.

Ideally, the topic sentence of a summary contains both the title of the article and the author's name, and one of those two elements is the grammatical subject of the sentence. In effect, this means that writers can use the preposition *in* with the title and *by* with the author but they cannot use both in their topic sentence, because a grammatical subject cannot be in a prepositional phrase. This is shown in the variations of a summary topic sentence given below.

**For a summary topic sentence:**

- Either the title or the author has to be the grammatical subject of the sentence.
- The grammatical subject cannot be in a phrase beginning with a preposition.
- The title of the article is singular (for subject–verb agreement).
- The title of an article or short story is written between quotation marks.
- The title and the author's name must be given in full, with no changes or mistakes.
- If the article was written by two authors, both names are given (and the verb is in the plural form if the authors are the subject of the sentence).
- Use a verb such as *say*, *tell*, *explain*, and *discuss* to introduce the main idea of the article (but avoid weak verbs such as *mention* or *refer to*).

Here are some examples of topic sentences for a summary paragraph:

a) "Fear Math, Not Numbers" by Peter Martyn argues that we should make a distinction between arithmetic and mathematics.

**correct topic sentence:**
The grammatical subject of the sentence is the title of the article.

b) In "Fear Math, Not Numbers," Peter Martyn argues that we should make a distinction between arithmetic and mathematics.

**correct topic sentence:**
The grammatical subject of the sentence is the author.

c) In "Fear Math, Not Numbers" by Peter Martyn argues that we should make a distinction between arithmetic and mathematics.

**incorrect topic sentence:**
The sentence lacks a grammatical subject because both the title and the author's name are in prepositional phrases.

| | |
|---|---|
| d) "Fear Math, Not Numbers" is by Peter Martyn. | **weak topic sentence:** It just gives the title and author with no information about the topic of the article. |
| e) "Fear Math, Not Numbers" by Peter Martyn. | **incorrect topic sentence:** It is an incomplete sentence (no verb). |
| f) In the article "Fear Math, Not Numbers" by Peter Martyn, the author argues that we should make a distinction between arithmetic and mathematics. | **wordy topic sentence:** Saying "the article," "by," and "the author" is unnecessary. |
| g) This article is about the distinction between arithmetic and mathematics. | **incorrect topic sentence:** The article is not identified. |
| h) Arithmetic is different from mathematics. | **incorrect topic sentence:** It does not show that this is a summary and does not identify the article. |
| i) This article was very interesting. | **incorrect topic sentence:** It does not identify the reading, it does not say what the article is about, and it gives an opinion. |
| j) This is a summary of the article "Fear Math, Not Numbers" by Peter Martyn. | **incorrect topic sentence:** This is an announcement instead of a topic sentence. |

## Exercise 8.4

Here is a 227-word summary of "White Tops, Grey Bottoms," by Bev Akerman (Unit 15, pages 339–40). Eliminate unnecessary phrases and sentences, and reduce wordiness to make the summary less than 100 words:

In the article "White Tops, Grey Bottoms," by Bev Akerman, the author explains her objections to the strict dress codes at her children's public school in Montreal. The author gives examples of the problems of the dress code, which is too strict. Her son was sent home from school for having an untucked shirt. Akerman had to wear a uniform when she was in school, but things have changed. Akerman complains that students have to wear specific brands of uniforms. The uniforms are in dull colours like grey and white. These colours are boring and do not let the students express their creativity. Bev Akerman also makes a complaint that the money that the parents are collecting from the sale of the clothing is used to pay for items that the school board should pay for, such as musical instruments and school computers. Moreover, uniforms are a cop-out for parents. The parents do not want to deal with their children wearing inappropriate clothing, so they defer to the schools to take the heat and regulate their children's appearance. Uniforms are a way of making public schools seem like elite private schools, but Akerman prefers the diversity inherent in the public school system where there are many different kinds of students. Her son's school should concentrate on educating the students. It is far too concerned with their appearance.

**A good summary**

- is clear to anyone who has not read the original article or story
- gives only the main ideas of the original, without unnecessary details or examples
- is a paraphrase, with no quotes from the original
- tells the reader it is a summary in the first sentence by identifying the original work
- is concise, meeting word limits
- covers all the major points of the article
- does not give the summary writer's opinion of the original

## Writing about Readings

In your English course, you may be assigned a variety of writing tasks based on a reading. It is important that you have a clear idea of what each task entails, so here is a reference list:

**Reading comprehension questions** (explained below): usually short answers, in full sentences, in your own words (in other words, paraphrased)

**Summary** (explained in the previous section): the main ideas of the reading, usually in a paragraph

**Literary analysis** (explained below): close examination of the writer's techniques or the elements of fiction (such as plot, theme, and characters); could be in a paragraph or an essay

**Personal response** (explained below): your opinion of the reading; usually less structured

**Paragraphs and essays** (examples shown in Units 4–6 and Appendices C and D): writing on a topic related to what is said in the reading (not necessarily the main idea); see examples of topics in the Discussion and Assignments sections following each reading in Part 2

## Answering Reading Comprehension Questions

Short-answer comprehension questions are a good way for instructors to test both your reading and your writing skills. Your answers may be marked for both content and language use.

Paraphrasing is an important part of comprehension tests because you cannot paraphrase properly if you do not understand what has been said. If you copy the author's words directly, your instructor cannot tell how much you understand. Even a person with very little English could be lucky enough to find and copy the right sentence to answer the question.

On a reading test, you have to understand both what the author is saying in the reading and what the question is asking. Look for key words such as *describe*, *compare*, and *explain*, and make sure your answer fulfills the requirement. If it is a two-part question, do not neglect half the question. Check to see how many marks each question is worth to make sure you say enough but not too much. For example, a three-mark question asking you to explain the author's thesis should be two to three sentences—not an extended paragraph summarizing the whole article.

One way to get your answer on the right track is to use a few words from the question. For example, if the question asks, "Why does the father encourage the waiters to learn English?" you can start by saying, "He encourages them because . . . ."

Each of the reading selections in Part 2 of this text is accompanied by comprehension questions that will allow you to practise answering such questions.

Here is an example of a reading comprehension question and answer for "Fear Math, Not Numbers" in Unit 9 on pages 260–61:

> Why does Peter Martyn think it is important to keep the distinction between arithmetic and mathematics?
>
> He thinks it is important because understanding arithmetic is part of our everyday lives. People need to understand basic addition, subtraction, multiplication, and division to do tasks such as figuring out the correct change for a purchase. Mathematics, on the other hand, requires the higher-level work with numbers that scientists and engineers use.

## Literary Analysis

You may be called upon to write a literary paragraph or essay in which you analyze what a writer did in a short story, novel, or play. You might have to discuss plot, symbolism, or theme or compare two literary works. What students find most difficult about this task is doing actual analysis and not just retelling the plot. You can keep on track if you remember what you learned about academic paragraphs— begin each paragraph with your main idea, an argument. Then you use examples from the text to support what you said. Compare the two sample paragraphs on the next page.

In "Why My Mother Can't Speak English," the story begins with the old mother wanting to get her citizenship because she is afraid of being deported and of losing her old age pension. After a disappointing interview with a Citizenship clerk, the narrator recounts the reasons why his mother never learned the English language. While the father in the story encourages the Chinese waiters to learn English, he discourages his own wife from doing so because he is afraid of losing control over her. More interesting is the revelation that the mother does not want to learn because she thinks she may be changed. However, the story ends somewhat happily: The mother does get her citizenship, and she wants to show her achievement to her dead husband at the cemetery.

**incorrect:**
This is just a plot summary. It retells the story but does not do any analysis.

In "Why My Mother Can't Speak English," Garry Engkent presents some complex reasons for the difficulty immigrant women have in learning a new language. First, learning English opens up the new world to women, and some men have trouble accepting that. For example, the husband does not permit his wife to learn English because he can control her if she cannot speak the language. Moreover, he is afraid that she will learn the ways of white women, something he cannot accept. Second, the wife is reluctant to become more than merely functionally literate in the restaurant because she is afraid that English may change her cultural identity. The writer underscores the point that language is more than a medium of communication.

**correct:**
This paragraph focuses on a point—explaining why immigrant women experience difficulty learning the new language. The supporting details for this point are from the story.

## Writing a Personal Response

In your writing course, you may be asked to write a personal response to a reading. It could be a simple paragraph explaining your reaction to what you read or a fully developed essay with a thesis—it depends on what is specified in the assignment.

Unless you are specifically asked to include a summary of the reading in your personal response, a summary is not required in this type of writing because it is assumed the reader of your response has read the original. Moreover, a summary and a personal response are two quite different pieces of writing: Summaries should not include your opinion of what you read, but a personal response calls on you to do exactly that.

Instead of making a bland statement such as "I enjoyed the story because it was interesting," say something specific. Here are some example statements that you could include in a personal response:

> I enjoyed reading "Why My Mother Can't Speak English" because the story reminded me of my own grandmother, who is also stubborn about hanging onto her culture.

"The Case against Bottled Water" gave me information I had not known and made me rethink my own habit of drinking bottled water. The authors gave compelling arguments and supported each point they made with clear examples and facts, such as the actual cost of the water.

A personal response is an opportunity for you to do critical thinking of what you read and to state and support your personal opinions of the article or story.

## Building Reading Skills

- Read as often as possible. For instance, read when you have to wait, such as at the doctor's office or in a line-up for service. Keep reading material handy, whether it is a paperback or magazine in your bag or an e-book on your smartphone or tablet.
- Join the public library to gain access to a wide range of materials, both print and electronic.
- Vary your reading diet. Read both fiction and non-fiction. Read both short works like newspaper articles and long ones like novels. Read opinions that you do not agree with.
- For readings assigned for school, read them more than once. Look up unfamiliar words in the dictionary. Summarize the readings in your notes.
- Read attentively, paying attention to the use of language.
- Use a dictionary, but use it judiciously—do not stop to look up every unfamiliar word, because you will lose the flow of your reading. If you can follow the general meaning, keep reading.
- Keep a reading journal. Writing something about the reading will help you remember it. You can record your thoughts, a brief summary, or vocabulary notes.
- For non-fiction, read popular treatments of subjects you are interested in. Many science and social science books are written for a lay (non-professional) audience.
- Get into the newspaper habit. Daily newspapers offer articles of interest for everyone, and they are often available online.
- Read books at a level you are comfortable with. They should be challenging enough to enable you to build your skills but not too difficult that they make the reading a chore.
- Try children's literature or books written for teenagers. Some of these books are quite sophisticated. Moreover, the classic books are part of a shared culture and are often referred to. Learning this shared culture is especially important for ESL students.
- Check out simplified novels if you find other novels difficult. They are written at different reading levels and can be found in the public library.
- Try different kinds of literature. Give the book or article a fair chance, but if you decide it is not for you, try something else.
- Ask your instructors and librarians for advice and book recommendations.

# PART 2

# Reading Selections

# UNIT 9

# Education

## Unplug the Digital Classroom

*by Doug Mann*

1      We are entering an age when the "digital delivery of course content can free faculty in traditional institutions to engage in direct dialogue and mentorship with students."

2      So says the Ontario government's 2012 white paper on education, "Strengthening Ontario's Centres of Creativity, Innovation and Knowledge." Professors muse that the classroom must "evolve or die" to become more "fun and engaging" for the modern student.

3      Such views are misinformed at best, crude propaganda for Apple and Microsoft at worst. The use of digital technology in higher education has promoted ignorance, not knowledge, and severely degraded basic reading, writing and thinking skills. It's time to hit the off button.

4      One problem with the most enthusiastic futurists is that too many of them haven't spent any time in the classroom in the last decade. If they had, they'd realize that digital technology is already omnipresent there, used by both students and professors. Almost all undergraduate students in North America are addicted to texting on their smartphones and checking their Facebook pages on an hourly basis. Almost all professors use computers, projectors, Power Point presentations and the Internet as part of their lectures. Calling for more digital technology in education today is like calling for more white people in the Republican party.

5      The real question is how computers, smartphones and iPods are used, and whether these uses contribute anything to the main goal of higher education: to improve students' minds and characters by helping them to learn facts, debate ideas and understand the world better. The answer, for the most part, is no—study after study shows that digital technology has dumbed down higher education. They may make education more "fun" and "engaging." But that's only saying that they've turned education into a form of entertainment. Writing essays, reading difficult texts or figuring out complex mathematical problems have never been "fun"—and never will be.

6    On the plus side, the use of the computer as a delivery device for texts and images is largely a positive development. Gone are the nights spent in the bowels of the university library looking through card catalogues and the social science index for books and articles. It's also useful from a teacher's point of view to be able to display images and video via classroom computers when teaching things like fine art, comics and film.

7    Laptops in the classroom are much more of a problem. Yes, one student in 10 actually uses them to look up relevant facts and issues, but the other nine are using classroom Wi-Fi to check their Facebook pages, email or celebrity websites. Portable computers combine all four of the general functions of digital technology: information delivery, peer communication, entertainment and procrastination. Cellphones concentrate on the last three functions and have no pedagogical purpose.

8    Anyone who has walked to the back of a university classroom and looked at what students are actually looking at on their various screens will abandon any sense that digital technology plays a positive role in the classroom. Facebook and celebrity websites dominate their screens.

9    What's especially frustrating when we hear the blind support for digital technology bruited in government white papers and the mass media today is the refusal to acknowledge the substantial empirical research over the last 15 years that questions the value of such technology. Mark Bauerlein's *The Dumbest Generation* contains literally dozens of studies that show how digital technology has helped to create a generation of proud bibliophobes who avoid complex knowledge like the plague.

10    Jean Twenge and Keith Campbell's *The Narcissism Epidemic* shows how celebrity culture, the web 2.0 and soft parenting have accelerated young people's sense of self-esteem beyond all reasonable boundaries of actual achievement. The mass culture tells them that everyone can be a star, facts be damned. Digital narcissists don't care about their inability to read and write English or their ignorance of a range of basic historical and political facts.

11    My solution? Hit the off button in as many places as we can. Turn off Wi-Fi in the classroom, restricting it to student lounges scattered across campus. Create a schoolwide policy that bans the use of cellphones during lectures and seminars. Since texting has become an addiction for many, treat cells like cigarettes: if you want to text, do it outside. Ban the use of social networking websites during class. Stop promoting Internet-managed distance-education courses: these are cheap imitations of the real thing. Digital technologies can be great delivery devices. But what they too often deliver has nothing to do with education.

[6 October 2012]

## Notes

Mann's reference to "calling for more white people in the Republican party" [4] means that there is already too much technology in the classroom. The Republican Party is the right-wing, conservative political party in the United States. It is criticized for the lack of diversity among its membership. Most Republicans are white.

## Comprehension

1. What is Mann's main argument?
2. What supporting evidence does he offer for his main argument?
3. What does the Ontario government propose in its 2012 white paper?
4. Why does Mann refer to these views as "crude propaganda"?
5. How is digital technology used in the classroom now?
6. What are the advantages of using digital technology in the classroom, according to Mann?
7. What do students use their laptops for in the classroom?
8. Mann refers to two books. What do the authors say?
9. Explain "celebrity culture, the web 2.0 and soft parenting" [10].
10. What is Mann's final suggestion?

## Discussion

1. Discuss the ways you have seen digital technology used in the classroom by both the instructor and the students. What was effective? What did not work well?
2. How has the use of digital technology affected you?
3. Do you think Mann's opinion of digital technology in the classroom is too negative? Is this essay just an anti-technology rant from the older generation? Or are his arguments justified?
4. Is it realistic to think that education should be fun and entertaining?
5. Mann says that cellphones "have no pedagogical purpose" [7]. Do you agree? How could cellphones be used in class?
6. Discuss the statement: "The mass culture tells them that everyone can be a star, facts be damned" [10]. Consider, for example, celebrities such as Justin Bieber who started their careers with YouTube videos. Does this mean that anyone actually can become famous?
7. What kind of limits should be placed on students' use of digital devices such as smartphones in the classroom?

## Assignments

1. Studies show that students learn differently from digital devices than from printed books. Research this topic, and write a comparison essay.
2. Do students waste their time on celebrity news and social media? Write an essay explaining your point of view.
3. Mann says the main goal of education is "to improve students' minds and characters by helping them to learn facts, debate ideas and understand the world better" [5]. Write an essay explaining what the purpose of education is.
4. How should instructors make class more appealing to the digital generation?

## Paraphrase and Summary

1. Paraphrase: "We are entering an age when the 'digital delivery of course content can free faculty in traditional institutions to engage in direct dialogue and mentorship with students'" [1].

2. Paraphrase: "Anyone who has walked to the back of a university classroom and looked at what students are actually looking at on their various screens will abandon any sense that digital technology plays a positive role in the classroom" [8].

3. Write a one-paragraph summary of the article. Use no more than 100 words.

## Structure and Technique

Mann begins by quoting and referring to a government publication in his first two paragraphs. This is a common technique to establish the topic. It sets up his argument—his disagreement with the position taken in the report. How effective do you find this opening?

Note how Mann uses the two books to support his argument. He says the work is based on "substantial empirical research."

In his argument essay, Mann uses many long sentences of explanation. However, he also uses conversational expressions to make his essay more accessible to the average reader. Note the fragment ("My solution?") [11] and the use of *yes* [7] and *no* [5]. He also uses *you* and command sentences in his conclusion. These colloquialisms would not be acceptable in an academic essay.

## Language Study

### Definitions

Use the context from the reading to match each word to its definition:

| | |
|---|---|
| 1. bowels, *n* [6] _____ | a) based on scientific testing |
| 2. bruite, *v* [9] _____ | b) being everywhere |
| 3. degrade, *v* [3] _____ | c) delaying something for later |
| 4. empirical, *adj* [9] _____ | d) false or misleading information used by an institution |
| 5. mentorship, *n* [1] _____ | e) having someone work as an advisor and role model |
| 6. muse, *v* [2] _____ | |
| 7. omnipresent, *adj* [4] _____ | f) make something worse |
| 8. pedagogical, *adj* [7] _____ | g) related to education |
| 9. plague, *n* [9] _____ | h) serious infectious disease |
| 10. procrastination, *n* [7] _____ | i) spread, as for news |
| 11. propaganda, *n* [3] _____ | j) student working on a bachelor's degree in university |
| 12. undergraduate, *adj* [4] _____ | k) the lowest or deepest part of something, such as a basement |
| | l) think, imagine |

### Word Focus

#### addicted [4]

The verb *addict* is rarely used in the active form. For instance, we would not say, "Tobacco addicts many people." Instead, we would use the passive voice: "Many people are addicted to tobacco." We use the passive participle, *addicted*, to describe the people but the adjective form, *addictive* and its opposite *non-addictive*, to describe the substances. The noun forms are *addict* for the person and *addiction* for the state. A common error is to confuse *addicted* and *addictive*. Examine these example sentences:

> He is a drug addict. He is addicted to crystal meth, which is a very addictive substance. However, he is going to enter a treatment facility for his addiction.

### bibliophobe [9]

The word *bibliophobe* is a combination of two Greek roots. The root *biblio-* means books and shows up in the words *bibliography* and *Bible*. The combining form *–phobe* refers to a fear or dislike. Thus, a bibliophobe is someone who dislikes books.

The form *–phobe* refers to a person, and *–phobia* refers to the fear itself, while *–phobic* is the adjective ending. Here are examples of words that use this root word:

> technophobe: someone who dislikes technology

> claustrophobic: describing someone who is afraid of enclosed spaces

> arachniphobia: fear of spiders

The opposite of *–phobe* and *–phobia* is *–phile* and *–philia*, referring to a lover or love of something, respectively. The combining forms *–mania* and *–maniac* can also refer to an obsession for something. Here are some examples:

> bibliophile: someone who loves books

> Sinophilia: the love of Chinese culture and things

> kleptomaniac: someone who obsessively steals things

There are hundreds of obscure words formed with the *–phobe* and *–phile* roots attached to Latin and Greek words. Even though they are not in common use, they are entertaining to examine. You can easily do a search on the Internet for a list of phobias and philias. See if you can find out the meaning of *triskaidekaphobia*, for instance.

### narcissism [10]

*Narcissism* refers to self-love. A *narcissist* is a person obsessed with himself or herself. The words come from the Greek myth of Narcissus and Echo. See the definition paragraph on pages 164–65 to find out more.

### Word Families

Fill in the chart with the corresponding parts of speech:

| NOUN | VERB | ADJECTIVE | ADVERB |
|------|------|-----------|--------|
| achievement [10] | | | n/a |
| | | digital [1] | |
| | dominate [8] | | |

| NOUN | VERB | ADJECTIVE | ADVERB |
|---|---|---|---|
| imitation [11] | | | |
| knowledge [3] | | | |
| | promote [3] | | n/a |
| | n/a | | severely [3] |
| value [9] | | | |

## Collocations and Expressions

Discuss the meanings and usage of the following expressions:

hit the off button [3]
avoid something like the plague [9]
on the plus side [6]
on an hourly basis [4] (Note that hourly is an adjective in this expression, but it can also be an adverb.) (Other time words can also be used in this expression—daily, weekly, monthly, and yearly.)

## Sentence Structure Analysis

Identify the main subject and verb in the following sentences. Identify the modifiers—adjectives, adverbs, phrases, and clauses—and what they modify.

1. "The real question is how computers, smartphones and iPods are used, and whether these uses contribute anything to the main goal of higher education: to improve students' minds and characters by helping them to learn facts, debate ideas and understand the world better." [5]
2. "Gone are the nights spent in the bowels of the university library looking through card catalogues and the social science index for books and articles." [6]

## Fear Math, Not Numbers

*by Peter Martyn*

1 Words matter. They indelibly colour our perceptions.

2 Take the overdue revival of debate about the value of memorizing addition, subtraction and multiplication tables in school curriculums. The problem lies in the use of the word "math."

3 For reasons not clear to me, simple arithmetic—addition, subtraction, multiplication, division—has come to be called math. It's cursed a couple of generations of otherwise intelligent, creative people with an ungrounded and unnecessary fear of numbers.

4    In his classic 1946 essay Politics and the English Language, George Orwell decried his contemporaries' "lack of precision" in their use of words (not to mention their reliance on outdated metaphors and bland euphemisms). The situation has not improved.

5    We can't blame Twitter, with its admirable and disciplined brevity. Common use of the one-syllable, four-letter "math" for mathematics predates not only the advent of social media, but for all intents and purposes, the Internet itself. Perhaps the misnomer comes from an understandable disinclination to use polysyllabic vocabulary. After all, Orwell did admonish us to "Never use a long word where a short one will do."

6    Actual "math" is difficult for many. The Oxford English Dictionary defines it as "the abstract science of number, quantity and space." It's not arithmetic.

7    The distaste for true math often begins in high school. Geometry is not so difficult. Algebra and trigonometry are harder. And many of us are thrown under the bus of calculus, never to walk again among mathematicians.

8    That is the point where people begin to say they "can't do math."

9    When children hear their parents and teachers trash-talking "math," meaning anything to do with numbers, those adults are inadvertently contributing to a dangerous dumbing-down. We need facility with numbers, without having to refer to a calculator or an app.

10   Some foresee mental faculties we don't use succumbing to atrophy, becoming vestigial, like the appendix. Columbia professor Tim Wu has suggested, in two recent New Yorker pieces, that unused mental faculties will eventually disappear through a process of "biological atrophy."

11   But if you can't do simple arithmetic in your head, how do you know if you're getting short-changed at the store? How do you know whether the politicians debating your next tax bill make sense—and how do they know whether their aides' figures add up? These are important things to be able to do on the fly, but they don't require mathematics. Arithmetic suffices.

12   Around the walls of my grade-school classroom was a wooden picture rail, from which hung posters or student art. Above it were construction-paper cutouts with arithmetic exercises: $3 + 3 =$, $7 \times 11 =$ and so on. Whenever our attention wandered, Miss Cline would take her wooden pointer and stride the room, aiming its tip at the questions and calling on us at random. Woe betide those who couldn't answer—they would spend the next several evenings at home memorizing.

13   Memorization, drills. They sound like something from the 19th century, and in fact they are. But recent research using functional magnetic resonance imaging shows that brains change as subjects memorize the solutions to numerical problems, getting quicker with practice.

14   So get out those addition, subtraction and multiplication tables. Memorize them, if you were deprived of that brain exercise in grade school. And teach a child. It will improve your mental agility, and it's not math.

[3 April 2014]

## Comprehension

1. What is Martyn's thesis?
2. Explain the first paragraph of the reading.
3. What is the difference between mathematics and arithmetic? Is it possible to be skilled at one and not the other?
4. Explain Martyn's opinion of Twitter.
5. Why do we need to be able to do arithmetic in our head?
6. Why is mathematics less useful than arithmetic in our daily lives?

## Discussion

1. Discuss Martyn's first two sentences. Give examples of how language determines how something is perceived.
2. Do you have math anxiety? Why or why not?
3. How did you learn arithmetic and mathematics in school? Did your studies focus on memorization or on problem solving? Were the methods effective?
4. What learning methods did you use for other subjects? For example, languages are often taught with drills and memorization. Do you think the methods used were effective? How would you change the education you had?
5. Now that we have calculators on our smartphones, is it necessary to be able to do arithmetic in our heads? Discuss.
6. What else do we depend on our smartphones to "remember" for us? For example, do you know your family members' and friends' phone numbers by heart? What information would you lose if you lost your phone? What is the danger of this?
7. What are the benefits of rote learning and drills? What should students actually memorize?
8. Does Martyn follow Orwell's advice to "Never use a long word where a short one will do"? Can you think of any instances in the article where he didn't follow this advice? If so, what are they? Which shorter words could he have used in those cases?

## Assignments

1. Write an essay arguing that it is (or is not) still important to be able to do arithmetic in our heads without technical aids.
2. How does Twitter affect language use? Write an illustrative essay.
3. The way that math is taught in school is a controversial subject. Some people favour more drill and memorization, while others argue that students need to understand math concepts and do problem solving. Research the topic, and write an essay explaining your point of view.

## Paraphrase and Summary

1. Paraphrase and explain: "And many of us are thrown under the bus of calculus, never to walk again among mathematicians" [7].

2. Paraphrase: "When children hear their parents and teachers trash-talking "math," meaning anything to do with numbers, those adults are inadvertently contributing to a dangerous dumbing-down. We need facility with numbers, without having to refer to a calculator or an app" [9].
3. Write a one-paragraph summary of the article. Use no more than 100 words.

## Structure and Technique

Discuss Martyn's tone in this article. Is his language and style academic or conversational or a mixture of both? Explain your answer, and discuss the effect of the tone.

## Language Study

### Definitions

Use the context from the reading to match each word to its definition:

| | |
|---|---|
| 1. bland, *adj* [4] _____ | a) accidentally, without meaning to do something |
| 2. brevity, *n* [5] _____ | b) did not have something |
| 3. contemporaries, *n* [4] _____ | c) dislike, feeling that something is unpleasant |
| 4. decried, *v* [4] _____ | d) in a way that is impossible to forget or to remove |
| 5. deprived, *v* [14] _____ | e) lacking colour or interest |
| 6. distaste, *n* [7] _____ | f) people of the same age or era |
| 7. inadvertently, *adv* [9] _____ | g) strongly criticized |
| 8. indelibly, *adv* [1] _____ | h) using few words |
| 9. misnomer, *n* [5] _____ | i) without a good foundation |
| 10. ungrounded, *adj* [3] _____ | j) wrong name for something |

### Word Focus
#### difficult [6, 7]

The adjective *difficult* is used in the reading to describe math and, more specifically, geometry. The word *difficult* and its synonyms and antonyms can cause problems for some language learners when they try to use these adjectives to describe people and come up with incorrect sentences such as "I am difficult to learn English" or "college students are easy to look for jobs." To add the element of a person, the preposition *for* is used: "Math is difficult for me."

Practise using these words by writing answers to the following questions. Vary your wording by using synonyms for *difficult* and *easy*.

a) What subject do you find difficult in your program?
b) In gym class, what was the easiest activity or sport for you? Was this also the one you enjoyed the most?
c) What do you find easy in writing essays, and what do you find difficult?

### Word Families
Fill in the chart with the corresponding parts of speech:

| NOUN | VERB | ADJECTIVE | ADVERB |
|---|---|---|---|
| | | admirable [5] | |
| | | creative [3] | |
| | | dangerous [9] | |
| | debate [11] | | |
| | | functional [13] | |
| | memorize [2] | | |
| | refer (to) [9] | | |
| reliance [4] | | | |
| | suffice [11] | | |

### Collocations and Expressions
Discuss the meanings and usage of the following expressions:

> to come to be [3]
> for all intents and purposes [5]
> to throw somebody under the bus [7] (Note: This was used in the passive voice in the article.)
> trash talk [9]
> to dumb down [9]
> to get short-changed [11]
> on the fly [11]
> at random [12]
> woe betide [12] (Note: an old-fashioned expression)

### Verb Tense and Form
1. *It's* can be a contraction of *It is* or *It has*. Which one is it in "It's cursed" [3]? Explain.
2. Explain the use of the modal verb *would* in Paragraph 12: "Miss Cline would take . . ." What meaning does it have?
3. What verb form is Martyn using in all these instances: "Take" [2] and "get out," "memorize," and "teach" [14]? Explain what the purpose of this verb form is.

### Tackling a Difficult Sentence
Sometimes as you are reading, you will be stopped by a sentence with unfamiliar words and a complex structure. If you understand what is being said from the

context, you can just continue reading. Sometimes, however, the sentence may be critical for understanding the text, so you have to spend the time to analyze and decode the sentence. Some techniques for analyzing such sentences are given below. The example sentence is a quotation from the reading:

> "Some foresee mental faculties we don't use succumbing to atrophy, becoming vestigial, like the appendix." [10]

1. **Read surrounding sentences to get the context.** Martyn repeats the idea with more detail in the following sentence, where he uses the phrase "will eventually disappear" along with repeating some of the words. This points to a similarity of meaning between "succumbing to atrophy" and "disappear."

2. Because this sentence has a lot of unfamiliar words, **use your dictionary to find the definitions**:

   foresee (*v*): to think something is going to happen in the future
   mental faculties (*n*): mental abilities (imagination, language skills, etc.)
   succumb (*v*): to lose out to something
   atrophy (*v*): to become weak and useless
   vestigial (*adj*): remaining as the last part of something that used to exist
   appendix (*n*): a small bag of tissue attached to the large intestine (Note: It is helpful to know that this is a body part humans don't really need.)

3. **Isolate the core of the sentence** by identifying modifying phrases and clauses:
   Some foresee mental faculties [we don't use] succumbing to atrophy, [becoming vestigial,] [like the appendix].

4. **Identify the subject and verb**:

   subject: some (people)
   main verb: foresee

5. **Use your dictionary to check the structure the main verb takes**:

   to *foresee* sb/sth doing sth
   I just didn't foresee that happening. [*Oxford Advanced Learner's Dictionary*]

   Knowing the pattern of use for the verb *foresee* helps you to see why *succumb* is in the −*ing* form and how it fits in the sentence.

6. Finally, **paraphrase** the sentence to check your understanding:
   Some people think that our mental abilities will weaken and perhaps disappear if we do not use them.

## Sentence Structure Analysis

Identify the main subject and verb in the following sentences from the article. What are the phrases and clauses, and what do they modify?

1. "Around the walls of my grade-school classroom was a wooden picture rail, from which hung posters or student art." [12]

2. "When children hear their parents and teachers trash-talking 'math,' meaning anything to do with numbers, those adults are inadvertently contributing to a dangerous dumbing-down." [9]

3. "Common use of the one-syllable, four-letter 'math' for mathematics pre-dates not only the advent of social media, but for all intents and purposes, the Internet itself." [5]

## Why Study Liberal Arts?

The worlds of the liberal arts and the sciences are at loggerheads today. Students of the humanities seem to be poles apart from science and math students. Moreover, the prevailing wisdom is that university students studying literature, history, philosophy, or music are wasting their time and money and that those who want a job had better study engineering and computer science. Governments follow this precept by making cuts to arts programs, deeming them an expensive luxury item. However, engineers and scientists can benefit greatly from more education in the arts.

The very term "humanities" shows that these subjects stress people skills—skills that are sorely needed in the scientific community. The study of literature can foster empathy; tech designers can use empathy to understand their users and thus create cellphones suitable for older people, for example. Second, because liberal arts courses require essay-writing, students develop their critical thinking and communication skills—skills that all professionals need. Scientists who have taken drama courses, for instance, have stronger public speaking skills and can better present their ideas at conferences. Story-telling is a fundamental teaching skill—a skill learned through the study of literature. Teaching or instructing others is something most people have to do at some time, in any profession. Moreover, learning another language can also help scientists communicate with others.

Students in the sciences can broaden their thinking by taking liberal arts courses. Today science and technology is highly specialized, resulting in narrow fields of view. Scientists need to take a break and step away from their field once in a while to get perspective. A knowledge of history can show scientists how human knowledge was built on the discoveries of previous researchers and give them insight into the future. For instance, Steve Jobs took a course in calligraphy that gave him an appreciation of the aesthetics of typefaces and influenced his ideas for the design of Apple products. Philosophy courses can make scientists consider the ethics of their decisions.

Finally, arts and sciences should not be viewed as an either/or proposition. A strong correlation has been found between mathematical, musical, and language skills. It stands to reason that training in music can enhance other abilities. Neurological studies also show that human brains respond fundamentally to art. Moreover, careers can span both areas. Leonardo da Vinci was not only one of the greatest artists of all time, he was also a scientific genius. Some fields, like the social sciences, depend on both sciences and arts. Linguistics, for example, encompasses a scientific view of language in its many branches. For instance, neurolinguistics studies how language is stored in the brain, and phonetics and phonology show how human beings make and combine sounds.

While today's world does demand a high degree of specialization, it is a mistake to focus too narrowly on a scientific field of inquiry without appreciating what the arts provide to humanity. Educators understand this when they "force" students to take courses outside their primary field of interest. Too many students, however, do so grudgingly, complaining about having to take an English course. They should embrace the opportunity to broaden their experience and learning, which will ultimately make them better at their jobs.

## Additional Topics

1.  Choose a program or subject that you think deserves more time and attention in school, and write an essay arguing your point. For example, should there be more physical education and sports classes?
2.  What are the dangers of over-specialization? Why do students need courses outside their area of study? Write an essay focusing on one field. For example, you can argue why medical students should study literature and philosophy.
3.  Write an essay comparing two kinds of education that you are familiar with. For example, you can compare high school and college, two different courses or programs, or Canadian education with that in another country.
4.  Studies show that women are having more academic success than men. For instance, female students outnumber males at Canadian universities. Write an essay explaining either causes or effects of this trend.
5.  It has been argued that boys and girls learn differently. Should there be separate schools or separate classes in elementary or secondary education? Support your position.
6.  Find out about alternatives to public schools in your province. What kind of private schools are allowed? What are the regulations on home schooling? Choose one alternative to public school, and argue for or against it. Or argue in favour of the public school system for all students.
7.  What should students take into consideration when choosing a program? Is it more important to follow their passions or to study courses that they think will lead to a job? Explain why.

# UNIT 10

# Work

## Lots of Ways to Make Canada Fairer

*by Carol Goar*

1   The rules of the game used to be clear. You got a good education, found a job with a future, rented an apartment, started a family, bought a home, equipped your kids with the tools to succeed and saved for your retirement. It worked for five generations of Canadians. It is not working for the sixth.

2   Today's young people are living in a world of precarious work, globalization, outsourcing, retrenchment at all levels of government and rising household debt. Even if they get a good education, they might not get a job. Even if they find work, it is likely to be short-term contract employment. Even if they make a decent living, they'll be priced out of the housing market. Even if they want to save for their retirement, there's no money left when the bills are paid.

3   For baby boomers, this is a strange new world. They don't know how to prepare their children for it.

4   An increasing number are revisiting the idea of a basic income guarantee for all Canadians. They never thought they'd endorse universal income redistribution by the state. But they don't see any other option.

5   In fact there are alternatives. They haven't been talked about since 2006 when Stephen Harper became prime minister, vowing to cut taxes, downsize government, impose market discipline on the public sector and allow the private sector to bring in thousands of pliant temporary foreign workers, but they still exist. With an election approaching, it's time to widen the conversation, look at the policies that he jettisoned and the tools being tested in other countries.

6   This list of possibilities is by no means exhaustive. It is meant to get people thinking and dispel the sense of powerlessness they feel.

7   Progressive taxation was used for almost a century to prevent the richest segment of the population from amassing a disproportionate share of the nation's wealth. Since the mid 1980s, policy-makers have reduced the number of tax brackets under the guise of simplification and created hundreds of loopholes

allowing wealthy individuals to pay little or no tax. As executive compensation hit stratospheric levels, the government did nothing.

8    By adding a couple of new high-income tax brackets and cleaning up the loopholes that are draining billions of dollars from the public treasury, Canada's next government could mitigate the growth of inequality and use the new revenue to restore the safety nets that have been shredded.

9    After the Great Depression, Canada created unemployment insurance to tide workers over between jobs. It worked well for the baby boom generation (1946–1965). But their children (born 1972 to 1992) entered a very different labour market. Employers preferred contractors to employees, part-time and casual work became more common, temporary agencies burgeoned. Rather than adjust the system, Ottawa restricted access to benefits. Today, the majority of Canadian workers are excluded from the program.

10    By modernizing the employment insurance system, a new government could keep people afloat between jobs, stabilize their lives and moderate the swings of the business cycle.

11    Until 1996, Canada had a federal minimum wage. It applied only to industries regulated by Ottawa, but it set a national benchmark. Today, each province establishes its own wage floors. All 10 of them are below the poverty line.

12    Ottawa can't dictate provincial labour standards. But it can set an example. By reinstating the federal minimum wage at or above the poverty line—which would mean at least $12.75 per hour—it could exert upward pressure.

13    In other countries, the state is the lead investor in far-sighted projects that spawn new industries, create good jobs and spur lasting economic growth. That used to happen in Canada too: Ottawa took a risk on Bell Northern Research (later Nortel), an early pioneer of digital communication; spearheaded the development of the Canadarm, inspiring generations of scientists and engineers; and created Atomic Energy of Canada (AECL) to explore the vast potential of nuclear energy in everything from medicine to power generation.

14    Under Harper, government labs closed, scientists fled, the very idea of government-led innovation fell out of favour. But a new government could revive it, using any national challenge—building modern infrastructure, moving to a low-carbon economy, adapting to an aging population—as the springboard.

15    The point is that Canada's next generation is not doomed to a future of insecure low-wage work in an increasingly polarized nation. It is a choice.

[11 March 2015]

## Notes

The *public sector* refers to the areas of the economy controlled by the government, while the *private sector* does not have direct government control. Teachers and doctors, for instance, are in the public sector since they receive their income from government institutions—school boards and post-secondary institutions and the health care plan. (This distinction is also used in public and private schools (see "White Tops, Grey Bottoms," pages 339–40).)

A *tax bracket* [7] is a range of income that is taxed at a certain rate. For instance, an income over $140,000 could be taxed at 30 per cent. *Progressive taxation* [7] means that the more money you have, the more tax you pay.

The social *safety net* [8] refers to the government programs that exist to help people survive. It includes health care, unemployment insurance, and welfare.

The *poverty line* [11] is the minimum income needed to acquire the necessities of life—food, shelter, and utilities like heat and power. The poverty line for single people is different from the poverty line for a family. It can also vary depending on location. For example, it costs more to live in Toronto than in Halifax and more to live in Iqaluit than in Saskatoon.

## Comprehension
1. What does Goar mean by the "rules of the game?" [1]
2. What are the problems that young people today face? Explain why these problems exist.
3. What changed in 2006? Explain the effect of each of these policies.
4. How do businesses try to avoid paying taxes?
5. Why is unemployment insurance no longer effective?
6. What is the problem with the minimum wage today?
7. What has changed in the relationship between the government and science and innovation?
8. What is Goar's opinion of the Harper government? How does she show this?

## Discussion
1. Goar says that parents equipped their kids "with the tools to succeed" [1]. What do you think these tools are? What do you think parents should do to ensure their children's success in life?
2. What is the role of the government in employment issues? Consider, for example, health and safety and minimum wage.
3. How would you change the tax system in Canada? Explain why.
4. Do you think this article is a fair assessment of the Harper government? Explain. What do you think the Liberal government will do?
5. What do you think could improve the employment situation in Canada?

## Assignments
1. Should the minimum wage be increased? Write an essay explaining your viewpoint.
2. Write an essay explaining why students should learn about politics.
3. Consider the advantages and disadvantages of contract work instead of full-time positions from three points of view—the workers', the employers', and society's. Write an essay on one of these six aspects, such as the advantages for the worker or the disadvantages for society.

272

4. Goar refers to the government's desire to "impose market discipline on the public sector" [5]. Should schools function as a business? Some institutions refer to their students as "clients." Write an essay explaining the problems of this approach to education.

## Paraphrase and Summary

1. Paraphrase: "Even if they make a decent living, they'll be priced out of the housing market" [2].
2. Paraphrase: "With an election approaching, it's time to widen the conversation, look at the policies that he jettisoned and the tools being tested in other countries" [5].
3. Paraphrase: "This list of possibilities is by no means exhaustive. It is meant to get people thinking and dispel the sense of powerlessness they feel" [6].
4. Write a one-paragraph summary of the article. Use no more than 100 words.

## Structure and Technique

Writers repeat phrases or structures for a purpose. What effect does the repetition of the sentence beginning "even if" have in Paragraph 2?

Note how Goar varies her sentence structure and length, with some long, complex sentences and some short, simple sentences. Examine where the short sentences are used. What is the effect?

## Language Study

### Definitions

Use the context from the reading to match each word to its definition:

| | |
|---|---|
| 1. benchmark, *n* [11] _____ | a) an opening that allows someone to get around a law |
| 2. burgeon, *v* [9] _____ | b) begin to grow rapidly |
| 3. endorse, *v* [4] _____ | c) divide into two opposite and opposing groups |
| 4. infrastructure, *n* [14] _____ | |
| 5. loophole, *n* [7, 8] _____ | d) easily influenced and controlled by others |
| 6. mitigate, *v* [8] _____ | e) extremely high or great |
| 7. outsource, *v* [2] _____ | f) make a situation less harmful or serious |
| 8. pliant, *adj* [5] _____ | |
| 9. polarize, *v* [15] _____ | g) make exist; give birth to |
| 10. spawn, *v* [13] _____ | h) make something happen faster |
| 11. spur, *v* [13] _____ | i) publicly support something |
| 12. stratospheric, *adj* [7] _____ | j) send work out to another company or another country |
| | k) standard to judge by |
| | l) systems and structures that a country needs to work, such as roads and the power grid |

## Word Focus
**precarious [2]**

The adjective *precarious* is often used to describe a person or an object that can easily fall over, something that is unstable. It is now used to describe employment situations—jobs that can easily be lost, as when contracts expire.

The term *precariat* was coined to describe the class of people in precarious employment such as contract workers and part-timers. It is a *portmanteau* term—a word formed from the merging of two other words, in this case *precarious* and *proletariat* (a term used in socialist writing to describe a class of workers who work for wages and do not own property).

## Word Families
Fill in the chart with the corresponding parts of speech:

| NOUN | VERB | ADJECTIVE | ADVERB |
|------|------|-----------|--------|
| | dictate [12] | | |
| | | exhaustive [6] | |
| globalization [2] | | | |
| inequality [8] equality | | | |
| innovation [14] | | | |
| | | progressive [7] | |
| risk [13] | | | |
| safety [8] | | | |
| | stabilize [10] | | |
| | widen [5] | | |

## Word Parts
Discuss the meaning of these words by looking at their parts:

       disproportionate [7]
       modernizing [10]
       powerlessness [6]
       redistribution [4]
       reinstating [12]
       retrenchment [2]
       revisiting [4]
       simplification [7]

Usually, you can take off prefixes and suffixes to identify the root of the words and thus make them easier to understand. Sometimes, however, a word might be more familiar with the affixes than without. For example, the word *guise* [7] is related to *disguise*, which is the more common word. Check your dictionary for the difference in meanings.

## Collocations and Expressions

Discuss the meanings and usage of the following expressions:

to make a decent living [2]
strange new world [3]
to tide someone over [9]
to fall out of favour [14]

## Sentence Structure Analysis

1. Identify the main subject and verb in the following sentence. Identify the modifiers—adjectives, adverbs, phrases, and clauses—and what they modify. What is the parallel structure used?

   "By modernizing the employment insurance system, a new government could keep people afloat between jobs, stabilize their lives and moderate the swings of the business cycle." [10]

   Sentences that start with *by* can be difficult for writers to structure correctly. Review Reducing Clauses to Phrases, pages 86–87. Consider these example sentences:

| | |
|---|---|
| By walking to school, it can save money. | **incorrect**<br>*it* cannot walk to school. |
| By walking to school, students can save money. | **correct**<br>Here the participial phrase works because students are doing the walking. (This is the same structure we see in the quotation: the government is doing the modernizing.) |
| Walking to school can save money. | **correct**<br>The gerund phrase *walking to school* is the subject of the verb phrase *can save*. |

2. Analyze the following sentence. Start by identifying the subject and verb. What does *they* refer to in the sentence? Find the parallel structure—what are the four verbs in a list?

   "They haven't been talked about since 2006 when Stephen Harper became prime minister, vowing to cut taxes, downsize government, impose market discipline on the public sector and allow the private sector to bring in thousands of pliant temporary foreign workers, but they still exist." [5]

# If the Artists Starve, We'll All Go Hungry

*by Elizabeth Renzetti*

1    Let's say you wear a big hat and had one of the most infectious, popular songs of the year. You're Pharrell Williams, and your song *Happy* was played 43 million times on the music-streaming service Pandora. Pretty sweet, huh? Except, according to the website Fusion, Mr. Williams made about $25,000 in royalties from Pandora for those 43 million clicks.

2    And that's Pharrell, who sits atop music's golden throne. If he's earning tiny digital royalties, what does that say for the artists further down the chain, in the grubby realm of mere mortals? Toronto songwriter Diana Williamson, who recently moved back from L.A., told me about a song she'd co-written that had reached 260,000 downloads and made it to No. 3 on the Billboard dance chart. She hadn't seen a penny in royalties. To complain about rip-off downloading, she said in an interview, is to invite "abuse from the mob. But if those fans were bakers, they wouldn't be giving away their croissants for free."

3    After 20 years in the music business, she says she's seeing songwriters "leaving in droves. If you can't make a living, if you can't afford go to the dentist, you're going to leave." This is a lament you'll hear from artists everywhere these days: We can't afford to do this anymore. The well has dried up. Freelance rates are what they were when the first Trudeau was in power. Rents rose, and royalties fell. Novelists are becoming real-estate agents; musicians open coffee shops.

4    The evidence of this culture shock is in front of our eyes, in the shuttered book shops and video stores and music clubs, yet it's remarkably unremarked upon. Artists don't actually like to complain publicly about their lot in life, knowing the inevitable backlash from those who still believe that creating is not "a real job."

5    I mean, they're artists. They're supposed to suffer, right? It's this very prejudice that has allowed "a great Depression" to go on right under our noses for the past decade without any outcry, American journalist Scott Timberg argues in his new book, *Culture Crash: The Killing of the Creative Class*. All the other victims of the ragged economy receive sympathy, apart from artists. "We produce and export creativity around the world," Mr. Timberg writes. "So why aren't we lamenting the plight of its practitioners? . . . When someone employed in the world of culture loses a job, it's easier to dismiss or sneer at their plight than when it happens to, say, a steel worker or an auto worker."

6    Mr. Timberg outlines the gutting of the average artist's income over the past decade. With most attention focused on the lucky, minuscule minority—the Rowlings, the Beyoncés—what has gone unnoticed is that a weak economy and rapid technological change have been ruinous for many creators. Incomes have fallen, jobs have disappeared and the formerly grotty centres of cities are now too posh for all but the wealthiest artists (at one point, he interviews a violinist with the Santa Barbara Symphony who cannot afford to live in Santa Barbara).

7    When the artists go, a whole ecosystem goes with them—publicists and roadies, critics and video-store clerks. Yet it's gone unlamented, for complex reasons. Artists don't generally like to moan about their economic plight, for fear

of seeming ungrateful or mercenary. They are perhaps the only class of humans, apart from criminals, whom we begrudge a decent living. Their work should be reward enough, suffering is their historic lot, and on and on. This, Mr. Timberg rightly argues, is BS.

8      Do we value the role of artists (and their handmaidens) enough to ensure that they can actually continue to create? Or do we just want to be left with the *American Idol* winners and the trust fund babies? For things to change, we'd have to acknowledge that artists have a right to aspire to the security of a middle-class life, as much as any accountant or teacher. Second, we have to return to a place where people are paid for the fruits of their labour, whether they're making a car or a song.

9      Because I'm not Merlin, I'm not entirely sure how that will be accomplished. But we can start with the words of David Byrne, genius songwriter and outspoken advocate of getting paid, who put it this way: "Philosophically, I think the issue is: Do we always do what is best for the consumer in the short run, or do we think more long-term about our culture and quality of life?" That's not a question for people who make the art, but for the rest of us who have become used to not paying for it.

[19 January 2015]

## Notes

Renzetti refers to "the Rowlings, the Beyoncés" [6]. J.K. Rowling is the famous, and wealthy, author of the Harry Potter books. Beyoncé is a huge singing star. Both are at the top of their professions. Renzetti uses a plural form to include other stars like them.

The time reference "when the first Trudeau was in power" [3] refers to the years when Pierre Trudeau was prime minister of Canada (1968–79 and 1980–84). His son, Justin Trudeau, was elected leader of the Liberal Party in 2013 and became Prime Minister on November 4, 2015.

Merlin [9] is the magician who guided King Arthur in the British legend.

## Comprehension

1. How much in royalties is Pharrell Williams making per click?
2. What point is Williamson making when she mentions bakers and croissants? Is this a good comparison?
3. What are the attitudes many people have toward artists? Explain.
4. In Paragraph 5, the economy is described as "ragged." Look up the different meanings of *ragged*. Do you think this is a good word to describe the modern economy? Explain the picture the word paints.
5. What point is Renzetti making when she refers to J.K. Rowling and Beyoncé [6] and to *American Idol* winners and the trust fund babies" [8]? Explain.
6. Why are artists important to the economy as a whole?
7. Explain what point Renzetti is making in her concluding sentence.

## Discussion

1. Do you think $25,000 is fair pay for the song "Happy"? Why or why not?

2. How should artists get paid? In the past, artists, such as Mozart and Shakespeare, had patrons, either wealthy individuals or organizations that funded their work. Today, there is barely any financial support for the arts. If artists are not earning a living wage from selling their works, should we develop other ways to support them, or should we increase the amounts they get from the systems already in place (such as giving Pharrell Williams more money per click)? Should artists use crowdsourcing and ask fans for donations?

3. Discuss and debate the ramifications of downloading music, streaming videos, and photocopying textbooks. Are these acceptable practices? Why do so many people not consider these actions the same as stealing? Explain people's attitudes.

4. Do you consider larger economic decisions when you purchase something, or is the cost your only consideration? For instance, do you support Canadian artists and Canadian companies?

5. Considering how little artists get paid, discuss what drives them to create their work.

6. How important are the arts in your life? Discuss what impact music, the movies, dance, literature, art, and the theatre have on you personally.

7. Would you want a career in the arts? Explain why or why not.

8. Why do you think that many people consider the work that artists do to be relatively easy? Why do so many non-artists think they could do the work?

## Assignments

1. Research the average earnings of actors, musicians, writers, and visual artists (such as painters and sculptors). Choose one profession, and write a report explaining how they are paid.

2. Watch the music video for Pharrell Williams's song "Happy." Write a review, explaining why it became such a hit.

3. Renzetti refers to the "ecosystem" surrounding artists' work [7]. Choose one artistic profession (such as acting, music, dance, writing, or painting), and consider the wider economic benefits of the work performed by the artists, such as tourist dollars. Write an essay explaining the effects.

## Paraphrase and Summary

1. Paraphrase: "The evidence of this culture shock is in front of our eyes, in the shuttered book shops and video stores and music clubs, yet it's remarkably unremarked upon" [4].

2. Paraphrase: "If he's earning tiny digital royalties, what does that say for the artists further down the chain, in the grubby realm of mere mortals?" [2]

3. Write a one-paragraph summary of the article. Use no more than 100 words.

## Structure and Technique

Renzetti starts with a specific example of an underpaid artist. She uses an example that most of her audience would likely be familiar with and even puts the audience in the artist's shoes with the use of *you*: "Let's say you wear a big hat and had one of the most infectious, popular songs of the year. You're Pharrell Williams, and your song 'Happy' was played 43 million times on the music-streaming service Pandora." This gets the readers' attention and allows them to relate to the points she goes on to make.

## Language Study

### Definitions

Use the context from the reading to match each word to its definition:

1. backlash, *n* [4] _____
2. begrudge, *v* [7] _____
3. grotty, *adj* [6] _____
4. lament, *n* [3] _____
5. mercenary, *adj* [7] _____
6. minuscule, *adj* [6] _____
7. plight, *n* [5, 7] _____
8. posh, *adj* [6] _____
9. roadie, *n* [7] _____
10. shuttered, *adj* [4] _____
11. sneer, *v* [5] _____

a) closed
b) dirty and unpleasant
c) expression of sadness
d) fancy and expensive
e) feel unhappy that someone has something you do not think he or she deserves
f) only interested in the money they will be paid
g) show a lack of respect for someone through one's facial expression or tone of voice
h) someone whose job is to help with the equipment when musicians travel
i) strong negative reaction by many people against something that has happened
j) very bad situation or trouble that someone is in
k) very small

### Word Focus

**suppose**

*Suppose* essentially means "to think," with a touch of uncertainty. The verb is often followed by a noun clause. It can also be used to introduce a hypothetical idea, "Let's suppose . . ."

*Suppose* is commonly used in a kind of passive voice structure, *to be supposed to*, that functions like a modal verb showing expectation and obligation. The verb *to be* can be either simple present (*am, is, are*) or past (*was, were*), and the *to* is followed by the base form of the verb (as a modal verb is).

Examine the differences of meaning and use of *suppose* in these examples:

| | |
|---|---|
| "They're supposed to suffer, right?" [5] | meaning: People expect artists to suffer. (passive voice, present tense) |
| I suppose that he could have misplaced the file. | meaning: I think that this is a possibility. (active voice, used with noun clause) |
| We are supposed to change those figures to metric. | meaning: Somebody wants us to change the figure. |
| I was supposed to pick him up at four, but I forgot. | meaning: I was told (or it was arranged) that I would pick him up, but I didn't. |

The logical relationship between this modal structure and the base meaning of the verb *suppose* may be confusing, but expectation is based on belief, or what somebody thinks, so that "he is supposed to wait there" has the basic idea that somebody *thinks* that he should wait there.

A common error is to leave the *d* off the end of the past participle *supposed*. For example, someone may write, "He was <u>suppose</u> to leave the keys." This error occurs because the writer is confused by the pronunciation: The sound of the *d* disappears next to the *t* of *to* (just as the *d* sound in the expression *used to* tends to disappear in speech).

## Word Families

Fill in the chart with the corresponding parts of speech:

| NOUN | VERB | ADJECTIVE | ADVERB |
|---|---|---|---|
| abuse [2] | | | |
| creativity [5] creation | | | |
| | dismiss [5] | | |
| | | economic [7] economical | |
| | | infectious [1] | |
| | | | philosophically [9] |
| publicist [7] publicity | | | |
| | | ruinous [6] | |
| security [8] | | | |
| sympathy [5] | | | |

## Collocations and Expressions

Discuss the meanings and usage of the following expressions:

> in front of one's eyes [4]
> (right) under one's nose [5]
> leaving in droves [3]
> to make a living [3]
> the well has dried up [3]
> fruits of their labour [8]

## Conversational Expressions

Note Renzetti's use of conversational style:

> "Let's say . . ." [1]
> "Pretty sweet, huh?" [1]
> "I mean, they're artists. They're supposed to suffer, right?" [5]

Discuss the meaning and use of each of these phrases and sentences. What makes them conversational? Give other ways of expressing the same meaning. What effect do these conversational expressions have in the article?

In the expression "pretty sweet," is *pretty* an adjective or an adverb? What is the difference in meaning between the adjective and the adverb? Which usage is more common? Why do you think so? What can the adjective *pretty* be used to describe?

## Sentence Structure Analysis

1. Renzetti uses quotations in her article. Examine how she integrates them into her writing and the punctuation she uses. How are the quotations in Paragraphs 2 and 3 different from those at the end of Paragraphs 5 and 9? Note the quotation marks around the phrases "a real job" [4] and "a great Depression" [5]. Which of these phrases is a quotation attributed to an actual person? Explain the use of the quotation marks in the other case.

2. Identify the main subject and verb in the following sentences. Identify the modifiers—adjectives, adverbs, phrases, and clauses—and what they modify.

   a) "With most attention focused on the lucky, minuscule minority—the Rowlings, the Beyoncés—what has gone unnoticed is that a weak economy and rapid technological change have been ruinous for many creators." [6]

   b) "When the artists go, a whole ecosystem goes with them—publicists and roadies, critics and video-store clerks." [7]

## No Tips, Please

In North American restaurants, diners are expected to tip their servers. The going rate is between 10 and 20 percent of the bill. This gratuity system is so ingrained that wait staff is paid less than minimum wage on the assumption that their earnings are supplemented by tips. While tips are supposed to be voluntary, in effect, people in the service industry are practically demanding tips—even those who traditionally do not receive them. However, instead of extending the practice to supplement the poor wages of even more workers, the practice of tipping should be abolished.

Tipping is a practice that just does not make sense. If the purpose is, as commonly understood, "To Insure Promptness," then the money would be better given as a bribe before service. In addition, the speed of service depends more on the efficiency of the kitchen than on the work of the server. Furthermore, who gets tipped and who does not is an arbitrary system. Many jobs today are in the service industry, but only a few in the sector regularly receive gratuities. Even in food service, the system makes no sense. Someone who brings food to the table in a restaurant gets tipped handsomely, while someone who hands food over a counter in a cafeteria gets nothing. Both employees interact with customers, and both work hard. All workers deserve to be paid fairly for their labour—by their actual employer.

The practice of tipping taints the whole dining experience. Servers size up customers, giving more attention to those they think will tip well. Customers realize they are being judged and treated according to their potential generosity. Wait staff have been known to discriminate against people they think will tip less—such as non-drinkers and people from Asian cultures (where tipping is not a common practice). Some customers even endure the stress of having servers hover over them as they pay. Even calculating a fair gratuity can put pressure on diners, especially if they have imbibed enough to make their math skills questionable.

The tipping system leads to many kinds of abuse. Servers are asked to tip out a percentage of their sales. If they were unlucky enough to have a series of low-tipping customers, they could end up losing money. Sometimes, restaurant management even takes some of the gratuities, a practice that defeats the purpose of the tip in the first place. Moreover, gratuities are not reported on T4 slips, and much of the money is given in cash. As a result, this income is part of the underground economy—most of the money is not reported for income tax purposes.

It is clear that the unfair practice of tipping needs to be eliminated. Instead, restaurants can raise their meal prices, give all their staff a living wage, and make it clear that the establishment has a no-tipping policy. If this catches on, most people would be on board. Even the servers who make much more than others in the service industry would recognize that eliminating tipping is the right thing to do.

## Additional Topics

1. What factors determine how rate of pay is established? For example, why does a daycare worker make less than a zookeeper? How important are criteria such as education, training, years of experience, and the prestige inherent in the job?
2. Employers look for many ways to reduce labour costs, such as outsourcing work overseas, hiring foreign workers, using interns, and offering only contract work. Choose one of these practices, and explain the causes or the effects in an essay.
3. While the average Canadian worker makes about $50,000 a year, CEOs in Canada can make 200 times what their employees earn. Write an essay arguing that CEOs are worth millions of dollars or that they are not worth it.

4. The argument has been made that instead of giving welfare and unemployment benefits, the government would be better off making sure everyone has a "living wage." The organization Living Wage Canada explains the benefits of this policy on its website. Write an essay agreeing or disagreeing with this policy. Or you can write an essay on the likelihood of this policy being adopted. What would stand in its way?

5. Young people desperate to get a foothold in the job market may take unpaid internship positions. Some of these are short practicums that are credited as part of their school work. However, in some cases, employers take advantage of free labour without offering interns valuable experience or a realistic chance of being hired at the company. Moreover, the laws governing internships are weak. For instance, interns may not have injury compensation coverage. Research the topic of internships, and choose one issue for an argument essay. For example, you could argue that all interns should be paid at least minimum wage or explain that internship only benefits graduates from rich families.

6. Since 2007, women have outnumbered men in the workforce in Canada, yet women still get paid less. Choose one specific issue concerning women in the workforce, and write an essay stating your point of view. For example, you could write about the glass ceiling, about women in top management, about women in science and technology fields, or about discrimination or harassment.

7. While underground economies (unlicensed and untaxed) have always existed, websites and phone apps have facilitated the growth of what is now referred to as "the sharing economy." For instance, instead of staying in a hotel, tourists can rent an apartment they find on the service Airbnb. Instead of hailing a taxi, people can get a ride in a private car with a service like Uber. Apps can also put you in touch with people who are willing to clean your house, take care of your children, and do home repairs. Choose one of the issues surrounding the sharing economy for an essay. You can focus on a specific service and explain its advantages or disadvantages; you can argue whether these services are fair competition or not; or you can explore the effects these services have on the economy.

# Money

## Why Pay More? To Be Conspicuous

*by Peter Singer*

1    When Radoslaw Sikorski, Poland's Foreign Minister, went to Ukraine for talks last month, his Ukrainian counterparts reportedly laughed at him because he was wearing a Japanese quartz watch that cost just $165. A Ukrainian newspaper reported on the preferences of Ukrainian ministers, several of whom have watches that cost more than $30,000. Even a Communist member of Ukraine's parliament, the Rada, was shown wearing a watch that retails for more than $6,000.

2    The laughter should have gone in the opposite direction. Wouldn't you laugh (maybe in private, to avoid being impolite) at someone who pays more than 200 times as much as you do, and ends up with an inferior product?

3    That is what the Ukrainians have done. They could have bought an accurate, lightweight, maintenance-free quartz watch that can run for five years, keeping virtually perfect time, without ever being moved or wound. Instead, they paid far more for clunkier watches that can lose minutes every month, and that will stop if you forget to wind them for a day or two (if they have an automatic mechanism, they will stop if you don't move them). In addition, the quartz watches also have integrated alarm, stopwatch and timer functions that the other watches either lack or employ only as a design-spoiling, hard-to-read effort to keep up with the competition.

4    Why would any wise shopper accept such a bad bargain? Out of nostalgia, perhaps? A full-page ad for Patek Philippe has Thierry Stern, the president of the company, saying that he listens to the chime of every watch with a minute repeater that his company makes, as his father and grandfather did before him. That's all very nice, but since the days of Mr. Stern's grandfather, we have made progress in time-keeping. Why reject the improvements that human ingenuity has provided to us? I have an old fountain pen that belonged to my grandmother; it's a nice memento of her, but I wouldn't dream of using it to write this column.

5    Thorstein Veblen knew the answer. In his classic *The Theory of the Leisure Class*, published in 1899, he argued that once the basis of social status became wealth itself—rather than, say, wisdom, knowledge, moral integrity or skill in battle—the

rich needed to find ways of spending money that had no other objective than the display of wealth itself. He termed this "conspicuous consumption." Veblen wrote as a social scientist, refraining from rendering moral judgments, although he left readers in little doubt about his attitude toward such expenditure in a time when many lived in poverty.

6      Wearing a ridiculously expensive watch to proclaim that one has achieved an elevated social standing seems especially immoral for a public official in a country where a significant portion of the population still lives in real poverty. These officials are wearing on their wrists the equivalent of four or five years of an average Ukrainian's salary. That tells Ukrainian taxpayers either that they are paying their public servants too much, or that their public servants have other ways of getting money to buy watches that they would not be able to afford otherwise.

7      The Chinese government knows what those "other ways" might be. As the International Herald Tribune reports, one aspect of Beijing's campaign against corruption is a clampdown on expensive gifts. As a result, according to Jon Cox, an analyst at Kepler Capital Markets, "it's no longer acceptable to have a big chunky watch on your wrist." The Chinese market for expensive watches is in steep decline. Ukrainians, take note.

8      Wearing a watch that costs 200 times more than one that does a better job of keeping time says something else, even when it is worn by people who are not governing a relatively poor country. Andrew Carnegie, the richest man of Veblen's era, was blunt in his moral judgments. "The man who dies rich," he is often quoted as saying, "dies disgraced."

9      We can adapt that judgment to the man or woman who wears a $30,000 watch or buys similar luxury goods, like a $12,000 handbag. Essentially, such a person is saying; "I am either extraordinarily ignorant, or just plain selfish. If I were not ignorant, I would know that children are dying from diarrhea or malaria, because they lack safe drinking water or mosquito nets, and obviously what I have spent on this watch or handbag would have been enough to help several of them survive; but I care so little about them that I would rather spend my money on something that I wear for ostentation alone."

10     Of course, we all have our little indulgences. I am not arguing that every luxury is wrong. But to mock someone for having a sensible watch at a modest price puts pressure on others to join the quest for ever-greater extravagance. That pressure should be turned in the opposite direction, and we should celebrate those, like Mr. Sikorski, with modest tastes and higher priorities than conspicuous consumption.

[13 May 2013]

## Notes

Patek Philippe is a high-end Swiss watch-making company. The company's website explains what a minute repeater is with this definition:

> A repeater is a complication in a mechanical watch that chimes the time on demand by activating a push or a slide-piece. Different types of repeater allow the time to be heard to varying degrees of precision; from

the simple quarter-repeater which merely strikes the number of hours and quarters, to the minute repeater which sounds the time down to the minute using separate tones for hours, quarter-hours and minutes.

Originating before widespread use of electricity, they allowed the time to be determined in the dark and they were also used by the visually impaired. Today minute repeaters, one of the most complex repeater mechanisms, are coveted by collectors and watch lovers alike as rare masterpieces of precision mechanical engineering.

Andrew Carnegie (1835–1919) was a famous American industrialist and philanthropist. He made his money in the steel industry and was responsible for establishing many public libraries with his charitable donations.

## Comprehension

1. Why did the Ukrainian ministers laugh at the Polish foreign minister?
2. What are the advantages of quartz watches over the ones that the Ukrainian ministers were wearing?
3. What is Singer's main argument?
4. Why does Singer call it immoral to spend thousands of dollars on a watch? [5]
5. Explain what Singer means when he says, "That tells Ukrainian taxpayers either that they are paying their public servants too much, or that their public servants have other ways of getting money to buy watches that they would not be able to afford otherwise" [6]. What is he referring to?
6. Explain what Singer means when he says, "The Chinese market for expensive watches is in steep decline" [7].
7. Explain this statement: "But to mock someone for having a sensible watch at a modest price puts pressure on others to join the quest for ever-greater extravagance" [10].
8. What is conspicuous consumption? Explain Veblen's argument [5].

## Discussion

1. What kind of consumer are you? Do you love to shop? Are your tastes modest and practical? Do you care what other people think of your purchases? How important is style and fashion in your purchases? Do you indulge in conspicuous consumption?
2. Singer says, "I am not arguing that every luxury is wrong" [10]. What kind of luxuries do you think are justified? Explain why.
3. Explain Carnegie's statement, "The man who dies rich dies disgraced" [8]. Do you agree? Explain why or why not.
4. How much should people donate of their time and money to charitable causes? Give guidelines.
5. Discuss designer knock-offs. Would you buy one—such as a fake Rolex? What are some of the problems? Consider issues such as copyright and quality.
6. Are watches even worth wearing now? Many people just refer to their cellphones to find out the time. Compare analog and digital timepieces—which are better, and why?

7. Singer says, "Why reject the improvements that human ingenuity has provided to us? I have an old fountain pen that belonged to my grandmother; it's a nice memento of her, but I wouldn't dream of using it to write this column" [4]. Is new technology always better? For instance, some people argue that vinyl records have a better sound than CDs or digital recordings. Some writers insist on writing by hand or on a manual typewriter. Discuss the advantages of older technologies.

## Assignments

1. Choose one luxury item, and argue whether or not this item is worth buying (by those who can afford it) in a paragraph or a short essay. You can discuss specific brands or just the item in general. Consider whether it is the quality of the item that makes it worthwhile or whether it's just ostentation. Example items: luxury cars (like a Ferrari or Porsche), designer shoes, designer hand-bags, expensive watches (like Rolex).
2. Singer talks about a fountain pen being a nice memento of his grandmother. Similarly, pocket watches are often handed down as heirlooms. What would you appreciate as a keepsake of your grandparents? Write a paragraph describing the item and explaining why it is meaningful.
3. The Andrew Carnegie Dictum says that one should spend the first third of one's life getting all the education one can, the next third making all the money one can, and the last third giving it all away for worthwhile causes. Discuss this dictum in an essay. Is it an ideal way to spend one's life?
4. Consider Veblen's argument that "once the basis of social status became wealth itself—rather than, say, wisdom, knowledge, moral integrity or skill in battle—the rich needed to find ways of spending money that had no other objective than the display of wealth itself" [5]. Discuss this statement in an essay.
5. Singer refers to "one aspect of Beijing's campaign against corruption" [7]. Corruption among politicians and bureaucrats is a serious problem in many countries. Write an essay about political corruption. Focus on effects or solutions. Narrow your topic to a specific area—perhaps a place or an industry such as construction.

## Paraphrase and Summary

1. Paraphrase Andrew Carnegie's saying, "The man who dies rich dies disgraced" [8].
2. Paraphrase this statement: "Wearing a ridiculously expensive watch to proclaim that one has achieved an elevated social standing seems especially immoral for a public official in a country where a significant portion of the population still lives in real poverty" [6].

## Structure and Technique

Note the different uses of quotations in the article. Paragraphs 7 and 8 include quotations by identified speakers (Cox and Carnegie, respectively). However, in Paragraph 9, Singer gives a hypothetical quotation—it is not directly quoting something that someone actually said. What is the effect of this "quotation"? Rephrase what he is saying so that it is not in the first person.

In addition, Singer uses quotation marks around "other ways" in Paragraph 7; in a sense, he is actually quoting himself because this refers back to his use of the words "other ways" in the previous paragraph. In Paragraph 5, the quotation marks around "conspicuous consumption" show that it was a coinage by Veblen. Now, *conspicuous consumption* is an accepted expression in English, and you would not need to quote it to use it.

## Language Study

### Definitions
Use the context to match each word to its definition:

1. blunt, *adj* [8] _____
2. chime, *n* [4] _____
3. clampdown, *n* [7] _____
4. clunkier, *adj* [3] _____
5. counterpart, *n* [1] _____
6. expenditure, *n* [5] _____
7. indulgence, *n* [10] _____
8. ingenuity, *n* [4] _____
9. integrated, *adj* [3] _____
10. nostalgia, *n* [4] _____
11. ostentation, *n* [9] _____
12. rendering, *v* [5] _____
13. retails (for), *v* [1] _____
14. virtually, *adv* [3] _____

a) a ringing sound
b) a treat, some pleasure you allow yourself
c) almost, practically
d) amount of money spent
e) combining many parts that work well together
f) display of wealth to show off to other people
g) feeling of affection for something in the past
h) heavier, more awkward to wear or use
i) making, expressing
j) sells for, costs in a retail store
k) skill at inventing and coming up with new ideas
l) someone who has the same job but in a different location
m) sudden action taken to stop illegal activity
n) very direct, saying exactly what you think without trying to be polite

### Word Focus
#### afford [6], spend [5, 9]
The verbs *afford* and *spend* are relatively easy to understand, but they can cause problems in writing, especially for English language learners. Both are transitive verbs, which means they take direct objects. The direct objects for *spend* usually refer to money or time. The verb *afford* is almost always used with *can*, *could*, or *be able to*, often in the negative. It can also be followed by an infinitive. Even though *afford* is a transitive verb, it is not used in the passive voice.

Study these example sentences, identifying direct objects and verb forms:

1. She could not afford a designer purse, so she bought a knock-off. She spent only $20.
2. They spent several hours trying to identify the problem, but they could not afford to lose another day on the project.
3. Jason cannot afford a new car, so he is shopping for a used one.
4. Even if they save for 10 more years, they will not be able to afford to buy a house.
5. She does not want to spend more than $2000 on the trip.

## Word Families
Fill in the chart with the corresponding parts of speech:

| NOUN | VERB | ADJECTIVE | ADVERB |
|---|---|---|---|
| | celebrate [10] | | n/a |
| corruption [7] | | | |
| | employ [3] | | n/a |
| indulgence [10] | | | |
| knowledge [5] | | | |
| progress [4] | | | |
| | | social [5] | |

Explain the difference in pronunciation between *progress* [n] and its verb form.

## Collocations and Expressions
Discuss the meanings and usage of the following expressions:

keeping time [3, 8]
to end up with something [2]
to keep up with somebody [3]
would not dream of doing something [4]

## Sentence Structure Analysis
1. Identify the main subject and verb in the following sentences. Identify the modifiers—adjectives, adverbs, phrases, and clauses—and what they modify.
   a) "They could have bought an accurate, lightweight, maintenance-free quartz watch that can run for five years, keeping virtually perfect time, without ever being moved or wound." [3]
   b) "Wearing a ridiculously expensive watch to proclaim that one has achieved an elevated social standing seems especially immoral for a public official

in a country where a significant portion of the population still lives in real poverty." [6]

2. Note how the *so . . . that* structure is used in this sentence: "but I care so little about them that I would rather spend my money on something that I wear for ostentation alone" [9]. After the word *so*, an adjective or adverb can be found; in this case, it is the adverb *little*, completed by the phrase *about them*. In the *so . . . that* construction, *that* introduces a clause; in this sentence, the subject of the clause is *I*, and the verb is *would spend*. Paraphrase the sentence using another *so . . . that* structure.

This sentence also illustrates the use of *would rather* to show preference. Because the *would* is contracted in speech and the sound is almost lost, many people barely recognize that the *would* is necessary to the sentence. They sometimes mistakenly write sentences such as "he rather go" instead of "he'd rather go" or "he would rather go."

## Online Gambling a Way to Rip off the Poor

*by Leonard Stern*

1   To disapprove of gambling is considered quaint, a bit like railing against pool tables and rock 'n' roll. Gambling was traditionally classified as a "vice," an old-fashioned word that conjures up tedious moralizing.

2   I'll try not to moralize, or at least not to be tedious, in discussing the plan of provincial governments to expand Internet gambling operations.

3   British Columbia raised the weekly betting limits for its online casino games to $9,999. Quebec figures that in a couple of years, revenue from online gambling will add some $50 million to the treasury. The Atlantic provinces are getting into the game.

4   Perhaps, in a self-interested way, this is something that non-gamblers like me should celebrate. I ought to encourage my own province of Ontario also to expand its state-run gambling enterprise, so that all the good things that the government does, from which I derive personal benefit, will be even more heavily subsidized by others.

5   Let the loser who takes forever at the gas station sorting through his lottery tickets, thus making me late for work when all I want to do is pay for a fill-up—let him pay for my health care.

6   A 2008 survey showed that about seven per cent of Ontario adults believe that "gambling is an easy way to make money." Nine per cent believe that "the more you gamble, the more likely you are to win a lot of money." You don't have to be a student of probabilities to know how wrong they are.

7   While a lot of people gamble now and then, the habitual gamblers—the ones who provide much of the revenue that governments reap—constitute a small percentage of the population, perhaps the nine per cent who believe gambling is a way to make money. So part of me wants to say nine per cent of Ontarians are delusional and we shouldn't feel bad about taking their money and using it to buy MRI machines for the rest of us.

8    Let's be honest. This nine per cent who provide so much revenue and who believe gambling is a way to get rich are an unsympathetic lot. I was taught that the secret to financial security was education and hard work. If some people try to use the casino as a short cut, then they deserve to lose their money.

9    Or maybe the problem isn't that they're lazy. If they really believe they can make money gambling, they might be plain stupid.

10    Lots of data suggest that a disproportionate amount of gambling revenue comes from the uneducated class. The province might as well take their money because these people aren't competent to spend it wisely anyway.

11    That's the cynical view. As I said, I'm not immune to it, especially when I'm stuck behind a guy buying $50 worth of lottery tickets who would be better off spending the money on winter boots for his toddler.

12    The ethical view, however, is that exploiting the poor is wrong. Economists talk about gambling as a regressive tax, a tax on those who can least afford it.

13    One Canadian study found that the highest rates of compulsive gambling show up in aboriginal communities. There are U.S. data going back 20 years showing that state lotteries raise much of their money from disadvantaged minorities.

14    Last year in Britain, a new study was released showing that manual labourers and the unemployed are significantly more likely to play the national lottery, a finding that has caused some controversy because the lottery is helping to pay for the London 2012 Olympic Games.

15    It's tempting to call for governments to exit the gambling business altogether—tempting, but impractical. In Canada, the provinces are too dependent on the revenue. There's also the unseemly paternalism of trying to protect people—especially poor people—from themselves. Gambling isn't the only unhealthy behaviour that correlates with low income and education. In a free society people are allowed to make dumb choices.

16    But governments should be aware that gambling revenue is morally compromised. In a 2006 paper, the Ottawa-based Vanier Institute of the Family argued persuasively that governments have played an important role not just in sanitizing and legitimizing gambling, but in creating the demand for it.

17    Remember the hype surrounding Lotto Super 7? The marketing targeted those foolish, desperate people who believe everyone is entitled to be rich, that you don't have to work for it and that anyone can be a winner.

18    It's enough that our governments are in the gambling business. The least they could do is not promote so aggressively the unhealthy fantasies that fuel it.

[18 February 2010]

## Notes

For much of Canada's history, most gambling activities were illegal, but in 1969 a Criminal Code amendment opened the door for government-run lotteries and casinos. Now the federal government and provincial governments take in billions of dollars from gambling activities. Hospitals use this money to fund research projects and their everyday activities. In essence, the money from gambling supplements the government's income from taxes. People do not want to pay taxes, but many of them do not mind buying lottery tickets; this is why lotteries are often referred to as "a tax on the stupid."

In his first paragraph, Stern is referring to changing social attitudes toward gambling and other activities that can be considered immoral behaviour—acts such as gambling, drinking, smoking, prostitution, and drug use. What society tolerates is reflected in its laws, and these laws vary widely from country to country and over time. For example, laws determine where alcohol can be sold and drunk, the age of drinkers, and bar hours. Quebec has more liberal drinking laws than Ontario, which in turn is more liberal than many American states. Even shopping on a Sunday can be considered wrong in some societies. Stern mentions rock 'n' roll music, which used to be considered immoral. Today, many jurisdictions in North America are moving toward decriminalization and even legalization of marijuana use. On the other hand, smoking was once widely accepted in Canada, but now smokers are treated as social outcasts. It is interesting to look at the different attitudes towards such "sins" and "vices." (See Assignment Topic #2.)

## Comprehension

1. What is Stern's position on gambling? Explain what he is feeling conflicted about. What conclusion does he come to?
2. Why do governments run lotteries, casinos, and other gambling businesses? Where does the money go?
3. Explain the point Stern is making when he says, "You don't have to be a student of probabilities to know how wrong they are" [6].
4. Who tends to gamble more?
5. Why can't the government quit running gambling activities?
6. What kind of "unhealthy behaviour" and "dumb choices" [15] is Stern referring to, besides gambling?
7. What is Stern referring to in his last sentence?

## Discussion

1. Is it immoral for governments to make so much money from lotteries and casinos? Could governments get out of the gambling business? What would happen if they did? Would gambling cease to exist?
2. Are people who buy lottery tickets stupid, as Stern suggests? Discuss.
3. Stern says that he was taught "that the secret to financial security was education and hard work" [8]. Do you agree with this view? Why or why not?
4. It has been argued that hospitals especially should not run lotteries because gambling addiction is a mental illness and hospitals should not be encouraging it. Do you agree or disagree? Explain your point of view.
5. Why are young people particularly susceptible to gambling addictions?
6. Why is online gambling worse than other kinds of gambling for those who are addicted?

7. Gambling is often referred to as "gaming." What is the effect of using this word?
8. Discuss the commercials and other advertisements used to promote lotteries and casinos. What advertising techniques are used? Are the ads effective? Are they misleading?

## Assignments

1. Research the history of gambling in Canada. Write an illustrative essay showing how attitudes toward gambling changed over time: what was once considered a sin or a vice is now considered a form of entertainment.
2. Consider the points made in the second Note above. Write an essay comparing two different views of one "immoral activity" (such as drinking or smoking). You can base your comparison on either time or place. For instance, you can compare attitudes toward and laws concerning alcohol use in Canada to those in Saudi Arabia. Or you can look at the differences between attitudes today and those during Prohibition in 1920s America.
3. Write an essay comparing two kinds of gambling activities (such as online gambling, buying lottery tickets, or playing poker). Consider which is more addictive, for example, or which has some element of skill.
4. Research the odds of winning various lotteries and gambling activities. Give an oral report to the class.
5. Write an essay about the effects of gambling addictions.
6. Write a paragraph analyzing a particular advertisement for a casino or lottery.
7. Many casinos are found on Native reserves and are run by First Nations organizations. Research these casinos, and write an essay explaining either the advantages or the disadvantages of such gambling operations.

## Paraphrase and Summary

1. Paraphrase: "To disapprove of gambling is considered quaint, a bit like railing against pool tables and rock 'n' roll. Gambling was traditionally classified as a 'vice,' an old-fashioned word that conjures up tedious moralizing" [1].
2. Paraphrase: "This nine per cent who provide so much revenue and who believe gambling is a way to get rich are an unsympathetic lot. I was taught that the secret to financial security was education and hard work. If some people try to use the casino as a short cut, then they deserve to lose their money" [8].
3. Write a one-paragraph summary of the article. Do not exceed 100 words.

## Structure and Technique

Note the language Stern uses to show his conflicted feelings. He starts Paragraph 4 with "Perhaps" and says "I ought to." In Paragraph 7 he says, "part of me wants to say." After he refers to "the cynical view" [11], he says he is "not immune" to having this view—which is not exactly saying that he holds that view. Explain how Stern makes his own viewpoint clear. Where does he stand on the issue?

## Language Study

### Definitions
Use the context to match each word to its definition:

1. compulsive, *adj* [13] _____
2. conjure up, *v* [1] _____
3. cynical, *adj* [11] _____
4. delusional, *adj* [7] _____
5. derive, *v* [4] _____
6. hype, *n* [17] _____
7. paternalism, *n* [15] _____
8. quaint, *adj* [1] _____
9. tedious, *adj* [2] _____
10. vice, *n* [1] _____

a) advertising and publicity that usually exaggerates the qualities of something
b) boring
c) evil or immoral behaviour
d) fooling yourself; having a false belief
e) nice in an old-fashioned way
f) not caring that something might hurt others
g) system in which the government tries to protect citizens without giving them freedom of choice (like a father)
h) that is difficult to stop or control
i) to get something from something
j) to make something appear in your mind

### Word Focus

**to rail against something [1]**
This expression is relatively formal and not that common today. The verb *rail* (and the related noun *raillery*) is different from the noun *rail* used for iron bars and train tracks. Check to see how the word is shown in your dictionary. For instance, is it a separate entry, or is it given as an alternative meaning under the entry for *rail*?

**disapprove [1], disproportionate [1], disadvantaged [13]**
Note the use of *dis-* as a negative prefix. Explain the meaning. What part of speech is each word? Check for other forms of the words (both with and without the negative prefix) to explore the word families.

**sanitizing [16]**
The verb *sanitize* comes from the Latin word for health, *sanitas*, which can refer to both physical and mental health. It can therefore be confusing sorting out the many English words that come from this source word. *Sanitize* means to make something really clean, especially removing bacteria, but it can also refer to making something less offensive or unpleasant (as it is used in the article). The two lists below show the basic meanings, but check the dictionary definitions for any words you are unsure of.

Words relating to health and hygiene: **sanitation, sanitary, sanitize**

Words referring to mental health: **sane, insane, sanity, insanity, sanitarium**

### Word Families

Fill in the chart with the corresponding parts of speech:

| NOUN | VERB | ADJECTIVE | ADVERB |
|------|------|-----------|--------|
| | n/a | | aggressively [18] |
| | | dependent [15] independent | |
| | n/a | desperate [17] | |
| fantasy [18] | | | |
| | | immune [11] | n/a |
| | legitimize [16] | | |
| | | | morally [16] |
| | | | persuasively [16] |
| | promote [18] | | n/a |
| | | | significantly [14] |
| | | sympathetic unsympathetic [8] | |

### Collocations and Expressions

Discuss the meanings and use of the following expressions:

> to get into the game [3]
> to be better off [11]
> to create a demand for something [16]
> the least someone can do [18]

### Sentence Structure Analysis

1. Identify the main subject and verb in the following sentences. Identify the modifiers—adjectives, adverbs, phrases, and clauses—and what they modify.
   a) "While a lot of people gamble now and then, the habitual gamblers—the ones who provide much of the revenue that governments reap—constitute a small percentage of the population, perhaps the nine per cent who believe gambling is a way to make money." [7]
   b) "There's also the unseemly paternalism of trying to protect people—especially poor people—from themselves." [15]
2. Note the structure in the phrase "the more you gamble, the more likely you are to win" [6]. English uses a "the . . . , the . . ." structure with comparative

forms of adjectives or adverbs to show that one thing depends on another. Note the use of the comma between the phrases. Study these examples:

a) The more he tries to help, the more mistakes she makes.
b) The more he thinks about it, the less he understands.
c) The hungrier she gets, the grumpier she is.
d) The fewer participants there are, the higher the cost will be.
e) The later they arrive, the less time we will have.

## False Economy

Thriftiness and careful shopping are generally seen as virtues. No one likes to spend more money than they have to. However, economy taken to extremes turns people into cheapskates: they begrudge every penny that comes out of their wallets and do not appreciate true value. This can become a social problem, and even a national characteristic, rather than just a personality quirk. The mindset of many Canadians today is dominated by cheapness, affecting retail products, news and entertainment, and public infrastructure.

By making their buying decisions based on price alone, Canadians create problems on a national scale. They want to buy inexpensive items, such as $10 T-shirts, but these goods are produced in overseas factories with cheap labour and unsafe working conditions. As a result, factories in Canada close down, putting Canadians out of work. Salespeople are also losing their jobs as retailers lose business to online shopping. Consumers often choose to buy cheaper products, such as books, online—even if they have visited the retail stores to make their selections beforehand. Widespread unemployment means less money pumped into the economy in both spending and taxes. It also creates a vicious circle because as jobs are lost, people are unable to afford better goods. In addition to these economic problems, the choice of cheap goods causes environmental problems. These products do not last long and have to be replaced. For example, while hand-crafted furniture can last for more than 100 years, modern furniture made of particle board and melamine becomes garbage in less than 10 years. It ends up in the landfill, and replacement items have to be bought. Stress on the environment occurs both in the manufacturing process as well as in the disposal of the item.

Canadians are no longer willing to pay for their news and entertainment. The Internet has fooled them into thinking that they can get everything free. They download music, movies, television shows, and books. They get their news from free online sources to avoid paying subscription fees. These practices hurt many industries. Movie producers have to fight the pirating and the subsequent loss of their income. Musicians and writers lose royalties from their work. Newspapers fold because of the lack of subscriptions and ad revenues. With less money going to the creators, the quality of products also suffers. The industries are less inclined to make the required investments for superior products. For example, ground-breaking investigative news stories cost a lot of money for researchers' and journalists' time. Cheap news is put out quickly on social media and blogs, but it lacks the fact-checking and thoughtful analysis of older media.

Canadians particularly resent paying taxes, thinking of it as the government picking their pockets rather than as citizens paying for necessary services. This attitude has changed the civic discourse, where politicians now consider voters taxpayers rather than citizens and spending any public money is seen as a careless or even evil action. Aging infrastructure, including roads and water systems, is not being maintained as it should be because that costs too much money. This means that eventually it will cost even more to replace the structures. With less tax revenue, cities cannot afford to upgrade their transit systems, yet citizens are deluded into thinking they can get subways for free. Many new public buildings are cheap and ugly because no one wants to pay for impressive edifices, yet beautiful architecture is the face of a city and attracts visitors as well as making a better environment for citizens.

Cheapness is an illness that is destroying the country. Canada needs leaders to be honest, to tell the citizens that they will only get what they are willing to pay for, and that an investment in quality is well worth the money. Canadians should not be a people that, as Oscar Wilde said, "know the price of everything and the value of nothing."

## Additional Topics

1. How should discretionary income be spent? Write an essay giving advice to young adults.
2. Discuss the advantages or the disadvantages of a cashless society. Consider how easily the one-cent coin was phased out. Is it time to go completely electronic and get rid of coins and bills?
3. What is the best way for financial literacy to be learned? How should children be taught about the meaning of money? Are young adults in Canada financially illiterate? Do they understand the use of credit and the value of saving? Explain.
4. Henry Ford was famous for establishing modern manufacturing and for paying his workers enough so that they could afford to buy one of his cars. Find out more about Ford's ideas about money, or research another famous businessperson such as Bill Gates or Timothy Eaton. What were their attitudes toward money based on? Were they philanthropic? Were they considered ruthless businessmen?
5. Choose one major retailer, and explain its failure (or success) in the marketplace. Here are examples for you to consider: Eaton's, Sears catalogue shopping, Target Canada, Canadian Tire, WalMart.
6. Choose one product (such as athletic shoes, textbooks, or fast-food hamburgers), and research its pricing. Find out how much it costs for the materials, the labour, the retailer, the taxes, and the profits. Write a report.

# Technology

## Turning the Table on Instagram

*by Emma Teitel*

1   Last year, American celebrity chef Anthony Bourdain opened up to a tabloid about one of modern life's most common social practices, or—depending on whom you're talking to—one of its biggest transgressions. When asked what he thought about "food instagramming"—photographing your meal at a restaurant and uploading the pictures onto social media—he explained that while he does this "all the time," he isn't particularly fond of the practice. "It's a dysfunctional, even aggressive practice," he said. "Why do we instagram pictures of our food? To make people feel really bad. You don't want people eating dinner with you when you instagram a picture of your food. You want them to be eating a bag of Cheetos on their couch in their underpants. It's a passive-aggressive act." In other words, much like other popular online pastimes—posting jealousy-inducing travel photos to your Facebook page or pictures of the diamond ring your fiancée just gave you—instagramming your food is an easy, detached way of saying, "My life is better than yours." Bourdain's philosophy on this subject may be highly cynical, and a bit snooty, especially for a man who has the luxury of being around photo-worthy culinary masterpieces all the time. But he's not alone.

2   Last week, an anonymous poster claiming to be a Manhattan restaurateur argued in the "Rants and Raves" section of New York's Craigslist page that photographing food at restaurants is not only rude and self-indulgent, but a blight on customer service. The poster, who has since deleted his now-viral rant (it racked up more than 750,000 shares on Distractify in one weekend), claimed to have studied security footage at his midtown restaurant from the last 10 years, and concluded that smartphone use at the table has drastically increased wait times in his restaurant, to the point where some customers were so busy looking at their phones and photographing their food that when they were finally ready to take a bite, their food was cold and the server had to reheat it.

3   According to his survey, "26 out of 45 customers spend an average of three minutes taking photos of food," and "14 out of 45 customers take pictures of each other with the food in front of them. This takes, on average, another four minutes, as they must review and sometimes retake the photo. Nine out of 45 customers sent their food back to reheat." The whole food-photo ordeal, he alleged, can add, on average, up to five wasted minutes of a server's time.

4       Whether any of this is true we will likely never know.

5       Matty Matheson, the executive chef at Toronto's popular Parts and Labour restaurant, acknowledges that smartphone and Instagram use sometimes delays service in his restaurant. "I see customers tell servers to 'come back to us' because they're on the phone," he says. But he argues that the positives generally outweigh the negatives. Instagram is, after all, free publicity for any business.

6       What's most interesting, however, in this extremely low-stakes debate isn't the dubious data presented by an anonymous Craigslist poster, but the enormous popularity of the post and the speed at which it was shared. Clearly, fictitious or not, people were excited by the notion that public smartphone use had disrupted life as they knew it. There was a possibility that their annoyance with amateur Internet food photography had suddenly been validated by cold, hard facts. So, of course, they did what any mature social media-wary people would do in the year 2014: They shared the story on social media.

7       Instagramming your food and digitally documenting the finer things in life may be passive-aggressive, as Bourdain claims, but so is modern Internet life in general. The truth is that we've all turned inward—not just those of us who ignore our dates while we photograph food, but those of us who have a problem with the ubiquity of public smartphone use, too. Some of us may believe social media is inherently anti-social and destructive, yet it appears that the only forum where we feel truly comfortable expressing this discontent is on social media itself. (There is no greater proof of this irony than the huge success of British writer Gary Turk's short film *Look Up*, about the dangers of excessive social media use. It now has more than 44 million views on YouTube and 44,000 comments.) Rarely do any of us, ballsy enough to take on the habits of the young, tell a friend or a stranger that his incessant instagramming—at the dinner table or anywhere—is a rude, annoying waste of time. A more interesting and prudent study might be one that determines how many customers actually say something—in real life—when the practice annoys them.

8       Whether we like it or not, etiquette has undergone a radical makeover in the last five years. However, the biggest loss we've suffered as a social civilization may not be manners or the art of conversation, but the art of public confrontation.

[11 August 2014]

## Notes

*Passive-aggressive* is a term from psychology that can be hard to explain and to understand. The words *passive* and *aggressive* are essentially opposites. The term refers to someone being angry but not expressing that anger openly, instead choosing to do something negative somewhat secretly. Look online for examples of passive-aggressive behaviour, and discuss. Choose which example you think best describes this kind of behaviour.

## Comprehension

1. What is Instagram, and how is it used?
2. Explain the term *social media*. What does it include?
3. Explain what Anthony Bourdain thinks of the practice of instagramming meals. What is Teitel's opinion of Bourdain's view?

4. Explain how taking photos of food can affect restaurant service. How can it benefit a restaurant?
5. What point is Teitel making in Paragraph 6? Explain the irony in "they did what any mature social media-wary people would do in the year 2014: They shared the story on social media."
6. What does Teitel mean when she says "we've all turned inward" [7]?
7. Explain what Teitel means when she says, "the biggest loss we've suffered as a social civilization may not be manners or the art of conversation, but the art of public confrontation" [8].

## Discussion
1. Do you instagram your meals? Why or why not? What do you think of the practice?
2. Teitel refers to "jealousy-inducing travel photos" on Facebook [1]. Is posting to social media just showing off? Explain.
3. Do you think that customers taking photos of food is an actual problem in restaurants?
4. How has the smartphone changed the way people behave in public? Is this behaviour acceptable?
5. How do you use social media? Do you think social media are a time-waster or a valuable tool? What are your favourite apps?
6. Do you agree that people are now less able to confront people personally? Would you consider this a social problem? Discuss.

## Assignments
1. Write an essay explaining why people want to share their lives on social media.
2. Write an essay explaining the effects of easy access to cameras. For example, tourists are so busy taking photographs of the view that they do not take time to admire it. (It has been shown that people remember better if they look at something instead of photographing it.)
3. Technology changes the way we deal with people because it protects us from personal interaction. For example, pedestrians do not treat each other as rudely as drivers do; road rage happens because drivers are "hidden" in a car. People post rude comments anonymously online—things they would never say in person to someone. Some people even break up with their partner by text message. Take one example of such actions, and in an essay explain why it happens, what it leads to, or what should be done about it.
4. Watch Gary Turk's YouTube video *Look Up*. Write a one-paragraph review of the video.

## Paraphrase and Summary
1. Paraphrase: "much like other popular online pastimes—posting jealousy-inducing travel photos to your Facebook page or pictures of the diamond ring your fiancée just gave you—instagramming your food is an easy, detached way of saying, 'My life is better than yours'" [1].

2. Paraphrase: "What's most interesting, however, in this extremely low-stakes debate isn't the dubious data presented by an anonymous Craigslist poster, but the enormous popularity of the post and the speed at which it was shared" [6].

3. Write a one-paragraph summary of the article. Use no more than 100 words.

## Structure and Technique

Note that Teitel clearly gives her opinions in this article, but she makes no personal references to herself. She does not have to say "I think" or "in my opinion." Go through the article and examine how she presents points of view—hers and others' views.

How does Teitel show that she doesn't believe the anonymous poster she discusses in Paragraphs 2–4? Discuss the words she uses to show this lack of belief.

## Language Study

### Definitions

Use the context to match each word to its definition:

| | |
|---|---|
| 1. ballsy, *adj* [7] _____ | a) allowing yourself something you do not need |
| 2. blight, *n* [2] _____ | b) angry, critical speech |
| 3. dubious, *adj* [6] _____ | c) careful and sensible |
| 4. incessant, *adj* [7] _____ | d) common existence, seeming to be everywhere |
| 5. inherently, *adv* [7] _____ | e) difficult experience |
| 6. ordeal, *n* [3] _____ | f) doubtful, not proven |
| 7. prudent, *adj* [7] _____ | g) naturally part of something |
| 8. rant, *n* [2] _____ | h) newspaper that tends to report gossipy, sensational news |
| 9. self-indulgent, *adj* [2] _____ | i) not stopping |
| 10. snooty, *adj* [1] _____ | j) showing a lot of courage and determination |
| 11. tabloid, *n* [1] _____ | k) snobbish, thinking you are better than others |
| 12. transgressions, *n* [1] _____ | l) something that has a bad effect on something |
| 13. ubiquity, *n* [7] _____ | m) something that is against the rules |

### Word Focus

#### instagram [1]

Instagram is the name of a social media app used on mobile phones. Note that the word is capitalized when it is used as the proper noun (the actual name of the app) in Paragraph 5. However, it is not capitalized when used as a verb in Paragraphs 1 and 7. The verb refers to the practice of taking a photo and posting it online with Instagram. It is common for words to change part of speech in English, such as the practice of "verbing" nouns.

When the name of a brand becomes a regular word, it reflects a certain status—that the word has been accepted into the language as more than a proper noun. For example, the search engine is called Google, but the verb *to google* is now used to refer to online searches in general.

Social media are powerful forces that have made many changes to the language. For example, because of the influence of Facebook, the word *like* is used as a countable noun to say that something received a number of "likes."

Can you find other examples of word changes influenced by modern technology?

### server [3]

The word *server* is a good example of how language adjusts to reflect social change. The words *waiter* and *waitress* were more commonly used in the past, but *server* is the preferred term now because it is gender-neutral. The term *waitstaff* is also used.

In the same way, *flight attendant* has replaced *steward* and *stewardess*. Feminine forms such as *actress* have dropped out of usage in favour of *actor* for both sexes. In small groups, discuss other such changes in terminology to describe people. Make a list of some gender-neutral terms and the words they replaced.

### allege [3]

*Allege* is a verb that means to state something is a fact but without actual proof. The word is used a lot in crime reporting because it cannot be said that someone committed a crime before that person is convicted in court. Thus, "the alleged killer" means that there is strong evidence the person is the killer but that it has not yet been proven legally.

### Word Families

Fill in the chart with the corresponding parts of speech:

| NOUN | VERB | ADJECTIVE | ADVERB |
|---|---|---|---|
| | argue [2] | | |
| | believe [7] | | |
| | | comfortable [7] | |
| confrontation [8] | | | |
| | | | digitally [7] |
| | | excessive [7] | |
| | | fictitious [6] | |
| | | | finally [2] |
| popularity [6] | | | |
| | | public [6] | |
| | | social [1] | |

## Sentence Structure Analysis

Identify the main subject and verb in the following sentences. Identify the modifiers—adjectives, adverbs, phrases, and clauses—and what they modify.

1. "Bourdain's philosophy on this subject may be highly cynical, and a bit snooty, especially for a man who has the luxury of being around photo-worthy culinary masterpieces all the time." [1]
2. "However, the biggest loss we've suffered as a social civilization may not be manners or the art of conversation, but the art of public confrontation." [8]

## Maybe It's Time to Rewire and Unplug the Next Generation

*by Gwyn Morgan*

1  A decade has passed since BlackBerry led the transformation of mobile phones into e-mail and Internet access devices. By the end of 2014, more than 1.7 billion of global mobile phone users–some 40 per cent–will own smartphones.

2  In that breathtakingly brief period, the smartphone has transformed society in unimaginable ways. The most widely cited impacts are social. Pervasive e-mail and text messaging, the phenomenal popularity of Facebook, Twitter, Instagram and YouTube plus the vast amount of information accessible through search engines see many users virtually unable to avoid using their smartphone for more than a few minutes. This condition has become known as Internet addiction. It infects children as young as two years and it's well on its way to infecting a large part of the post-smartphone generation.

3  What does this have to do with business? A great deal, since those who grew up in the age of smartphones will eventually comprise Canada's entire workforce. How can people who've spent almost every waking minute fixated on their gadgets learn thinking skills such as problem solving, strategic planning and disciplined time management? Psychological studies don't paint an encouraging picture.

4  When we go online, we enter an environment that promotes cursory reading and hurried, distracted thinking. Surprisingly, one of the clearest enunciations of the problem comes from an Internet veteran. Two years ago, Joe Kraus, a partner at Google Ventures, sounded the alarm. "We are creating . . . a culture of distraction where we are increasingly disconnected from the people and events around us and increasingly unable to engage in long-form thinking. People now feel anxious when their brains are unstimulated . . . We threaten the key ingredients behind creativity and insight by filling up all our gap time with stimulation."

5  With Facebook, Twitter and other cellphone interactions, this is surely the most socially connected generation in history. But as personal as these seem to be, they shield the user from face-to-face interaction. And given the opportunity for face-to-face interaction, users often prioritize their phones over the people right in front of them.

6  "We are lonely, but fearful of intimacy. Digital connections offer the illusion of companionship without the demands of friendship. We expect more from

technology and less from each other," says Sherry Turkle, an MIT Professor who studies technology and society.

7      This helps explain why employers are finding young recruits very bright, but awkward and deficient when working in teams or interacting with customers.

8      Studies by psychologists and neurobiologists point to the conclusion that the Internet device revolution is actually rewiring brains. Mr. Kraus puts it this way: "We're radically overdeveloping the parts of our quick thinking, distractible brain and letting go of the long-form thinking, creative contemplative, solitude-seeking, thought-consolidating pieces of our brain atrophy by not using them . . . that's both sad and dangerous."

9      It's dangerous from a social standpoint because constantly distracted people who are incapable of long-form thinking will have difficulty managing their lives. And it's dangerous economically because business success in a globally competitive world requires undivided focus, analytical accuracy, creative problem solving, innovative thinking and team-working skills.

10     The Internet brain seeks to fill all "gap" time tweeting, texting, e-mailing, following Facebook "friends" and, if there's any spare minutes left, playing video games. Is it possible to rewire the Internet-addicted brain? I wouldn't be surprised to see "Internet withdrawal" retreat centres emerge as a new business opportunity. And businesses should be adding "long-form thinking" to employee development programs. The survival of their enterprises may depend upon it.

[1 December 2014]

## Notes

Gwyn Morgan is a business writer. This is why he asks "What does this have to do with business?" [3]. He is anticipating that his audience will be wondering why he starts by talking about social change brought about by technological change.

## Comprehension

1. What is Morgan's thesis?
2. What is the point Morgan is making in the first paragraph?
3. Explain what Kraus means by "a culture of distraction" [4].
4. What is meant by "gap time" [4]?
5. What are the "key ingredients behind creativity and insight" [4]?
6. What is the problem with the social connections that are common today?
7. What do employers see as a problem with the young people who are being hired today?
8. What does Morgan recommend in his conclusion?

## Discussion

1. Discuss Turkle's pronouncement that we "expect more from technology and less from each other" [6]. What does she mean? Do you agree? Give examples of such behaviour.
2. What are the signs of Internet addiction?

3. How do you fill your "gap time"?
4. Do you agree with Morgan that addiction to the Internet and electronic gadgets is causing serious social and economic problems? Explain.
5. Morgan argues that the younger generation needs to be rewired and unplugged. He sees their dependence on technology as a weakness. However, is it realistic to change a whole generation? Maybe the workplace has to adapt to this generation. Discuss.
6. Morgan suggests a future for "'Internet withdrawal' retreat centres" [10]. What other kinds of services do you think our technology-dependent society could use? Propose a possible business.

## Assignments
1. In an essay, compare digital friendships to traditional ones.
2. Choose one skill that is important in today's workplace. In an essay, explain its importance and how it is affected by the use of communication technology.
3. Is the use of digital media changing our thinking or just our behaviour? Write an essay arguing your point of view.
4. Morgan describes the online environment as one "that promotes cursory reading and hurried, distracted thinking" [4]. Studies show that people read differently online and that they remember more from paper books. One report is "The Reading Brain in the Digital Age: The Science of Paper versus Screens," by Ferris Jabr (*Scientific American*, 11 April 2013). Write a research essay on the differences between reading on paper versus reading on digital media.

## Paraphrase and Summary
1. Paraphrase: "And given the opportunity for face-to-face interaction, users often prioritize their phones over the people right in front of them" [5].
2. Paraphrase: "And it's dangerous economically because business success in a globally competitive world requires undivided focus, analytical accuracy, creative problem solving, innovative thinking and team-working skills" [9].
3. Write a one-paragraph summary of the article. Use no more than 100 words.

## Structure and Technique
The first two paragraphs are an introduction, giving background information and setting up Morgan's arguments. He is moving from facts to opinions. How effective is this introduction? What else could he have done to introduce his argument?

Discuss Morgan's use of pronouns. Note that he avoids *you*, but uses a collective *we*. He does not use *I* until the end. How effective is this? What tone does the pronoun use give the article?

Note how Morgan uses the opinions of others. How does he show that these people's opinions are valuable? He quotes others but does not give full references for the quotations as you would have to in an academic journal article.

## Language Study

### Definitions
Use the context to match each word to its definition:

| | |
|---|---|
| 1. atrophy, *v* [8] _____ | a) always thinking or focusing on one particular thing |
| 2. comprise, *v* [3] _____ | b) become weak from not being used |
| 3. contemplative, *adj* [8] _____ | c) come out as |
| 4. cursory, *adj* [4] _____ | d) consist of, make up |
| 5. deficient, *adj* [7] _____ | e) existing everywhere |
| 6. emerge, *v* [10] _____ | f) lacking something |
| 7. fixated, *adj* [3] _____ | g) make something most important |
| 8. pervasive, *adj* [2] _____ | h) person who has recently joined an organization |
| 9. prioritize, *v* [5] _____ | i) thinking quietly and seriously about something, meditating on something |
| 10. recruit, *n* [7] _____ | j) without paying enough attention to details |

### Word Families
Fill in the chart with the corresponding parts of speech:

| NOUN | VERB | ADJECTIVE | ADVERB |
|---|---|---|---|
| access [1] | | | |
| | | analytical [9] | |
| | avoid [2] | | |
| | | competitive [9] | |
| creativity [4] | | | |
| | | fearful [6] | |
| | | global [1] | |
| | infect [2] | | |
| | | unimaginable [2] imaginable imaginative | |
| management [3] | | | |
| | | strategic [3] | |

## Word Parts

Discuss the meaning of these words by looking at their parts:

breathtakingly [2]
neurobiologists [8]
overdeveloping [8]
unimaginable [2]

## Collocations and Expressions

Discuss the meanings and use of the following expressions:

have something to do with something [3]
it's well on its way to . . . [2]
to sound the alarm [4]

## Sentence Structure Analysis

1. Identify the main subject and verb in the following sentences. Identify the modifiers—adjectives, adverbs, phrases, and clauses—and what they modify.
   a) "Studies by psychologists and neurobiologists point to the conclusion that the Internet device revolution is actually rewiring brains." [8]
   b) "When we go online, we enter an environment that promotes cursory reading and hurried, distracted thinking." [3]

2. If you overload a sentence with too many modifiers, phrases, or clauses, you can lose track of the basic sentence structure. This can result in an ungrammatical sentence and one that is confusing to the audience. In speech, this is not too much of a problem because listeners are used to following sentences that ramble or change direction. Transcripts of actual speech show many false starts, hesitations, and repetitions; speech is far from the polished form we see in written language. Journalists who report what people say often have to clean up sentences to make them readable.

   An example of an overloaded sentence that ran away from the author is Joe Kraus's statement below. Analyze and discuss the quoted sentence to determine the core and the modifiers. Why is the sentence problematical? Discuss ways to improve the sentence.

   > "We're radically overdeveloping the parts of our quick thinking, distractible brain and letting go of the long-form thinking, creative contemplative, solitude-seeking, thought-consolidating pieces of our brain atrophy by not using them . . . that's both sad and dangerous." [4]

## Technology and the Generational Divide

Communication technology such as the smartphone has become an indispensable tool all over the world. Astonishingly, according to a 2013 UN study, more people in the world have access to cellphones than to toilets. The utter domination of cellphones has taken less than 20 years. Millennials, those born after 1980, have had access to the technology from their teen years and even before. Their parents, the baby boomers, were the first generation to grow up with television, but most did not start using computer technology until they were well into adulthood. The differing experiences of these two generations has created a disconnect. Millennials and boomers have far different attitudes toward the technology they both use.

Young people and their parents use technology differently in their social spheres. Millennials depend on being able to contact their friends instantly. They arrange get-togethers on the fly and invite friends to come and join them by sending text messages. Boomers, on the other hand, tend to arrange social events ahead of time with fixed time and place. Cellphones provide only a back-up contact method to confirm or change plans. Once they do meet their friends, millennials have a hard time dragging their attention away from their phones. Instead of conversing, they may be looking at the screen together watching streaming video. They may even be busy sending messages to others rather than talking to the friends that are actually there. Boomers prefer talking to their friends face-to-face.

Technology has created a generation of multi-taskers with shorter attention spans than their parents. The Internet experience is made up of a never-ending trail of distractions—other links to click, beeps announcing new messages, and games and videos to fill downtime. Constantly dealing with so much calling for their attention, millennials have faith in their ability to multi-task. They are more likely to think they can drive and text at the same time, for instance. Ultimately, millennials find it hard to stay focused on one subject and get bored easily. Their parents are not unaffected by the assault of technological distraction, but they are better able to turn it all off when they need to. Boomers can more easily enjoy pursuits such as reading a novel or watching a movie that does not change to another frenetic scene every few seconds.

While boomers do rely on their cellphones for both work and social purposes, their children have evolved a dependence on their gadgets that forms an unbreakable bond. Millennials argue that they cannot turn off their phones in class because their family might have to contact them in an emergency (their teachers scoff at the likelihood of this happening—their definition of "an emergency" is much more narrow than their students'). Millennials depend on their phones instead of their memory, and much of their memory is visual—so they will take pictures of what they need to remember. Boomers tend to write down important information. Dependence also leads to trust: millennials are less likely to worry about their phones getting hacked or compromised, while their parents do not completely trust modern technology. Boomers have also come to depend on technology, but they remember a world without such gadgets and so can find other ways to do the same tasks. For example, a boomer could figure out the change for a cash purchase, while a millennial would be helpless if the computerized cash register broke down—and probably would not even make a cash purchase in the first place.

While both boomers and millennials have had their lives irrevocably changed by technological developments, the age people are exposed to the technology makes a big difference. Those who acquire technologies as adults can easily remember how to live without the gadgets. Looking into the future is much more difficult than remembering the past. The social change wrought by technological advancement would have been impossible to predict a generation ago, so preparing for a future more than a couple of years ahead is beyond our ability. Technology is changing our world, and we can just go along for the ride and adapt as we can.

## Additional Topics

1.  Is a prohibition against cellphones in school unfair? Discuss.
2.  Explain young people's reliance on their communication devices. Use strong arguments that would convince the skeptical older audience.
3.  Are people today too dependent on communication technology?
4.  Are online relationships as satisfying as face-to-face ones? Explain.
5.  How do people use cellphones and other technology to insulate themselves from human interaction? For example, does using earbuds or headphones send a "do not talk to me" message? When does this insulation become hiding and thus potentially dangerous? For instance, anonymous Internet posters make hurtful and even obscene comments that they would never make if their identities were known.
6.  Are we moving toward less dependence on the written word? For example, text messages can be sent with emoji instead of words, and traditional written instructions are being replaced by ones that rely on icons to communicate the message. Discuss advantages and disadvantages of the change to more visual communication.
7.  Laws and regulations cannot keep up with the rapid pace of technology. For instance, the laws protecting traditional mail do not apply to email; cyberbullying is a new kind of crime; privacy laws do not cover drones looking into your windows; and copyright laws cannot handle the type of electronic copying that is done today. Choose one such case, and discuss how the laws should treat the case.
8.  How does access to cellphones change lives in developing countries?
9.  What new devices do you foresee being developed, and how would they change our lives?
10. Both pedestrians and drivers risk their lives because of their use of smartphones and other electronic devices. Write an essay explaining the problem or an essay giving solutions.
11. "Inattentional blindness" occurs when someone is engaged in a certain task and does not register or actually see something within his or her field of vision. One famous test is the gorilla experiment in which viewers did not see the person in the gorilla suit because they were concentrating on something else in the video. (You can look up this experiment and view the video online.) Although most laws allow drivers to use hands-free devices while driving, studies show that this practice is as dangerous as driving under the influence of alcohol. Take a position on this issue, and write an essay arguing your point of view. For example, you can argue that the laws should be amended to include a prohibition on hands-free devices, or that car manufacturers should not have so many distracting devices in cars, or that drivers need to use such devices despite the risk.

# The Environment

## The Case against Bottled Water

*by Sean Petty and Justin Trudeau*

1    Canadians have long been proud of the mighty rivers and beautiful lakes that make this country one of the greatest repositories of fresh water on the planet. So, it's a sad statement about our society that we are increasingly choosing to drink bottled water, often from foreign companies.

2    A recent Statistics Canada study found that three in 10 Canadian households used bottled water as their main source of drinking water in 2006. The study results are surprising, as there are so many good reasons to avoid drinking bottled water.

3    Many Canadians buy bottled water because they think it's safer and healthier than tap water. Certainly, advertising by bottled water companies—dominated by images of pristine glaciers and mountain streams—leaves consumers with that impression. The reality is that Canada's water supply—with rare exceptions—is extremely safe. Furthermore, according to Health Canada, there is no evidence to support the belief that bottled water is any safer than tap water. Indeed, if anything, our tap water may well be safer and healthier than bottled varieties.

4    The municipal water supply is more stringently tested than bottled water supplies. In Canada, the CBC reports that local water supplies are inspected every day while bottled-water plants are inspected just once every three years. In addition, according to MSN News, water-bottling plants are required to test for coliform bacteria just once a week whereas most municipal water systems test for the bacteria several times a day.

5    Consumers should also consider the safety and health risks posed by the bottles themselves. Many plastic water bottles are made using the chemical polyethylene terephthalate or PET. A recent study by Dr. William Shotyk, the Canadian director of the Institute of Environmental Geochemistry at the University of Heidelberg, found PET bottles leach a dangerous toxin called antimony into the water they contain. The study found that the levels of antimony rise the longer water stays in the bottle.

6     Before reaching for bottled water, Canadians need to think about the serious environmental consequences of their water choice. These include: release of millions of tons of carbon dioxide into the atmosphere from manufacturing, transport, and marketing, which contributes to global warming; depletion of scarce energy and water resources; release of toxic chemicals into our air, land, and water; and absorption of poisons into the food chain.

7     According to the Pacific Institute, the energy required to produce plastic water bottles for the American market alone in 2006 was equivalent to more than 17 million barrels of oil and created 2.5 million tons of carbon dioxide.

8     Producing bottles consumes a huge amount of water too, with the Pacific Institute estimating it takes three litres of water to produce one litre of bottled water.

9     It also takes energy to fill the bottles; ship them by truck, train, boat, or plane to the consumer; refrigerate them; and recover, recycle, or dispose of the empty bottles. The Pacific Institute estimates the total amount of energy used to provide a bottle of water to the consumer could be equal to filling 25 per cent of that bottle with oil.

10     Unfortunately, most empty bottles—more than 85 per cent according to the David Suzuki Foundation—are thrown into the trash. These bottles don't just disappear—they either get buried in the landfill or they're incinerated. The buried bottles take up to 1000 years to biodegrade and may leak toxic additives into the groundwater. The incinerated bottles release toxic chemicals into our air. Moreover, some of the bottles make their way into our oceans, where they break down into increasingly tiny pieces and can enter the food chain when they're eaten by marine animals and birds.

11     The economics of bottled water are as startling as the health and environmental considerations. While we don't tend to think of it in this way, buying bottled water is an incredibly expensive habit: a bottle of water costs more than a litre of gasoline. If we buy a bottle a day for a toonie from the vending machine, we're spending more than $700 a year on water.

12     What's more, bottled water is an example of price gouging at its most outrageous. More than one-quarter of the bottled water consumed by Canadians is nothing more than filtered tap water. Two of the top-selling brands in Canada are Dasani, which is owned by Coca-Cola, and Aquafina, which is owned by its beverage rival PepsiCo.

13     As Pepsi was forced to admit last year, both brands take the water they bottle directly from municipal water systems; Dasani uses water from Calgary and Brampton taps while Aquafina uses tap water from Vancouver and Mississauga.

14     Shocking, isn't it? These companies are taking our tap water, which on average in Canada costs us less than one-tenth of a cent per litre, filtering it, although it is already perfectly clean, and selling it back to us at a markup that can be several thousand times its original price.

15     What's perhaps even more galling is that not only is the consumer paying exorbitant prices for filtered tap water but the taxpayer is also heavily subsidizing

these companies on the back end by allowing them to draw water from municipal systems that were built with their tax monies.

16      From a marketing perspective, bottled water is unquestionably one of the great success stories of modern times. However, from a social, environmental, and economic perspective, the success of bottled water has created a myriad of problems.

17      Responding to these problems, governments, universities, schools, companies, and restaurants around the country have stopped buying and selling bottled water. They are thinking before they drink. You can too.

[11 August 2008]

## Comprehension

1. What is the main argument of this article?
2. Why do so many Canadians drink bottled water?
3. Why is tap water safer than bottled water?
4. Why is plastic an environmental hazard?
5. Where do many bottled water companies get their water from?
6. Why do the authors say that bottled water producers are gouging consumers?
7. Why do the authors say that bottled water is a marketing success?

## Discussion

1. Do you drink bottled water? How often? Why? Will this article change your practice?
2. Are the authors' arguments sound? Give counter-arguments.
3. What can people do in their everyday lives to lessen environmental damage?
4. Is it feasible to stop the use of bottled water? Are there occasions when its use is justified, such as when travelling or buying take-out food? Discuss.
5. Do you feel pressured to follow more environmentally sound practices?

## Assignments

1. Although ideally products are designed and made to meet human needs, often the need is as manufactured as the product. Petty and Trudeau show that bottled water is unnecessary. Consider another product for which the perceived need is exaggerated. Write an essay explaining why.
2. While consumers should reduce their use of bottled water, an outright ban on the product would be going too far. In an essay, explain when bottled water is necessary, giving guidelines for its use.
3. Petty and Trudeau say that "Canada's water supply—with rare exceptions—is extremely safe" [3]. One of those exceptions was the contamination of drinking water in Walkerton, Ontario, in May 2000. Research the event, and write an essay or give an oral report explaining the causes or the results.

4.  Petty and Trudeau call Canada "one of the greatest repositories of fresh water on the planet" [1]. This fact makes Canadians take fresh water for granted. What happens as a result of this attitude?

## Paraphrase and Summary

1.  Paraphrase: "Many Canadians buy bottled water because they think it's safer and healthier than tap water. Certainly, advertising by bottled water companies—dominated by images of pristine glaciers and mountain streams—leaves consumers with that impression" [3].
2.  Paraphrase: "What's perhaps even more galling is that not only is the consumer paying exorbitant prices for filtered tap water but the taxpayer is also heavily subsidizing these companies on the back end by allowing them to draw water from municipal systems that were built with their tax monies" [15].
3.  Write a one-paragraph summary (no more than 100 words) of this article.

## Structure and Technique

Petty and Trudeau's essay follows a similar structure to that of an academic essay even though it is more journalistic in style. Specifically, it has the short paragraphs necessary for newspaper-writing. The article has a clear thesis, three main arguments, and two supporting points for each argument. Identify these elements in the essay, and write them in the following outline.

Thesis:

1.  Main argument:
    a)  Supporting point:
    b)  Supporting point:

2.  Main argument:
    a)  Supporting point:
    b)  Supporting point:

3.  Main argument:
    a)  Supporting point:
    b)  Supporting point:

Consider the three main arguments. Are they presented in a logical and effective order? Which argument do you consider the strongest? Would you use the same order? Explain why or why not.

Note how the authors show other people's opinions in Paragraph 3. They use the phrases "they think" and "leaves consumers with that impression," but then they say "The reality is . . ." More on distinguishing opinions can be found in Unit 8, page 234.

## Language Study

### Definitions

Use the context to match each word to its definition:

| | |
|---|---|
| 1. biodegrade, *v* [10] _____ | a) burned up |
| 2. depletion, *n* [6] _____ | b) change back to a natural state through the action of bacteria |
| 3. exorbitant, *adj* [15] _____ | |
| 4. galling, *adj* [15] _____ | c) making somebody angry because of an unfair situation |
| 5. gouging, *n* [12] _____ | |
| 6. incinerated, *adj* [10] _____ | d) much too high (usually used with cost) |
| 7. leach, *v* [5] _____ | |
| 8. pristine, *adj* [3] _____ | e) reduction in the amount of something to the point that there is not enough |
| 9. startling, *adj* [11] _____ | |
| 10. stringently, *adv* [4] _____ | |
| | f) remove a chemical from something as the result of water passing through it |
| | g) strictly |
| | h) surprising, shocking |
| | i) taking too much money from somebody with no justification |
| | j) very clean, pure |

### Word Focus

#### bottled water

In the phrase "bottled water," *bottled* is an adjective—the past participle formed from the verb *to bottle* (which means to put liquid in a bottle), so it refers to water that has been put in a bottle and is sold that way. However, students sometimes write "bottle water" by mistake. This expression would not mean the same thing—it would refer to water that would be put in a bottle, but it is not a usual expression at all.

"A bottle of water" would refer to a specific bottle and is therefore countable. You can say, "I want to buy three bottles of water." "Bottled water" is not countable because water and other liquids are not countable. When Petty and Trudeau want to refer to a single bottle, they say "a bottle of water" [9].

When people say something like "I want a water," it is not really grammatical—it is considered an ellipsis, a short form, standing for "a bottle of water." This is similar to the way people say "let's go for a coffee"; it is a short form for "a cup of coffee."

Petty and Trudeau also refer to "plastic water bottles" [5]: This refers to the bottles that are used for water. They refer to the factories as both "bottled-water plants" [3] and "water-bottling plants" [4]; these terms are synonymous, but "water-bottling" has more emphasis on the action of putting the water in the bottles. Note that both these adjectives are hyphenated.

Go through the article to check the use of the words *bottle* and *water*. Look at the verb forms and determiners that show that *bottle* is countable while *water* is uncountable. (See pages 208–9 for more on countable and uncountable nouns.)

### subsidize [15]

*Subsidize* is a verb. The participles *subsidizing* and *subsidized* are used as adjectives. What are the two noun forms? Fill in the correct forms of the verb or the noun in the blanks in the sentences. What adverb collocates with the adjective *subsidizing* in the reading?

    a)  There are too few _____ daycare spaces.

    b)  After the rule infractions, they decided to withdraw the _____.

    c)  The provincial government _____ the education costs.

    d)  Family farms would not survive without _____.

### toxic [6]

What is the opposite of the adjective *toxic*?

Here are four definitions corresponding to four different nouns related to the word *toxic*. Use your dictionary to find the word for each definition.

    a)  a poisonous substance:
    b)  the scientific study of poisons:
    c)  blood poisoning, infection of the blood:
    d)  the quality of being poisonous:

### municipal [4]

The adjective *municipal* refers to city government. What is the noun form? What other adjectives ending in *–al* are used to describe levels of government in Canada? Give the noun form of each.

### myriad [16]

The expression "a myriad of" is similar to "a host of," which is discussed in the Word Focus note on page 321.

### toonie [11]

Every day new words are invented. Some catch on while others don't—this can make for some fascinating stories.

    The one-dollar coin was introduced in Canada on 30 June 1987. While many coins and bills have nicknames (such as *penny, nickel, dime, quarter, buck*), these names are not officially designated by the Royal Mint or the Bank of Canada. The one-dollar coin is officially referred to as a "one-dollar coin."

The image on the first one-dollar coin was of the Canadian bird, the common loon. It did not take long for people to start calling the coin "a loonie." The word *loonie* is now firmly established in the Canadian lexicon. (Be careful of the spelling so as not to confuse *loonie* with *loony*, which means "crazy" and is a short form of *lunatic*.)

The loon, however, was not the first-choice design for the coin. The coin was supposed to feature two voyageurs in a canoe, showing the importance of the fur trade in Canada's history. However, the master dies for the coin were lost in transit to the Mint in Winnipeg. To prevent counterfeiting, the Mint used a different design. It is interesting to ponder what the nickname of the coin would have been with the original design. It is safe to say that a nickname would not have been so easily coined.

This brings us to the story of the word *toonie*, which is not as interesting a tale, but the word would not exist if it were not for *loonie*. The two-dollar coin was introduced on 19 February 1996. It featured a polar bear. Many suggestions were bandied about for a nickname: "doubloon" (as in "double loon") or "bearback." However, *toonie*, a combination of *two* and *loonie*, won out.

## Word Families

Fill in the chart with the corresponding parts of speech:

| NOUN | VERB | ADJECTIVE | ADVERB |
|------|------|-----------|--------|
| | | beautiful [1] | |
| belief [3] | | | |
| choice [6] | | | n/a |
| | consider [5] | | |
| | | economic [16]<br>economical | |
| | | | perfectly [14] |
| | produce [7] | | |
| | n/a | proud [1] | |
| risk [5] | | | |
| | | sad [1] | |
| | | safe [3] | |
| success [16] | | | |

## Word Parts
Discuss the meaning of these words by looking at their parts:

increasingly [10]
unquestionably [16]

## Collocations and Expressions
Discuss the meanings and usage of the following expressions:

to leave somebody with an impression (How is this different from "to impress somebody"?)
to support a belief that (How is this different from "to believe"?)
to pose a risk

## Sentence Structure Analysis
1. Analyze the structure of the following passage. Identify the main subject and verb and the antecedent of the pronoun *these* in the second sentence. Explain the use of the colon and semicolons.

   "Before reaching for bottled water, Canadians need to think about the serious environmental consequences of their water choice. These include: release of millions of tons of carbon dioxide into the atmosphere from manufacturing, transport and marketing, which contributes to global warming; depletion of scarce energy and water resources; release of toxic chemicals into our air, land and water; and absorption of poisons into the food chain." [6]

2. Identify the main subject and verb in the following sentences. What are the phrases and clauses, and what do they modify?
   a) "However, from a social, environmental and economic perspective, the success of bottled water has created a myriad of problems." [16]
   b) "According to the Pacific Institute, the energy required to produce plastic water bottles for the American market alone in 2006 was equivalent to more than 17 million barrels of oil and created 2.5 million tons of carbon dioxide." [7]

3. Compare the use of *as* in these two sentences from Paragraph 2:
   a) "A recent Statistics Canada study found that three in 10 Canadian households used bottled water <u>as</u> their main source of drinking water in 2006."
   b) "The study results are surprising, <u>as</u> there are so many good reasons to avoid drinking bottled water."

   What is the difference between the two uses of *as*? Which of the two could be replaced by another word? Which words would work as a replacement?

   Analyze the two sentences. Find the core of the sentence (the main subject and verb). Identify clauses and phrases.

# Battle of the Bag

*by Peter Shawn Taylor*

1 It could be worse. Cathy Cirko could be the official spokesperson for the Somali Brotherhood of Pirates, or the Mosquito Breeders Association. As it is, Cirko is vice-president of the Canadian Plastics Industry Association and the country's chief advocate of plastic shopping bags.

2 The once-ubiquitous plastic bag has quickly become an environmental bogeyman in Canada. Earlier this month, citing concerns over litter and landfill, Toronto launched the country's first municipal bylaw requiring all stores to charge a five cents per bag fee to discourage their use. Several retail chains—including Home Depot and Canada's largest grocer, Loblaw Co. Ltd.—have taken the fee nationwide. Emboldened by the speed with which this policy has moved, environmental groups are now talking of the day when plastic bags will seem as repellant as in-flight smoking sections. "It's taking off everywhere as people realize this is the next right thing to do," says Steven Price, the senior conservation director of the World Wildlife Fund.

3 Tasked with the unenviable job of defending plastic bags in the face of this momentum, Cirko has fought back with a host of independent scientific studies and government data that appear to undercut the substantive arguments made against the bags. "Even if we assume every plastic bag went straight to the dump, it would only represent 0.2 per cent of the 25 million tonnes we send to landfills annually," she says, citing federal and provincial documentation. And she points to a 2007 Decima poll that found more than eight out of 10 Canadians reused their shopping bags for household garbage or pet waste.

4 She also notes a 2006 City of Toronto street litter audit that examined 4300 individual pieces of garbage at 300 sites citywide. Of this total urban detritus, just six were plastic retail shopping bags. That's 0.15 per cent of total litter.

5 "Bags are not a litter issue, and they are not a landfill issue," she says. "And we have the numbers to show that. Unfortunately, this has become an emotional issue rather than a debate based on facts. It is very frustrating." She argues municipal efforts would be better directed towards recycling plastic rather than discouraging its use.

6 Glenn de Baeremaeker, a Toronto councillor, is the architect of his city's bag bylaw. The ardent environmentalist disputes the notion that bags are a minor issue. "Nothing is insignificant," he says. "We are drowning in a sea of garbage. So we are coming after plastic bags, and we are coming after everything else that's bigger as well." From disposable coffee cup lids to consumer electronics, it is all in his sights. De Baeremaeker argues that beyond the practical benefits of reducing landfill usage, if only by a tiny amount, his campaign is emblematic of a broader issue. "The plastic bag is a symbol of our wasteful and gluttonous lifestyle. It all has to change."

7 Still, it's hard to escape the sense that the plastic bag crusade is largely a political statement. The bags, for instance, are frequently held up as the biggest blight on the world's oceans. But this month, the United Nations Environmental

Programme (UNEP) released a major report on marine waste which cited garbage cleanups along the Mediterranean Sea showing plastic bags accounted for just 8.5 per cent of total marine litter. Cigarettes and cigars were 37 per cent, plastic bottles, 10 per cent. With respect to entanglement of marine life, a 2007 study identified fishing nets, lines, and ropes as being responsible for over 70 per cent of such incidents. Plastic bags, including garbage and shopping bags, caused less than 10 per cent. The report recommended that bag use be "discouraged" in coastal areas. Instead, the executive director of the UNEP, Achim Steiner, issued a press release calling for a sweeping worldwide ban on "pointless" plastic bags. Based on the evidence, a ban on fishing line, plastic bottles, or cigarettes would make more sense.

8    Then there's the possibility that, regardless of the symbolism, throwaway plastic bags might simply be better than the alternatives. Cirko also commissioned two independent labs to examine the health implications of replacing plastic shopping bags with reusable woven "green" bags. Bags randomly obtained from shoppers were tested for bacteria, yeast, mould, and E. coli. The results were then interpreted by Dr. Richard Summerbell, the former chief of medical mycology for Ontario.

9    The tests found surprisingly high levels of bacteria in two-thirds of the reusable bags. One-third had levels above those set for safe drinking water. The fact that some people used the bags to carry items other than food—gym clothes or beer empties—greatly increased the risk.

10    "This study provides strong evidence that reusable bags could pose a significant risk to the safety of the food supply if used to transport food from store to home," Dr. Summerbell concluded. He recommended that all meat be double-wrapped before being placed in reusable bags and that the bags themselves be washed and discarded regularly. None of the throwaway bags were found to be contaminated in any way.

[2 July 2009]

## Notes

In 2012, the City of Toronto rescinded the bylaw making retailers charge for plastic shopping bags and voted against a proposed ban on their use. However, some grocery store chains and other stores continue to charge for shopping bags.

Not mentioned in the article, but important to understand, are other problems that surface in the battle against the plastic bag. Biodegradable bags do not work well unless they are placed in composting; they contaminate the recycling stream. People who do not have grocery bags to recycle as bags for their garbage may turn to buying bags especially for these purposes; these garbage bags, however, are made with more plastic and are only used once, which is more wasteful.

## Comprehension

1. Explain the first sentence. What does *it* refer to?
2. Who is Cathy Cirko?
3. What is being done to reduce the use of plastic bags?

4. What are the main arguments that Cirko gives? What does she mean when she says "this has become an emotional issue" [5]?
5. What is de Baeremaeker's position? How does he justify it?
6. What point is being made with all the figures given in the article?
7. What is the problem with reusable grocery bags?

## Discussion

1. Although Taylor presents both sides of the argument, he reveals a bias. What is his opinion about plastic bags? How do you know?
2. Discuss Taylor's reference to the made-up groups: "the Somali Brotherhood of Pirates" and "the Mosquito Breeders Association." What point is he making? Is the point made effectively?
3. Where do you stand on the plastic bag issue? Do you use reusable bags? Why?
4. What kind of controls should be placed on plastic bags? Should they be banned? Could an education program be enough to curtail use? Should there be no controls?
5. Do you think it was right to target plastic bags in this way? Is there any pollution that you think is worse?

## Assignments

1. Write an essay giving your opinion on the controls on plastic bags.
2. Write an essay on either the benefits or the problems of one specific kind of recycling.
3. Choose one garbage problem (such as excessive packaging, discarded electronic equipment, or paper diapers), and suggest solutions in an essay.

## Paraphrase and Summary

1. Paraphrase: "The once-ubiquitous plastic bag has quickly become an environmental bogeyman in Canada" [2].
2. Paraphrase: "Tasked with the unenviable job of defending plastic bags in the face of this momentum, Cirko has fought back with a host of independent scientific studies and government data that appear to undercut the substantive arguments made against the bags" [3].
3. Paraphrase: "Glenn de Baeremaeker, a Toronto councillor, is the architect of his city's bag bylaw. The ardent environmentalist disputes the notion that bags are a minor issue. 'Nothing is insignificant,' he says. 'We are drowning in a sea of garbage. So we are coming after plastic bags, and we are coming after everything else that's bigger as well.' From disposable coffee cup lids to consumer electronics, it is all in his sights" [6].
4. Write a one-paragraph summary of this article. Use no more than 100 words.

## Structure and Technique

Taylor reports on other people's words, findings, and opinions. Note how he uses both quotes and indirect speech. (You can refer to Unit 8, pages 244–45, for an explanation of these forms.) Are the quotes effective? Are there any that should be indirect speech instead?

Taylor starts his article with an attention-grabbing sentence, "It could be worse," which forces people to read the second sentence to find out what the *it* refers to. He repeats the verb form *could be* to show that he is expanding on the first sentence. In an academic essay, however, you should start your body paragraphs with nouns, not unidentified pronouns, to make your writing clear.

## Language Study

### Definitions

Use the context to match each word to its definition:

| | |
|---|---|
| 1. advocate, *n* [1] _____ | a) campaign to get something done; long war |
| 2. ardent, *adj* [6] _____ | b) disagree with something |
| 3. audit, *n* [4] _____ | c) existing everywhere |
| 4. blight, *n* [7] _____ | d) having strong positive feelings for something |
| 5. bogeyman, *n* [2] _____ | e) leftover bits; waste material |
| 6. crusade, *n* [7] _____ | f) monster; somebody or something that people think is evil |
| 7. detritus, *n* [4] _____ | g) official examination of the standard of something |
| 8. dispute, *v* [6] _____ | h) person who publicly supports something |
| 9. emblematic, *adj* [6] _____ | i) something that spoils or damages something |
| 10. ubiquitous, *adj* [2] _____ | j) that represents or is a symbol of something |

### Word Focus

#### cite [2, 7], site [4], sight [6]

The words *cite*, *site*, and *sight* are homophones (words that sound the same) that can be easily confused. Here is a chart, partially filled in, to help you distinguish the three words. Fill in the blanks. Use your dictionary when you are not sure.

| | Cite | Sight | Site |
|---|---|---|---|
| Part of speech | | noun (usually) | |
| Basic meaning | | | location |
| Related words | citation (noun) | | |

Fill in the blanks with *cite*, *sight*, or *site*:

a) The environmental study did not approve of the proposed _____ of the factory.

b) Double-decker _____-seeing buses are popular among tourists in many large cities.

c) Students must be careful to correctly _____ their sources when they are writing a research essay.

d) It is not wise to rent a place _____ unseen.

e) The web _____ was taken down after many people complained.

## host [3]

English has a few expressions that follow the pattern "a _____ of" and mean "many." Taylor refers to "a host of independent scientific studies" [3], and in the first article of this unit, Petty and Trudeau refer to "a myriad of problems" [16]. Both of these expressions are formal English. In contrast, "a lot of" is a conversational expression that should be avoided in academic writing. "A number of" can be used in both academic and conversational English.

All four expressions take a plural form of the verb (as in "a number of mistakes were made") even though by strict grammatical rules they could be considered singular. Compare this to the sentence "each of the students needs a book" where a singular form of the verb is used.

## green [8]

Taylor refers to "reusable woven 'green' bags." The word *green* is often used to describe actions or products that are better for the environment. There can be confusion with the reference to green as just a colour. This confusion was played on with reusable shopping bags that had the slogan "This is a green bag" printed on them whereas they were actually black in colour.

## Word Families

Fill in the chart with the corresponding parts of speech:

| NOUN | VERB | ADJECTIVE | ADVERB |
|------|------|-----------|--------|
| argument [3] | | | |
| benefit [6] | | | |
| | | disposable [6] | n/a |
| | | emotional [5] | |
| | identify [7] | | |
| | | political [7] | |
| safety [10] | | | |
| | | significant [10] | |

## Word Parts

Discuss the meaning of these words by looking at their parts:

> emboldened [2]
> unenviable [3]
> undercut [3]
> reused [3]
> insignificant [6]
> disposable [6]
> entanglement [7]
> reusable [9]

## Sentence Structure Analysis

1. Note the use of the verb form *be* in the sentences with the verb *recommend*:

   a) "The report recommended that bag use <u>be</u> 'discouraged' in coastal areas." [7]

   b) "He recommended that all meat <u>be</u> double-wrapped before being placed in reusable bags and that the bags themselves <u>be</u> washed and discarded regularly." [10]

   In formal styles of English, verbs such as *demand, insist, recommend,* and *require* take the base form of the verb in the *that* clause. This is called the subjunctive; in English, its use is slowly dying out. In less formal styles, which word would replace *be* in the above sentences?

   Discuss the structure of the sentences and the verb forms used in these sentences and in the additional examples below:

   c) She insisted that he take the earlier train.

   d) They demanded that the candidate be approved by the vetting committee.

   e) The agreement required that the manager review the recommendations before the changes could be implemented.

2. Identify the main subject and verb in the following sentences. Identify the modifiers—adjectives, adverbs, phrases, and clauses—and what they modify.

   a) "Emboldened by the speed with which this policy has moved, environmental groups are now talking of the day when plastic bags will seem as repellant as in-flight smoking sections." [2]

   b) "Tasked with the unenviable job of defending plastic bags in the face of this momentum, Cirko has fought back with a host of independent scientific studies and government data that appear to undercut the substantive arguments made against the bags." [3]

   c) "Based on the evidence, a ban on fishing line, plastic bottles, or cigarettes would make more sense." [7]

   Note the similarity of the sentence structure: Each sentence starts with a phrase describing the subject of the sentence—it is important that the phrase does in fact describe the grammatical subject, as shown here:

   a) Environmental groups are emboldened by the speed . . .
   Environmental groups are now talking of the day . . .

   b) Cirko is tasked with the unenviable job . . .
   Cirko has fought back . . .

c) A ban would be based on the evidence . . .

A ban . . . would make more sense . . .

Refer back to Reducing Clauses to Phrases (pages 86–87) if you need more help understanding this sentence structure.

## It's Not Easy Being Green

The environmental movement has done a good job informing people about the need to be kinder to the earth. Canadian students learn the three R's—reduce, reuse, and recycle—in elementary school, and they influence their parents to be more conscious of environmental damage in their everyday lifestyle. However, Kermit the Frog's lament "It's not easy being green" can be applied to consumers' attempts to reduce harm to the environment. Despite their best intentions, people run into problems trying to follow such practices as recycling goods, reducing consumption, and buying environmentally friendly products.

Although recycling may be the most visible victory of the environmental movement, it is often impractical. Not everything can be reused or recycled. As anyone who has tried to downsize knows, it is often hard to find a new home for items such as furniture and books—even charities do not want them. It feels wasteful to throw things in the garbage, but sometimes that is the only option. Recycling actually takes energy to collect, sort, clean, and ship items. Most important, there may not even be a market for the recycled goods. Metal, glass, and paper usually can be more easily recycled than plastics, which vary greatly in composition and type. People feel good about recycling, but most do not realize that some of the items they have so carefully placed in blue boxes get dumped into landfills by municipalities because recycling can be costly.

Although one solution to the problems of reusing and recycling is to buy less in the first place, this is also easier said than done. People should buy goods that do not need to be replaced as often, but the market is flooded with cheaply made stuff, and it is hard to find or even recognize better quality goods. Appliances and furniture do not seem to last as long as they once did, and the cost of fixing them can outweigh the cost of replacing them. The high-tech industry tempts consumers with newer, flashier gadgets, causing people to throw out perfectly usable cellphones after only months of service. In addition, conscientious consumers are stymied when they try to avoid excessive packaging; if they want an item, they get the styrofoam, oversize packages, and unopenable clamshell plastic cases with it.

Even the products that are presented as "greener" choices have their dark side. For example, compact fluorescent bulbs contain mercury, which makes disposal tricky. Batteries from some electric cars can also be toxic. Plastic shopping bags are considered an environmental scourge, but reusable green bags are contaminated with bacteria, and bans on the bag force people to buy bags for their garbage instead of reusing the ones from the grocery store. Local fruits and vegetables do not have to travel as far, but if growing conditions are not as favourable, more water and fertilizer may have to be used to produce them. Moreover, choosing truly eco-friendly products is difficult because many companies use misleading claims on their packaging; this established practice even has its own term, "greenwashing." For example, the term "all natural" is not a regulated term, so it can fool buyers. Consumers would need extensive education to ensure that they are making environmentally sound choices.

From the purchases shoppers make to the way they dispose of products, environmentally conscious decision-making is fraught with difficulty. However, this does not mean that people should just throw up their hands in surrender. They need to do what they can because the environment is so important. They must complain to manufacturers and government agencies about systemic problems such as greenwashing and over-packaging.

## Additional Topics

1. Canadians today spend less time outdoors. How can this affect their awareness of environmental damage?
2. Most Canadians depend on their personal vehicles for everyday transportation. How can they limit environmental damage from their cars?
3. Write an essay comparing the environmental situation in Canada with that in another country you are familiar with. You can compare people's attitudes, government actions, or the state of pollution.
4. Some people follow vegan diets (which do not allow any animal products) for environmental as well as health reasons. Write an essay about the advantages or disadvantages of veganism (or vegetarianism).
5. Research a huge garbage problem, such as the Great Pacific Garbage Patch or space junk, and explain the problem.
6. When considering global warming, many people confuse weather and climate. Write a definition paragraph explaining the difference.
7. Choose one environmental problem, and write an essay explaining causes or effects.

# Citizenship

## No Hyphen for Me

*by Salim Sachedina*

1   On July 16, I will be celebrating 47 years in Canada. I could delay writing this article, in anticipation of a rounder figure—say, half a century. But at my somewhat advanced age, it is better to act in the present.

2      I was among the first wave of immigrants to arrive in Canada after 1962, when the government abolished the previous, racist immigration policies with a more balanced merit-based approach.

3      I remember landing in Toronto on a sunny Saturday afternoon in 1967. My benefactors and friends, Pat and Geri Clever, came to pick me up at the airport. They'd sponsored me and my family, sight unseen, to Canada (a story in itself—but one I will save for another day).

4      My first memories of Toronto remain vivid to me. The TD Centre was under construction; the new City Hall had just opened a year earlier; and the old Canadian Imperial Bank of Commerce building on King Street West was the tallest building in the British Commonwealth.

5      But otherwise, Toronto was a dull city then, a poor cousin to the dynamic and progressive Montreal. Those were the days when we Torontonians went to Buffalo, N.Y., to have some fun.

6      I lived in an apartment complex north of Maple Leaf Gardens with my first wife, Farida, and our son Abdul, who was almost two years old when we arrived here. I remember that when we took a walk on Yonge Street, my wife, clad in a sari, caused a few heads to turn. Many had never seen a woman dressed that way before. Toronto has indeed come a long way. That year, the 1966–67 hockey season, was the last time the Maple Leafs won the Stanley Cup. Hockey was new to me. But if I had known then how long it would be until the event repeated itself, I would have indulged more in the celebration.

7      There are two stages to the immigration process—the physical and the emotional. The former is achieved as soon as one sets foot in the new land. The latter can take decades. Unless one achieves both, there will always be a longing

for one's home country, where the sun is thought to shine brighter; the sky bluer; the sea warmer.

8    Achieving emotional immigration depends on one's purpose. Immigrants who come with no other goal except to get rich will never settle fully as an immigrant until that goal is achieved. But in my case, the goal was to live in a country that was politically stable, offered law and order, and provided an opportunity for children to get the education they deserve. These advantages became available to me the moment I set my foot in this great land. I never looked back. This was home, I told myself.

9    I quickly started to adopt the values of my new environment—which meant discarding certain notions I'd brought from overseas. When I think of issues connected to culture and values, I use the analogy of a glass of water filled to the rim. You can't add anything fresh to it unless you are willing to dump out some of the existing contents.

10   Canada's history became my history. I started to learn more about my new country—its history, its arts and literature, its political structure. I even picked a favourite prime minister: Sir Wilfrid Laurier.

11   I stopped seeing myself as a hyphenated Canadian, even if my double identity is of interest to demographers and pollsters (and to politicians who seek to package their politics to suit my presumed tendencies). I have no use for the religious and ethnic leaders who have resolved to live in a fish-bowl under the pretext of multiculturalism. As Laurier would say: "I am a Canadian first, last and all the time." In time, the lyrics of Gordon Lightfoot, Stompin' Tom Connors and Joni Mitchell became as relevant to me as songs by Lata Mangeshkar and Mohammed Rafi about social injustices in my father's homeland of India. The narratives by Margaret Atwood about Canadian life now resonate as well as Moyes Vasanji's stories echoed my early days in Tanzania.

12   I remarried, to a wonderful woman named Honey. She is Jewish and I, a Muslim. Canada is one of the few countries where such a union could not only take place but also flourish without danger or controversy.

13   I have never taken Canada for granted. And I have shared my love and appreciation of this country with all of my four children: Abdul, Najeeb, Jeremy and Hamida. I am also proud to say that I have never missed voting in an election—municipal, provincial or federal.

14   Canada is no Utopia. I know that. No human institution is. The country has built-in conflicts, between English and French. Its historical treatment of Aboriginal peoples is shameful, not to mention more mundane problems of governance and equity.

15   Yet at the same time, Canadians are resolved to go forward and tackle these problems, in a spirit of respect and harmony. We exhibit those qualities far more often than not.

16   I love my country. There is no other like it, and certainly no other place I would rather live. On Canada Day weekend, I will be one of those proudly standing on guard "for thee."

[28 June 2013]

## Comprehension

1. Explain the title.
2. When did Sachedina come to Canada? What made his arrival possible?
3. What does Sachedina mean by a "merit-based approach" [2]?
4. What is the picture that Sachedina paints of Toronto? How was it different from what it is today?
5. Explain what Sachedina means by the two stages of the immigration process.
6. Explain the author's analogy in Paragraph 9. Do you think what he says is valid?
7. Why would Sachedina's ethnic identity be of interest to demographers, pollsters, and politicians? Discuss.
8. What did Sachedina do to become Canadian?
9. Why is Sachedina proud to be living in Canada?
10. What is Sachedina referring to in the last five words of the article?

## Discussion

1. Do you think Sachedina had the right approach to immigration? Discuss.
2. What makes a successful immigrant?
3. Discuss the various reasons that people immigrate to Canada.
4. Does the reason that an immigrant comes to Canada make it easier to adapt to the new life? For instance, does an immigrant fleeing a war-torn country find it easier to settle than one who is coming for economic reasons? Discuss.
5. What kind of values do you think are better discarded by new immigrants to Canada? What kind of values should be retained?

## Assignments

1. What factors determine how easily immigrants adapt to living in Canada? Write an essay.
2. Write an essay explaining why it is important to vote in elections.
3. Research one of the Canadian icons Sachedina mentions in Paragraph 11, and write a paragraph explaining why that person is important to Canada. Or choose another notable Canadian, and explain why that person is important.
4. Sachedina says Laurier is his favourite prime minister. Who would you pick? Explain why.
5. Write an essay comparing the personal essay "No Hyphen for Me" and the short story "Why My Mother Can't Speak English" (pages 353–58). Choose one basis of comparison. For example, you could discuss the differences between the citizenship experiences of the mother in the story and those of Sachedina.

## Paraphrase and Summary

1. Paraphrase: "But otherwise, Toronto was a dull city then, a poor cousin to the dynamic and progressive Montreal" [5].
2. Paraphrase: "There are two stages to the immigration process—the physical and the emotional. The former is achieved as soon as one sets foot in the new land. The latter can take decades. Unless one achieves both, there will

always be a longing for one's home country, where the sun is thought to shine brighter; the sky bluer; the sea warmer" [7].

3. Write a one-paragraph summary of the article. Use no more than 100 words.

## Structure and Technique

This is a personal essay in which the author tells something of his own life story. "Why My Mother Can't Speak English" (pages 353–58) is also the story of an immigrant, but it is autobiographical fiction told in a short story. Both are narratives, but a short story is told much differently from a personal essay. Note the use of dialogue in the short story. The short story also covers a shorter amount of time but in more detail. Discuss the differences in narration.

## Language Study

### Definitions

Use the context from the reading to match each word to its definition:

| | |
|---|---|
| 1.  abolish, *v* [2] _____ | a)  be officially responsible for an immigrant to Canada, giving financial support if necessary |
| 2.  benefactor, *n* [3] _____ | |
| 3.  clad, *adj* [6] _____ | |
| 4.  demographer, *n* [11] _____ | b)  be successful and happy |
| 5.  equity, *n* [14] _____ | c)  dressed in, clothed in |
| 6.  flourish, *n* [12] _____ | d)  garment made of a long, thin cloth wrapped around the body, worn by women in South Asia |
| 7.  mundane, *adj* [14] _____ | |
| 8.  pollster, *n* [11] _____ | |
| 9.  sari, *n* [6] _____ | e)  be in harmony with |
| 10.  sponsor, *v* [3] _____ | f)  not interesting or exciting; ordinary |
| 11.  resonate, *v* [11] _____ | g)  officially end a practice of something |
| 12.  tackle, *v* [15] _____ | h)  person who gives money or other support to someone or something |
| | i)  person who studies population |
| | j)  situation where everyone is treated fairly and equally |
| | k)  someone who determines public opinion by asking questions |
| | l)  try to solve a difficult problem |

### Word Focus

#### even [10, 11]

*Even* is an adverb used to strengthen or intensify. It is used just before the surprising part of a statement.

> Even John was pleased with the results.
> I even got my nails done.
> I couldn't even see the stitching; it was so fine.
> She started working even faster when the bell rang.

*Even though* is stronger than *although* but is used in the same way. A common ESL error is to use *even* as a conjunction, but it cannot stand alone to join sentences—it must have an accompanying conjunction to make *even though*, *even if*, or *even when*.

> Even if the mini-skirt does come back into fashion, I wouldn't be caught dead wearing one.
> Even though Monica spent a fortune on her outfit, she didn't look half as good as Rachel.

Alter the following sentences by adding the word *even*. See in how many positions *even* will fit in each sentence. You might have to make slight alterations to the sentence:

a) If Fred had notified us a day earlier, I would have been able to fix the problem with less effort.

b) Although Fatima couldn't see the alterations, she approved the new design as a better choice.

c) I had to follow the template, so I couldn't use Jamie's suggestions.

d) If I raised the hemline and took in the seams, the dress wouldn't look better.

## Word Families

Fill in the chart with the corresponding parts of speech:

| NOUN | VERB | ADJECTIVE | ADVERB |
|---|---|---|---|
| appreciation [13] | | | |
| | | bright [7] | |
| construction [4] | | | |
| | | political [10] | |
| | repeat [6] | | |
| respect [15] | | | |
| | | rich [8] | |
| | | shameful [14] ashamed | |
| | | stable [8] | |
| | | warm [7] | |

## Collocations and Expressions

Discuss the meanings and usage of the following expressions:

> live in a fish-bowl [11]
> sight unseen [3]
> set foot in [7]
> take something for granted [13]

## Sentence Structure Analysis

Identify the main subject and verb in the following sentences. Identify the modifiers—adjectives, adverbs, phrases, and clauses—and what they modify.

1. "Immigrants who come with no other goal except to get rich will never settle fully as an immigrant until that goal is achieved." [8]
2. "When I think of issues connected to culture and values, I use the analogy of a glass of water filled to the rim." [9]

## Attention, Dual Citizens: Canada Can No Longer Afford Our Divided Loyalty

*by Rudyard Griffiths*

1 I have to make a confession: I am a citizen of the United Kingdom of Great Britain and Northern Ireland.

2 Yes, even though I have just written a book declaring how special it is to be a Canadian and admonishing Canadians to be better citizens, I am one of the more than three million of us who hold a second passport. Mine entitles me to vote in British elections, attend, at reduced cost, some of the world's finest universities and, should I wish, leave Canada to work and live in Britain hassle-free.

3 It also bestows on me the rights of full membership in the European Community, so I could conceivably take up residence in Tuscany, vote for the next president of Slovenia or accept a job, if my Ontario high-school French were up to it, with the Académie française. And, like all dual citizens, I can confer these benefits on my children and spouse.

4 In not-so-subtle ways, my British passport represents a kind of standing invitation, should things not work out for me in Canada, to take part in one of the world's great social, political and economic experiments. There is something undeniably impressive about the fact that half a billion Europeans are fashioning a common civic identity from 27 states, 23 languages and a $17-trillion economy.

5 But I have come to the conclusion that Canada will not survive the coming decades in its current form if more and more of its Canadian-born citizens continue to live, as I have, with the mental gymnastics of dual citizenship.

6 As I argue in *Who We Are: A Citizen's Manifesto*, the scale and complexity of the challenges Canada will soon face are like nothing we have experienced in living memory. When the social and economic effects of our fast-aging population and rapid climate change begin to hit home—starting in 2020 and then intensifying relentlessly as we move toward the mid-century mark—it is inevitable that Canadians' collective flight-or-fight instincts will kick in.

7 Those who choose to fight will respond to the stresses racking our society with a spirit of solidarity and self-sacrifice. Others, driven by the flight instinct, will act out of self-interest and self-preservation. Which of these two instincts ultimately triumphs depends, in no small part, on how we each imagine our place in Canada.

8    I became a dual citizen a decade ago for sentimental, rather than practical, reasons. I wanted to acknowledge how choices made by my parents and grandparents had helped to shape my life.

9    But I cannot deny that it introduced an element of doubt as to whether my allegiance to Canada is, in fact, unconditional.

10    Who is to say that after living for another decade in a country struggling to cope with rapid ecological change, the financial burdens of a greying society or some yet-unfathomed crisis, I will not end up finding a convenient rationale to justify leaving for William Blake's "green and pleasant" land?

11    We all must decide, whether our families have been here for generations or only a few years, that Canada is where we will make our collective stand. If we are to thrive in the difficult period that lies ahead, there can be no opting out when the going gets tough.

12    We may be called upon to make many sacrifices, which will be especially difficult for those who are not rooted in Canada by a strong sense of history or place, and are quick to judge the value of citizenship by the access it provides to the highest quality of life for the fewest obligations. As a result, I believe it's essential for the country's long-term well-being that it return to a version of the pre-1977 practice of annulling the citizenship of Canadian adults who voluntarily and formally acquire the citizenship of another country.

13    At this point, the measure should apply only to natural-born citizens (whether living at home or abroad) with at least one parent who is a Canadian citizen.

14    Such a law would have two important objectives. It would impress on those born here that there is no opt-out clause in their social contract with Canada.

15    It also would let all aspiring citizens know that assuming Canadian citizenship has an important, permanent and unavoidable consequence: The children you have once you become a citizen will be Canadian and nothing more.

16    That said, I do not believe it is reasonable to mandate that newcomers to Canada renounce the citizenship of their homelands. First-generation immigrants feel far more pressure to retain a second passport. It allows them to visit their extended families unimpeded and to keep up business relationships that may be integral to their livelihood here—and to the Canadian economy, which benefits from these global links.

17    But for the 750,000 Canadian-born adults who voluntarily became dual citizens, plus the millions of second-generation Canadians who will be born in the coming decades and, for the most part, will be legally entitled to claim a second citizenship, the time has come to acknowledge that dual citizenship does Canada a disservice.

[7 March 2009]

## Notes

Rudyard Griffiths is the co-founder of the Dominion Institute. This article is adapted from his book *Who We Are: A Citizen's Manifesto*. Griffiths was born in Canada but acquired his dual citizenship because he had a parent born in Britain.

Each country has different, and sometimes complicated, rules as to who is considered a citizen. For instance, a country's government may confer official citizenship on anyone born in that country and may extend it to children and even grand-children of their citizens, even if the children were born elsewhere. In addition, immigrants can become citizens of their new country through naturalization; immigrants who have permanent resident status can apply for Canadian citizenship after three years in the country. Some countries, like Canada, allow dual citizenship. For instance, immigrants can keep the citizenship of their country of birth even after they are naturalized as Canadian citizens. Second-generation immigrants born in Canada can acquire citizenship from their parents' native country.

Griffiths is quoting from the last line in William Blake's poem "Jerusalem": "In England's green and pleasant land" [10]. The poem is sung as a well-known English hymn and anthem.

## Comprehension
1. What citizenships does Griffiths hold?
2. Why does he use the word *confession* in his first sentence?
3. What are the advantages of having British citizenship?
4. Explain what Griffiths means by "one of the world's great social, political and economic experiments" [4].
5. Griffiths refers to two specific challenges that Canada faces in the coming years. What are they?
6. Why does the author think that first-generation immigrants should be allowed to have dual citizenship but not the second-generation?

## Discussion
1. Do you agree with Griffiths? Should second-generation Canadians not be allowed to hold dual citizenship? Would you renounce a second citizenship?
2. If you have dual citizenship, where do your loyalties primarily lie? Explain why.
3. Is attachment to a home country more than eating the food and cheering for the sports teams? Discuss. What does patriotism mean in a global society?
4. Do you think Griffiths will give up his British citizenship? Explain why or why not.
5. Griffiths imagines different places he could live in Europe. If you could live anywhere in Europe, where would you choose to reside? Why?
6. What makes Canada such an attractive destination for so many immigrants?

## Assignments
1. What are the responsibilities of a Canadian citizen? Explain in an essay.
2. Write an essay arguing for or against dual citizenship.

3. Griffiths refers to the European Union as "one of the world's great social, political and economic experiments" [4]. However, this article was written in 2009, and it could be argued that the experiment is currently not going so well. Choose a recent problem Europe is facing, such as the dissatisfaction of foreign workers or the economic strains of poorer countries on the union. Write an essay explaining how the problem affects the whole union.

4. Dual citizenship is a controversial issue. Consider the following questions, and choose one issue for an argument essay. Specific examples are given to help you research the question.

   a) How much should Canada do to get its citizens out of trouble when they are in a country where they also hold citizenship? Consider cases such as the evacuees from the war in Lebanon in 2006 and Mohamed Fahmy imprisoned in Egypt in 2013.

   b) Should high-ranking politicians and government officials be allowed to keep dual citizenship? Consider, for example, former Governor General Michaëlle Jean (2005) and NDP Leader Thomas Mulcair (2012).

   c) How are dual citizens treated differently than other Canadians? Consider the 2015 cases of Zakaria Amara and Saad Gaya and the Harper government's *Strengthening Canadian Citizenship Act*.

## Paraphrase and Summary

1. Paraphrase: "But I have come to the conclusion that Canada will not survive the coming decades in its current form if more and more of its Canadian-born citizens continue to live, as I have, with the mental gymnastics of dual citizenship" [5].

2. Paraphrase: "Who is to say that after living for another decade in a country struggling to cope with rapid ecological change, the financial burdens of a greying society or some yet-unfathomed crisis, I will not end up finding a convenient rationale to justify leaving for William Blake's "green and pleasant" land?" [10].

3. Write a one-paragraph summary of the article. Use no more than 100 words.

## Structure and Technique

Griffiths starts with a personal example: He has dual citizenship. After four paragraphs explaining the advantages, he changes direction. Discuss how he accomplishes it. Does he offer clues before Paragraph 5, or is his twist a surprise to the reader?

Note that in Paragraph 11 Griffiths introduces an inclusive *we*. What effect does this have on his argument?

## Language Study

### Definitions

Use the context to match each word to its definition:

| | | | |
|---|---|---|---|
| 1. admonishing, *v* [2] _____ | | a) | continued support for a person or institution |
| 2. allegiance, *n* [9] _____ | | b) | give somebody an honour or a right |
| 3. conceivably, *adv* [3] _____ | | c) | make or shape something |
| 4. confer, *v* [3] _____ | | d) | make somebody do something officially |
| 5. disservice, *n* [17] _____ | | e) | not obvious |
| 6. fashion, *v* [4] _____ | | f) | possibly |
| 7. hassle-free, *adj* [2] _____ | | g) | something harmful to someone or something |
| 8. mandate, *v* [16] _____ | | h) | telling someone that he or she has done something wrong |
| 9. relentlessly, *adv* [6] _____ | | i) | win, succeed |
| 10. subtle, *adj* [4] _____ | | j) | without being stopped or blocked |
| 11. triumph, *v* [7] _____ | | k) | without problems or trouble |
| 12. unimpeded, *adv* [16] _____ | | l) | without stopping, refusing to give up |

### Word Focus

**opt out [11, 14]**

The verb *opt* means to choose; it is related to the noun *option*. It can be followed by *for*, *against*, *in*, or *out*, or it can be followed by an infinitive (as in "he opted to refuse the transfer").

Phrasal verbs, such as *opt out*, are written as separate words, but they are hyphenated when they become adjectives or nouns. If the nouns become established as compounds, they may lose the hyphen. Study these examples:

> He opted out of the excursion to see the Mayan temple.
> There are no provisions for anyone to opt out.
> The opt-out box has to be checked.
> The instructor asked the students to hand out the assignment instructions.
> That instructor gives his class too many hand-outs.
> We need to log off when we finish the work, but the log-off instructions are complicated.
> My daughter likes to dress up. She has a trunk full of dress-up clothes.

## Word Families

Fill in the chart with the corresponding parts of speech:

| NOUN | VERB | ADJECTIVE | ADVERB |
|---|---|---|---|
|  |  | collective [6, 11] |  |
|  | * | convenient [10]<br>inconvenient |  |
|  |  | financial [10] |  |
|  |  |  | formally [12] |
|  |  | impressive [4] |  |
|  | intensify [6] |  |  |
| invitation [4] |  |  |  |
|  | opt [11] |  |  |
| rationale [10]<br>rationalization |  |  |  |
|  |  |  | voluntarily [12] |

*Note that the verb is a negative form.

## Sentence Structure Analysis

Identify the main subject and verb in the following sentences. Identify the modifiers—adjectives, adverbs, phrases, and clauses—and what they modify.

1. "Those who choose to fight will respond to the stresses racking our society with a spirit of solidarity and self-sacrifice." [7]
2. "But for the 750,000 Canadian-born adults who voluntarily became dual citizens, plus the millions of second-generation Canadians who will be born in the coming decades and, for the most part, will be legally entitled to claim a second citizenship, the time has come to acknowledge that dual citizenship does Canada a disservice." [17]

## What Makes a Good Voter

Voting is important in a democracy and an obligation of every citizen. However, turnouts in Canadian elections are embarrassingly low, averaging about 60 percent of eligible voters. Moreover, many voters put little thought into their support for a candidate, some just voting along party lines or casting a ballot for the incumbent. However, civic engagement is every citizen's duty. Good voters must educate themselves, think critically, and vote strategically.

First, voters need to be well-informed. They need to know the issues and the candidates. The best way to do this is to read the newspaper regularly. Newspapers report on local, provincial, and national issues, giving more information than television news shows can ever cover. Journalists' investigative reporting uncovers scandals and crimes such as outrageous expenses claimed by politicians. In addition to factual stories, newspapers contain op-ed pieces, regular columns, and letters to the editor analyzing the political issues and offering a wide range of opinions. Voters can also read campaign literature and watch debates. The more information they acquire, the better informed they will be when they cast their vote.

Using their amassed knowledge, voters must develop critical thinking skills. Politicians pander to the voters and make promises based on what they think will get them elected, so voters need to evaluate the validity of different claims. For example, vowing to build a subway without increasing taxes is a claim that defies common sense and economic logic. When something sounds too good to be true, it probably is. Therefore, voters have to decide when and which politicians are playing fast and loose with the facts.

Good voters may also have to vote strategically. In provincial and federal elections, Canadians do not cast a vote for the premier or the prime minister; they can only decide who their riding representative will be. The leader of the party with the most elected representatives in the House then comes into power. Therefore, both the individual candidate and political party are important to consider. Voters have to weigh many factors to make their decision. They have to know how to play the politics game. By voting with their heart, they may split the vote and help elect a candidate that might be harmful to their interests. For instance, citizens who strongly believe the environmental issues facing us today are of utmost importance may favour Green Party policies, but if the Green Party candidate has little chance of gaining a seat, environmentalists might be better off casting a vote in favour of another candidate who also values the environment, perhaps a Liberal or New Democrat, in order to prevent another less environmentally conscious candidate from taking the riding.

Being a responsible voter does take effort. Casting a ballot is an important part of living in a democracy. It is a responsibility that should not be taken lightly, especially in consideration of the many countries around the world that do not hold free elections. With more emphasis on civics in school curricula, students can be taught to recognize their right and responsibility to vote.

## Additional Topics

1. Research a specific group of immigrants, such as the Vietnamese boat people or the Irish in the 1850s. Summarize why they came to Canada, how they were treated, and how they fared.
2. Write an essay explaining how you think new immigrants to Canada should be chosen. What should be the most important criteria?
3. What should be the criteria for being granted citizenship in Canada? For example, how long should immigrants have been residents of Canada? How well should they be able to speak English or French? What type of test should

they pass? Write an essay detailing what you think are reasonable criteria, explaining why.

4.  Should Canadian citizenship be taken away from someone? Under what circumstances?

5.  The citizenship oath has been challenged in court because it requires swearing allegiance to the Queen. Should those seeking Canadian citizenship be required to swear this oath? Write an essay arguing your point of view.

6.  Should high-calibre athletes from other countries be fast-tracked for Canadian citizenship so that they can compete for Canada in the Olympics?

7.  Should amnesty be granted to illegal residents, especially children, if they have been living here for many years and contributing to our society?

8.  On 20 July 2015, the Ontario Court of Appeal agreed with the federal Conservative government that ex-pats living abroad for more than five years could not vote in federal elections. Should all Canadian citizens have the right to vote?

# Clothing

## White Tops, Grey Bottoms

*by Bev Akerman*

1    Not long ago, my 15-year-old son received a detention. He had to stay after school not for inappropriate language or behaviour but because his shirttail was untucked. Although I usually allow room for some embellishment—and even, at times, truth-twisting—in his version of events, I believe him on this one. And that's because I've become acquainted with the Uniformists. In Quebec, they're among the parents, teachers, and school administrators on the governing boards that run the schools.

2    My three children, all in the public system, go to elementary and high schools with strict dress codes. I've never been completely in favour of all this uniformity. When I was in kindergarten in 1965–66, I had to wear a navy, box-pleated tunic to school. Not long after that, the school abandoned this requirement because, according to the then-latest thinking, wearing a uniform stifled self-expression and creativity. Now, the received wisdom is quite different: uniforms are supposed to "create an environment conducive to learning" and a sense of "community among students." Fair enough, I suppose, given the intense, competitive consumerism and cliquishness that plague many schools today.

3    Still, I have a number of questions, starting with: How much uniform is uniform enough? All my kids and all their schoolmates wear some variation of white shirts and grey flannel skirts or slacks. The school my 15-year-old attends also insists on a particular brand of shoe. I can understand requiring a certain style, but no one has yet explained to me why one make should be sanctioned. Meanwhile, both schools keep changing which style of shirt they deem acceptable. Oxford, T-shirt, polo— who can keep track? And the latest dictates: monograms on collars or pockets.

4    So why all the white and grey? Do we want our schools to be sensory deprivation zones? I see nothing wrong with letting a child wear a blue, pink, or yellow shirt as long as it's in the prescribed style. Besides, there's the environmental degradation that keeping white shirts white is causing—I'd never used bleach before my kids entered these schools!

5    I have other concerns. Our high school has a devoted cadre of volunteers who run the uniform store, generating tens of thousands of dollars a year. This money is put toward many things that really are the school board's responsibility: new musical

instruments, a fresh coat of paint more than once every seven years, equipment for classrooms, computers, libraries, etc. It also gets spent on extras: lavish graduation exercises, an unbelievable number of academic prizes for graduates, European exchange trips. So requiring students to wear uniforms, in effect, functions as an invisible school fee, over and above the taxes we all pay. Maybe if we were more up-front about this we'd demand more money from our governments, or at least that our school boards make better use of the existing funds.

6     The surprising truth is most parents I speak with feel the uniforms are a blessing: they are relieved to not have daily arguments about appropriate dress. As for the school officials, it seems one reason they've chosen a particular monogrammed shirt is that it's only available in adult sizes. The previously acceptable shirt was also available in children's sizes, which on some high school girls were extremely tight and skimpy.

7     But I question whether we are really doing our kids any favours by abdicating our authority to the school bureaucracy. Parents need to face head-on the challenges these uniforms try to cover over with grey flannel. If we have a problem with the downright sluttish dress of some of our daughters, tattoos, body piercing, or outlandish hair colour, we should deal with these things ourselves. Buck up, people! Learn to say, "No, that is not appropriate dress for school. When you are a responsible adult, you can choose whether or not to conform to society's expectations." No further explanation necessary.

8     Finally, I suspect the Uniformists have a secret motivation behind their fashion agenda: it makes public schools resemble, in the most superficial way, the exclusive private schools that pepper my Montreal neighbourhood. I simply do not share that aspiration. We should be proud that our kids go to public schools, where all races, religions, and socio-economic groups form a community—just like the real world they will eventually enter.

9     My kids love their schools. And I'm grateful for all the hard work the decimated custodial staff, devoted teachers, concerned administrators, and dynamic parent volunteers put in. I know—and so does my son—that by his age, he shouldn't be wandering about with his shirttail hanging out. But I wish the administration was more concerned with the originality of my kids' minds and less concerned about the conventionality of their dress. In the final analysis, shouldn't their education be more about content and less about form?

[7 March 2005]

## Notes

The terminology for different kinds of schools differs from country to country and even from province to province in Canada. History explains the split between public schools and separate schools. When Canada became a country in 1867, there were two main ethnic groups—English Protestants and French Catholics—so two public school systems were set up according to both language and religion.

As Canada became multicultural, some provinces were left with the legacy of the split system. In Ontario, for example, the schools serving English Protestants became the public system for students of all religions, with a further division into

French and English systems depending on linguistic area. The separate school system is essentially for those of the Catholic faith but not exclusively so. However, other religious groups do not have public school funding, although private schools may be established for specific religious groups.

Private schools in Ontario do not receive tax funding, so parents pay hefty school fees to send their children there. While private schools can be religion-oriented, many are elitist institutions, the kind referred to by Akerman as "exclusive" [8].

School uniforms are more commonly worn in private and separate schools than in the public system.

## Comprehension

1. What is the main argument in this article?
2. Why did Akerman's son receive a detention? What is her complaint about this?
3. What is the author's personal experience with uniforms?
4. What argument for wearing uniforms does she accept as valid?
5. What objections does she have to the colours of uniforms?
6. Explain her complaint about what the funds from selling uniforms are used for.
7. What objections does she have to parents letting the schools dictate what is acceptable clothing?
8. What does she see as an advantage of the public school system?

## Discussion

1. Do you think more Canadian schools should adopt uniforms? Why or why not? Discuss your experience with school uniforms.
2. Do Canadians dress too casually? Consider work as well as school.
3. What is your opinion about "tattoos, body piercing, or outlandish hair colour"?
4. Should religious schools be funded by the government? Why or why not?
5. Are private schools better than public schools? Discuss the advantages and disadvantages of both kinds of education.
6. Akerman refers to the "intense, competitive consumerism and cliquishness that plague many schools today" [2]. Discuss this statement. Is it true? How does consumerism and cliquishness manifest itself? What are the problems they cause?
7. Consider the educational necessities and luxuries Akerman lists in Paragraph 5. What do you think are the basics that should be covered in government funding? What are luxury items that could be paid for through parents' and students' fund-raising activities?

## Assignments

1. Write an essay for or against uniforms in high school.
2. In an essay, explain how appearance can affect a person's life. You may want to narrow the topic down to focus on one aspect such as clothing choice, physical features, or body art.
3. Write a classification essay explaining different cliques that existed in your high school.
4. Are teenagers today too materialistic? Write an essay explaining your view.

5. What rules and guidelines should parents set down for their teenagers' appearance? Explain your choices.
6. Write a paragraph (or essay) comparing business suits and school (or work) uniforms.

## Paraphrase and Summary

1. Paraphrase, in impersonal, academic English: "Buck up, people! Learn to say, 'No, that is not appropriate dress for school. When you are a responsible adult, you can choose whether or not to conform to society's expectations.' No further explanation necessary" [7].
2. Paraphrase: "But I wish the administration was more concerned with the originality of my kids' minds and less concerned about the conventionality of their dress. In the final analysis, shouldn't their education be more about content and less about form?" [9].

## Structure and Technique

This essay is less formal than an academic essay would be. It contains personal references, sentence fragments, sentences that begin with conjunctions, exclamation marks, overuse of questions, and conversational expressions. Identify examples of this type of usage, and explain what could be used instead in an academic essay.

This essay clearly gives the author's opinions. Notice the repeated use of *I*. She starts many of her points with phrases like "I question," "I suspect," and "I have other concerns." This emphasizes that she is disagreeing with the school policies.

The author moves from relating a specific incident that happened with her son to other problems. Explain how she gets to other problems. What are the logical connections?

## Language Study

### Definitions

Use the context to match each word to its definition:

| | |
|---|---|
| 1. embellishment, *n* [1] \_\_\_\_\_ | a) added details to a story that are not true but make it more interesting |
| 2. stifled, *v* [2] \_\_\_\_\_ | |
| 3. conducive, *adj* [2] \_\_\_\_\_ | b) to bother or annoy somebody or something |
| 4. plague, *v* [2] \_\_\_\_\_ | |
| 5. sanctioned, *v* [3] \_\_\_\_\_ | c) allowing something to happen easily |
| 6. deem, *v* [3] \_\_\_\_\_ | d) consider, think |
| 7. dictates, *n* [3] \_\_\_\_\_ | e) give up one's responsibility for something |
| 8. lavish, *adj* [5] \_\_\_\_\_ | |
| 9. abdicate, *v* [7] \_\_\_\_\_ | f) large, impressive, expensive |
| 10. superficial, *adj* [8] \_\_\_\_\_ | g) officially accepted or approved |
| | h) on the surface only, not deep |
| | i) rules, regulations |
| | j) stopped from happening or developing |

## Word Focus

### conventionality [9]

*Conventionality* is an example of a noun made from an adjective, *conventional*; another noun form is *convention*. Use your dictionary to find the different meanings of *convention*. Which meaning is the one that relates to the meaning of *conventionality*?

### cliquishness [2]

*Cliquishness* is a noun formed from an adjective (*cliquish*) formed from a noun (*clique*). Another adjective form is *cliquey*. *Clique* is usually pronounced "cleek" although some people pronounce it as "click." The word refers to a small, exclusive group of people and generally is used for the groups formed in high school. It has a negative connotation. The word is originally French (as you can tell by the *−que* ending).

Paragraph 5 has another French word for a group of people. Find the word, check its meaning, and determine how it is different from the word *clique*.

### uniform and dress

The word *uniform* is primarily an adjective meaning "of one form." It became a noun to refer to army uniforms (and then other uniforms) as a shortening of "uniform dress." Note that the noun *uniform* is countable, as in "he wears a uniform to work."

You won't find the word *Uniformist* in your dictionary. Akerman has essentially made the word up. It is a proper noun (it starts with a capital letter). In English, the *−ist* ending denotes a person who believes in something, so Akerman is using the word to describe those in favour of school uniforms and a strict dress code.

Note that even schools without uniforms can have a dress code. The term *dress code* (which is a compound noun) refers to clothing rules in general. For example, T-shirts printed with obscene slogans are not allowed in most schools' dress codes.

The word *dress* can be confusing. It is both a verb and a noun, and the noun has a different meaning depending on whether it is used as a countable or uncountable noun. Study these example sentences and the use of the word in the reading.

| | |
|---|---|
| She hates wearing a dress. | *dress* as a countable noun refers to a woman's article of clothing |
| She prefers casual dress. | uncountable use of *dress* to refer to clothing in general |
| The play was presented in modern dress. | uncountable use of *dress* to refer to clothing in general |
| I don't know how to dress for the party. | *dress* as a verb |
| He likes to dress up for special occasions. Ken refuses to dress up for the Halloween party. | *dress up* is a phrasal verb meaning to dress in special clothing such as formal clothes (the opposite is *dress down*) or to dress in a costume. |
| She'll be ready soon. She is just getting dressed. | *to get dressed* means to put on clothing |

See also the note on *clothes/clothing* on pages 348–49.

### Word Families

Fill in the chart with the corresponding parts of speech:

| NOUN | VERB | ADJECTIVE | ADVERB |
|---|---|---|---|
| creativity [2] | | | |
| | | competitive [2] | |
| variation [3] | | | |
| | | acceptable [3] | |
| | prescribe [4] | | |
| responsibility [5] | n/a | | |
| | | unbelievable [5] believable | |
| argument [6] | | | |
| | | exclusive [8] | |

### Collocations and Expressions

Discuss the meanings and usage of the following expressions:

> to receive/get/have a detention [1]
> to run a school (or other institutions) [1]
> to be in favour of something [2]
> to keep track of something [3]
> to see nothing wrong with something [4]
> money put toward something [5]
> to do somebody a favour [7]
> to face something head on [7]
> buck up [7] (informal, idiom)

### Sentence Structure Analysis

1. Identify the main subject and verb in the following sentences. Identify the modifiers—adjectives, adverbs, phrases, and clauses—and what they modify.
   a) "If we have a problem with the downright sluttish dress of some of our daughters, tattoos, body piercing or outlandish hair colour, we should deal with these things ourselves." [7]
   b) "Although I usually allow room for some embellishment—and even, at times, truth-twisting—in his version of events, I believe him on this one." [1]
2. Identify the part of speech of the words underlined in the following sentences. Explain how the sentence structure tells you the function of the word. Both words are more commonly used in another part of speech. Which one?

a) "...it makes public schools resemble, in the most superficial way, the exclusive private schools that <u>pepper</u> my Montreal neighbourhood." [8]
b) "I can understand requiring a certain style, but no one has yet explained to me why one <u>make</u> should be sanctioned." [3]
3. Akerman uses parenthetical dashes in Paragraphs 1, 3, 4, 8, and 9. Review the section Hyphens and Dashes," page 99, and then study how she uses them in her sentences.

## Why Arcade Fire Fans Should Rise to the Occasion and Say Yes to the Dress Code

*by Robert Everett-Green*

1   Dress codes used to be a way of indicating what kind of place or event you were going to. Now the term is almost a form of abuse, as shown by the ruckus raised when Arcade Fire said that people attending its forthcoming shows should come in "formal attire or costumes."

2   Nothing the Montreal band has done, said, written or recorded has had such sneeringly bad press, though from my years as a music writer I know that rock critics tend to resent any clothing more formal than a faded band T-shirt.

3   They're missing the point this time, which is that a dress code can create an occasion, by getting people to do something in harmony with a lot of others they don't know.

4   An audience that dresses for a show is an engaged audience, especially when the code is as open as "formal attire *or costumes*." The wonder isn't that Arcade Fire put out such a request, but that other bands don't.

5   We already have a massive public event with a dress code that is universally accepted. It's called Halloween, and I'll bet that a lot of people grousing about Arcade Fire's call for costumes didn't raise a murmur when the pumpkins were out, just a couple of weeks earlier.

6   Last weekend I attended another event at which everyone dressed to rule, and no one complained about it. WORN Fashion Journal's periodic Black Cat Ball is a black-and-white affair, and few people who go to the Toronto event fail to execute some riff on that simple contrast.

7   It would be a very different party if they didn't. The thought and effort that go into making your appearance a variation on a common theme give the ball the feeling of a creative social experience.

8   A lot of people at the Black Cat Ball dressed to stand out, which is contrary to the traditional purpose of dress codes, especially at the formal end of the spectrum. "Formal and semi-formal clothes leave less leeway for individuality, hence less room for error," says my 1954 copy of *Esquire Etiquette*. Dress codes were a way of defusing anxiety, not stirring it up.

9   When clothing started to become less formalized, a decade or so after that book was published, dress codes started to seem more like the universal dad's way of spoiling the fun. Restaurants that keep racks of jackets and ties to impose

on men who arrive without them are the worst thing that ever happened to dress codes.

10    The second worst is probably the kind of hedged terminology—"casual black tie," for example—that sets up a puzzling dissonance about what is expected.

11    But where a dress code has an organic origin or is well-established, it can be hard to displace. The Queen's annual race meeting at Ascot has been held since 1711, and is "the last large-scale court occasion with strictly enforced dress rules," writes Philip Mansel in his 2005 book, *Dressed to Rule: Royal and Court Costume from Louis XIV to Elizabeth II*.

12    Women at Ascot must wear "formal day dress with a hat"; for men, "black or grey morning dress with top hat is required." In 1968, these rules were relaxed so that men could wear a business suit, but the change was abandoned after two years, "since so few men wanted to wear it."

13    Presumably they felt that without formal dress, Ascot wouldn't be Ascot. What people wear is a key part of the event.

14    That's what Arcade Fire had in mind: to get its audience to help make the occasion with the clothes. "It just makes for a more fun carnival when we are all in it together," they said. A similar idea is visible at any goth or metal concert, where fans tend to dress within a carefully structured code without prompting.

15    From the outside, a uniform look among people who attach themselves to a kick-it-over sensibility in music can seem comical, but from the inside, it's part of the experience, part of being in the crowd and with the band.

16    Arcade Fire's error, apparently, was to ask. But what they're asking seems to me a great idea, and could make these concerts among their most satisfying.

17    Say yes to dress codes, rock fans. You have nothing to lose but your inhibitions.

[2 December 2013]

## Notes
Arcade Fire is an acclaimed rock band from Montreal.

Ascot refers to a town in Berkshire, England, where the Queen's special horse race, The Royal Ascot, occurs each year.

"Black-and-white affair" refers to formal parties where people wear only black and white.

## Comprehension
1. What did Arcade Fire do, and what was the reaction?
2. What is the thesis of this article?
3. What three specific examples does Everett-Green draw on to make his point about the value of dressing up?
4. Explain "the traditional purpose of dress codes" [8].

5. Explain the point the author is making in Paragraphs 9–11. Explain the distinction he is making when he disapproves of the restaurant "racks of jackets and ties" [9] and "hedged terminology" [10] but approves of "a dress code that has an organic origin or is well-established" [11].
6. How did Ascot change its dress code in 1968 and then in 1970?
7. Explain "Goth or metal concert" [14]. How do fans of these types of music tend to dress?

## Discussion

1. Do you agree with Everett-Green? Why or why not?
2. Are events like concerts and theatre presentations special enough to require less casual clothing? Discuss what you think is appropriate attire.
3. Do you think Canadians dress down too much?
4. What do you think is suitable work attire for an office? Are you in favour of casual Fridays? Why or why not?
5. What is your personal style of clothing? Why do you prefer such clothes?
6. Do you enjoy Halloween? Do you like wearing a costume? Explain why or why not.

## Assignments

1. Clothing terminology can be confusing. Much of it relies on minor distinctions. For instance, how does a tuxedo differ from a regular suit? Write a paragraph comparing two similar articles of clothing.
2. The Ascot horse races are famous events in England. Look up "Ascot dress code." Write a paragraph summarizing what the dress code specifies.
3. Halloween has become a major holiday in North America. Research its origins and customs and how it has changed over the past generation. Write an essay explaining the evolution of Halloween as a holiday.
4. Write a paragraph explaining "cosplay" (short for "costume play") among science fiction and fantasy fans.
5. Write a comparison essay on two different styles of music culture, such as goth, heavy metal, punk, or grunge.
6. Write an essay explaining the importance of dressing appropriately for events.

## Paraphrase and Summary

1. Paraphrase: "That's what Arcade Fire had in mind: to get its audience to help make the occasion with the clothes. 'It just makes for a more fun carnival when we are all in it together,' they said" [14]. Be sure to use indirect speech for the quotation.
2. Paraphrase: "a dress code can create an occasion, by getting people to do something in harmony with a lot of others they don't know" [3].
3. Write a one-paragraph summary of the article. Do not exceed 100 words.

## Structure and Technique

Note how the author takes a specific news story (criticism of Arcade Fire's request that concert-goers dress up) and uses it to make general statements about formal and special attire. This is a common journalistic technique, since a journalist's job is to relate news events to a wider context.

Everett-Green quotes the Arcade Fire pronouncement twice, in the first paragraph and in the fourth. But in the second quote, two words are italicized. What is the point of the italics?

## Language Study

### Definitions

Use the context to match each word to its definition:

| | |
|---|---|
| 1. dissonance, *n* [10] _____ | a) complain |
| 2. grouse, *v* [5] _____ | b) feelings of shyness |
| 3. inhibitions, *n* [17] _____ | c) happening in a slow and natural way |
| 4. leeway, *n* [8] _____ | d) improvisation; a variation on a theme |
| 5. murmur, *n* [5] _____ | e) in a way that shows no respect |
| 6. organic, *adj* [11] _____ | f) lack of agreement |
| 7. riff, *n* [6] _____ | g) noisy argument |
| 8. ruckus, *n* [1] _____ | h) say something in a soft, quiet voice |
| 9. sneeringly, *adv* [2] _____ | i) range of related qualities or ideas |
| 10. spectrum, *n* [8] _____ | j) room or freedom to change something |

### Word Focus

#### clothes/clothing

The words *cloth*, *clothes*, and *clothing* can be difficult for students to use correctly. *Clothes* and *clothing* are synonyms, but *clothes* is often more specific to the owner, and *clothing* is more general. Both words are nouns, but *clothes* is a plural form with no corresponding singular, and *clothing* is uncountable. *Cloth* refers to the material used to make clothes and is not the singular of *clothes*.

Fill in the correct word (more than one word may be possible):

a) After his growth spurt, all his _____ were too small.

b) Her wedding dress is made of some shiny _____, perhaps satin.

c) She was still wearing her work _____ when we met.

d) I need a damp _____ to clean this mess up.

e)  The immigrant family needed to buy winter _____.

f)  The _____ store has re-opened after the fire.

Here are some other words that refer to clothing: *apparel, attire, dress, garment, wear,* and *wardrobe.* Find out the difference in meaning and usage. For example, which words are countable? Write a sentence for each word. See also the note on the words *uniform* and *dress,* page 343.

### few [6]

The determiner *few* can be tricky to use correctly. First, it is used with countable nouns, while *little* is used with uncountable nouns. The determiners *much* and *many* show the same distinction.

Examine the following example sentences, and mark each noun as countable or uncountable:

> She has few friends and little interest in keeping them.
> A few students complained that there was too much homework.
> Many people attended the party, so it was crowded and there was too much noise.
> Because so many applications had to be processed, much time was lost.

The second characteristic to note is that *few* and *little* change in connotation if the indefinite article *a* is used before the determiners.

Note the differences in connotation:

| | |
|---|---|
| Few people attended the after-party. | focusing on the negative—not many |
| A few people attended the after-party. | focusing on the positive—some |
| I have little time now, so I'll have to do it later. | focusing on the negative—not enough |
| I have a little time now, so I can do it. | focusing on the positive—enough |
| Fortunately, few people were lost. | focusing on the positive—not many were lost |
| Unfortunately, a few people were lost. | focusing on the negative—some were lost |

Thus, "few people who go to the Toronto event fail to execute some riff on that simple contrast" [6] is saying that most people who attend wear the appropriate clothing. Note that you have two negative expressions here: "few people" and "fail to."

## Word Families
Fill in the chart with the corresponding parts of speech:

| NOUN | VERB | ADJECTIVE | ADVERB |
|---|---|---|---|
| abuse [1]* | | | |
| | accept [5] | | |
| | | | carefully [14] |
| | create [3] | | |
| | execute [6] | | n/a |
| | | formal [1] informal | |
| harmony [3] | | | |
| | indicate [1] | | |
| individuality [8] | | | |
| | resent [2] | | |
| variation [7] | | | |

*Note the pronunciation of the different parts of speech for this word.

## Collocations and Expressions
Discuss the meaning and usage of the following expressions:

to rise to the occasion [title]
used to be [1]
to raise a ruckus [1] [This was used in the passive voice in the article.]
bad press [2]
to miss the point (of something) [3]
(to do something) to rule [6]
to stand out [8]
to leave leeway for something [8]
room for error [8]
strictly enforced [11]
nothing to lose [17]

## Sentence Structure Analysis
1. Identify the main subject and verb in the following sentences. Identify the phrases and clauses, and determine what they modify.
   a) "Arcade Fire's error, apparently, was to ask." [16]

b) "The thought and effort that go into making your appearance a variation on a common theme give the ball the feeling of a creative social experience." [7]

c) "What people wear is a key part of the event." [13]

2. Explain the use of the modal verb *would* in the following sentences. What kinds of sentences are these? Paraphrase and explain each sentence.

a) "It would be a very different party if they didn't." [7]

b) "Presumably they felt that without formal dress, Ascot wouldn't be Ascot." [13]

## The Lure of Costumes

Dressing up in costumes is more than just child's play. Most cultures have traditions such as theatre, masquerades, and pageants. In North America, Halloween has become a billion-dollar industry, mostly driven by adults' costumes and parties. In addition, the popularity of superhero comic books has led to conventions where many fans indulge in "cosplay"—dressing up as their favourite fantasy character. Wearing costumes has become a widespread activity because it allows people to extend their hobbies, take on new identities, and garner attention.

Instead of just reading fantasy books and watching movies or television shows, fans of different genres can go a step further into actually acting out life in their favourite world. Wearing replica uniforms, history buffs can take part in battle re-enactments. The Society of Creative Anachronism allows people to pretend to live in medieval times. Fans of the television show *The Walking Dead* can sport ghoulish makeup and lurch down the street in a zombie walk. Live Action Role Play (LARP) allows people to play games in character, perhaps imagining a post-apocalyptic world. Dressing up adds another dimension to the fans' enjoyment of their fantasy.

People are also attracted to costumes because they can become someone different from their ordinary selves. The clothing, along with masks and makeup, not only changes a person's appearance but also permits him or her to shed inhibitions. Actors point out that costuming is an important part of their craft, that they can assume the character's traits more readily as soon as they get dressed and made up. Shy people, especially, find it easier to interact with others if they are wearing a mask or makeup. They may have dull everyday jobs, but they can become superheroes when they go to conventions. Costume-wearing becomes escapism.

Costumes also offer people a chance to be in the limelight. Other people clamour to take selfies with costumed characters. For those in costume, there is a great feeling in being noticed, in being the centre of attention, in being worthy of a shared moment with strangers. Moreover, since many of the costumes are homemade, the wearers get to show off and take pride in their handiwork. Costume competitions allow the wearers to bask in admiration and even profit from prizes. Wearing a costume can even lead to a way to make a living. Costumed characters have become part of the landscape in places such as Times Square where they get paid for posing for photographs with tourists.

Wearing costumes has always been part of human history, but its recent popularity shows its range of possibilities and the benefits wearers garner from the outfits. The trend shows no signs of abating. It is fed by an entire industry, spanning the manufacture of costumes to the blockbuster movies centring on comic book heroes and villains. Modern adults do not want to abandon their toys as they grow up.

## Additional Topics

1. Choose an item of clothing that has significance in a religion, such as a nun's habit, the yarmulke, the hijab, the niqab, the burqa, or the Sikh turban. Explain the significance of the item and any controversy surrounding it.
2. Is women's clothing oversexualized? Discuss.
3. In today's marketplace, it is difficult to find gender-neutral clothing and toys. Girls are supposed to wear pink and play with dolls. Boys' clothes are festooned with trucks and robots. Even toys like building blocks are divided into girls' and boys' versions. In an essay, discuss the causes or effects of such marketing.
4. Write a paragraph describing your best Halloween costume.
5. Watch the movie *The Devil Wears Prada*. Write a review of the movie. Or write an essay agreeing or disagreeing with the movie's central argument about the importance of the fashion industry.

# Fiction Readings

## Why My Mother Can't Speak English

*by Garry Engkent*

1   My mother is 70 years old. Widowed for five years now, she lives alone in her own house except for the occasions when I come home to tidy her household affairs. She has been in *gum san* for the past 30 years. She clings to the old-country ways so much that today she astonishes me with this announcement:

2   "I want to get my citizenship," she says as she slaps down the *Dai Pao*, "before they come and take away my house."

3   "Nobody's going to do that. This is Canada."

4   "So everyone says," she retorts, "but did you read what the *Dai Pao* said? Ah, you can't read Chinese. The government is cutting back on old age pensions. Anybody who hasn't got citizenship will lose everything. Or worse."

5   "The *Dai Pao* can't even typeset accurately," I tell her. Sometimes I worry about the information Mother receives from that bi-weekly community newspaper. "Don't worry—the Ministry of Immigration won't send you back to China."

6   "Little you know," she snaps back. "I am old, helpless, and without citizenship. Reasons enough. Now get me citizenship. Hurry!"

7   "Mother, getting citizenship papers is not like going to the bank to cash in your pension cheque. First, you have to—"

8   "Excuses, my son, excuses. When your father was alive—"

9   "Oh, Mother, not again! You throw that at me every—"

10   "—made excuses, too." Her jaw tightens. "If you can't do this little thing for your own mother, well, I will just have to go and beg your cousin to . . ."

11   Every time I try to explain about the ways of the *fan gwei* she thinks I do not want to help her.

12   "I'll do it, okay? Just give me some time."

13   "That's easy for you," Mother snorts. "You're not 70 years old. You're not going to lose your pension. You're not going to lose your house. Now, how much *lai-shi* will this take?"

14      After all these years in *gum san* she cannot understand that you don't give government officials *lai-shi*, the traditional Chinese money-gift given to persons who do things for you.

15      "That won't be necessary," I tell her. "And you needn't go to my cousin."

16      Mother picks up the *Dai Pao* again and says: "Why should I beg at the door of a village cousin when I have a son who is a university graduate?"

17      I wish my father were alive. Then he would be doing this. But he is not here, and as a dutiful son, I am responsible for the welfare of my widowed mother. So I take her to the Citizenship Court.

18      There are several people from the Chinese community waiting there. Mother knows a few of the Chinese women, and she chats with them. My cousin is there, too.

19      "I thought your mother already got her citizenship," he says to me. "Didn't your father—"

20      "No, he didn't."

21      He shakes his head sadly. "Still, better now than never. That's why I'm getting these people through."

22      "So they've been reading the *Dai Pao*."

23      He gives me a quizzical look, so I explain to him, and he laughs.

24      "You are the new generation," he says. "You didn't live long enough in *hon san*, the sweet land, to understand the fears of the old. You can't expect the elderly to renounce all attachments to China for the ways of the *fan gwei*, white devils. How old is she, 70 now? Much harder."

25      "She woke me up this morning at six and Citizenship Court doesn't open until 10."

26      The doors of the court finally open, and Mother motions me to hurry. We wait in line for a while.

27      The clerk distributes applications and tells me the requirements. Mother wants to know what the clerk is saying so half the time I translate for her.

28      The clerk suggests that we see one of the liaison officers.

29      "Your mother has been living in Canada for the past 30 years, and she still can't speak English?"

30      "It happens," I tell the liaison officer.

31      "I find it hard to believe that—not one word?"

32      "Well, she understands some restaurant English," I tell her. "You know, French fries, pork chops, soup, and so on. And she can say a few words."

33      "But will she be able to understand the judge's questions? The interview with the judge, as you know, is a very important part of the citizenship procedure. Can she read the booklet? What does she know about Canada?"

34      "So you don't think my mother has a chance?"

35      "The requirements are that the candidate must be able to speak either French or English, the two official languages of Canada. The candidate must be able to pass an oral interview with the citizenship judge, and then he or she must be able to recite the oath of allegiance—"

36      "My mother needs to speak English," I conclude for her.

37    "Look, I don't mean to be rude, but why didn't your mother learn English when she first came over?"

38    I have not been translating this conversation, and Mother, annoyed and agitated, asks me what is going on. I tell her there is a slight problem.

39    "What problem?" Mother opens her purse, and I see her taking a small red envelope—*lai-shi*—I quickly cover her hand.

40    "What is going on?" the liaison officer demands.

41    "Nothing," I say hurriedly. "Just a cultural misunderstanding, I assure you."

42    My mother rattles off some indignant words, and I snap back in Chinese: "Put that away! The woman won't understand, and we'll be in a lot of trouble."

43    The officer looks confused, and I realize an explanation is needed.

44    "My mother was about to give you a money-gift as a token of appreciation for what you are doing for us. I was afraid you might misconstrue it as a bribe. We have no intention of doing that."

45    "I'm relieved to hear that."

46    We conclude the interview, and I take Mother home. Still clutching the application, Mother scowls at me.

47    "I didn't get my citizenship papers. Now I will lose my old age pension. The government will ship me back to China. My old bones will lie there while your father's will be here. What will happen to me?"

48    How can I teach her to speak the language when she is too old to learn, too old to want to learn? She resists anything that is *fan gwei*. She does everything the Chinese way. Mother spends much time staring blankly at the four walls of her house. She does not cry. She sighs and shakes her head. Sometimes she goes about the house touching her favourite things.

49    "This is all your dead father's fault," she says quietly. She turns to the photograph of my father on the mantle. Daily, she burns incense, pours fresh cups of fragrant tea, and spreads dishes of his favourite fruits in front of the framed picture as is the custom. In memory of his passing, she treks two miles to the cemetery to place flowers by his headstone, to burn ceremonial paper money, and to talk to him. Regularly, rain or shine, or even snow, she does these things. Such love, such devotion, now such vehemence. Mother curses my father, her husband, in his grave.

50    When my mother and I emigrated from China, she was 40 years old, and I, five. My father was already a well-established restaurant owner. He put me in school and Mother in the restaurant kitchen, washing dishes and cooking strange foods like hot dogs, hamburgers, and French fries. She worked seven days a week from six in the morning until 11 at night. This lasted for 25 years, almost to the day of my father's death.

51    The years were hard on her. The black-and-white photographs show a robust woman; now I see a withered, frail, white-haired old woman, angry, frustrated with the years, and scared of losing what little material wealth she has to show for the toil in *gum san*, the golden mountain.

52    "I begged him," Mother says. "But he would either ignore my pleas or say: 'What do you need to know English for? You're better off here in the kitchen. Here

you can talk to the others in our own tongue. English is far too complicated for you. How old are you now? Too old to learn a new language. Let the young speak *fan gwei*. All you need is to understand the orders from the waitresses. Anyway, if you need to know something, the men will translate for you. I am here; I can do your talking for you.'"

53    As a conscientious boss of the young male immigrants, my father would force them out of the kitchen and into the dining room. "The kitchen is no place for you to learn English. All you do is speak Chinese in here. To survive in *gum san*, you have to speak English, and the only way you can do that is to wait on tables and force yourselves to speak English with the customers. How can you get your families over here if you can't talk to the Immigration officers in English?"

54    A few of the husbands who had the good fortune to bring their wives over to Canada hired a retired school teacher to teach a bit of English to their wives. Father discouraged Mother from going to those once-a-week sessions.

55    "That old woman will get rich, doing nothing. What have these women learned? *Fan gwei* ways—make-up, lipstick, smelly perfumes, fancy clothes—like whores. Once she gets through with them, they won't be Chinese women any more—and they certainly won't be white, either."

56    Some of the husbands heeded the words of the boss, for he was older than they and had been in the white devils' land longer. These wives stayed at home and tended the children, or they worked in the restaurant kitchen, washing dishes and cooking *fan gwei* foods, and talking in Chinese about the land and the life they were forced to leave behind.

57    "He was afraid that I would leave him. I depended on him for everything. I could not go anywhere by myself. He drove me to work, and he drove me home. He only taught me to print my name so that I could sign anything he wanted me to, bank cheques, legal documents . . ."

58    Perhaps I am not Chinese enough any more to understand why my mother would want to take in the sorrow, the pain, and the anguish and then to recount them every so often.

59    Once I was presumptuous enough to ask her why she would want to remember in such detail. She said the memories didn't hurt any more. I did not tell her that her reminiscences cut me to the quick. Her only solace now is to be listened to.

60    My father wanted more sons, but she was too old to give him more. One son was not enough security he needed for old age. "You smell of stale perfume," she would say to him after he had driven the waitresses home. Or, to me, she would say: "A second mother will not treat you so well, you know," and, "Would you like another mother at home?" Even at that tender age, I knew that in China a husband could take a second wife. I told her that I didn't need another mother, and she would nod her head.

61    When my father died five years ago, she cried and cried. "Don't leave me in this world. Let me die with you."

62    Grief-stricken, she would not eat for days. She was so weak from hunger that I feared she wouldn't be able to attend the funeral. At his graveside, she chanted

over and over a dirge, commending his spirit to the next world and begging the goddess of mercy to be kind to him. By custom, she set his picture on the mantel and burned incense in front of it daily. And we would go to the cemetery often. There she would arrange fresh flowers and talk to him in the gentlest way.

63    Often she would warn me: "The world of the golden mountain is so strange, *fan gwei* improprieties, and customs. The white devils will have you abandon your own aged mother to some old age home to rot away and die unmourned. If you are here long enough, they will turn your head until you don't know who you are, what you are—Chinese."

64    My mother would convert the months and the days into the Chinese lunar calendar. She would tell me about the seasons and the harvests and festivals in China. We did not celebrate any *fan gwei* holidays.

65    My mother sits here at the table, fingering the booklet from the Citizenship Court. For thirty-some years, my mother did not learn the English language, not because she was not smart enough, not because she was too old to learn, and not because my father forbade her, but because she feared that learning English would change her Chinese soul. She only learned enough English to survive in the restaurant kitchen.

66    Now, Mother wants *gum san* citizenship.

67    "Is there no hope that I will be given it?" she asks.

68    "There is always a chance," I tell her. "I'll hand in the application."

69    "I should have given that person the *lai-shi*," Mother says obstinately.

70    "Maybe I should teach you some English," I retort. "You have about six months before the oral interview."

71    "I am 70 years old," she says. "*Lai-shi* is definitely much easier."

72    My brief glimpse into mother's heart is over, and it has taken so long to come about. I do not know whether I understand my aged mother any better now. Despite my mother's constant instruction, there is too much *fan gwei* in me.

73    The booklet from the Citizenship Court lies, unmoved, on the table, gathering dust for weeks. She has not mentioned citizenship again with the urgency of that particular time. Once in a while, she would say: "They have forgotten me. I told you they don't want old Chinese women as citizens."

74    Finally, her interview date is set. I try to teach her some ready-made phrases, but she forgets them.

75    "You should not sigh so much. It is bad for your health," Mother observes.

76    On the day of her examination, I accompany her into the judge's chamber. I am more nervous than my mother.

77    Staring at the judge, my mother remarks: "*Noi yren.*" The judge shows interest in what my mother says, and I translate it: "She says you're a woman."

78    The judge smiles "Yes. Is that strange?"

79    "If she is going to examine me," Mother tells me, "I might as well start packing for China. Sell my house. Dig up your father's bones, I'll take them back with me."

80    Without knowing what my mother said, the judge reassures her. "This is just a formality. Really. We know that you obviously want to be part of our Canadian society. Why else would you have gone through all this trouble? We want to

81      welcome you as a new citizen, no matter what race, nationality, religion, or age. And we want you to be proud—as a new Canadian."

81      Six weeks have passed since the interview with the judge. Mother receives a registered letter telling her to come in three weeks' time to take part in the oath of allegiance ceremony.

82      With patient help from the same judge, my mother recites the oath and becomes a Canadian citizen after 30 years in *gum san*.

83      "How does it feel to be Canadian?" I ask.

84      "In China, this is the eighth month, the season of harvest." Then she adds: "The *Dai Pao* says that old age pension cheques will be increased by nine dollars next month."

85      As we walk home on this bright autumn morning, my mother clutches her piece of paper. Citizenship. She says she will go up to the cemetery and talk to my father this afternoon. She has something to tell him.

[June 1985]

## Notes

This story is autobiographical fiction. It is based on true events, but these events have been dramatized in the story-telling.

Second-generation immigrants are those born or raised in Canada, like the son in the story. Many have a first language that is different from their mother tongue. (*Mother tongue* refers to the language first learned and still understood, usually their parents' native language. *First language* means the language the person is most comfortable speaking.) Most second-generation immigrants become very comfortable in English or French, especially as they progress through their schooling in that language. They do not develop their ability to speak their mother tongue in the same way. For example, they might be able to talk about history and do math in English but only talk about household concerns in their native language. A common situation is that the immigrant parents speak their mother tongue to their children, but the children answer back in English or French. In this story, the son cannot read Chinese but does speak to his mother in Chinese.

Unlike other ethnic groups, the Chinese were not encouraged to establish families in Canada. While the men were welcome as workers, Canadian immigration policies such as the Head Tax (1885–1923) and the Chinese Exclusion Act (1923–47) prevented them from bringing over family members. This is why the father in the story was in Canada before his wife and son.

## Comprehension

1. Why does the mother want to get her citizenship?
2. Describe the process by which the mother gained her citizenship.
3. Why did the mother want to use *lai-shi*? Why did the son not want her to do that?

4. What was the father's attitude toward immigrants learning English? What double standard did he have?

5. What reasons contribute to the mother's not learning English? What is the most important reason she does not learn?

6. Explain the author's reference to the mother's "Chinese soul."

7. What is ironic about the last bit of dialogue in the story—the last exchange between the mother and son?

8. How does the writer make the story humorous?

## Discussion

1. How realistic is the portrayal of the mother? Do you know any immigrants like her?

2. Are the mother's fears justified? Why or why not?

3. What is the most important factor in learning a second language? Could the mother have overcome her age and her husband's disapproval had she really wanted to?

4. What are some of the problems faced by immigrant women learning English?

5. What kinds of conflicts are common between first- and second-generation immigrants?

6. Discuss the immigration and citizenship procedures in Canada. Use examples of the experience of friends, family, or yourself.

7. Different cultures have different rituals for mourning the dead. Discuss different funeral and mourning customs you are familiar with. For instance, in Western cultures, black is the colour of mourning, while in some Asian cultures, white is traditionally worn.

## Assignments

1. What factors determine how well an immigrant assimilates? Explain these factors in an essay.

2. What factors determine how much a second-generation immigrant will keep his or her mother tongue? Explain these factors in an essay.

3. Research the history of the Chinese in Canada (or that of another immigrant group). Write a report on the factors that played a part in their settlement. Alternatively, write an essay comparing two immigrant groups.

4. Write an essay explaining the process of becoming a Canadian citizen.

5. What are the rights and responsibilities of Canadian citizenship? Is Canadian citizenship too easy to obtain? Should dual citizenship be allowed? Write an essay on one of these issues or another issue related to Canadian citizenship.

6. Review the information given in *Discover Canada: The Rights and Responsibilities of Citizenship*, the booklet given to people studying to become citizens (available on the website of Citizenship and Immigration Canada). Is it a good introduction to Canada? What do you think of the coverage? Is there any other information you think should be included in the booklet?

## Paraphrase and Summary

1. Paraphrase: "Perhaps I am not Chinese enough anymore to understand why my mother would want to take in the sorrow, the pain, and the anguish and then to recount them every so often" [58].
2. Paraphrase: "She turns to the photograph of my father on the mantle. Daily, she burns incense, pours fresh cups of fragrant tea, and spreads dishes of his favourite fruits in front of the framed picture as is the custom. In memory of his passing, she treks two miles to the cemetery to place flowers by his head-stone, to burn ceremonial paper money, and to talk to him. Regularly, rain or shine, or even snow, she does these things" [49].
3. Write a summary of the story. Do not exceed 150 words.

## Structure and Technique

### First Person, Unnamed Narrator

This story is told in first-person narration: *I.* The narrator's name is not given. Note that this story is fiction, so the *I* is a character, and you cannot refer to him as "Garry Engkent." Instead, you can call him "the son" or "the narrator."

In first-person narration, the *I* tells the story from the *I* perspective, not from a general one. The reader gets only the narrator's way of seeing or interpreting an action and must trust that what the narrator says is valid and true. Often, the reader identifies with the narrator.

### Present-Tense Narration

Although most stories are told in the simple past tense, the use of the present tense brings a sense of immediacy. How effective is the use of the present tense in this story? Compare this to the past-tense narration used in pages 363–64 the other readings in this unit.

### Dialogue

Much of this story is told in dialogue. Look at the punctuation used and the wording that sets up the speech. When a new speaker begins, there is a new paragraph.

### Use of Foreign Words

Words from a foreign language that are not a standard part of English are generally printed in italics. Engkent uses words in Chinese to add flavour to the story. The author knows that his audience will not know what these words mean; even Chinese-speaking readers would be unlikely to know this particular dialect. Therefore, he gives the readers many clues to help them figure out the meaning.

The most common technique is to put the translation in apposition. This means it is set off by commas. For example, in "for the toil in *gum san*, the golden mountain" [51], Engkent shows that the translation of *gum san* is "golden mountain," which is the way the Chinese referred to Canada and the United States. (The term reflects the fact that the first Chinese came to North America as part of the gold rush.)

Context is also important for understanding the meaning of the words. Note how the meaning of *Dai Pao* gradually becomes clearer. The first clue is that it is something the mother "slaps down" [2]. The capital letters show that it is a proper noun, the official name of something. Finally, the meaning is given as "that bi-weekly community newspaper."

Look at all the Chinese words in the text, and find the clues the author gives you. Figure out what each word means. Sometimes the translation or definition does not come with the first use of the word in the story.

## Language Study

### Definitions

Use the context to match each word to its definition:

| | |
|---|---|
| 1. astonish, *v* [1] _____ | a) answer back angrily |
| 2. clutch, *v* [46] _____ | b) emotional comfort |
| 3. glimpse, *n* [72] _____ | c) hold tightly |
| 4. heed, *v* [56] _____ | d) memories |
| 5. misconstrue, *v* [44] _____ | e) misunderstand |
| 6. obstinately, *adv* [69] _____ | f) pay attention to, follow advice |
| 7. reminiscences, *n* [59] _____ | g) quick look at something |
| 8. retort, *v* [70] _____ | h) something that represents a feeling or event |
| 9. robust, *adj* [51] _____ | i) strong and healthy |
| 10. solace, *n* [59] _____ | j) stubbornly |
| 11. token, *n* [44] _____ | k) surprise, shock |
| 12. trek, *v* [49] _____ | m) take a long, hard walk; hike |

### Word Focus

#### welfare [17]

The noun *welfare* has the same parts as the word *farewell*. The verb *to fare* means to progress and get on, so *welfare* means the well-being of someone. Note that in Canada we also use the word *welfare* as a short form for "welfare benefits," the government payments people receive if they cannot earn their own living. We say someone is "on welfare." Check the dictionary for other meanings of the word *fare* and its homophone *fair*.

#### grief-stricken [62]

The compound adjective *grief-stricken* has a variation of the past participle of the verb *strike*, which is also used in *poverty-stricken* and *panic-stricken*. The more commonly used past participle is seen in such compounds as *awe-struck* and *thunderstruck*. See if you can find other compounds. For example, *horror-struck* and *terror-stricken* are mentioned in the language note for *horrified* on pages 365–66.

#### conscientious [53]

The words *conscience* (n) and *conscious* (adj) are sometimes confused because they sound almost the same and both concern mental states. Your conscience is the voice inside your head that tells you whether something is right or wrong. If you listen to your conscience and do the right thing, you can be considered *conscientious* (adj). If you are conscious, it means you are awake and aware. Related words include *unconscious* (adj), *subconscious* (n), and *consciousness* (n). Use your dictionary to find definitions, example sentences, and other uses of the words.

## Word Families

Fill in the chart with the corresponding parts of speech:

| NOUN | VERB | ADJECTIVE | ADVERB |
|---|---|---|---|
| appreciation [44] | | | |
| | explain [11] | | n/a |
| | | | finally [26] |
| formality [80] | | | |
| | | helpless [6] | |
| information [5] | | | |
| instruction [72] | | | |
| security [60] | | | |
| | suggest [28] | | |
| | tighten [10] | | |

## Collocations and Expressions

Discuss each of the following expressions. How clear is the meaning? Is it idiomatic? How useful is the expression?

>  to cut back on [4]
>  little you know [6]
>  to have a chance (at something) [34]
>  to stare blankly at something [48]
>  to be better off [52]
>  to cut somebody to the quick [59]
>  to gather dust [73]

## Sentence Structure Analysis

Identify the main subject and verb in the following sentences. Identify the modifiers—adjectives, adverbs, phrases, and clauses—and what they modify.

1. "There are several people from the Chinese community waiting there." [18]

2. "As a conscientious boss of the young male immigrants, my father would force them out of the kitchen and into the dining room." [53]

3. "The booklet from the Citizenship Court lies, unmoved, on the table, gathering dust for weeks." [73]

## Soap and Water

*by Urs Frei*

1    The other day a man walked into the store, carrying a cat. I don't know which I noticed first, the cat or how the man was crying. The cat was his, I guess. Its legs were mangled, and blood was dripping through his fingers. He was crying so hard he didn't notice that this wasn't a vet hospital anymore.

2    "I need you to put my cat to sleep," he said.

3    There he stood, dripping onto the carpet. We had three customers in the store. Of course they were staring.

4    "The vet moved out last month, sir," I said. I came around the counter to show my concern. But also to move him out of there. You have to understand, we'd only been open a month. "We sell computers."

5    The man was silent. The cat was crying low, strange cries.

6    "Where's the vet?" he said.

7    "Where'd that vet go?" I said. Robert, one of my sales reps, was staring back at me. It was a pointless question, actually, because I knew the vet hadn't moved anywhere near. I was pretty sure there was no vet within a mile. "Have a look in the phone book," I told him.

8    The man was sobbing again. I couldn't decide if the best thing to do would be to ask him to step outside or if this would antagonize the customers. I had a closer look at him. He had earrings in both ears. His hair was shaved on the sides of his head. He was wearing a leather jacket, and it was hard to say for sure, but he seemed handsome, the kind of man who would talk about his successes with women. What was he doing crying about a cat?

9    The stock boy had heard the cat and come in from the stock room. He wasn't supposed to be in the store.

10    Robert said, "There's a vet over on K- road."

11    K- road was the other side of town.

12    "Should I call them?" he said. "They have a pet ambulance, it says here."

13    "Call the pet ambulance," I said. "Get that pet ambulance over here."

14    The stock boy wasn't a boy at all. He was a Mexican man, about 40 years old, named Ricardo, who spoke almost no English. He was wearing dirty blue jeans and a blue work shirt. Also, he wasn't legal. He was taking off his shirt. I thought, Lord in heaven—Lord in heaven. There was that cat, dripping on my new carpet, and there was the stock boy, taking off his shirt.

15    He walked up to the man, spreading the shirt on his palms, and took the cat, and wrapped it in the shirt. The man said nothing. Ricardo turned his back so that no one could see, but everyone heard the snap as he broke the cat's neck. The cat

went silent. One of the customers, a lady, made a horrified sound. Then Ricardo, with his head bowed, handed the cat back, along with his shirt.

16     I was glad I'd got that in about the pet ambulance. You have to understand that this was before I learned that blood comes out easily with just soap and water. It was that lady customer who told me.

———————————————

[Autumn 1997]

## Notes

The stock boy "wasn't legal," which means he didn't have proper status from the immigration department.

## Comprehension

1. Describe the narrator: male or female? age? occupation?
2. Is the narrator portrayed as an admirable character? Support your answer.
3. What is the setting for the story? Why is this significant? Could this story happen somewhere else with the same impact?
4. Why did the man with the cat come into the store?
5. What do you think had happened to the cat? Support your answer.
6. Explain the narrator's description of the man with the cat. What does the way the man is described say about the narrator?
7. What is the narrator concerned about?
8. What is the narrator apologizing for in the last paragraph?
9. Compare the narrator and the stock boy. How do their different backgrounds explain their reactions?
10. What is the significance of the title?

## Discussion

1. What would you do in this situation?
2. Could you competently kill an animal if necessary? Could you, for example, kill a chicken, clean it, and prepare it for dinner? Could your parents do it? Could your grandparents? What has changed? Does this matter?
3. Do Canadians care too much about their pets? Consider, for example, people who have severe allergies and yet refuse to get rid of their pets.
4. How far would you go to save the life of a pet? Would you pay thousands of dollars for surgery, for example?
5. How does the narrator fit the stereotype of a computer expert?
6. What is this story saying about modern society? Is this a valid criticism?

## Assignments

1. Write an essay explaining the criteria that should be considered for euthanasia for animals and/or humans.
2. Have Canadians become too urbanized, like the computer store owner? Have we lost touch with nature? Write an essay explaining the problems this causes. Or write an essay arguing that it does not matter.

3. Take one of the controversial issues surrounding animal rights, and discuss it in an essay. For example, how should farming practices be changed to be more humane? Or are vegans going too far?

4. Consider the problems of illegal immigrants. Canadians rely on them for cheap labour, but Canadian immigration favours educated immigrants, many of whom have trouble getting jobs that suit their education level. Some people argue that illegal immigrants should be given amnesty since they have established themselves here, often having children born in Canada and therefore Canadian citizens. Yet they live in an underground economy and cannot avail themselves of simple services such as health care and education. Suggest a possible solution, and discuss it in an essay.

## Paraphrase and Summary

1. In one short paragraph, summarize what happens in the story.
2. Write a one-sentence description of each character, paraphrasing what the narrator says.

## Structure and Technique

1. The author has used first-person narration, with an unnamed narrator. What is the effect of this type of narration in this story?
2. The author gives us the narrator's internal dialogue. How does this reveal the narrator's personality?
3. The story hinges on an implied contrast between the narrator and the stock boy. Should this contrast have been made more explicit?

## Language Study

### Word Focus

#### vet [1], rep [7]

Both *rep* and *vet* are short forms of longer words. What does each word stand for in the story? What other words use the same short forms?

#### legal [14]

One of the sentences describing Ricardo says, "he wasn't legal." This refers to his immigration status. The terminology for immigrant status varies, and the connotation can be quite different depending on the term used. For example, *illegal immigrant* is more negative than *undocumented immigrant*. Moreover, Americans use the term *alien*. Discuss the different terminology describing immigration and citizenship status.

As for the adjective *legal*, what other words are in its word family? What are the noun, verb, and adverb forms? What word is the opposite of *legal*?

#### horrified [15]

From the noun *horror*, we have the adjectives *horrific*, *horrible*, *horrendous*, *horrid*, and *horror-struck* (or *horror-stricken*) and the corresponding adverbs *horribly* and *horrendously.* The adjectives *horrified* and *horrifying* are participles of the verb *horrify.* All have come down from a Latin verb which meant "to tremble."

Fill in the blanks with an appropriate word from this word family:

a)  Even though she did not believe in ghosts, she found the spooky atmosphere in the old house truly _____ .

b)  The bystanders were _____ by the brutal attack.

c)  At Halloween, all the television stations show _____ movies.

d)  That is a _____ colour.

e)  The collision was _____ . It left several people with severe injuries.

Using these sentences as examples and referring to a dictionary when necessary, discuss the different uses of these words. For instance, which words can be used to describe the person feeling the emotion, and which words can be used to describe what is causing the feeling? Which adjectives seem stronger in meaning?

The word family for *terror,* a synonym of *horror,* shows a similar pattern of forms and usage: the verb *terrify* (with the participles *terrified* and *terrifying*); adjectives *terrific, terrible, terror-struck* (or *terror-stricken*); and the adverb *terribly. Terror* has also spawned *terrorize, terrorist,* and *terrorism.* However, one of the words derived from *terror* has changed meaning completely and is now used to describe something that is good. Which word is it? Discuss any other differences in meaning between corresponding words in the two families. Which corresponding synonyms from *terror* can be used in the blanks of the example sentences above? What other synonyms could be used?

## Connotation

The man wants someone to "put my cat to sleep" [2]. This is an example of a euphemism. When people talk about their pets, they use this expression. The man would not ask someone to "kill" his cat or "put it to death."

There are many expressions to refer to killing and dying. Some are euphemisms; some are idioms. Some terms can be used to refer to animals; some are used for people.

Here are some examples of words and expressions. Discuss these and other terms you are familiar with.

1.    euthanasia, mercy killing, to pull the plug, to put down
2.    kill, murder, assassinate, foul play, manslaughter
3.    homicide, suicide, genocide, patricide
4.    die, pass away, kick the bucket, be six feet under

## Sentence Structure Analysis

1.  Explain the use of parallel structure in the sentence:

> "There was that cat, dripping on my new carpet, and there was the stock boy, taking off his shirt." [14]

2. In the sentence below there are four verb forms, one different from the others. Identify the subject and the main verbs. Explain the function of the other verb form. How else could the sentence have been structured? Which word is not necessary grammatically? Explain the use of the commas.

> "He walked up to the man, spreading the shirt on his palms, and took the cat, and wrapped it in the shirt." [15]

## Tempest in the School Teapot

Excerpt from Chapter XV, *Anne of Green Gables*, by L.M. Montgomery

1  Mr. Phillips was back in the corner explaining a problem in algebra to Prissy Andrews, and the rest of the scholars were doing pretty much as they pleased, eating green apples, whispering, drawing pictures on their slates, and driving crickets, harnessed to strings, up and down the aisle. Gilbert Blythe was trying to make Anne Shirley look at him and failing utterly, because Anne was at that moment totally oblivious, not only of the very existence of Gilbert Blythe but of every other scholar in Avonlea school and of Avonlea school itself. With her chin propped on her hands and her eyes fixed on the blue glimpse of the Lake of Shining Waters that the west window afforded, she was far away in a gorgeous dreamland, hearing and seeing nothing save her own wonderful visions.

2  Gilbert Blythe wasn't used to putting himself out to make a girl look at him and meeting with failure. She should look at him, that red-haired Shirley girl with the little pointed chin and the big eyes that weren't like the eyes of any other girl in Avonlea school.

3  Gilbert reached across the aisle, picked up the end of Anne's long red braid, held it out at arm's length, and said in a piercing whisper:

4  "Carrots! Carrots!"

5  Then Anne looked at him with a vengeance!

6  She did more than look. She sprang to her feet, her bright fancies fallen into cureless ruin. She flashed one indignant glance at Gilbert from eyes whose angry sparkle was swiftly quenched in equally angry tears.

7  "You mean, hateful boy!" she exclaimed passionately. "How dare you!"

8  And then—Thwack! Anne had brought her slate down on Gilbert's head and cracked it—slate not head—clear across.

9  Avonlea school always enjoyed a scene. This was an especially enjoyable one. Everybody said, "Oh" in horrified delight. Diana gasped. Ruby Gillis, who was inclined to be hysterical, began to cry. Tommy Sloane let his team of crickets escape him altogether while he stared open-mouthed at the tableau.

10  Mr. Phillips stalked down the aisle and laid his hand heavily on Anne's shoulder.

11  "Anne Shirley, what does this mean?" he said angrily.

12        Anne returned no answer. It was asking too much of flesh and blood to expect her to tell before the whole school that she had been called "carrots." Gilbert it was who spoke up stoutly.

13        "It was my fault, Mr. Phillips. I teased her."

14        Mr. Phillips paid no heed to Gilbert.

15        "I am sorry to see a pupil of mine displaying such a temper and such a vindictive spirit," he said in a solemn tone, as if the mere fact of being a pupil of his ought to root out all evil passions from the hearts of small imperfect mortals. "Anne, go and stand on the platform in front of the blackboard for the rest of the afternoon."

16        Anne would have infinitely preferred a whipping to this punishment, under which her sensitive spirit quivered as from a whiplash. With a white, set face, she obeyed. Mr. Phillips took a chalk crayon and wrote on the blackboard above her head.

17        "Ann Shirley has a very bad temper. Ann Shirley must learn to control her temper," and then read it out loud so that even the primer class, who couldn't read writing, should understand it.

18        Anne stood there the rest of the afternoon with that legend above her. She did not cry or hang her head. Anger was still too hot in her heart for that, and it sustained her amid all her agony of humiliation. With resentful eyes and passion-red cheeks she confronted alike Diana's sympathetic gaze and Charlie Sloane's indignant nods and Josie Pye's malicious smiles. As for Gilbert Blythe, she would not even look at him. She would never look at him again! She would never speak to him!

[1908]

## Notes

Unlike most of the other reading selections in this textbook, this is an excerpt from a longer work. Excerpts are often harder to understand because the context is missing. Some of the context is usually explained in notes.

The most famous Canadian book in the world is undoubtedly *Anne of Green Gables* by Lucy Maud Montgomery. It was first published in 1908 and is the first in a series of books about Anne Shirley. When the book begins, Anne, who is then 11 years old, comes from an orphanage in Nova Scotia to live with Matthew and Marilla Cuthbert, an elderly brother and sister who need help on their family farm in Prince Edward Island. Anne has red hair (which she is very sensitive about), a lively imagination, a keen intelligence, a tendency to daydream, and a talent for getting into trouble. Her best friend is Diana.

Avonlea school is a one-room rural school, typical of that day. Children from six to 16 study in the same classroom. Students write on slates (small, individual black-boards). Girls often wear their hair in long braids, which are irresistible to boys; a typical prank is to dip the braid in an ink bottle. This scene takes place early in the school year, on the first day Gilbert is at school.

Note that Mr. Phillips misspells Anne's name on the blackboard—another thing that Anne is sensitive about.

## Comprehension
1. Why was the teacher oblivious to what the students were doing?
2. What was Anne doing during the class?
3. What did Gilbert do to provoke Anne? Why did he do it?
4. What was Anne's reaction to Gilbert's provocation?
5. How was Anne punished? How did she react to the punishment?
6. Who were Anne's friends in the classroom? How were their reactions to Anne's punishment different?

## Discussion
1. Who was most at fault in this incident?
2. Is Anne's anger at Gilbert justified? Did she overreact?
3. Do you think she deserves her punishment?
4. How is this school scene different from what one would expect today?
5. What would modern students do if their teacher was preoccupied or out of the classroom?
6. What kind of teasing went on in school when you were a child? When does teasing cross the line to bullying?
7. What were common methods of discipline in your school? How effective were they?
8. What do you imagine happened to Anne and Gilbert afterwards? Do you think she ever spoke to him again?

## Assignments
1. Write a narrative retelling the basic story but updating it to modern times. For instance, the students could be using tablets instead of slates.
2. Write a paragraph comparing a modern classroom to the one in the story.
3. Read the book *Anne of Green Gables*. It can easily be found in the library or online. Write a book report.
4. Watch the 1985 TV miniseries "Anne of Green Gables" starring Megan Follows. Write a review of the series.
5. Research the book's fame and position in Canadian literature. Find out about the role of the story in the tourist industry of Prince Edward Island. Do you find this interest surprising, or is the book's fame justified? Write an essay.
6. In small groups, act out the scene in class. Do not read or memorize the text; feel free to interpret it. Compare your version to the one in the 1985 miniseries.

## Paraphrase and Summary

1. In less than 75 words, summarize the main action of the story.
2. Paraphrase: ". . . Anne was at that moment totally oblivious, not only of the very existence of Gilbert Blythe but of every other scholar in Avonlea school and of Avonlea school itself. With her chin propped on her hands and her eyes fixed on the blue glimpse of the Lake of Shining Waters that the west window afforded, she was far away in a gorgeous dreamland, hearing and seeing nothing save her own wonderful visions" [1].
3. Paraphrase: "Anne returned no answer. It was asking too much of flesh and blood to expect her to tell before the whole school that she had been called 'carrots'" [12].
4. Paraphrase: "Anger was still too hot in her heart for that, and it sustained her amid all her agony of humiliation. With resentful eyes and passion-red cheeks she confronted alike Diana's sympathetic gaze and Charlie Sloane's indignant nods and Josie Pye's malicious smiles" [18].

## Structure and Technique

Explain Montgomery's technique in these sentences: "And then—Thwack! Anne had brought her slate down on Gilbert's head and cracked it—slate not head—clear across." Does the word "thwack" give a good idea of the sound? Why is the verb ("had brought") in the past perfect tense? Is the use of parenthetical dashes effective? Is it humorous? Would it be as effective if Montgomery had instead written "cracked her slate and not his head"?

## Language Study

### Definitions

Use the context to match each word to its definition:

| | |
|---|---|
| 1. slate, *n* [1] _____ | a) brief look, a partial view |
| 2. harnessed, *adj* [1] _____ | b) completely |
| 3. utterly, *adv* [1] _____ | c) easily upset and excited |
| 4. oblivious, *adj* [1] _____ | d) evil, showing hatred |
| 5. propped, *adj* [1] _____ | e) feeling anger and surprise because of unfair treatment |
| 6. glimpse, *n* [1] _____ | |
| 7. gorgeous, *adj* [1] _____ | f) high, loud, unpleasant sound |
| 8. piercing, *adj* [3] _____ | g) not noticing anything |
| 9. indignant, *adj* [6, 18] _____ | h) shake, be affected |
| 10. hysterical, *adj* [9] _____ | i) small chalkboard in a wooden frame that schoolchildren used to write on |
| 11. quiver, *v* [16] _____ | |
| 12. malicious, *adj* [18] _____ | j) strapped together |
| | k) supported |
| | l) very beautiful |

## Word Focus

### used to [2]

The structure *used to* is very common in English, but it is often written or formed incorrectly. For example, a common spelling mistake is to leave off the *d* on *used*; this occurs because the *d* sound is not distinct—it slides into the *t* sound.

It is important to distinguish the two *used to* expressions, in both form and meaning.

**used to do:** for an action in the past

> He used to smoke, but he quit.
> The building used to house a veterinarian's office.

**be used to doing:** expresses the idea of being accustomed to something

> The students were used to staying up late to finish assignments.
> The dog is used to being fed at the same time every day.

It is important to pay attention to the different verb forms used. To express the idea of an action in the past, *used to* is followed by a verb in the base form (with no endings) to complete the idea. To express the idea of a habit, a form of the verb *to be* (such as *is* or *was*) is followed by *used to* and then a gerund (*–ing* form).

Note the differences:

| | |
|---|---|
| I used a credit card to open the door. | the verb *to use* in its basic meaning |
| A credit card can be used to open the door. | passive voice construction with the verb *to use* |
| I used to work long hours, but now I have a new job. | past action |
| I'm used to working long hours, so I don't mind my new shifts. | showing a habitual action and being accustomed to it |

Explain which meaning of *used to* is shown in this sentence from the reading: "Gilbert Blythe wasn't used to putting himself out to make a girl look at him and meeting with failure" [2].

Note that one of the definitions in the Definitions exercise above can be interpreted in two ways and thus pronounced with two different stresses, depending on whether the verb *used* is considered part of the expression *used to* or not: "small chalkboard in a wooden frame that schoolchildren used to write on." When the past action is meant, *used to* is pronounced together as one unit.

### horrified [9]

Here the adjective is used to describe *delight*. What does "horrified delight" mean? Do you consider this word combination to be unusual? Discuss the meaning and effect. Compare this to the other uses of *horrified* and its related words on pages 365–66.

## Word Families

Fill in the chart with the corresponding parts of speech:

| NOUN | VERB | ADJECTIVE | ADVERB |
|------|------|-----------|--------|
|  |  | angry [6] |  |
|  | confront [18] |  |  |
| delight [9] |  |  |  |
|  |  | enjoyable [9] |  |
|  |  |  | equally [6] |
|  |  | resentful [18] |  |
|  |  | sympathetic [18] |  |

## Collocations and Expressions

Discuss the meanings and usage of the following expressions:

to do as one pleases [1]
to put oneself out to do something [2]
to be inclined to be something [9]
at arm's length [3] [Note that in this reading, the expression is used literally. More commonly today, the expression is used to talk about a figurative distance.]
with a vengeance [5]
to ask too much of somebody [11]
flesh and blood [11]
to speak up [12]
to pay no heed to somebody/something [14]
to have a bad temper, to control one's temper [17]
to hang one's head [18]

## Language Change

*Anne of Green Gables* was written more than 100 years ago, and the language reflects this. Much of the wording sounds old-fashioned. For instance, the words *scholars* [1] and *pupil* [15] for students are not as common today.

Here are some words that you may know but may not recognize in the way Montgomery uses them. Look them up in the dictionary, go through the various meanings of the words, and find the definition that fits the usage in the reading:

afford [1], fancies [6], legend [18], quench [6], primer [17], save [1]

### Sentence Structure Analysis

1. Examine the structure of this sentence. Divide it into the two main clauses, and identify the different phrases and what they describe.

   "Mr. Phillips was back in the corner explaining a problem in algebra to Prissy Andrews, and the rest of the scholars were doing pretty much as they pleased, eating green apples, whispering, drawing pictures on their slates, and driving crickets, harnessed to strings, up and down the aisle." [1]

2. Change the sentence structure of "Gilbert it was who spoke up stoutly" [12] to one that would be commonly used today. What effect does the original sentence have? In other words, why does Montgomery start her sentence with "Gilbert"?

## Michael's New Toy

*by Linwood Barclay*

1    The two women stood in the doorway between the kitchen and the dining room, arms folded, watching with cautious interest as the 10-year-old boy played with his model trains.

2    He had taken over the dining-room table, where he had set up a couple of loops of track, a passenger station and sidings on top of a green tablecloth. He was consumed, at this moment, with placing the wheels of some coaches on the tracks. It was a delicate task, getting the flanges just so on the insides of the rails.

3    The boy's mother, Edna, said to her friend, Sandra, "Michael's absolutely loving the trains. He hasn't stopped playing with them since Frank and I bought him the set last week. I don't want him down in the basement, where it's damp and he might catch a chill, and there's no spot for it in his bedroom, so we thought we'd let him set up here. It's not like we ever eat in here anyway, except at Christmas."

4    "Sure," said Sandra. "I get that." She lowered her voice to a whisper. "So no trouble since you got him interested in trains?"

5    Edna shook her head. "Not a one. I've been keeping a count of how many matchbooks we've got in the drawer and none of them have disappeared."

6    "That's encouraging," Sandra said. "That last time, when he set those bins of trash on fire out back of the house, you nearly lost the place."

7    Edna nodded. "It was a close one, that's for sure."

8    "Did the doctor say why he does that?"

9    "He said most kids are curious about fire, but there's a handful that take pleasure in it. They get a bit of a thrill."

10    "And Michael's one of those?"

11    Michael coupled two passenger cars together, then linked them to an engine. He plugged the transformer into a wall outlet, and made sure the two wires leading from the transformer were firmly attached to the terminal track.

12    Edna sighed. "We don't know for sure. If it was just the trash by the house, well, that'd be just one incident. But there was that fire in the classroom, and that thing with the little girl's shoelaces . . ."

13    "I heard about that. And the animals?"

14    Michael turned the throttle on the transformer and the train began to move. It circled the track, gaining speed.

15    Edna sighed. She really didn't want to talk about it. It was embarrassing, your child having all these problems. But at the same time, it was good to be able to share her troubles with someone.

16    "Well, again, we haven't had any incidents since we bought Michael the train set. It was the doctor's idea. Find something positive and fun for him to focus on."

17    "That's good then, isn't it?" Sandra said encouragingly. "It's all a question of pointing him in the right direction. Is old Mrs. Farnsworth next door still making a big issue over her cat?"

18    Edna gave her a sharp look. "She has so many of the damn things it's a wonder she even noticed one missing. If it hadn't been for the smell in the backyard, she might not have."

19    Sandra leaned her head so close she practically had it on Edna's shoulder. "He really grabbed hold of its neck and . . ."

20    Edna cut her off. "For all I know, he was just hugging it a little too tight. Young boys, sometimes they just don't know their own strength."

21    The train sped around the loop, so fast it was almost a blur. Michael had his chin on the table so he could watch the train at eye level.

22    Sandra whispered, "You must wonder, sometimes, what's going on inside his head. The things he must be thinking."

23    And what Edna was thinking, but did not say, was that she often really didn't want to know.

24    "The good thing is," Michael's mother said, "is that he's got his mind off dark things. He's really liking his trains. He's mesmerized by them. He and his father even went down to the station so Michael could watch how the tracks and the switches and whatever you call them all go together so he could make something just like that. We had to take him back to the store and buy more pieces of track and switches and . . ."

25    There was a sudden, loud, clatter. The train had fallen off the track and knocked the passenger station to the floor.

26    "Oh, dear!" Edna cried. "Are you okay?"

27    Michael looked at his mother and smiled. "I'm fine," he said. "It's okay." He bent down, picked up the station, and set it back on the table. Then he set about putting the train back on the tracks.

28    "What happened?" his mother asked. "Is it broken?"

29    "Nope," Michael said. "I was just running it too fast."

30    "But you're still having a good time?" she asked.

31    "Yup," he said. "I love it."

32    Edna smiled, and touched Sandra's arm. "The mums are going to have some tea now, Michael."

33    "Okay," he said.

34    Once the women were gone, Michael inspected his handiwork. He had taken just one match from one of the matchbooks in the kitchen drawer, from the middle of the pack where no one would notice.

35    He had placed it sideways on the track, thinking that, in size, it was pretty close in scale to a big piece of lumber. When the engine came around and the wheels caught it, the whole train went flying. Right into the passenger station.

36    Michael knew from his trip to the station with his father that there were several times a day, when people were waiting on the platform for a local train, that an express blew right through at high speed. He wondered if a real piece of wood, placed just right, would create the same result that it did right here on his dining-room table.

37    He could imagine the sound. Wheels scraping on rail. Cars buckling and crashing into each other. People screaming.

38    Michael'd had no idea trains could be this much fun.

[21 July 2012]

## Comprehension

1. Why was Michael given a train set?
2. Why is the train set up in the dining room?
3. Explain what trouble Michael has gotten into.
4. Why did the train fall off the track? [25]
5. How is Michael fooling his parents?
6. Why does Edna talk to Sandra about Michael's problems? How does she feel about sharing the problems?

## Discussion

1. Discuss the effect of the story. Did you like it? Were you caught up in it? Were you surprised by the ending? Do you think the story was well constructed? Explain your point of view.
2. What do you think is the likely setting for the story? Is it contemporary (modern day) or set in the past? Is it set in Canada? Discuss possible indications of setting.
3. Do you think Edna and Frank are good parents? Discuss.
4. What do you think is wrong with Michael?
5. Barclay leaves "that thing with the little girl's shoelaces" [12] unexplained. What do you think could have happened?
6. What leads people to violent tendencies and criminal acts? Is criminality learned or inherited? Discuss.

## Assignments

1. Write an essay naming and analyzing three techniques the author uses to tell the story.
2. Write a paragraph explaining what you think will happen in the future to Michael and his family.
3. Write an essay about the benefits of a specific hobby—either model trains or something similar. For example, you can talk about constructing dollhouses, building model planes, or setting up military dioramas.
4. Although the terms *psychopath* and *sociopath* are often used interchangeably, many psychiatrists say there are important distinctions. Look up some different definitions. Write a paragraph explaining what you think is the most important distinction between the two terms.

## Paraphrase and Summary

1. Paraphrase Edna's reason for setting up the train set in the dining room [3], using indirect speech (see pages 244–45 for more on indirect speech).
2. Paraphrase: "Edna sighed. She really didn't want to talk about it. It was embarrassing, your child having all these problems. But at the same time, it was good to be able to share her troubles with someone" [15].
3. Write a one-paragraph summary of this story. Use no more than 150 words.

## Structure and Technique

Barclay uses the dialogue between the mothers to reveal background information. How effective is this technique? Does it give the reader enough information?

Most of the story is told in dialogue, but Barclay shows what Edna is thinking, not just what she is saying. Which paragraphs show Edna's thoughts? What other words show her feelings? Are these a necessary supplement to the dialogue? Discuss Barclay's technique for expanding on the dialogue.

Barclay also turns the focus to what Michael is doing and, at the very end of the story, to what he is thinking. Why does he leave Michael's thoughts to the very end? What is the effect of the author's choice?

Linwood Barclay was a columnist for the *Toronto Star* before he became a well-known mystery writer. He is the author of "A Global Warming Deal to Do Nothing Still Possible" (pages 14–15). Compare his writing techniques in the newspaper article and in the short story.

## Language Study

### Definitions

Use the context to match each word to its definition:

1. buckle, *v* [37] _____
2. consumed, *adj* [2] _____
3. flange, *n* [2] _____
4. handiwork, *n* [34] _____
5. mesmerized, *adj* [24] _____
6. siding, *n* [2] _____
7. terminal track, *adj+n* [11] _____
8. throttle, *n* [14] _____
9. transformer, *n* [11] _____

a) bend under a weight or force
b) device that controls the power to the engine and therefore the speed
c) device that changes the high voltage from the wall outlet to a safer and lower voltage to power the train engine
d) flat end on the wheels that keeps them from falling off the rails
e) fully engaged in something, with complete attention on something
f) short railway track connected to the main track where trains are kept when they are not being used
g) so attracted to something that one cannot look away
h) something that someone has made or done
i) track that the transformer wires connect to, which powers the engine

### Word Families

Fill in the chart with the corresponding parts of speech:

| NOUN | VERB | ADJECTIVE | ADVERB |
|---|---|---|---|
| | | cautious [1] | |
| | n/a | curious [9] | |
| | | | encouragingly [17] |
| | imagine [37] | | |
| incident [12] | n/a | | |
| strength [20] | | | |
| trouble [4] | | | |

## Collocations and Expressions

Discuss the meanings and usage of the following expressions:

catch a chill [3] (catch a cold)
get someone's mind off something [24]
keep a count of [5]
not a one [5] (Note that this phrase is not grammatical, because the indefinite article *a* and the word *one* essentially mean the same thing.)

## Sentence Structure Analysis

The last sentence of the story contains a contracted auxiliary verb:

"Michael'd had no idea trains could be this much fun." [38]

What auxiliary verb does the *'d* stand for?

Examine the other verb tenses used in that section (Paragraphs 34–8), and explain the usage. For instance, where is the past perfect tense used, and why?

# Appendix A

Most students use email to communicate with their professors, and it is important to write messages that communicate effectively. Here are some guidelines.

## Using a Subject Heading

You should always give your email a brief, descriptive subject heading. "Hi, this is Jung" is not an appropriate subject heading. Be as specific as possible. Here are some examples: "question about midterm," "absence on Friday," and "appointment request."

## Identifying Yourself

Make sure that any email from you includes your full name. The recipient should be able to tell immediately whom the message is from. This should be evident from your email address. If it is not in the address, you may have to include it in your subject heading.

Do not start your message with "Hi, my name is May Novak. I'm one of your students." Instead, give your full name at the bottom of the email as a signature. You can also use an automatic signature with information about yourself, such as your title, address, and phone number.

You will generally be given a school email address; use it for correspondence with your instructor. It is not professional to send out email with an address like "sexyguy@hotmail.com," and the messages may end up in the trash as suspected spam. It is useful to have different email accounts: your school email, one for social contacts, and one to use with retailers, for instance.

## Including a Salutation

Letters generally start with a salutation, such as "Dear Professor Brown," but memos do not have salutations since the information at the top of the page gives the addressee's name. An email message is more like a memo since it includes "to," "from," and subject information. Therefore, salutations are considered optional in email. They are a good idea when you initiate an email conversation but unnecessary once you get into a back-and-forth exchange of information.

Email etiquette is still evolving. It seems that "Hi" with the person's name is becoming the common salutation in email messages. As North American business style has become more casual, first names are commonly used even in business communication. However, if you do not know the person, it is wise to be formal and use title and last name, especially if you are contacting your professor. In other words, say "Professor Chu" instead of using the professor's first name.

## Using Correct, Standard English

You can use abbreviations such as "U R" in chat messages or in email to your friends, but your mail to your instructor should be written in correct, Standard English—especially for an English course. Use a spell checker, and proofread carefully before you send your message.

## Making Your Message Clear and Concise

Like all writing, email messages should be clear and concise. No one wants to read a long, rambling message only to come to the end with no clear idea of what the sender wants.

Write an email message like a business letter. State right away what the purpose of your message is. You can give necessary details in subsequent paragraphs.

## Being Prudent

Before you hit the "Send" button, reread and rethink your message. Remember that email is recorded forever. Keep in mind that business email is legally the property of the institution, so your supervisor is entitled to read any message you send from a company address. If you are sending an emotional message, such as a response to an insult, save your message and read it again the next day before you send it.

## Reducing Email Traffic

Do not hit "Reply All" unless your information must actually go to every recipient on the list. For example, if someone is setting up a meeting, you probably do not have to tell everybody on that mailing list whether you will attend or not.

Do not request a "Received Receipt" unless it is absolutely necessary.

Do not let messages get longer and longer as the back-and-forth correspondence goes on. Delete any of the copied information from previous messages unless it is important reference information.

Print messages only if the hard copy is important as a reference. Copying and pasting the message into a word processing document allows you to control the way it is printed, so you can save paper, eliminate unnecessary parts, and increase the print size.

## Attachments

Your instructor will probably have definite preferences on whether or not work can be submitted electronically, so ask if your instructor does not tell you this in the course information. Some instructors prefer to get essays by email, while others are wary of opening attachments. Many instructors prefer assignments in hard copy so that they do not have to print your work (especially if they do not have access to school facilities for this purpose). If you have questions about your draft, you can copy and paste the text into the body of the message.

## School Policies

Your institution may have official policies for appropriate use of email. Check these policies for further information.

# Appendix B

## Following Format Guidelines

Presenting your work properly is important whether you are in elementary school, college, or the workforce. The two most important criteria for school assignments are that the work is easy to read and that it leaves the marker plenty of room for comments and corrections. Instructors with specific format guidelines generally make them clear with assignment instructions. Here are some common format guidelines:

- Type your assignments on a computer. The printout should be black ink (not faded) on medium-weight 8½-by-11-inch white paper.
- Use a plain type face in a size that is easy to read, such as Times New Roman, Arial, or Calibri 12 point. Do not use typefaces that look like printing or handwriting.
- Double-space your essay. (Set paragraph line spacing at 2.)
- Leave a one-inch margin on all sides of the page.
- Number your pages. MLA and APA formats require page numbers in the top right corner.
- Use only one side of the paper.
- Indent your paragraphs with five spaces, the default tab setting.
- Use left justification and a ragged right margin. (Full justification often results in large gaps between words.)
- Make sure your sentences are clearly shown with a capital letter at the beginning and a period at the end.
- Use one space after a period. Do not put spaces before periods or commas.
- Make sure your work is properly identified with the title of the assignment, your name and student identification number, the course code including section number, the date, and the professor's name. You may be asked to put this information on a separate cover page or on the top of the first page of the assignment. (The sample MLA essay in Appendix C shows the latter style, while the sample APA essay in Appendix D shows a cover page.)
- Avoid unnecessary artwork. Include illustrations only when necessary.
- Staple the pages together in the top left corner. Do not use a cover or folder unless your instructor has specifically asked for one.

# Appendix C

**Sample Research Essay in MLA Format**

Melissa Galliano

Professor T. Singh

English 101

14 April 2015

The Benefits of Reading Fiction

Curling up with a novel seems an old-fashioned pastime in the modern world of amusements such as cat videos and Twitter gossip. Students used to the brevity of modern communication may struggle with classic novels such as *A Tale of Two Cities* and *Treasure Island*. However, even short stories and contemporary novels seem to be too much work for students today—they would rather watch the movie. Moreover, educators are under pressure to reduce the study of literature in the classroom to focus more on marketable skills. However, fiction is more than entertainment: It is vital to human learning and development.

Fiction gets its primary legitimacy from the long-standing importance of story-telling in human life. Story-telling is practically hard-wired into our brains—after all, we spend our sleeping hours making up fiction in our dreams. The art of the

Galliano 2

narrative exists in every culture; it is "an almost certain part of our evolutionary heritage, having arisen as a response to the daily needs of survival in our hunter-gatherer ancestors" (Ingram). Telling stories is how our ancestors imparted important survival information. A story about a hunter evading a bear would teach listeners what to do if they came across a bear in the woods. Even today, with all our high-tech ways of accessing information, we remember facts better if they are told in a story. For example, a reader of historical fiction retains more facts about the time period than anyone reading a regular history textbook. In the classroom, teachers' anecdotes help students to retain information. It does not matter whether the stories are true or fantasy—we need the narrative to have it stick in our brains.

Fiction-reading is an important part of educational development. Students improve their language skills as they read. Fiction, specifically, offers readers a rich vocabulary, metaphors, and symbolism, all of which challenge the brain to understand what is being said. Reading a novel strengthens memory as readers have to follow a complicated plot, keep track of a range of characters, and remember details of settings. Moreover, fiction exercises the imagination. Readers have to picture the characters and settings from what the author reveals. Once books are made into movies, however, this power is taken away. For example, now that the Harry Potter books have been filmed, a reader would be unable to imagine his own Harry—he or she would only be able to see Daniel Radcliffe, the actor. In addition, fiction can challenge our critical thinking skills. Science fiction encourages us to think "what if," and mystery novels make us use our deductive skills to figure out "whodunit."

Even though fiction is not "true," it gives us real insights into our lives. For instance, in "Why My Mother Can't Speak English," an elderly woman who "feared that

Galliano 3

learning English would change her Chinese soul" teaches us what immigrants face in assimilation (Engkent 357). Malcolm Lowry's novel *Under the Volcano* takes us into the mind of an alcoholic. The lessons revealed in fiction can be life-altering, as evidenced by work in bibliotherapy. For example, book clubs in prisons are successful vehicles of rehabilitation, as attested to by an inmate who values the exercise:

> Reading a book, sure, there is adventure, there is escapism, lifting yourself out
> of this reality, which isn't always kind or welcoming. [But] it's in a purposeful
> and productive way. It's better than drugs. It's better than banging your head
> on the wall. It's safe and builds something, knowledge, empathy (Taylor).

Short stories and novels can thus guide us to a deeper understanding of our world.

Fiction-readers not only read books better—they also read people better. Neuroscientists have proved that these readers develop understanding and empathy. Brain scans show that words involving the senses and physical motion fire up the parts of the brain that are used for those senses and motions. "The brain, it seems, does not make much of a distinction between reading about an experience and encountering it in real life; in each case, the same neurological regions are stimulated" (Paul). This brain activity also shows that readers view fictional characters like real people and have an emotional response to them. The parts of the brain that we use to follow a narrative are also used in our own social interactions with people (Paul). The ability to understand people's motives and actions is an important part of emotional intelligence, a quality that is highly valued in the modern workplace. Fiction-readers can therefore use their people-reading skills to achieve success.

Reading fiction undoubtedly makes us smarter. The study of literature deserves a place in every language and writing course throughout our education.

Galliano 4

With the wealth of reading materials available today, instructors can find novels and stories suitable for each student. The habit of reading fiction should be cultivated in all students so that they carry on the practice throughout their life and can reap the many benefits.

## Works Cited

Engkent, Garry. "Why My Mother Can't Speak English." *Skill Set: Strategies for Reading and Writing in the Canadian Classroom.* By Lucia Engkent. 3rd ed. Don Mills: Oxford UP, 2016. 353–58. Print.

Ingram, Jay. "Once upon a Time, a Story Meant Survival." *Toronto Star*, 23 Dec. 2001: F.8. *Canadian Newsstand.* Web. 15 April 2015.

Paul, Annie Murphy. "Your Brain on Fiction." *New York Times*, 17 March 2012. Web. 14 April 2015.

Taylor, Kate. "The Book Club at the Big House." *Globe and Mail*, 22 Nov. 2014: R5. Print.

# Appendix D

## Sample Research Essay in APA Format

The Adolescent Brain

Andreas Lackner

York University

Prof. K. McKenzie

PSYCH 250: Patterns of Behaviour

21 March 2015

The Adolescent Brain

Parents and educators have always complained about the irrational and immature behaviour of teenagers and young adults, but today it seems worse. Adolescence—the period before adulthood—seems to extend to the age of 30 as the boomerang generation settles into their parents' basement after college or university. Many factors—such as economic conditions and the development of technology—play a role in this state of affairs, but a factor that is only being understood now is the neurological one. The human brain continues to develop beyond the legal age of maturity. Understanding the adolescent brain can help people to understand the behaviour of adolescents.

One predominant characteristic of adolescents is their heightened social sensitivity. Teenagers are very self-conscious and think that everyone is looking at them. They are mortified by minor embarrassments—even simple actions such as dropping a tray or tripping on stage. Adults can more easily shrug off criticism, but bullying and rejection by peers can be devastating to teens and young adults (Carman, 2012, p. A4). Humiliation on social media can even lead them to commit suicide. The development of the adolescent brain shows that social anxiety is part of a natural growth process:

> As the brain matures in adolescence, the prefrontal cortex assumes
> responsibility for many of the cognitive processes—such as reasoning,
> planning and behavior control—that are initially performed in the more
> primitive subcortical and limbic structures, she [Dr. Deborah Yurgelun-Todd]
> says. The development of the prefrontal cortex parallels improvements in
> cognitive control and behavioral inhibition as an adolescent transitions to
> an adult. Frontalization may underlie adolescents' growing ability to think

abstractly outside of themselves, and see themselves in the way others see them—which could contribute to the feeling of being constantly on stage and judged that many teens experience (Packard, 2007.)

As they mature, adolescents gain control of the social parts of their brain. It is part of the normal maturation process as children gradually individuate themselves from their parents and learn to act in a larger social arena.

Adolescents tend to take more risks than adults. They are more likely to drive recklessly—behaviour they pay for in higher car insurance rates. They try crazy stunts, such as diving off a cliff, especially under the influence of peer pressure. Again, this is due to the ongoing development of their brains: "Since both the wiring to the prefrontal cortex, and the insulation, is incomplete, teens often take longer to access their prefrontal cortexes, meaning they have a harder time making accurate judgments and controlling their impulses" (McMahon, 2015, p. 50). Hormones and neurotransmitters like dopamine also play an important role because they make risk-taking an immensely pleasurable activity (McMahon, 2015, p. 51). This activity is heightened when teens have an audience of their peers. For example, researchers found teens take more risks in a car-racing video game when they are watched by other teens (McMahon, 2015, p. 53).

Experimentation with drugs and alcohol is also common among teens and young adults. This can lead to addiction and serious social and mental problems. The experimentation can be considered another kind of risk-taking behaviour influenced by peer pressure, but more biological factors come into play. "The hormone THP, which is released by the body in response to stress, has a calming effect in adults, but actually seems to have the opposite effect in teens, increasing stress" (McMahon, 2015, p. 50).

ADOLESCENT BRAIN                                                      4

A higher level of stress may lead them to try drugs as a release in the first place. This is dangerous because the developing brain is more susceptible to damage from drugs and alcohol.

Parents and teachers need to understand adolescent brain development in order to guide young people through their tumultuous development. Adolescents' social anxiety and reactions to bullying cannot be dismissed as minor problems. Parents and educators have a delicate balancing act to manoeuvre—guiding adolescents away from behaviour that can lead to permanent damage while allowing them enough leeway to learn and mature to responsible adults.

ADOLESCENT BRAIN5

References

Carman, T. (2012, October 12). Bullying among teenage girls like "worst sort of brain torture." *Vancouver Sun*, p. A4. Retrieved from http://lcweb.senecac.on.ca:2075/docview/1112617690?accountid=28610.

McMahon, T. (2015, January 12). Inside your teenager's scary brain. *Maclean's*, pp. 48-53.

Packard, E. (2007, April). That teenage feeling. *Monitor on Psychology*, *38*(4). Retrieved from http://www.apa.org/monitor/apr07/teenage.aspx.

# Index

tense, of verbs, 25–7, 52–4, 162
textbooks, 230–1
thesauruses, 35, 45
thesis statements, 137–40
    identification of, 233–4
    as three-pronged, 138–40
    topic sentences and, 104–7
*they* (plural pronoun), as singular, 202–3
titles, 135–6, 233
*toonie*, 314–15
topic, choice of, 131
topic sentences
    for body paragraphs, 127, 145–7
    for summary paragraphs, 247–8
    thesis statement and, 104–7
*toxic*, 314
transition signals, 5, 6, 115, 119–20, 121
transitive verbs, 54, 62–3
"Turning the Table on Instagram" (Teitel), 297–8
typos (typographical errors), 193

uncountable nouns, 24, 208–9
*uniform*, 343
"Unplug the Digital Classroom" (Mann), 255–6
*used to*, 371

verbals, 60–2
verbs
    as describing actions or states, 25, 64
    endings/beginnings of, 25
    gerunds created from, 26, 60, 65
    gerunds/infinitives following, 65
    sentence structure and, 50, 62–7
    subject agreement with, 210–12
    tense/aspect of, 25–7, 52–4, 162
verbs, forms of, 25–7, 54–60
    active/passive voice, 54–6
    base form, 25–6
    errors in use of, 215
    infinitive, 25, 61–2, 65
    modal auxiliary, 50, 56–7, 69
    participles, 26–7, 61–2, 73, 180
    phrasal, 50, 57–8, 59
    transitive/intransitive, 54, 62–3

*vet*, 365
vocabulary. *See also* words
    errors in, 194
    expansion of, 47
    knowledge/use of, 21–2
    parts of speech, 24–8
    pronunciation, 22–3
    spelling, 23–4, 190, 195–8

*welfare*, 361
"What Makes a Good Voter," 335–6
"White Tops, Grey Bottoms" (Akerman), 339–40
"Why Arcade Fire Fans Should Rise to the Occasion and Say Yes to the Dress Code" (Everett-Green), 345–6
"Why My Mother Can't Speak English" (Engkent), 353–8
"Why Pay More? To Be Conspicuous" (Singer), 283–4
"Why Study Liberal Arts?," 266–7
words. *See also* vocabulary
    classes of, 28–9
    combinations of, 41, 75
    families of, 32–4
    foreign, 360–1
    formation of, 30–2
    as idioms/jargon, 37–8
    as inappropriate, 38–9
    as incorrectly chosen, 200
    meanings/connotations of, 35–6
    as often confused/misspelled, 195–7
    origins of, 23, 42–4
    unfamiliar, 39–40
writing. *See also* essays; rhetoric
    audience/purpose of, 4–5
    evaluation of, 18–19, 188–89
    principles of, 3–16
    process of, 16–18
    reading as important to, 3, 47, 252
    techniques of, 234–5
"writing by ear" errors, 194
written English. *See* spoken *vs.* written English

yes-or-no essay questions, 131
*you* (second person pronoun), 204–5

# Credits